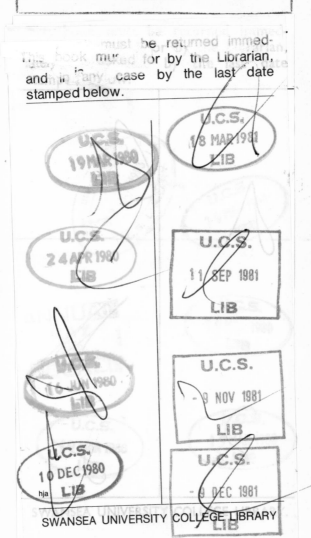

THE CLOTH INDUSTRY
IN THE WEST OF ENGLAND
FROM 1640 TO 1880

The Cloth Industry in the West of England from 1640 to 1880

J. de L. MANN

CLARENDON PRESS · OXFORD

1971

Oxford University Press, Ely House, London W.1

GLASGOW NEW YORK TORONTO MELBOURNE WELLINGTON
CAPE TOWN IBADAN NAIROBI DAR ES SALAAM LUSAKA ADDIS ABABA
DELHI BOMBAY CALCUTTA MADRAS KARACHI LAHORE DACCA
KUALA LUMPUR SINGAPORE HONG KONG TOKYO

PRINTED IN GREAT BRITAIN
BY WILLIAM CLOWES & SONS, LIMITED
LONDON, BECCLES AND COLCHESTER

PREFACE

THE fifteen years or so during which this book has been in preparation have seen an increasing stream of information about its subject flowing into County Record Offices. This stream has not dried up; since the book went to press it has been discovered that there were spinning jennies in Frome in 1784, and it now seems probable that a steam engine may have existed, also in Frome, at an earlier date than that given in the text for one in Trowbridge. No doubt this process will continue and may alter some of the conclusions arrived at.

I owe a great debt to the many people who have helped me with information and references, often from their own research. The greatest is to Mr. K. G. Ponting, whose knowledge of the trade and its history has saved me from many mistakes. Any that remain are my own responsibility. W. A. Miles, Assistant Commissioner for Handloom Weavers in Gloucestershire, remarked that no subject was more complicated than cloth; and though he may have known little of other industries, it is still true that wool, as an organic raw material, does offer problems which a historian who has never had experience of using it may easily overlook. My second and almost equally great obligation is to the County Record Officers of Gloucestershire, Wiltshire, and Somerset and to members of their staffs, who have been unfailingly helpful in pointing out documents which I should otherwise have missed. I am particularly grateful to Mr. K. H. Rogers of the Wiltshire Record Office upon whose extensive knowledge of the area round Trowbridge I have frequently drawn.

Where information given me by others is directly referred to in the text my obligations to them are acknowledged in the notes and are not repeated here. But I have also greatly benefited from conversations with Mr. Walrond, Curator of Stroud Museum, and with Mr. Hammond of Chalford, whose wide knowledge of families in the Stroud area has filled in for me some of the background of the Gloucestershire industry. Mr. J. F. Everett has enabled me to distinguish the various branches of the Everett family of Heytesbury. My debt to the

Revd. J. and Mrs. Wansey of West Lavington, Sussex, acknowledged in a previous publication, remains great, as also that to
Mrs. Hulls for information about the Wansey family. Lord
Methuen, Lord St. Aldwyn, and Mrs. Smith of Painswick
allowed me to visit their houses, and Messrs. Rawlings of Frome
their mill, in order to see documents in their possession; and I
am particularly grateful to Lord Methuen's archivist, Miss E.
Wade, for the help she gave me on my visits to Corsham Court.
Sir John Colfox allowed me to quote from the correspondence
of Thomas Colfox, now on loan in the Dorset County Record
Office, and I am indebted to Mrs. Hare of Frome Vauchurch
for letting me see these papers in the first instance. Mr. D. J.
Jeremy, now Curator of the Merrimack Textile Museum in the
U.S.A., told me of the information to be found in the archives
of the Bath and West Society. I am grateful to the Society and
to its honorary librarian for permission to consult them in its
library; and also to the editors of the *Wiltshire Times* and the
Stroud News and Journal for letting me see the files of newspapers
in their offices. I have also benefited from the courtesy of the
Directors of most of the remaining mills in the area in showing
me over them and making available any documents they
possess. Finally, the late Professor T. S. Ashton was kind
enough to read the first draft of part I; and I owe a great
deal to his interest and encouragement.

Melksham   J. de L. M.
June 1971

CONTENTS

ABBREVIATIONS

A.P.C.	*Acts of the Privy Council*
Arch. H.L.	Archives of the House of Lords
Arch. B. and W.	Archives of the Bath and West Society
B.G.A.S.	*Transactions of the Bristol and Gloucestershire Archaeological Society*
B.M.	British Museum
B.P.P.	*British Parliamentary Papers*
Cal. Treas.	*Calendar of Treasury (Papers or Books)*
C.J.	*Journals of the House of Commons*
C.R.O.	County Record Office
C.S.P.D.	*Calendar of State Papers Domestic*
Econ. Hist. Rev.	*Economic History Review*
E.H.R.	*English Historical Review*
Encycl. méth.	*Encyclopédie méthodique*
G.C.L.	Gloucester City Library
Glos. Inq. P.M.	*Gloucestershire Inquisitiones Post Mortem*
H.M.C.	*Historical Manuscripts Commission*
Ind. Arch.	*Industrial Archaeology*
J.C.T.P.	*Journal of the Commissioners for Trade and Plantations*
L.J.	*Journals of the House of Lords*
N. and Q.	*Notes and Queries*
Parl. Reg.	Parliamentary Register
P.L.	Public Library
P.R.O.	Public Record Office
V.C.H.	*Victoria County History*
W.A.M.	*Wiltshire Archaeological Magazine*
W.A.S.	Wiltshire Archaeological Society
Abst.	Abstract (Population Returns)
Ev.	Evidence
Lr.	Letter
Pop.	Population

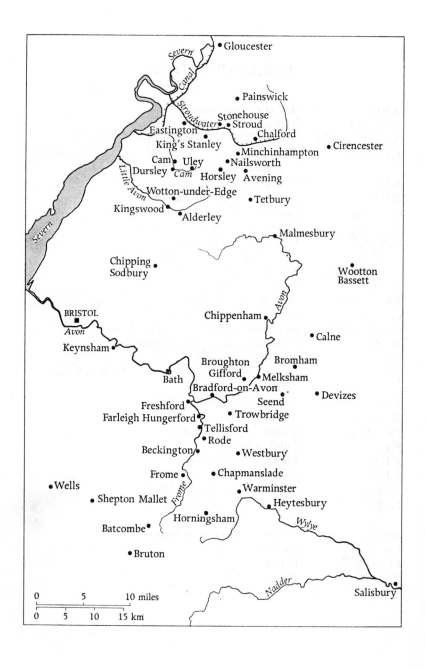

Severn

Gloucester

Painswick

Stroudwater
Stonehouse
Stroud
Chalford

Eastington
Cirencester
King's Stanley
Minchinhampton

Cam
Uley
Nailsworth
Dursley
Cam
Horsley
Avening
Wotton-under-Edge
Tetbury
Little Avon
Kingswood
Alderley

Severn

Malmesbury

Chipping
Sodbury
Wootton
Bassett

BRISTOL

Avon

Chippenham
Avon

Calne

Keynsham

Broughton
Gifford
Bromham
Bath
Melksham
Bradford-on-Avon
Devizes
Seend
Freshford
Farleigh Hungerford
Trowbridge
Tellisford
Rode
Beckington
Westbury
Frome
Chapmanslade

Wells
Warminster
Shepton Mallet
Heytesbury
Horningsham
Wylye
Batcombe
Frome
Bruton

Nadder
Salisbury

| 0 | | 5 | | 10 miles |
| 0 | 5 | 10 | 15 km | |

INTRODUCTION

THE area with which this book is concerned lies in the counties of Gloucestershire, Wiltshire, and Somerset, within an imaginary line drawn from just below Gloucester south-east to Wootton Basset in Wiltshire and then south to Salisbury; from Salisbury slightly north-west through Bruton to Shepton Mallet and Wells; and from thence northwards to the outskirts of Bristol, continuing through the Vale of Severn back to Gloucester.[1] The subject matter is almost entirely concerned with cloth in the narrow sense—material made from short carded wool, felted by the fulling mill, and finished by raising and shearing the nap to give a smooth surface in which warp and weft were so completely united that neither could be separately distinguished. Some of this cloth was narrow but the characteristic product of the area was broadcloth, from 54 to 63 inches wide, which needed two weavers to the loom. Variations on this early type of cloth began to appear in the eighteenth century but the manufacture remained essentially the same in most of its stages, and very different from that in which long combed wool was manufactured into worsteds.[2] Between the two came a variety of materials made with a worsted warp and a weft of carded wool. A large part of the 'new draperies' which began to appear in England in the sixteenth century were of this type and many were finished in the same way as cloth. Some of these were made in the area delineated above, but in much smaller quantities. Cloth was the aristocrat of the woollen industry. Except for the coarsest kinds it was more expensive than worsteds or any of the new draperies; and the voluminous body of contemporary literature concerned with that industry is mainly devoted to it. The new draperies, though collectively much more important in the

[1] Clothmaking was dying out in Gloucester itself by 1639, W. B. Wilcox, *Gloucestershire, A Study in Local Government 1590 to 1640*, p. 177, n. 93. Worsted stuffs were made in the northern suburb of Barton Regis up to the eighteenth century.

[2] For the difference between wool and worsted see K. G. Ponting, *The West of England Cloth Industry*, pp. 12–13.

export trade and probably at home as well, were for the most part allowed to develop in silence. They were made with cheaper wool and although (if it was a long wool) it was often spun very fine, the 'feel' of the material made from it was harsher than that of cloth entirely made of short carding wool.

It must be admitted that the line described above is rather arbitrarily drawn. From the later seventeenth century onwards cloth was produced within this area in far greater quantities than in any other part of southern or western England, and it had a large though gradually diminishing export trade. But many places outside it also made cloth and some continued to do so right up to the third quarter of the nineteenth century. Among the latter the more important were southern Somerset particularly Ilminster and Chard,[1] and Dorset with several centres, of which that at Sturminster Newton continued until about 1820.[2] The blanket manufacture at Witney in Oxfordshire flourishes at the present day. In other places the industry continued, gradually decaying, until the eighteenth century,[3] among them Bristol where there were several clothiers about 1730,[4] and even one who was bankrupt in 1841; but the greater part of what remained of the once important industry there seems to have been devoted to making worsted stuffs for use as curtains and upholstery.[5] None of these places except Witney was of any great importance, though Chard makes an unexpected appearance at the end of the eighteenth century; and the only centre outside Yorkshire and part of Lancashire which, after 1660, continued to produce cloth comparable with that of the region indicated was the city of Worcester where clothiers and weavers were incorporated under a charter of 1590. Something will be said of the industry there in the following pages.

In 1600 and throughout the previous century the clothiers of Gloucestershire, Wiltshire, and east Somerset had been distinguished from most of their neighbours by the degree of

[1] Pigot's *Directory of Somerset*, 1830 and 1842; Kelly's *Directory of Somerset*, 1875.
[2] *V.C.H. Dorset* ii. 360–2.
[3] See below, pp. 27–8.
[4] Bristol Poll Books (Bristol P.L.), 1722 and 1734.
[5] As may be seen from the names of the goods mentioned in a list of weavers' grievances, 1726, F. F. Fox and J. Taylor (eds.), *Some Account of the Guild of Weavers in Bristol*, pp. 64–6.

their concentration on unfinished, so-called 'white' cloth, mainly for export to Holland and Germany, whence, after being dyed and finished, it was transported all over Europe. In the early years of the seventeenth century about 60 per cent of this cloth came from Wiltshire. Gloucestershire followed with 27 to 28 per cent and a large part of the remainder came from Worcester.[1] The decline of this industry has been told elsewhere.[2] By 1640 exports, which had averaged about 60,000 pieces around the turn of the century,[3] had been halved,[4] amid a wealth of argument about the reasons for their decay. In fact, neither of the two most favoured explanations, high prices and bad making, lay at the root of it. The Thirty Years' War disrupted markets and altered the value of currencies, but production might have recovered if it had not been for competition at home and abroad. As it was, the cloth manufactures of France and Holland, now recovered from the Wars of Religion, were expanding, and the production of coarser cloth was spreading in Germany and Poland. Even more important, perhaps, was the competition of the New Draperies. None had quite the same close texture as cloth but they were lighter and cheaper, important qualities when the fashion for close-fitting garments and the rise of a middle class had created a demand for both these advantages.

There were other outlets than Holland and Germany for some of the cloth produced. Much Worcester and Gloucestershire cloth and some from Wiltshire was dyed and finished in London and Coventry[5] for other foreign markets. In 1640 it

---

[1] Figures from A. Friis, *Alderman Cockayne's Project and the Cloth Trade*, p. 129 and App. C. As explained in *V.C.H. Wilts.* iv. 151, the percentages depend on the method adopted for dividing consignments coming from two or more sources. Any alternative to that chosen by Dr. Friis would give Wiltshire a larger proportion. Some cloth produced on the Somerset side of the R. Frome probably passed as Wilts. cloth.

[2] B. E. Supple, *Commercial Crisis and Change in England, 1600–1642*; G. D. Ramsay, *The Wiltshire Woollen Industry in the Sixteenth and Seventeenth Centuries*; *V.C.H. Wilts.* iv. 148–55.

[3] J. Wheeler, 'A Treatise of Commerce' (1601), see J. Smith, *Chronicon Rusticum Commerciale or Memoirs of Wool* i. 118. In 1606 and 1614, boom years, the number was between 70,000 and 80,000 pieces, Friis, loc. cit.

[4] *C.S.P.D. 1639–40*, 417.

[5] Cf. the statement of Richard Wood of Woodchester in 1625 that most of his cloth was dyed and dressed in England but not in Glos., P.R.O., E. 134/2 Car. i, Easter 1626, no. 19. (I am indebted to Mr. J. P. Cooper of Trinity College, Oxford, for this reference.) For Coventry see *V.C.H. Warw.* ii. 255.

may be that nearly 10,000 pieces of western cloth dyed in the piece, mainly from Worcester and Gloucestershire, were being sent abroad, largely to the Mediterranean countries.[1] Stroud-water reds, long well known, had been much improved at the beginning of the century.[2] Other colours were also dyed in Gloucestershire on a fairly extensive scale, to judge from the number of dyers there in 1608;[3] and according to Fuller, who was in the county with the Royalist army during the Civil War, its cloth was 'as good as any in England, for fineness and colour'.[4] One Frome clothier, at least, had customers in France[5] (as was the case with many in southern Somerset); but the French authorities had placed many difficulties in the way of cloth exports from England in the early part of the century.[6] Wiltshire, however, had concentrated almost exclusively on unfinished cloth, and with the decline of this industry the eventual demise of clothmaking there might have seemed probable had it not been for a new type of cloth known as 'Spanish cloth' which rose to prominence in the later twenties.[7]

'Spanish cloth' is a most imprecise and confusing term which does not necessarily imply the use of Spanish wool. The cheaper

[1] According to Dr. Supple (op. cit., App. A, Table 10a). 5,180 dressed long-cloths in 'notional' terms, rather more in actual cloths, were exported in 1622 and most of these were Gloucestershire cloths. They appear to be the 'long plain lists' which figure in the Port Book for 1640 (P.R.O., E.190/43/4). Dr. Supple gives 3,926 'notional' cloths exported to northern Europe in that year (ibid., Table 10b) and to this must be added about 4,600 actual pieces to the Levant and some to other Mediterranean ports. About 1,000 pieces of 'short narrow lists' were also exported to the Levant in 1640 and many are marked 'red'. If these are Stroudwaters the total would reach over 9,000 pieces, without allowing for any of the latter which may have been sent to other places.

[2] *C.S.P.D. 1635*, 50.

[3] *Men and Armour for Gloucestershire in 1608* (compiled by John Smyth). See A. J. and R. H. Tawney, 'An occupational Census of the Seventeenth Century', *Econ. Hist. Rev.* v (1). 55. 27 out of the total of 36 dyers were in the main clothmaking area of whom 10 were on the Cam and Little Avon and 17 on Stroudwater. See R. Perry, 'The Gloucestershire Woollen Industry, 1100–1690', *B.G.A.S.* 66, 83, 91–2.

[4] T. Fuller, *The Worthies of England* (ed. 1811), i. 374.

[5] *A.P.C. 1619–21*, 376.

[6] See E. Moir, 'Benedict Webb, Clothier', *Econ. Hist. Rev.* (2nd. ser.), x(2). 260.

[7] The date of 1567, sometimes given for its first appearance, is that of a petition from immigrant weavers in Southampton making 'Spanish quilts', *C.S.P.D. Add. 1566–79*, 32. This seems to be a translation of the Dutch *Spaansche Decken*, which were fairly coarse products using Spanish lamb's-wool, N. W. Posthumus, *De Gescheidenis van de Leidsche Laken Industrie* iii. 756. There is no evidence that future developments stemmed from this manufacture. See also *V.C.H. Wilts.* iv. 153, n. 52.

varieties were made wholly of English wool,[1] while the more
expensive kinds contained Spanish in varying quantities. The
dearest, selling wholesale in the later thirties at 26s. to 28s. a
yard,[2] or even retail at 35s.,[3] may have been made of it entirely;
but up to a much later date it was customary to use some
English wool even in the better kinds.[4] The Spanish cloth
produced at this time was a medley or 'mingled' cloth in which
dyed wool of two or more colours was mixed before spinning.[5]
There was nothing new about this, for the greater part of
English coloured cloth seems to have been dyed in the wool[6] and
medleys had been known for a long time,[7] although Spanish
cloth was noted for several new shades of colour.[8] Its real
novelty lay in the fact that it was a well-made material of a
lighter weight than other cloth. It is not always realized how
heavy the old draperies were. The heaviest cloth made today,
that for men's overcoats, weighs $16\frac{1}{2}$ to $17\frac{1}{4}$ ounces to the square
yard. The weight of the cloth most commonly worn in England
in the early seventeenth century, that of Kent, Reading, or
Yorkshire, was fixed by statute at about $23\frac{1}{2}$ ounces per square
yard.[9] The varieties made in the west were rather lighter and
a square yard of fine cloth may have weighed 19 ounces, or one
of the coarsest kind, 'narrow list sorting-pack cloth', a little
under that figure when dyed and finished. Spanish cloth, a
much better material with a well-filled web, weighed when
first exported only about 16 ounces per square yard. It is often
classed with the new draperies and was an equally important
innovation, since it united the durability and fine finish of

---

[1] As with the cheap Devonshire Spanish cloth, below, p. xviii.

[2] P.R.O., C. 107/20, Sales Book of James Ashe.

[3] *C.S.P.D. 1635*, 27. Prices from 15s. 6d. to 28s. and even 45s. for scarlet are recorded elsewhere between 1621 and 1640, J. E. T. Rogers, *Agriculture and Prices in England* vi. 554–6.

[4] See below, p. 11.

[5] It is not until towards the end of the century that we find 'Spanish cloth mixed or of one colour', *London Gazette*, no. 1839 (1683).

[6] This was the case with Kentish, Reading, and Yorkshire cloth and with Suffolk blues. Very bright colours could not be obtained in this way as they would not survive fulling.

[7] P. Wolff, 'English Cloth in Toulouse, 1380 to 1450', *Econ. Hist. Rev.* (2nd ser.), ii(3). 291 The mingle-coloured cloth mentioned in 1616 (*A.P.C. 1616–17*, 112) probably came from Reading.

[8] P.R.O., C. 107/20, Sales Book of James Ashe. Cf. Supple, op. cit., p. 151.

[9] See App. II. (The weight given in *V.C.H. Wilts.* iv. 150, n. 25, is an error.)

which only cloth was capable with the lighter weight which wearers were coming to demand. The use of Spanish wool may have contributed to this in the more expensive varieties. It had been greatly improved in the reign of Ferdinand and Isabella[1] and the best quality was exceedingly soft and short in staple. An improved technique, however, must have been equally important[2] and is suggested by the fact that, although the term 'Spanish cloth' in the early seventeenth century always denotes a medley, not all medleys were Spanish cloth. If there was no difference in technique, it is difficult to see why the medleys at 7s. a yard made in Devonshire of a mixture of Devon and Irish wool[3] were 'Spanish', while those made at Reading and Newbury were expressly distinguished from it.[4]

It has been suggested that both the decline in the white cloth industry and the use of Spanish wool were due to the increasing coarseness of English wool, resulting from the enclosures of the sixteenth century.[5] The former can hardly be the case, though Wiltshire clothiers were well aware as early as 1586 that the wool they bought was coarser than it had been. Most of the 'sorting-pack cloth' made in the west was only of medium quality[6] and the complaints about its defects do not suggest that the raw material in itself was at fault.[7] All the evidence points to Spanish cloth having been developed in one or two small centres over a considerable period of time before 1620. Contemporaries believed that it had first been made by Benedict Webb of Kingswood, near Wotton-under-Edge;[8] and

---

[1] J. Klein, 'The Mesta', *Harvard Economic Studies*, 21.

[2] Cf. Webb's claim to have studied French and Italian processes (below, p. xix, n. 1).

[3] W. B. Stephens, *Seventeenth Century Exeter*, pp. 28, 49. This manufacture disappeared after the Civil War.

[4] P.R.O., S.P. 16/240/23.

[5] P. J. Bowden, 'Wool Supply and the Woollen Industry', *Econ. Hist. Rev.* (2nd ser.), ix(1). 53–5.

[6] See App. II.

[7] The passage about jobbers quoted by Dr. Bowden (loc. cit. 55, n. 2) does not indicate the use of coarser wool, but of a mixture of wools which would result in all the faults mentioned. There were singularly few complaints that cloth was coarser than it had been.

[8] Bodl. Lib. MSS. Aubrey, 2, fol. 144. The information came from Samuel Ashe, a son of James Ashe of Batcombe, who had been brought up in the industry. (P.R.O., C. 107/20, Sales Book of James Ashe.)

there seems no reason to doubt his claim that, after studying
clothmaking processes in France where he had lived as apprentice to a London mercer, he had begun, when living in Taunton
in the late 1580s, to make 'a sort of medley cloth which Mr.
William Stone a mercer in Cheapside delt with mee for and
cald them Spanish Clothes'.[1] This statement derives some
support from the facts that Spanish cloth is mentioned possibly
as early as 1590[2] and that in 1606 Spanish wool was being used
by 'some clothiers of Somerset and other countries'.[3] A centre
of its manufacture was, in fact, growing up in and around
Shepton Mallet,[4] where clothiers had previously used fine wool
from the Isle of Wight to make cloth for the Spanish market.[5]
After the ruin of this trade by the war with Spain at the end of
the sixteenth century some of them had turned to making a
thin blue cloth for export to Holland and Germany, where it
was further dyed and finished and worn by the 'better sort of
people';[6] and this experience with relatively fine wool was a
good preparation for the use of that from Spain. By 1640
several had made fortunes out of it.[7] It was John Ashe, son of
one of the foremost of these clothiers, James Ashe of Westcombe
in the parish of Batcombe between Bruton and Shepton Mallet,
who introduced it to the valley of the Bristol Avon, in the
twenties;[8] and the catastrophic decline in sales of white cloth
must have stimulated its production over a wider area. By 1630
its manufacture was well established round Kingswood (to
which Webb had returned before 1600), and in north-west

[1] G.C.L., S.Z. 23, 2 (4a). I am indebted to Mr. J. P. Cooper for this reference
also.

[2] P.R.O., S.P. 15/34/52. This is a list of woollen or part-woollen materials in
alphabetical order, later dated in pencil 1590. 'Spanish cloth' appears as an
afterthought at the end.

[3] P.R.O., S.P. 14/20/9* (quoted Supple, op. cit., p. 149). There is no other
evidence for its use outside Somerset, though Webb may have used it at Kingswood.

[4] R. Watts, *The Young Man's Looking Glass*, pp. 40–4.

[5] R. H. Tawney and E. Power, *Tudor Economic Documents* iii. 204.

[6] P.R.O., S.P. 14/20/9* See also *C.S.P.D. 1611–18*, 561 where the petitioner,
Barnard, came from Shepton Mallet.

[7] Watts, op. cit., p. 42.

[8] He made large purchases of land from his father-in-law, Henry Davison of
Freshford, between 1625 and 1630. Corsham Papers, nos. 1608, 1609, 2774. The
family at this time spelt its name Aish, Aysh, or Ash; the spelling adopted here is
that favoured by its descendants.

Wiltshire.[1] By 1640 exports from London, at over 12,000 pieces,[2] were interfering both with those of white cloth and of coloured cloth from other places.[3] Its popularity is attested by the imitation known as 'say-dyed cloth', woven white and dyed before fulling, the production of which was organized by the brothers William and Christopher Brewer who came from the Somerset side of the Frome valley;[4] but although say-dyed cloth bulks large in the records because of the complaints of the Spanish clothiers,[5] it does not appear to have been as important as they suggest,[6] and it vanished altogether after the Civil War.

In 1640 the whole industry was in transition. Markets had appeared abroad other than those controlled by the Merchant Adventurers and a large section of the industry in Gloucestershire and Worcester was making goods for them. Further south the Spanish cloth manufacture had already established itself. The prospects were far more promising than for those neighbouring counties which had made no change in the kind of material they manufactured. It was to its adaptability in this respect that the western cloth area owed its survival.

---

[1] *C.S.P.D. 1629–31*, 418. For Webb's presence in Kingswood in 1597 see *A.P.C.* xxvii. 221. The extent of its manufacture in north-west Wilts. may be seen from the proceedings against the market spinners who were said to furnish much of the coloured yarn. P.R.O., S.P. 16/243/23.

[2] Ramsay, op. cit., p. 141. Supple, converting the pieces into notional short-cloths, gives 13,517, op. cit., p. 267.

[3] *C.S.P.D. 1640–41*, 370.

[4] Ramsay, op. cit., pp. 104–5.

[5] *C.S.P.D. 1629–31*, 164; *1634–35*, 24–5; *1640*, 210–11.

[6] Only four clothiers living within a very small compass were summoned on the Spanish clothiers' complaint in 1634, *C.S.P.D. 1634–5*, 376. In 1640 the Merchant Adventurers said that most of the 27 clothiers who signed a petition in its favour (*C.S.P.D. 1640*, 188) only sold white cloth to the two Brewers who were the sole producers, and only one merchant dealt in it. P.R.O., S.P.16/456/39.

PART I

1640 to 1790

I

THE SUCCESS OF INNOVATION,
1640–1790

ALTHOUGH the Civil War affords a convenient date for a survey of the new direction which the trade was taking, it made no difference to that direction. It hastened the decline of the branch which produced white cloth for export by giving a further incentive to production in Holland and Germany,[1] but this decline had begun more than twenty years earlier and the transition to the making of coloured cloth had been under way for nearly as long. Individual clothiers may have been ruined by the war but the trade went on. Gloucestershire was seriously involved in 1643, but after Waller's relief of Gloucester in September of that year it was never entirely cut off from London. Wiltshire suffered more heavily, right up to 1645,[2] and plague was raging there in 1644 and 1646.[3] Nevertheless, whenever possible, convoys went up to London from all parts of the area sometimes by devious routes, though the cloth was occasionally seized by Royalist parties on the way.[4] The King's efforts to make Bristol and, later, Exeter marts for the sale of western cloth had little result, partly because the way to London was never totally blocked after Malmesbury fell to Parliament in May 1644, while that to Exeter often was;[5] but also because such a sudden and total change in the direction of the trade was impossible.[6]

[1] *Thurloe State Papers* v. 127. The growth in the production of cloth in Leiden may be seen from Table 110 in Posthumus, op. cit. iii. 930.

[2] *L.J.* vi. 637; C. H. Firth (ed.), *Ludlow's Memoirs* i. App. II.

[3] *H.M.C. Var.* i (Wilts. Q. Sess. Rolls), 111–12, 114; B. H. Cunnington *Records of the Court of Quarter Sessions in Wilts.*, pp. 158, 161, 172, 174–6, 211–12.

[4] *L.J.* v. 670, 699. This cloth, seized at Reading, was returned except for that belonging to John Ashe. 72 packs of Gloucestershire cloth were seized in 1643 by forces under the Earl of Northampton and suits for restitution were in progress ten years later, but the clothiers did not obtain satisfaction. *Bibliotheca Gloucestrensis*, ed. J. Washbourn Jr., i. 138; *H.M.C. 3rd Rept.* (H. of L. MSS.), 186a; *C.S.P.D. 1652–3*, 385–6; ibid. *1653–4*, 62; *L.J.* viii. 712; ix. 210, 318.

[5] *H.M.C. 5th Rept.* (H. of L. MSS.), 56.   [6] Ramsay, op. cit., p. 112.

Although the general sentiment among western clothiers seems to have been in favour of Parliament[1] most of them, whatever their sympathies, tried to avoid embroilment. The names of a few Royalists among them are known,[2] and some were prominent on the Parliamentary side, notably John Ashe of Freshford who lent large sums for its forces, helped to oppose the Commission of Array in Somerset and was later Chairman of the Committee for Compounding.[3] Prince Rupert's seizure of cloth from the Stroudwater clothiers cannot have endeared the Royalist cause to them.[4] The King's armies paid at Oxford, if clothiers could reach it,[5] or in notes redeemable at the end of the war. Parliament, being in control in London, was able to clothe its armies in a more normal way and there seems to have been no complaint of delayed payment.

We know little about recovery from war conditions. Cloth was needed after the war years and military requirements, including the growing use of red cloth for soldiers' coats,[6] resulted in some orders for Gloucestershire; while the whole area benefited in 1649 from the needs of the Parliamentary forces in Ireland.[7] On the other hand, the Merchant Adventurers' exports continued to fall, to under 20,000 pieces a year, it was said, in 1656.[8] In 1662 those of white cloth did not exceed 11,000[9] and those of coloured did not make up the deficiency. Indeed, in spite of the halving of the export duty at the Restoration from 6s. 8d. to 3s. 4d. per cloth,[10] total exports of long, short, and Spanish cloth from London to all destinations in 1662–3 were only 45,732 pieces, of which Germany and Holland

---

[1] *Bibl. Glouc.* i. 18; *H.M.C. 4th Rept.* (Duke of Sutherland's MSS.), 161b. The Parliamentary leanings of the north Wilts. towns may be seen from the many reports of disaffection after the Restoration.

[2] G.C.L. 16526 (Smyth Papers iii. 70); *Som. Arch. and Nat. Hist. Soc.*, 14. 62; *Cal. Ctee for Compounding* iii. 1972. Several other familiar surnames appear, but it is uncertain whether the owners were themselves clothiers.

[3] *Som. Arch. and Nat. Hist. Soc.* 14. 53 ff; S. W. Bates-Harbin, *Members of Parliament for the County of Somerset*, p. 158; *C.J.* iii. 211, 241; iv. 283, 619.

[4] *Bibl. Glouc.* ii. 185;

[5] Letter to Prince Rupert in possession of Messrs. Strachan & Co., Lodgemore Mills, Stroud.

[6] C. H. Firth, *Cromwell's Army*, p. 233.

[7] *C.S.P.D. 1649–50*, 343; ibid. *1650*, 570.

[8] *Thurloe State Papers* v. 127.

[9] B.M., Add. MSS. 25, 115, fol. 336.

[10] *C.J.* viii. 101; 12 Car. ii, c. 4.

together took over one-third.[1] In that year these two ancient markets of the Merchant Adventurers still took more cloth than any other single country, in spite of the heavy taxes to which it was subjected. The Dutch had been increasing impositions on English cloth since the beginning of the century in order to protect their own industry, and by 1652 white cloths were paying from £1. 16s. to £3. 1s. per piece. Medleys (the only kind of coloured cloth admitted) paid £1. 8s. 10d.[2] Taxes in Hamburg were lower; in 1652 cloths paid from 12s. to £1. 12s. sterling a piece.[3] This lower tax, together with the frequent Dutch wars and the withdrawal of privileges in Holland, resulted in making Hamburg the chief, and in time the only mart of the Merchant Adventurers, which, by the end of the century, had come to be known as the Hamburg Company.

The Company was far too valuable as a source of loans for Parliament to do other than preserve its monopoly,[4] but after the end of the Civil War there was a considerable period when its adversaries had the upper hand.[5] Cromwell's proclamation in its favour in 1656[6] probably did little to restore the position. After the Restoration its charter was renewed[7] but the trade was several times partially thrown open in the hope that more exporters might mean more buyers.[8] This, however, did little to increase exports to Holland and Germany, whether of finished or unfinished cloth. In 1699 the total exported from London was hardly greater than in 1662–3[9] and, although it rose a little in the years immediately following, it soon fell

---

[1] Figures from Michaelmas 1662 to Michaelmas 1663, Add. MSS. 36, 785.

[2] Add. MSS. 34, 326, fol. 36 ff. These taxes, set out in great detail by the Merchant Adventurers, differ somewhat from those given in *C.J.* viii. 149.

[3] *C.S.P.D. 1650*, 21 (i.e. 20s. to £2. 13s. 4d. Flemish, which was worth about three-fifths of sterling).

[4] *C.J.* iii. 236–7; *L.J.* vi. 255.

[5] Cf. its complaints of 'lack of countenance' by the Government, *C.S.P.D. 1652–3*, 136; also *Diary of Thomas Burton M.P.*, ed. J. T. Rutt, i. 308–10.

[6] *C.S.P.D. 1655–6*, 318, 340.

[7] P.R.O., P.C. 2/58, fol. 120; *Cal. Treas. Books 1660–67*, 140–1.

[8] *C.S.P.D. 1661–2*, 371; *1663–4*, 103; *1665–6*, 352,; *1670*, 510; *1673–5*, 420; *1676–7*, 26–7; P.R.O., P.C. 2/55, fol. 620; 2/58, fol. 518; 2/61, fol. 238; 2/62, fols. 173, 320, 341. Privileges were maintained for the mart towns of Dort and Hamburg.

[9] 15,597 pieces from London in 1699 (P.R.O., Customs 3/3) against 15,421 in 1662–3. Exports from the outports in 1699 added only another 1,576 pieces.

off again.[1] Most of the exports were of finished cloth. After 1709 the figure for white cloth only once reached 3,000 pieces and after 1722 was never much over 1,000.[2] Thus what had once been England's chief export petered out, amid frequent lamentations for its loss; but by the end of the century it was recognized by those who could consider the position dispassionately that its place had been taken by other kinds of woollen goods exported, for the most part, to other destinations.[3] Among these, western cloth played a substantial, though no longer a predominant part.

The greatest sufferer from the decline in white cloth exports was Wiltshire, which had been the largest producer. Possibly this was the reason why Fuller omitted it from his rather unsatisfactory list of counties producing woollen goods, although he later commended Wiltshire whites, while saying that medleys were most made in other shires.[4] Many places there took to the manufacture of such of the new draperies as were most akin to cloth. 'Cloth serges' were made everywhere, particularly in Calne and Devizes, which had previously been the centre of the white cloth industry, and also in the north-east of the county.[5] They had a reputation for durability,[6] but there seems to be no evidence for the story, which a German visitor heard from his Salisbury host in 1805, that the name of 'German serges' borne by those made in Devizes was derived from the fact that they had been introduced by Dutch immigrants in the reign of Queen Elizabeth.[7] It looks as if these

[1] 1701, 21,307 pieces; 1706, 18,408; 1710, 25,056; av. 1715–19, 9,743. On the other hand, exports of coarse cloth (dozens and kersies) from Yorks. via Hull do not appear to have declined and may have increased.

[2] See E. B. Schumpeter, *English Overseas Trade Statistics*, Table XIV.

[3] *H.M.C., H. of L. MSS.* (N.S.), v. 69–70; C. Davenant, *Works*, ed. Sir C. Whitworth, ii. 235.

[4] T. Fuller, *Church History of Britain* (ed. 1811), ii. 287; *Worthies of England* (ed. 1811), ii. 435. The latter was not true in 1662, but the information may have been collected at a much earlier date.

[5] *V.C.H. Wilts.* iv. 159. Cf. entries of apprentices to serge-makers in 'Wiltshire Apprentices and their Masters', ed. C. Dale, *W.A.S. Recd. Brch.* xvii, and lists of Quaker births etc., in *Wilts. N. and Q.* iii, iv, and v. Wilts. bays are mentioned in 1653, 1661, and 1665, kersies in 1658, (City of London Journals, vol. 41, fol. 197; vol. 46, fol. 74) but nothing more is heard of them.

[6] Defoe, *Compleat English Tradesman* (3rd. ed. 1732), i. 330; P. A. Nemnich, *Neueste Reise* (1807), p. 216. Either these or the druggets also made in Devizes were being exported to Italy in 1719, *C.J.* xix. 179.

[7] Nemnich, loc. cit.

serges may have been the refuge of many small clothiers or
weavers whose capital would not stretch to the making of
fully finished cloth, but who could manage to produce a
coarser material from cheaper wool; and it is possible that they
could be sold locally without the expense of sending them up
to London.[1] When druggets were introduced from France soon
after the Restoration, both the fine and the coarser varieties
were made in many places, sometimes by clothiers who produced cloth as well. Worsted was used for their warps, which
made them lighter than cloth, but they were almost indistinguishable from it;[2] and the fine sorts, made with Spanish wool,
were often worn by the gentry,[3] in spite of complaints that they
had gone out of fashion as soon as they came to be made in
England.[4] The making of these alternatives did not raise the
output to its former level; and it was in this period that the
production of Wiltshire fell to a permanently lower level than
that of Gloucestershire.

There is little evidence of the stages of decay. There was
much emigration to America and the West Indies from all the
western counties. The names of those who went from Bristol
as indentured servants are recorded from 1654 to 1683,[5] but
the number from clothmaking areas does not seem to be unusually large in comparison with that from other western
districts, and it would be rash to say that they all left because
there was no work for them at home. There are occasional
mentions of unemployment,[6] of ruined or empty fulling mills,[7]
or of high poor rates in certain districts.[8] The industry receded
from Tetbury and Marshfield on the high ground separating
the Stroudwater basin from that of the Bristol Avon; and the

---

[1] *C.S.P.D. 1683–4*, 84, where a serge seller in Devizes is mentioned as returning
pedlar's money to London.

[2] *V.C.H. Wilts.* iv. 159; D. Defoe, *A Tour through the whole Island of Britain*, ed.
G. D. H. Cole, i. 281.

[3] See below, p. 84 n. 1.

[4] *C.S.P.D. 1675–6*, 574; ibid. *1676–7*, 19.

[5] W. D. Bowman, *Bristol and America*.

[6] B. H. Cunnington, op. cit., p. 200; *H.M.C.Var.* i, 115, 144.

[7] Bodl. MSS. Aubrey ii, fol. 144; 'Progress Notes of Warden Woodward 1659–
1675', ed. R. L. Rickard, *W.A.S. Recd. Brch.* xiii. 56.

[8] *Wilts. Topographical Collections of John Aubrey*, ed. J. E. Jackson, p. 11. The statement relates to Calne and Chippenham in 1663 and Aubrey attributes the high
rates to enclosures.

importance of Cirencester as a clothmaking town greatly diminished.[1] The making of bays and stuffs was introduced there and woolstapling, woolcombing, and worsted spinning became staple industries. The three latter were the only ones to survive in Tetbury.[2] This decline is frequently ascribed to the want of water in these higher localities but seems to have been principally the result of the tendency towards concentration in certain districts, in the valley of the Bristol Avon and its tributaries, on Stroudwater,[3] and in an area on the Cotswold slopes extending southwards from Dursley to Chipping Sodbury. The attraction of the Avon valley for makers of Spanish cloth was particularly strong. William Brewer the second, who, according to Aubrey, drove 'the greatest trade for medleys of any clothier in England'[4] had left his native Lullington to settle in Trowbridge by 1651;[5] and the fine Spanish cloth industry which had distinguished Shepton Mallet and its neighbourhood in the thirties seems to have migrated to the county border.[6] The Wylye valley formed a south-east extension of this industrial area and led down to Salisbury, which continued to make white cloth in spite of occasional but exaggerated complaints of its decay.[7]

Dyeing and dressing were now established in the country, said the Merchant Adventurers in 1661,[8] and the separation of the clothworker's business from that of the fuller was rapidly being completed.[9] But this did not prevent large quantities of unfinished cloth from continuing to reach London. As late as

---

[1] S. Rudder, *History of Gloucestershire*, p. 345. One clothier was still there in 1840, *Repts. Asst. Commrs. Hdloom Weavers*, 1840, pt. 5 (H.C. 220), 416.

[2] Rudder, op. cit., p. 729. Both towns furnished yarn to Devon and Somerset, see the petitions for extending the post from Bristol to Wotton-under-Edge in 1699. *Cal. Treas. Papers* 1697–1701–2, 307–8.

[3] 'Stroudwater' comprises the valleys of Nailsworth, Painswick, Chalford, and Stroud, C. E. Watson, 'The Minchinhampton Custumal', *B.G.A.S.* 54, 374.

[4] Bodl. Libr., Aubrey MSS. 2., fol. 144.

[5] Trowbridge Parish Register, 1651.

[6] Clothiers in Shepton Mallet were said in 1692 to have suffered great losses from debts incurred by their factor Stroud, *The Clothier's Complaint*, p. 11. No doubt he was a member of the Strode family who were closely connected with the town.

[7] e.g. by A. Yarranton, *England's Improvement by Sea and Land*, p. 100.

[8] B.M., Add. MSS., 25, 115, fols. 341, 343.

[9] For the original practice see Fox and Taylor, *Some Account of the Guild of Weavers in Bristol*, p. 10. Cf. the very few men entered as shearmen in Smyth's Muster Roll of 1608 (see above, p. xvi, n. 3).

1747 the London woollen drapers were said to 'buy their cloths of one colour, white, from the Hall . . . and have them dyed and dressed in Town'.[1] These did not, of course, include cloths dyed in the wool, dark blues as well as medleys, which had to be bought fully finished in the country; but the makers of these cloths produced many whites as well. Worcester and Salisbury made them also, the latter producing what was possibly the finest cloth in England. At the end of the seventeenth century the very finest thin cloth . . . 'of the quality of what ladies wear for mourning'[2] was ordered by an Aleppo factor among other Salisburys, although a good deal of mourning cloth came from Holland where the black dye was said to be superior.[3] Bright colours could not be obtained except by dyeing in the piece and this was always a chancy business, best left to London dyers in the opinion of many merchants. Reds, however, were a Stroudwater speciality and the East India Company, whose usual practice was to buy whites for dyeing in London, made at least a partial exception in their favour.[4] So did Levant merchants, and in 1678 the true scarlet 'Bow dye', only introduced into England in 1640, was obtained by one of them from a Uley clothier.[5] It is a curious comment on the eighteenth-century belief that Stroudwater scarlets were the finest 'anywhere in England; perhaps in any part of the world'[6] that both these buyers had reverted by that time to having their reds dyed in London.[7] Blacks, greens, and blues were dyed in increasing quantities as time went on; and the cloth racks in the Stroudwater valley 'in their glorious colours of Scarlet, Crimson, Blue and a variety of other delightful colours'[8] were admired by eighteenth-century travellers; but the surviving letters and pattern books of clothiers and merchants up to late in the eighteenth century show that much unfinished cloth was despatched to Blackwell Hall factors from

---

[1] R. Campbell, *The London Tradesman*, p. 194.

[2] P.R.O., S.P. 110/20, fol. 43.

[3] *Mercator*, no. 130.

[4] Commonwealth Office Libr., Home Misc. 16, Dyers' Accounts for 1704, which show very few long Gloucesters dyed red, though many were exported.

[5] P.R.O., C.104/44, Waste Book of Jacob Turner, fol. 36.

[6] Defoe, *Tour* ii. 441.

[7] R. Heath, *Aleppo and Devonshire Square*, p. 112.

[8] J. Blanch, *Hoops into Spinning Wheels*, p. 9.

all over the region.[1] Gloucestershire white cloth for export was dressed in the country before dyeing,[2] which made the cloth cheaper but cannot have improved its quality.[3]

In the production of coloured cloth the area was divided into two regions. Clothiers in Wiltshire, East Somerset, and, to some extent, in the strip of land running from Dursley down to Kingswood in Gloucestershire, tended to make cloth dyed in the wool, while those of the Stroudwater basin dyed theirs in the piece. This may have corresponded in part with a geological difference affecting the water in the different regions, though this is not true of the two districts of Gloucestershire. The harder the water the more difficult it is to produce an even colour when dyeing in the piece. The streams which make up the Stroudwater system derive from a substratum of limestone with an admixture of Cotswold sands, and water from the latter is softer and more suitable for dyeing than that from the limestone. In the streams the two are mixed, but well water differs in different places as to the amount of solid matter it contains. No Gloucestershire water is really soft, but it is appreciably softer than what comes from the chalk, as much Wiltshire water does; though many of the streams issuing from the upper greensand on the north-west of Salisbury Plain have only a temporary hardness, much of which can be removed by boiling. Mendip water contains much lime, though there are softer springs near Shepton Mallet.[4] The property which was believed to make the water of the Stroud region so suitable for dyeing red has never been identified. All that can be said about it is that the water is not unsuitable for piece dyeing and that skill

[1] Wilts. C.R.O. 927, Clark Papers, Temple's Account Book (1736–8); Glouc. C.R.O., D.149, F114, Packer Lrs. (1760–9); 'Documents illustrating the Wiltshire Textile Trade in the eighteenth century', ed. J. de L. Mann, *W.A.S. Rec. Brch.* xix., no. 583 (1774).

[2] *C.J.* xv. 459 (1707), and see below, p. 43.

[3] But according to a French source it was desirable to dress thick cloth before dyeing it in the piece, since the dye did not penetrate to the bottom of the cloth and the hairs raised in rowing might be imperfectly dyed, *Encyclopédie méthodique, Manufactures, arts et métiers* i. 318. (All later references to this *Encyclopédie* are to Vol. i. of this section.)

[4] For all geological information I am indebted to Dr. R. P. Beckinsale's unpublished thesis in the Bodleian Library, 'A Geographical Survey of the Textile Industries of the West of England', pp. 1–6, 118, 162–3, 194–6, and also to an unpublished essay by D. Gowing, 'The Stroudwater Woollen Industry', a copy of which is in the Stroud Museum.

developed over a long period may have been an even more important element in the dyers' success than the nature of the water they used.

Spanish cloth was greatly improved after 1650. If any had been entirely made of Spanish wool before this date, the comments of contemporaries prove that it can have been very little. Even in the second half of the century most writers on the trade appear to have thought that it always contained some English wool.[1] The softness and short staple of Spanish wool made it difficult to spin a thread strong enough for warp; yet the Dutch had surmounted this obstacle and Dutch fine cloth was underselling English in 1660, even in England,[2] until a heavy duty made its import almost prohibitive. In 1674 it was reported from Poland that 'the Hollanders do in spinning, dressing, dyeing and pressing so far exceed ours ... that ... for one fine English cloth, twenty Hollands are sold here'.[3] It is not surprising that the idea of importing Dutch artisans to improve English cloth was in the air during the Commonwealth and immediately after the Restoration.[4] In 1658, Salisbury was considering the employment of a Dutchman 'for teaching the workhouse children in the Spanish trade',[5] and John Ashe's son-in-law, Paul Methuen of Bradford, had already introduced a spinner, Derricke or Richard Jonson, from Amsterdam about a year earlier.[6] It may have been a result of his success that in 1659 Methuen received from his brothers-in-law, who constituted the London firm of Ashe, 155 bags of Spanish wool,[7] a quantity far exceeding the eighty bags which were considered

---

[1] J. Smith, op. cit. i. 198 (1656); *C.S.P.D. 1675–6*, 375; J. Haynes, *A View of the Present State of the Clothing Trade*, p. 14. For Haynes's career see below, p. 77, n. 4.
[2] W. Cunningham, *Growth of English Industry and Commerce, Modern Times*, Pt. II. p. 918, App. D.
[3] P.R.O., S.P.88/13, quoted R. W. K. Hinton, *The Eastland Trade and the Common Weal in the Seventeenth Century*, p. 156.
[4] T. Violet, *The Advancement of Merchandize*, pp. 10–11; *C.S.P.D. 1661–2*, 80.
[5] R. Benson and H. Hatcher, *Old and New Sarum*, p. 441.
[6] W. H. Jones and J. E. Jackson, *Bradford-on-Avon*, annotated by J. Beddoe, p. 54. The date is usually given as 1659 when Methuen gave a bond to Bradford parish for him, but the counterpart in Lord Methuen's possession states that two children had been born since his arrival, Corsham Papers, no. 3249. Bradford-on-Avon did not acquire its distinguishing suffix until 1865 and in this book the mention of 'Bradford' always denotes Bradford, Wilts.
[7] P.R.O., C.107/18, Large Day Book, fols. 186, 198, 225–7, 241, 248, 262, 271, 280.

normal for a 'considerable' clothier in 1739.[1] It was left to William Brewer, fifteen years later, to sponsor a whole colony of Dutch workers; but most of them came in response to a royal proclamation offering a welcome to Dutch merchants or craftsmen, which was issued in 1672 during the Franco-Dutch war.[2] Twenty-nine 'Dutch clothiers', with their dependents, arrived via Ostend in 1673 and 1674 and were consigned to Brewer at Trowbridge with the injunction to look after them and the promise that the King would be responsible for them if they got into difficulties.[3]

The Dutch have remained mostly anonymous, since the names of the first party are not known, and of the second it has only been possible to discover with certainty David Celosse, who lived in Trowbridge from 1674 to 1697 and returned to Holland after the Peace of Ryswick.[4] There are traces of others. The royal promise may have been forgotten twenty years later, for the Trowbridge overseers were paying the relatively large sum of 10s. a week to 'Daniel the Dutchman' with two children in 1693.[5] 'Dutch' appears as a surname in Trowbridge Parish Registers in 1712 and in the Frome ratebook in 1728,[6] and is still found in Wiltshire. Jonson's descendants continued to live in Bradford, and it is known that Brewer established three other men there, whom he seems to have brought over himself.[7] The suggestion that some moved to Twerton (now part of

[1] Smith, op. cit. ii. 312.

[2] *C.S.P.D. 1672*, 210.

[3] *V.C.H. Wilts*. iv. 157. It is frequently stated, on the authority of Roger Coke (who is not very reliable), that they were Walloons who arrived in 1668 under the leadership of 'one Brewer whose parents were said to be English', *A Detection of the Court and State of England* (4th ed. 1719), ii. 161. Elsewhere he says they were all Papists (*Reflections upon the East Indy and Royal African Companies*, p. 20) which, if one may judge by David Celosse, was untrue. If he was referring to another party, it has left no trace in the west, though one was reported in Ostend in 1675, *C.S.P.D. 1675–6*, 236. The position is complicated by the fact that a John Brewer and a Martin Bruer were both naturalized in 1675, ibid., 585, 584.

[4] *C.S.P.D. 1697*, 279. He lived in what is now Polebarn Rd. Som. C.R.O. DD/PL 23. (I owe this reference to Mr. K. H. Rogers.) The others were Reyner Rubuis and Clare his son, Leonard Servey, Hendrick Goodman, and Daniel Hooke, P.R.O., P.C.2/64, fol. 48o.

[5] Wilts C.R.O., 712/12. Trowbridge P.L. Papers. This reference also comes from Mr. Rogers.

[6] Som. C.R.O., DD/LW, 36 (Nicholas Dutch). The burial of 'Marie Cornil, Dutchman's wife' also appears in Trowbridge Par. Reg. in 1692.

[7] *V.C.H. Wilts*. iv. 156. 'James Jonson alias Dutch' was apprenticed by the Poor Law authorities in 1732, Wilts. C.R.O., 77/166.

Bath) has been shown to be unfounded by the discovery that the men with Dutch or German names buried there between 1722 and 1740 were, in fact, German brass-founders.[1]

Although we do not know how most of the Dutch immigrants fared, they left their mark on the industry. They did not originate the making of fine cloth but they did much to improve it. They made better cards, an indispensable requisite for producing fine yarn. Dutch card leaves for scribbling are mentioned in Frome in 1706[2] and references to 'Dutch spinning' can be found in the books of a Trowbridge clothier in 1724.[3] We do not know in what way they improved methods of dressing, but it is probable that their technique helped to lower costs; in fact one contemporary gives the reduction as 40 per cent.[4] The very high prices which prevailed even after the Restoration[5] disappeared in the 1680s, and this was not the result, as some alleged,[6] of a fall in the price of Spanish wool. Contemporaries seem to have thought that the Dutch had most to teach in finishing, for the largest group of those who flocked into Bradford and Trowbridge in the later seventies were clothworkers.[7] As far as we know, there were no Dutch in Gloucestershire, but fifteen immigrants came from thence to the two Wiltshire towns, and the use of Spanish wool had spread north of Kingswood by 1677. John Iles, said to have been the first person to use it in Uley,[8] was selling Spanish cloth to the Levant merchant, Jacob Turner, in that year and so were other Gloucestershire clothiers, Samuel Purnell, John Blanch, and others whose names are not given and whose marks cannot be identified.[9] The men named came

[1] *V.C.H. Som.* ii. 416; See *Bath Chronicle*, 17 Nov. 1937, Art. by R. G. Naish.

[2] Som. C.R.O., Sess. Rolls 241/2.

[3] Wilts. C.R.O. 927, Clark Papers, Cloth Book of Usher & Jeffries. The term may mean yarn reeled on the Dutch reel which may have had different dimensions from the English one. It was still used in Trowbridge 140 years later. J. Bodman, *History of Trowbridge*, p. 23.

[4] R. Coke, *A Detection. . . .* ii. 161.

[5] 20s. a yard is recorded for fine Spanish cloth in 1674, but later prices in this range were only for grain colours or drabs (a fine heavy cloth).

[6] Smith, op. cit. i. 312. The high price of Spanish wool in 1660 given in this pamphlet is not borne out by other evidence. See below, p. 266, n. 6.

[7] *V.C.H. Wilts.* 157.

[8] *B.G.A.S.* xi. 200. The name is spelt Eyles, Iles, and Eeles, the latter consistently by Turner, but as he is designated as 'of Uley', the identification seems certain. For this spelling see M. A. Rudd, *Historical Records of Bisley with Lypiatt*, p. 392.

[9] P.R.O., C.104/44, Waste Book, esp. fols. 36, 89, where 'Spanish' are distinguished from 'Lemster' whites.

from the slopes of the Cotswolds, and the first mention of Spanish cloth in the Stroudwater region proper has not been found until 1691,[1] but it would be strange if Spanish wool had not been used there at an earlier date. Even in 1667 it could be said, in the preamble to an abortive bill to regulate the manufacture of 'broad woollen cloth of the New Draperies commonly called Spanish cloth' in the three counties, that 'the nature of the said manufacture is much changed in these late years and that the new Draperie is most in use in the counties aforesaid',[2] although this does not necessarily mean the employment of Spanish wool. Even at the end of the century it was very far from the case that, as one writer put it in 1699, 'no Cloth of above 10s. a yard white or 13s. per yard in mix'd Colours . . . hath one Dram of English wool therein'.[3]

The new cloth was not always approved of, except by its wearers. Its weight continued to decrease and by 1689 that of fine medleys and Salisbury whites was roughly between $10\frac{1}{2}$ and 12 ounces per square yard, about two-thirds of what it had been in the thirties.[4] Samuel Ashe (John's younger brother) was almost speaking the literal truth when he told Aubrey about 1680 that spinning had been so much improved in the last forty years that one pound of wool made twice as much cloth as before the Civil War.[5] But some thought that thinner cloth was a debasement of the manufacture;[6] and when the price of English wool was low, it was bad enough that the 'thin tentered broad cloths in which there is not one third part of the wool formerly spent'[7] consumed less of it, but it was still worse if the wool were Spanish, for the wearers might then be represented as slighting their country's produce in favour of outlandish luxuries.[8] Such objections were a tribute to the popularity of Spanish cloth, and they reinforce the impression

[1] *London Gazette*, no. 2653.

[2] Arch. H. L., 11 Nov. 1667; See below, p. 99.

[3] Smith, op. cit. ii. 43.

[4] See App. II.

[5] Bodl. Libr. MSS. Aubrey, 2, fol. 64.

[6] Smith, op. cit. i. 226, where Sir Josiah Child argues against this belief, Cf. *British Merchant*, ed. C. King, ii. 96.

[7] *C.S.P.D. 1677–8*, 37. Cf. ibid. *1675–6*, 376.

[8] Smith, op. cit. i. 316. The original pamphlet 'A Treatise of Wool and Cattel' makes a much more sustained attack, which is abridged by Smith. For its authorship see below, p. 72.

of the prosperity of its makers which is given by the comparative absence of complaints from them in a period full of complaints from other quarters. Relying largely on home consumption they were often prosperous when the rest of the industry was depressed, as in 1675 when the wearing of Spanish cloth by the King gave rise to a great sale.[1] Perhaps it is unsafe to assume prosperity from the absence of petitions, for most of those from other places reached Parliament in connection with bills about the illicit export of wool; and clothiers using, or purporting to use, Spanish wool had nothing to complain of in that respect. Nor did the Spanish clothiers work for the Levant Company which, as we shall see, organized several petitions, and they did participate in those relating to the Hamburg Company in the nineties.[2] Nevertheless, their silence on other occasions is remarkable, in view of the fact that by the end of the century exports of their cloth had declined by about one-third from the level of 1662–3[3] and were lower than they had been in 1640.[4] This was due to the imposition of tariffs or prohibitions in Flanders, France, and Portugal to check the taste for English cloth and nourish the native industry. The trade to France is particularly interesting in view of the clamour against French goods in the seventies. In 1662–3 the Spanish cloth sent there amounted to not much over 1,000 pieces. The doubling of the tariff in 1667 had reduced this figure considerably by 1668–9, but by 1675 it was rising again and between 1683 and 1686–7 it reached what was probably a higher total than ever before, at 4,000 to 5,000 pieces a year.[5] This is the more remarkable because the prohibition placed on nearly all French imports in 1678 must, one would think, have checked exports also; and the fact that over 4,000 pieces were exported in 1683–4, before the ban on imports was lifted at the accession of James II, testifies to a keen demand. In fact, the popularity of Spanish cloth was too much for the reviving French industry to face;

[1] *C.S.P.D. 1677–8*, 70.

[2] *C.J.* xi. 81; xii. 156; xiii. 99. See below, p. 18, n. 2.

[3] See App. I, Table A.

[4] They were over 12,000 pieces in 1640 (see p. xx), and only averaged some 10,000 in 1699–1701.

[5] M. Priestley, 'Anglo-French Trade and the Unfavourable Balance Controversy, 1660–1685', *Econ. Hist. Rev.* (2nd ser.), iv(1). 46. The figures are:

1683–4	4131 pieces ⎱	Priestley,	1685–6	4190 pieces ⎱	*Mercator*,
1684–5	4856 pieces ⎰	loc. cit.	1686–7	5077 pieces ⎰	nos. 63, 25.

and the tariff was again raised by one-third in 1687, with the result that exports fell to 781 pieces in the following year.[1] The ban on all trade with France imposed after the Revolution of 1688 removed the opportunity of testing whether consumption would have risen again in spite of the addition to the price. Yet there were still no complaints. It may have been felt that they were useless or even dangerous; but the majority of the clothiers and their factors were Whigs,[2] who must have found their political views running contrary to their economic interest. They sent up some petitions at the end of the century when Flanders prohibited the import of cloth in retaliation for the English prohibition of bone lace;[3] but, in spite of a speedy withdrawal of the latter, the Flemish market was never wholly regained.[4] Spanish cloth, however, found its best market at home and it is surprising that Davenant estimated home consumption for 1688 at only 10,000 pieces a year, though his figure of about 9,000 pieces for exports fits other statistics on this point.[5] In 1704, when exports were beginning to rise, it was said that 30,000 pieces a year were made,[6] and this seems to be a more probable estimate.

Gloucestershire, which had produced far less white cloth for export than Wiltshire, suffered correspondingly less from its decline. If the figure of nearly 10,000 pieces already given for exports of western cloth (apart from medleys) in 1640[7] is anywhere near the truth, much of the loss may have been made up before the Civil War began. Gloucestershire clothiers made no specific complaint during the Interregnum and just after the Restoration when the industry in general was extremely depressed. The representations from the county for a free Parliament in 1659–60, unlike those from Devonshire, Kent, Norfolk, and Yorkshire, made no mention of decay of trade.[8] Gloucestershire cloth was, in fact, already finding a satisfactory

---

[1] *Mercator*, no. 72.

[2] Cf. the remarks about them in *A Treatise of Wool and the Manufacture of it*.

[3] *V.C.H. Wilts.* iv. 158.

[4] *C.S.P.D. 1699–1700*, 128. Cf. Haynes, *Great Britain's Glory*, p. 17. English cloth was superseded by Dutch, especially by that from Limburg.

[5] C. Davenant, *Works* ii. 149.

[6] Smith, op. cit. (2nd ed.), ii. 256.

[7] See p. xvi, n. 1.

[8] The Gloucestershire petitions are in B.M. 190, g. 13, nos. 302 and 303. Cf. Cunningham, op. cit., App. E., pp. 921–7.

outlet in the Mediterranean and especially in the Levant; and its production was probably increasing.

As it became apparent that exports to Holland and Germany would never again reach their former level, attention began to be more continuously directed to the growth of foreign competition, nourished, as was almost universally believed, on smuggled exports of English wool.[1] However this opinion may have originated,[2] it was not justified in the seventeenth century as far as carding wool was concerned. Combing wool was another matter; but good carding wool of lower quality than the fine Spanish sorts imported into England could be obtained from many other parts of Europe besides Spain, while French wool was suitable for many of the cheaper kinds of cloth.[3] These facts made little difference to propagandists who, as was said later, discussed the question almost continuously 'in a Spirit of Romance on the one hand and of Credulity on the other'.[4] The mass of literature on the subject and the number of times it was discussed in Parliament, the procession of bills designed to make the precautions against smuggling more effective, and the constant ascription of depressions to 'the transportation of our Wool' compel sympathy for those Members of Parliament who in 1747 were said 'to make it almost a standing Rule . . . as often as this Subject is started for their Deliberation to take up their Hats and move off'.[5] Gloucestershire was far better off than most of the counties which had manufactured cloth before 1640, but its clothiers protested as loudly as any. Occasionally the petitions seem to have originated within the county. Some manufacturers, though not all, lost their stocks in the Fire of London[6] and the Plague must have had a depressing effect on home sales as well as on exports. It is not surprising that weavers, tuckers, and spinners should have been complaining about their poverty in the autumn of 1666;[7] and the clothiers' successful efforts in 1669 to make it a felony to steal cloth from the racks

---

[1] For the earlier history of this agitation see P. J. Bowden, *The Wool Trade in Tudor and Stuart England*, pp. 184–94.

[2] See below, pp. 259–60.

[3] *British Merchant* ii. 398–9, 430; *H.M.C., H. of L. MSS.* (N.S.), x. 142. These accounts are to be preferred to the denials of *Mercator*.

[4] Smith, op. cit. i. xi.

[5] Ibid. i. ii.

[6] *H.M.C. Portland* iii. 298

[7] *C.J.* viii. 633.

when drying[1] suggest an increase in that form of larceny which
may have been due to severe unemployment. The majority
of petitions, however, were got up by merchants or Blackwell
Hall factors in connection with contemplated legislation. In
the nineties the Hamburg Company was struggling to preserve
its privileges[2] and petitions for and against its exclusive right
to export cloth to Hamburg and its neighbourhood were, no
doubt, organized on one side by factors who dealt with members
of the Company and on the other by those whose clients came
from a wider circle.[3] The many petitions about 'running of
wool' were similarly organized,[4] and the statements made in
them about poverty and decay must be taken with a grain of
salt. They may testify to temporary setbacks but are no guide
to the general condition of the industry. Defoe's remarks on
the absurdity of believing the statements made in petitions
have much truth in them, even if they were themselves made as
propaganda for the commercial clauses of the Treaty of
Utrecht.[5]

From the fifties onwards the fortunes of the Gloucestershire
industry were becoming more and more involved with those of
the Levant Company; and the circumstances in which the
Company found itself had more effect on the clothiers' prosperity than any other single cause. Wiltshire clothiers also sold
some cloth to members of the Company but, with the exception
of those of Salisbury, they were less involved. By 1669 the
Levant equalled Holland and Germany together as a market
for English cloth,[6] and from 1671 to 1683 the exports averaged nearly 20,000 pieces a year,[7] but the trade was subject to

[1] *C.J.* ix. 116; 22 Car. ii, c. 5.
[2] The Act (1 Wm. and Mary, c. 32, 12) under which the privileges were removed
expired in 1693 and the clause relating to the Company was omitted from the
Continuation Act (4 and 5 Wm. and Mary, c. 31, 10), cf. *C.S.P.D. 1700–2 and
Add.*, 576. The Company fought hard for its privileges (cf. J. Houghton, *A Collection for the Improvement of Husbandry and Trade* i. 454) but in March 1698 a bill to
support it did not get beyond its first reading (*C.J.* xii. 157) and another attempt
in 1700 shared the same fate, *C.J.* xiii. 208.
[3] *C.J.* xi. 66; xii. 81. See above, p. 15, n. 2.
[4] Cf. *H.M.C. 4th Rept.* (R. Cholmondely's MSS.), 349. Lr. from J. Tily to John
Smyth, 1706, asking him to get his neighbours to sign such a petition.
[5] *Mercator*, no. 7.
[6] B.M., Add. MSS. 36, 785.
[7] *An Account of the Number of Woollen Cloths . . . exported by the Levant Company . . .
in 46 years from Xmas 1671 to Xmas 1717.*

considerable fluctuation. Usually the Company chartered its own general ships, but it occasionally deferred sending them; and when this happened it tried to prevent its members from exporting on other vessels. To effect a restriction of supply in order to keep up the price was a point to which the Company attached great importance, and the clothiers' protests went unheeded.[1] More cloth might have been sold if its members had operated more widely over the country instead of only in the three centres of Constantinople, Smyrna, and Aleppo, but attempts by Bristol merchants to broaden the Charter in order that they might be included met with no success.[2]

Curiously enough, the new draperies did not make much impression in the Levant.[3] Anatolia and Persia, to which many of the exports found their way, were cold countries in winter and the warmth of cloth was appreciated there. The trade was mainly in piece-dyed material, red, wine, violet, sky-blue, and the various greens, with a few 'pearl' and 'aurora'; and these, with a smaller quantity of cinnamon, wormwood, orange, lemon, and sea-green, known as 'Persian colours', were taken by merchants from Smyrna and Aleppo far into the interior of Asia. In the early years of the century the chief exports had been kersies and Suffolk cloth, but by the thirties cloth was superseding kersies, and western cloth, mainly from Gloucestershire, was catching up with that from Suffolk. In 1640 Suffolk still predominated,[4] but during the Commonwealth the Gloucestershire clothiers adapted themselves to the demands of the market and made their cloth longer and narrower,[5] with the result that it became very popular. Factors in Aleppo found western cloth the best and references to the desirability of Stroudwater reds are frequent in letters from thence in 1658–9.[6]

---

[1] *Reasons for preserving the Publick Market at Blackwell Hall and restraining the Levant Company . . . from deferring their Shipping as long as they please.*

[2] P.R.O., S.P.29/268/142; P.C.2/62, fols. 2, 26, 35.

[3] e.g. in 1690 over 30,000 cloths were exported but only 270 perpetuanas (serges) and in 1701 the numbers were 21,905 cloths to 4,908 perpetuanas, P.R.O., S.P.105/145, fol. 298.

[4] Port Book, 1640, P.R.O., E.190/43/4. If, as suggested above (p. xvi, n. 1), the 'short narrow lists' were Stroudwaters the addition of them to the 'long plain lists' would still leave a small balance in favour of the Suffolks.

[5] *C.J.* x. 169–70. One witness had first seen this cloth in 1652 and another said 'they came into request about 1657'.

[6] P.R.O., S.P.110/11 *passim*. Cf. G. Ambrose, 'English Traders at Aleppo', *Econ. Hist. Rev.* iii(2). 248.

Worcester whites were equally good[1] and Worcester was coming
to depend almost entirely on the Levant trade.[2] More Suffolk
than western cloth was still being exported in 1665[3] but by
1675 nearly 90 per cent of the exports were westerns and
'Suffolk' as a title had disappeared,[4] although it is probable
that most of the thousand odd pieces exported as 'long' and
'short' cloth came from thence. At the end of the century the
nomenclature in the port books settled down as 'short' and
'long' and it is no longer possible to distinguish the origin of
the cloth, but it is clear from other sources that western cloth
had conquered almost the whole field. Suffolk blues, which had
been in demand in 1634,[5] had almost entirely disappeared. The
popularity of reds, of which, among other things, the Turkish
fez was made,[6] gave Gloucestershire a great advantage.
Moreover the western cloth exported, though not called 'Spanish', was not so heavy as the Suffolk, which had remained
unaffected by the trend to lighter cloth in the west.[7] From 1677
to 1685 the Levant merchant Jacob Turner was still buying
some Suffolk cloth, blues, plunkets, and whites, the latter
rather cheaper than Gloucestershire whites; but he bought far
more western and particularly Gloucestershire cloth, both
white and red.[8] A little Suffolk cloth was still being exported
after 1700[9] but its blue cloth trade could be called lost as early
as 1681.[10]

The western cloth sent out in the sixties was of medium
quality, but by the next decade finer cloth, which in earlier
years seems only to have been sent for presents, was being exported in greater quantities. In 1676 the Company rejoiced to find

[1] Ambrose, loc. cit.
[2] Cf. *C.J.* x. 393.
[3] P.R.O., E.190/50/4. (Exports to Smyrna only, as the Port Book is not complete.)
The short Suffolks exceed the long western by about 200 cloths, but many cloths
were entered only as 'short' or 'long' and most of the long were probably also
Suffolks.
[4] P.R.O., E.190/62/1. The following year the proportion was only 75 per cent,
E.190/63/8. I am indebted to Mrs. Millard for figures from these three Port Books.
[5] P.R.O., S.P.110/10. fol. 16.
[6] Ambrose, loc. cit., 248, n. 4.
[7] *British Merchant* ii. 96.
[8] P.R.O., C.104/44, Waste Book.
[9] P.R.O., C.111/127, Pt. i, Ledger of Henry Phill, 7 May 1703.
[10] Smith, op. cit. i. 363. Suffolk was also losing the Eastland trade, Hinton,
op. cit., App. D.

that it 'grows into so good esteem', and it noted that Salisburys were now 'more plentifully exported than formerly'.[1] In the following year it noted that English cloth had gained a good reputation among the Turks, 'beyond the manufacture of other nations'.[2] This decade was a prosperous one for the Company; for the Dutch, their chief competitors in fine cloth, were hampered by higher customs duties in Turkey and above all by the war with France, which also prevented the French from expanding what up to that time had been a very modest share of the trade.[3] This buoyancy may have done something to offset the depression which followed the Stop of the Exchequer in 1672 and the outbreak of war with Holland, though sales to other quarters may have been difficult to effect.[4] Perhaps not too much should be made of the absence of any protest from the county against the export of white cloth in 1674, for such petitions were got up by dyers and clothworkers[5] who may not have had many clients in Gloucestershire at this time. But the Levant trade was itself depressed in the eighties by the Austro-Turkish war and the exactions of an oppresive Grand Vizier.[6] The average exports for the five years 1684–8 dropped by about 5,000 cloths a year[7] and this, together with the general recession of 1683–6, caused considerable distress. In 1687 Gloucestershire clothiers were complaining that their sales for the Levant had fallen from 800 cloths a week to under 500 and might go still lower.[8] Conditions improved in the years immediately following but King William's wars had an even more disastrous effect. The ships which should have gone out in the winter of 1691–2 were first detained for convoy until March 1693 and then nearly all sunk by the French off Portugal. Even those which survived and went out again the following year were scattered by a storm which sank four of them and

---

[1] P.R.O., S.P.105/114, fols. 23, 42.

[2] Ibid., fol. 94.

[3] A. C. Wood, *A History of the Levant Company*, pp. 98–100.

[4] See below, p. 68.

[5] There was a spate of petitions about this in 1674 in which Worcester joined but Gloucestershire did not, *C.S.P.D. 1673–5*, 316, and see *V.C.H. Wilts.* iv. 155. The petition from Coventry is addressed to a dyer, P.R.O., S.P.29/361/244.

[6] Wood, op. cit., pp. 105–6.

[7] *An Account of the Number of Woollen Cloths. . . .*

[8] *C.S.P.D. 1686–7*, no. 346. They ascribed the fall to the fact that in 1686 purchases for the Levant had dropped from 20,000 to 7,000 cloths.

drove the rest to incur heavy charges at Cadiz.[1] Sales were partially kept up by interlopers[2] and also by Armenian merchants operating from Surat, who were buying Gloucestershire cloth for Persia as early as 1690 and shipping it out on the East India Company's ships.[3] These activities may have alleviated the situation but bitter complaints came from every centre which supplied the Levant,[4] though the Company seem to have been successful in directing at least some of them to the door of its enemy the East India Company, on which, with the assistance of petitions from clothiers, it had already made some attacks.[5] They were motivated by the fact that raw silk from India competed with that from Persia so that the East India Company's imports made it impossible for the Levant Company to do as much trade as before.[6]

The East India Company had itself been exporting cloth since the beginning of the century.[7] Great efforts had been made to find a market in China, but sales could only be effected there under very discouraging conditions.[8] In 1681 the quantity exported had risen to 5,560 broadcloths besides some other woollens; but after the loss of Bantam to the Dutch and the

---

[1] *H.M.C., H. of L. MSS.* (N.S.), i. 104–6, 190 ff.

[2] See esp. P.R.O., S.P.105/145, fol. 225, where Richard Blackham represents himself as having exported over 18,000 cloths in 1692. Though this may be exaggerated, he was remembered with gratitude in Gloucestershire and was given an obituary notice (*Gloucester Journal*, 16 July 1728) where it is said that he sailed without convoy. He was knighted by William III.

[3] *C.J.* x. 563, 570; East India Co.'s Court Books, vol. 36 (B/40), fol. 39; J. Blanch, *An Abstract of the Grievances of Trade*, pp. 10–11, where they are called Persians and Grecians.

[4] *C.S.P.D. 1693*, 324.

[5] According to Sir J. Child (Smith, op. cit. i. 363–5) the Levant Co. managed to get the East India Co. included in the petitions from Glos. and Coventry complaining of both Companies in 1675 (*C.J.* ix. 376, 327; *Court Min. of the E.I. Co.*, ed. E. B. Sainsbury, x. 180–1, 238, 241). The petitions in 1693 asking that the E.I. Co. might be forced to export more often or that members of the Levant Co. might join in their privileges (P.R.O., P.C.2/75, fols. 205, 218; *C.J.* x. 647, 710) were, no doubt, inspired from the same source. Cf. Nathaniel Harley's remarks, *H.M.C. Portland* ii. 246–7.

[6] W. R. Scott, *Joint Stock Companies* ii. 135; Smith, op. cit. i. 366; *C.S.P.D. 1686–7* nos. 257, 346; *C.J.* x. 395.

[7] H. N. Stevens, *The Dawn of British Trade to the East Indies, 1599–1603*, p. 36. The dyers' accounts already quoted (Com. Office Libr., Home Misc. 16) show the same kind of cloth as was sent to the Levant.

[8] H. B. Morse, *The Chronicles of the East India Company trading to China, 1635–1834* i. Chs. iii–iv.

capture of Amoy and Formosa by the Manchus in 1682 the exports greatly declined.[1] This cloth also came largely from Gloucestershire where, in 1685, clothiers said that they usually sold the Company from 1,500 to 2,000 pieces a year.[2] Cloth could not be sold in India except to Europeans; and the most hopeful market remaining was Persia where the Armenians from Surat were already established. The idea that the Persian market could be secured for cloth sent up from India was in the minds of the Directors[3] when they were forced in 1693, as a condition of renewing their Charter, to give bonds to export English goods to the value of £100,000 by January 1694 and and another £50,000 by the following April, of which half were to be woollen goods.[4] Their subsequent attack on this market infuriated the Levant Company[5] and ensured that the new Charter did less than had been expected to increase total exports of woollen goods to the East. It did, however, establish the principle that the Company's resources must be engaged to support the English woollen manufacture, even at a loss to itself. Although the western clothiers did not develop quite the same dependence upon the Company as later characterized the Devon serge manufacturers or the Norwich stuffmakers, the trade in cloth, all of which came from the west and most of it from Gloucestershire, became large enough to make a great difference to the total output of the area. Here again the import-ance of cloth is surprising. One would have thought that the lighter bays or stuffs would have been the obvious choice for a hot climate, but the quantity of stuffs and cloth rashes sent out in 1693–4 was only about four-fifths of that of cloth. In view of its higher price the latter formed nearly 80 per cent of the value of the woollen goods sent out and, indeed, the bond could not have been executed without it.[6]

From 1694 trade markedly improved, assisted by the state

[1] *C.S.P.D. 1686–7*, 432.

[2] Ibid., 346. Worcester and Salisbury probably furnished most of the remainder.

[3] S. A. Khan, *The East India Trade in the Seventeenth Century*, pp. 248–50. Cf. Home Misc. 36, Pt. II, fols. 32 (Contract with Coja Panous Calendar, 11 Mar. 1694/5), 40 (Lr. from Sir J. Child 11 May 1695).

[4] P.R.O., P.C.2/75, fols. 243–4.

[5] Wood, op. cit., pp. 115–17.

[6] The quantities exported between Feb. 1694 and May 1697 were: broadcloth, 20,377 pieces, cloth rashes (a kind of serge) 1015 pieces, stuffs 15,514 pieces. Their value was, cloth £222,860, rashes, £8,095, stuffs, £49,434. Home Misc. 36, fol. 246.

of the coinage and inflation due to war finance.[1] The recoinage of 1696 affected prices and lowered exports. They rose again after the Peace of Ryswick but the large quantities sent out in 1698 were too great for the markets to absorb and the price of raw materials showed little decline from the war level.[2] There was much discontent in the last years of the century, evinced, as far as Gloucestershire was concerned, by the continuing agitation against the Blackwell Hall factors,[3] the petitions against wool broggers[4] and demands that the second East India Company should also be forced to export woollen goods.[5] No part of the area was directly concerned in the controversy over the import of Indian silks and calicoes, for these did not compete with cloth nor with such serges and druggets as were made there; but clothiers in both counties were again roped in by their factors to express diverging opinions, according to which Company they traded with, over the East India Company's imports of raw silk[6]—a question which was to remain in contention for many years to come. The century ended with the removal of the remaining duty on woollen materials exported, in the hope of encouraging the manufacture.[7]

In 1702 the Board of Trade and Plantations reported that total exports of woollen goods were worth over a million pounds more than in the sixties, but that the increase was chiefly in the new draperies.[8] It escaped them on this occasion (although this error was rectified later)[9] that the earlier figures referred only to London and that this fact was responsible for much of the apparent increase. It is possible, however, to separate exports from London from those of the outports at the end of the century; and a comparison of the year 1662–3 with the average of the years 1699–1701[10] shows that the quantity of cloth exported from London in the later period had risen by about 29 per cent. This increase was entirely due to the very

---

[1] C. Davenant, *Works*, ed. Whitworth, i. 95.

[2] J. de L. Mann, 'A Wiltshire Family of Clothiers', *Econ. Hist. Rev.* (2nd ser.), ix(2). 247–8.

[3] See below, pp. 74–5.　　　　　　　　[4] See below, p. 262.

[5] *C.J.* xii. 423; xiii. 6.　　　　　　　　[6] Ibid. xi. 529, 623, 657, 659.

[7] 11 and 12 Wm. III, c. 20.　　　　　　[8] *H.M.C., H. of L. MSS.* (N.S.), v. 69.

[9] C. Davenant, *Works* v. 351; *H.M.C., H. of L. MSS.* (N.S.), x. 146.

[10] See App. I, Table A. Average exports for 1699–1701 may be slightly exaggerated owing to over-entries in 1701 after the removal of the export duty, but Davenant thought this affected mainly the new draperies, *Works* v. 443–5.

large rise in long cloth of which nearly treble the quantity was exported, reflecting the increase in the Mediterranean and East India trades. Short cloth, on the other hand, showed a decrease of over a thousand pieces while Spanish cloth had fallen by 36 per cent. The outports at this date exported hardly anything under the heading of 'cloth' and confined themselves to the new draperies and to the coarser varieties of the old, such as kersies and dozens, in both of which their exports greatly exceeded those from London.

A report of the Board in 1716 still treats long, short, and Spanish cloth—the 'fine draperies' as Davenant called them,[1] though most were not really very fine—as coming entirely from the west.[2] A very large portion must have done so, but it would be unsafe to conclude that no other part of the country furnished any of the 62,000 pieces which is the average annual figure exported under these heads in 1699–1701. Yorkshire's production was still mainly kersies and dozens, but Yorkshire cloth had been sent to the Levant in the seventeenth century, though not, it was said, very profitably.[3] Reading and Newbury were still exporting, though probably not much,[4] and a small quantity still came from Suffolk. Other places such as north and south Somerset, Dorset, and Witney also made cloth, some of which may have been sent abroad. One may perhaps calculate an average figure for western exports for the years 1699 to 1701 of about 54,000 pieces per annum,[5] which is not much larger than the quantity exported in 1640[6] and is, of course, well below the figure of 60,000 pieces said to have been the average annual export of white cloths alone at the beginning of the century. Production was, however, concentrated in a much smaller area, and there had been a great increase in

[1] Ibid. v. 445.

[2] P.R.O., S.P.35/5/38. The number of 'western Cloths' given in this document corresponds closely with the total of broad, long, short, and Spanish cloths in Schumpeter, op. cit., Table XIV (though that for northern double dozens does not). The figures given in Smith, op. cit. ii. 153 (rather differently arranged) are much lower and must have been manipulated for political purposes.

[3] P.R.O., S.P.110/20, fols. 19, 41. J. Haynes, *A View* . . . , p. 85, and see below, p. 37, n. 4.

[4] *C.J.* xiii. 52.

[5] For the figures on which this total is based see App. V.

[6] Taking white cloth exported at 30,000 pieces (see p. xv, n. 4), coloured western cloth at 10,000 pieces (p. xvi, n. 1) and Spanish cloth at 12,000 pieces (p. xx) we get a total of 52,000 pieces.

home consumption, for western cloth had nearly superseded that from Kent and Berkshire as the general wear of gentry and middle classes alike, though lighter materials, such as druggets, serges, and worsted stuffs seem often to have been worn as well, the stuffs especially by women and children.

Seventeenth-century statistics are not likely to be accurate, but it is possible to construct, from various sources, an estimate for the annual production of the western cloth-manufacturing region, including Worcester, of some 80,000 to 90,000 cloths,[1] which is not incompatible with a figure of 54,000 pieces for export. Even at this figure the part played by the western cloth industry in the production of woollen goods hardly justified the attention it received. The value of the cloth exported in 1700 was less than half that of the new draperies and just over 25 per cent of the total for the main woollen[2] piece goods. This proportion would probably be considerably lower if home consumption could be taken into account. The middle and upper classes wore western cloth, but the mass of the people wore serge, coarse druggets, kersies, or the coarse Yorkshire cloth known as 'dozens'. However long they may have made their clothes last, their numbers ensured that their total consumption must have been greater than that of the more well-to-do. The relatively minor place of western cloth in the woollen industry can also be seen from a table of net profits from the aulnage for 1686–8.[3] Gloucestershire's £600 and Wiltshire's £300 must be contrasted with the £1,500 estimated for Devonshire (mainly serges) and the £1,600 for Lancashire and Yorkshire together. Even if figures for Worcester and east Somerset could be added to make up the western total,[4] it is improbable that they would bring it much above £1,300 or nearly 18 per cent of the total of £7,340. In fact, western cloth received far more attention than the size of the industry would justify; partly because it was regarded as the ancient manufacture of England and partly, perhaps, because contemporaries

---

[1] See App. V.

[2] See App. I, Table B.

[3] *H.M.C.* xiv, App. 6 (H. of L. MSS.), 42.

[4] Worcestershire produced £150 of which perhaps half was for Kidderminster stuffs. The figure for Somerset was £800 but it does not look as if more than £300 would have come from our area. Between 3,000 and 4,000 Worcester cloths went yearly to Blackwell Hall from 1713 to 1719, see below, p. 32.

were hypnotized by its relatively high value per piece. It was not even remotely true that 'there are many more People employed and much more Profit made and Money imported by this Manufactory alone than by all the other Manufactories in England joined together',[1] but it was very generally believed.

The account of profits from the aulnage also shows how many small clothmaking enterprises were still scattered about the country at the end of the eighties. They were all gradually decaying. Suffolk, which produced £250 for cloth and says, could still muster seventy clothiers to sign a petition about the Levant trade in 1686,[2] but the disasters of the nineties must have hastened its decline. The production of cloth in Coventry, which had also depended upon the Levant, was nearly at an end by that time,[3] perhaps as much from the competition of Gloucestershire cloth as from the Levant Company's troubles. Kent only produced £30, although the manufacture did not die out there until the middle of the eighteenth century.[4] Reading was said to have only twelve clothiers left in 1681 where previously there had been one hundred and sixty.[5] Druggets and shalloons took the place of cloth over the rest of Berkshire and Hampshire,[6] although Newbury was still producing coarse cloth in the early eighteenth century and isolated clothiers were scattered about both counties until the end of it.[7] Oxfordshire only produced £35, all for broadcloth, which is surprising in view of the prosperity of the Witney industry.[8] Cloth was still made in north Somerset along the Quantock hills to Minehead, and in north Devon, but the only other

---

[1] Smith, op. cit. i. 371.

[2] *C.S.P.D. 1686–7*, 520. Says to be dyed in Holland and sent on to Germany were said to be the chief trade of Suffolk in 1676, P.R.O., S.P.29/379/5.

[3] *V.C.H. Warw*. ii. 255; *C.S.P.D. 1686–7*, 519.

[4] C.C.R. Pile, 'Cranbrook and the Clothmakers', *Cranbrook Notes and Records*, no. 2 (Oct. 1951), p. 11.

[5] 'Britannia Languens', in J. R. McCulloch, *Early English Tracts on Commerce*, (1952 ed.), p. 403. Both Reading and Newbury suffered from the interruption of trade with Flanders in 1699, *C.J.* xii. 553, 584; xiii. 114.

[6] *V.C.H. Berks*. i. 393–4; *Hants*. v. 487. Shalloons were a cheap worsted material sometimes glazed, often used for lining.

[7] *C.J.* xvi. 512. One clothier came from Fordingbridge to Chippenham in the 1780s, *Ev. on Woollen Trade Bill*, 1803 (H.C. 95), p. 363.

[8] A. Plummer, *The Witney Blanket Industry*, p. 5. One or two clothiers were left in Burford in the first half of the eighteenth century, R. H. Gretton, *Burford Records*, pp. 371, 397.

southern county producing it in any quantity was Dorset where profits of £120 came partly from serges and bays. Besides these areas, which had once been of much greater importance, several other counties yielded small sums for cloth, probably only for local consumption. All in all, the market for cloth had shrunk enormously and western clothiers, who had been the first to adapt themselves to the new conditions, were able to satisfy the whole demand for the better qualities. The only place where fine cloth could be got was the west, and up to the end of the seventeenth century and beyond it all kinds except the coarsest were far better made there than elsewhere. By picking up most of what remained of the inland trade for cloth, the western cloth area had found a supplement to its export trade which in the case of Wiltshire and east Somerset had already become of greater importance and was eventually to do so in Gloucestershire also.

The first twenty years of the eighteenth century were, all in all, the most prosperous which the area had experienced since the beginning of the seventeenth century; but while exports of Spanish cloth reached their peak in the second decade, those of long cloth were already beginning slightly to decline.[1] The East India Company did not find the trade to Persia very satisfactory,[2] and after its new charter in 1698 had altered the figure for exports of English goods to one-tenth of the total value of its exports,[3] the level for cloth fell to an average of under 6,000 pieces annually between 1702 and 1713–14,[4] and to under 3,000 from 1714 to 1719.[5] The Levant Company's exports revived at the end of the century and it regained a share of the Persian market, though it constantly complained about

---

[1] See App. I, Table C. The gloomy statements of the Blackwell Hall factor, Josiah Diston, in 1715 about the decay in the manufacture of medleys over the last twenty years are likely to be coloured by political prejudices and could hardly have been more erroneous, but there may be more truth in his colleague's statement that coarse woollens had decayed in Gloucestershire by one-third in the past two or three years, since exports to Turkey had been low in 1713 and 1714, *J.C.T.P.* 1714–18, pp. 95–6.

[2] S. A. Khan, op. cit., p. 268.

[3] *Cal. Treas. Papers* ii. 188.

[4] P.R.O., C.O.390/12, fol. 32. The figure of 65,123 broadcloths is said to cover 12 years but elsewhere (fol. 3) the dates are given as 29 Sept. 1702 to 29 Sept. 1713 which probably means the season beginning then.

[5] Averaged from Custom House Ledgers. The average is lowered by surprisingly small figures in 1715.

competition from India. Ominous signs of the rise of French trade to Turkey were, however, beginning to appear and between 1708 and 1715 the quantity of cloth from thence surpassed that from England by 3,000 or 4,000 pieces a year.[1] The Company's attitude to this competition varied from self-confidence[2] to alarm;[3] but the impression given by its Court Book for the period is that, while it was busy hunting down interlopers who sent in goods by way of Leghorn, it was not much worried about foreign competitors.[4] The French, who did not operate as a Company, spread over a much larger area than the English, but the latter were in a stronger position in the three places where the Levant Company had factories, Constantinople, Smyrna, and Aleppo.[5] The policy of restricting exports in order to keep up prices continued to cause clothiers much annoyance, especially in 1718 when shippings were suspended altogether in order to give time for the exports of the past two years to be taken off the market.[6] In each of the two following years, however, 23,000 to 26,000 pieces were sent out and it looked as if the good days of the seventies were returning.

Exports of Spanish cloth began to increase after 1703. By 1708 they had passed the level of 1663 and they rose steadily, with very few setbacks,[7] to a peak of over 25,000 pieces in 1717. This advance was an over-all achievement in all the markets where Spanish cloth was sold—from a little over 6,000 pieces to over 10,000 in northern Europe and from not much more than 2,000 to nearly 11,000 in Portugal and the Mediterranean. The war and the effect of war finance on the exchanges, as

[1] P. Masson, *Histoire du commerce français dans le Lévant au XVIIIe siècle*, pp. 476–7. French exports averaged 21,800 pieces between 1708 and 1715, while those of the Levant Company for the seven years from 1705 to 1712 averaged only 17,464, and from 1713 to 1717, 16,053, *An Account of the Number of Woollen Cloths. . . .* French cloths may, however, have contained fewer yards than English.

[2] *H.M.C., H. of L. MSS.* (N.S.), v. 99 (1702); P.R.O., S.P.105/115 (no pagination), Lr. to Ambassador 19 Aug. 1709.

[3] *H.M.C., H. of L. MSS.* (N.S.), x. 118; P.R.O., C.O.390/12, fol. 45.

[4] P.R.O., S.P.105/116, 20 Dec. 1710 and several references later.

[5] Masson, op. cit., pp. 364–5.

[6] *The Case of Several Members of the Levant Company; The Case of the Levant Company.* J. Noake, *Worcester in Olden Times*, p. 23, gives the petition of the Worcester Company of Clothiers against this policy.

[7] The lower exports of 1711 to 1713 (see below, p. 35, n. 4) meant very little for Spanish cloth, only a decrease of some 2,000 pieces from the large exports of 1710.

well as the elimination of competition in some places, must have been partly responsible for this rise, but it continued for some years after the peace of 1713. If the Customs figures can be trusted, remarkably little of it was due to the Methuen Treaty with Portugal in 1703, which had regained the Portuguese market for cloth, forbidden (with a few trifling exceptions) since 1677. The discovery about 1705 of new gold mines in Brazil gave Portugal an increased capacity to purchase English goods for its colonies[1] and total exports of cloth rose to over 8,000 pieces in the peak year of 1710. Only some 2,500 pieces of this was entered as Spanish cloth, though it is quite possible that the entries may have been confused with the 4,000 pieces of short cloth;[2] but, if the original entry is correct, it was a comparatively small amount to defend against the proposed commercial clauses of the Treaty of Utrecht which, it was feared, might mean repudiation of the Methuen Treaty without any countervailing advantage from freedom to trade with France.[3] Although the whole agitation may have been mainly a political move, the clothiers were probably right in supposing that this freedom would not have given them much advantage. It was alleged that Spanish cloth, as containing material foreign to the country where it was made, would have been again prohibited in France;[4] and even had it been admitted, the French manufacture had greatly improved in the twenty-five years which had elapsed since Spanish cloth had found a good market there. The fear that the accession of a French King to the throne of Spain would mean great advantages for France in the purchase of Spanish wool[5] had proved unfounded, but the carriage of it to Languedoc was cheaper than to England and, in the eyes of English clothiers, this advantage combined with

---

[1] H. E. S. Fisher, 'Anglo-Portuguese Trade, 1700–1770', *Econ. Hist. Rev.* (2nd ser.), xvi(2). (Dec. 1963), 224 ff. Bays, of course, were of much greater importance.

[2] P.R.O., Customs 3/13. The figures are for Portugal and Madeira. In their petition against the Treaty (*C.J.* xvii. 379) the Gloucestershire clothiers mentioned fine cloth, which would have come under the heading of short cloth. For possible confusion between the headings see p. 38.

[3] See D. A. E. Harkness, 'The Opposition to the 8th and 9th Articles of the Commercial Treaty of Utrecht', *Scottish Hist. Rev.* xxi. 221–3, 226.

[4] *British Merchant* i. 150–1. *Mercator*, no. 6, maintained that it would be admitted under the 1664 tariff (40 l. instead of 55 l. per piece).

[5] P.R.O., C.O.388/15, no. 110; *H.M. C.,H. of L. MSS.* (N.S.), x. 465; *J.C.T.P.* 1712–13, pp. 414–15.

lower French wages to put French cloth in a strongly competitive position. Yet they certainly attached too much importance to the Methuen Treaty. Experience in Spain, where English trade began to flourish when the high duties imposed in 1713 were removed by the Treaty of Madrid two years later,[1] shows that even without a privileged position the quantity of cloth sent there was not much less, and sometimes more, than that exported to Portugal, except in time of war;[2] but in 1713 this could not have been foreseen.

Up to the end of the second decade of the eighteenth century no fears of Yorkshire competition appear to have troubled the minds of western clothiers. For many years Yorkshire merchants had been doing an immense trade in kersies and the coarse broadcloth known as 'dozens' to Germany, and also to Russia and America. They were also being exported to the Mediterranean[3] but the amount of Yorkshire cloth sent from London is uncertain, since it is unknown (except in the case of the Levant, to which it went as 'cloth') whether it was entered in the Custom House under the heading of 'cloth' or of 'dozens'.[4] London merchants both exported it via Hull[5] and had it sent direct to their London warehouses,[6] but very little came independently to London in this period. A return from Blackwell Hall showing cloth received there between 1713 and 1719 gives an average of only 266 'horse-packs' of Yorkshire cloth annually, at most 2,660 pieces or perhaps half that number.[7] This return shows that the annual average of western cloth received at the Hall over the seven years in question was

---

[1] J. MacLachlan, *Trade and Peace with Old Spain*, pp. 54–75.

[2] From 1715 to 1718 Spanish cloth exported to Spain averaged 3,127 pieces a year against 1,725 pieces exported to Portugal, but rather more cloth of all kinds was sent to Portugal than to Spain. Selling conditions, however, were more difficult in Spain, see MacLachlan, op. cit., p. 75.

[3] Leeds was one of the places which feared for its Portuguese trade in 1713 (see Harkness, loc. cit.) and Yorks. cloth was exported to Italy in the same year, *H.M.C., H. of L. MSS.* (N.S.), x. 143.

[4] At Hull Leeds broadcloth was entered as 'dozens' (information kindly supplied by Dr. R. G. Wilson of the University of E. Anglia). Very little material from the Outports was entered as 'cloth' before 1760.

[5] As did Henry Phill in 1703–4, see P.R.O., C.111/127, Pt. I.

[6] Defoe, *Tour* ii. 614.

[7] P.R.O., C.388/12, Pt. 3, no. 400. The normal pack of western cloth contained 5 pieces, but Yorkshire packs may have been larger. The number received diminished from 520 packs in 1713 to 156 packs in 1719.

36,487 medleys, 23,102 pieces of Gloucestershire cloth, 733 Wiltshires excluding medleys, and 3,445 pieces from Worcester, a total of 63,767 cloths or 27,280 other than medleys. The exports of long and short cloths, however, averaged nearly 45,000 pieces a year during this period, so that it is obvious that much white and piece-dyed cloth can never have come to Blackwell Hall at all. Even if the Yorkshires and Suffolks (average for the latter 776 pieces), the only other types of cloth mentioned, had all been exported, they would not have made up the quantity, even without allowing for home consumption. Indeed, we might expect that by this time Blackwell Hall would be losing ground as a marketing centre. The East India Company ordered by sample and many other merchants got their cloth for export direct from clothiers, in which case it never appeared in Blackwell Hall at all. The figure for medleys, on the other hand, is more than twice the quantity exported; but they were not sent to India or the Levant which probably accounts for the fact that more of them in proportion reached Blackwell Hall than was the case with other varieties of cloth. There was also a large sale for them in the country, though it can hardly be true that, as alleged in 1714, almost half of what was made was sold at country fairs.[1] We might, however, be justified in believing that at least 40,000 pieces of medleys a year were being made during this period, an addition of ten thousand or so to the estimate for 1704. In Wiltshire the twenty years at the beginning of the century were looked back to as a golden age, in which clothiers could amass fortunes of £40,000 to £50,000 apiece.[2] Defoe enthusiastically chronicled the growth of the Avon valley towns,[3] which had already begun in Bradford by 1672 and continued both there and in Trowbridge after the arrival of the Dutch. Most of the immigrants came from villages and towns not more than twenty miles away.[4] Bradford spread up its northern hill, and in the 1690s Anthony Methuen was letting out his estate at the top of it for industrial housing.[5] The expansion of Trowbridge is

[1] *The Drapers' Bill . . . with the Clothiers' Objections* (1714), p. 5.
[2] Defoe, *A Plan of the English Commerce*, p. 84.
[3] *H.M.C. Portland* iv. 244 (1705); Defoe, *Tour* i. 281.
[4] Wilts. C.R.O., 77/23 and 206/50, Settlement Certificates for Bradford and Trowbridge.
[5] Corsham Papers, nos. 2253, 2262, 2265–8, 3252, 3256–7.

attested by the number of cottages erected on the extensive commons surrounding the town.[1] Frome, which was predominantly a place of small clothiers using English wool, was the largest of all; but 'Common Fame', as Defoe put it, made a great exaggeration in estimating that its population had grown by ten thousand in the twenty years before 1726.[2] In 1713 forty-four clothiers from Trowbridge, twenty-five from Bradford, fifty-four from Frome, and thirty-three from adjacent villages, 156 in all, signed a petition to the House of Lords against the commercial clauses of the Treaty of Utrecht.[3] There were, of course, a number of other centres such as Shepton Mallet, Westbury, Warminster, Chippenham, and Devizes, as well as Salisbury where, seven years later, 197 people connected with the industry signed a petition asking for the prohibition of printed calicoes.[4] It looks as if there may have been between 200 to 250 fairly substantial manufacturers of cloth in Wiltshire and east Somerset in the early eighteenth century, besides the very small men who, as we know from later evidence, existed in all the towns; and there were also sergemakers, drugget makers, and, in Salisbury, flannel makers. Unfortunately we have no figures for a hundred years earlier with which we can compare this estimate; but it is not inconsistent with the production of about 35,000 medleys and perhaps 10,000 whites a year.[5]

The figure of 50,000 cloths produced annually in Gloucestershire which was given in 1712,[6] even if exaggerated, shows that there had been a considerable increase since the beginning of the seventeenth century. For the period between 1686 and 1711 the names of 376 clothiers are known, mainly from signatures to petitions,[7] and it is very improbable that we know them all.

---

[1] I owe this observation to Mr. K. H. Rogers. Cf. *Gents. Mag.* ix. 205.

[2] Defoe, *Tour* i. 281.

[3] Arch. H.L., 1713, 4 June, no. 3010 (3).

[4] Arch. H.L., 1720, 25 Apr., no. 575. 30 clothiers besides several clothworkers were admitted to the freedom of the City between 1680 and 1720 (Salisbury City Books i. 252, Index) but there were others not free.

[5] Quite substantial clothiers in the eighteenth century did not make much over 200 cloths a year and the average was certainly lower. Some of the 40,000 medleys estimated above would have come from Glos. Wiltshire probably furnished all the whites exported and, to judge from later clothiers' books, a number of whites to be dyed in London as well.

[6] Sir R. Atkyns, *The Ancient and Present State of Gloucestershire*, p. 78. See App. V.

[7] Also from R. Bigland, *Gloucestershire Collections*, and other sources.

They were not all active at the same time, but it would seem that there must have been 350 to 400 at least, in the first decade of the eighteenth century.[1] Some were said to make 1,000 pieces a year,[2] but the average was very much lower. In 1718–22 William Palling of Painswick was sending to London about 230 cloths a year of the type exported to India and the Levant and he was a well-to-do man;[3] there would be nothing surprising in the presence of many small producers whose annual production was well under a hundred cloths. To produce 50,000 cloths a year (if this figure is not exaggerated) would have needed well over 3,000 looms,[4] and, as weavers seldom produced a cloth in the minimum time, the existence of another 500 is probable. On the basis of Smyth's figures for 1608 which suggest a total of 280 to 290 clothiers,[5] and of the statement made in 1622 that there were upwards of 1,500 looms in the county,[6] it looks as if the number of looms must at least have doubled and the number of clothiers increased by a hundred or more during the later seventeenth century. But, if this view is correct, what are we to make of a statement by Richard Stephens of Chavenage, who, in December 1693, considered that the clothing trade in the three counties had greatly decreased, 'the mills not near so well employed as formerly', although he conceded that there were parishes where new ones had been built and trade had increased.[7] It is probable however, that, as far as Gloucestershire is concerned, he was contrasting the current situation not with

---

[1] 738 persons stated to be clothiers signed a petition from Glos. in favour of the Levant Company in 1720 but many may have been in family partnerships and a few are identifiable as coming from north Wilts. Arch. H.L., 5 Apr. (Petition read 25 Apr.).

[2] *Camden's Britannia.* Translated with additions and improvements by Edmund Gibson D. D. 1695 (4th ed. 1772), p. 283. This was one of the additions to the original work.

[3] Palling Papers (see below, p. 68, n. 4).

[4] See App. III for the basis of this calculation.

[5] Smyth (see above, p. xvi, n. 3) gives the names of 207 clothiers some of whom lived well away from the main clothing area. If we add a quarter for those who failed to appear (in accordance with his own estimate), plus a number for those who were not bound to do so because of age or infirmity, the total might be about 280–90.

[6] *C.S.P.D. 1619–23*, 358. The original document says '1500 at least'.

[7] B. M., Loan Colln., 29/187, fol. 208, Lr. of 9 Dec. 1693. The situation of the Levant Co. had produced a severe depression just at this time. (The summary of this letter in *H.M.C. Portland* iii. 548, gives very little idea of its contents, see below, p. 105.)

the early part of the century, of which he would only have known by hearsay, but with the flourishing period in the seventies when the Levant trade was at its height. Other evidence suggests that the increase of mills was taking place in the Stroudwater basin where, in 1712, Chalford Bottom was 'a remarkable place for the great number of clothing mills and the great quantity of cloth made there and in the neighbourhood'.[1]

There is not much reason to think that Gloucestershire's trade was still expanding after 1700, although the war must have created a demand for uniform cloth; but the county was certainly enjoying a period of fairly stable prosperity. Complaints were remarkably few, nor did Parliament discuss the smuggling of wool with the same frequency as in the preceding years. Even in 1711, which has been called one of the worst years of the century,[2] it was only Wotton-under-Edge and Frome which made any mention of distress among all those places which sent up petitions in connection with the efforts of the Frome cardmakers to prevent the resale of old cards.[3] The fall in exports after 1710 was made much of by the Whigs in order to discredit the Tory administration of the last years of Queen Anne, but in reality this fall was far less than represented.[4]

The end of this period, the years from 1719 to 1721, again saw a recession in the export trade owing to the outbreak of war with Spain.[5] Exports of Spanish cloth decreased all round after 1717, probably because markets were glutted as a result of the huge exports of that year. Medleys sent to Blackwell Hall fell from 38,164 pieces in 1718 to 32,772 in the following year; and over 20,000 pieces were unsold at the end of it, a much higher number than at any year's end since 1713. Gloucestershire cloth showed a lower fall, and the resumption of the Levant Company's exports, many of which did not pass through the Hall, may have meant that the level of production was not much lowered. Nevertheless many places there were petitioning

---

[1] Atkyns, op. cit., p. 283.

[2] T. S. Ashton, *Economic Fluctuations in England 1700–1800*, p. 141.

[3] *C.J.* xvi. 471, 513.

[4] See P.R.O., S.P.35/5/23. By grouping the years in twos the fall was made to look larger than it was. Some of it was due to recession after the very large exports of 1710.

[5] Ashton, op. cit., p. 143.

in 1719 for the enforcement of apprenticeship[1] and against truck, and Gloucestershire clothiers joined in protests from all over the kingdom against the wear of printed calicoes;[2] but behind the petitions the hand of the Levant Company can again be detected, not only in the familiar argument that calicoes interfered with the silk industry, but also in the fact that there were none from Trowbridge, Bradford, or Frome, although exports of Spanish cloth were lower than they had been for many years. Prosperity returned in 1722, but the period of growth was nearly over and the next fifty years were to see increasing competition at home and abroad.

[1] *C.J.* xix. 181.

[2] ibid. 178–9, 184, 189, 204. Cf. the petitions to the House of Lords from Gloucestershire, Worcester, Salisbury, and some other places on the same subject in 1720 (Arch. H.L., 1720, 5 Apr.) and the less numerously signed petitions from Glos. about the desirability of silk buttons in 1721, Arch. H.L., 1721, 19 Apr. (Petition read 24 Apr.).

II

DECLINE AND RECOVERY, 1720–1790

AFTER 1720 the western cloth industry entered upon a long period of fluctuation. From 1721 to 1730 the annual average of cloth exports fell by over 11,000 pieces from the level of the previous decade. After a slight rise in the thirties, it subsided still lower in the forties; and no improvement was apparent until the Seven Years' War. The vast exports to which this gave rise did not last after the peace; but up to 1780 the figures remained higher than from 1721–50 by 20–30,000 pieces per annum.[1] This increase, however, came from Yorkshire, in spite of fluctuations in the growth of the woollen branch of the industry there in these years.[2] The trade from Hull to Portugal and the Mediterranean ports was increasing and in 1737 the interference of coarse Yorkshire cloth in the Spanish and Portuguese trades was noted as a detriment to the finer cloth of the west.[3] About 1720, after some more or less unsuccessful attempts,[4] Yorkshire cloth began to meet with some success in the Levant,[5] probably because the clothiers set themselves to imitate 'the Gloucestershire white cloths bought for the Dutch and Turkey trades';[6] and the result was a formidable competitor in the cheapest section of the trade known as 'Londra'. By the forties the quantity of Yorkshire cloth sold there was certainly considerable.

Even if the Yorkshire cloth industry stagnated over the

---

[1] See App. I, Table C.

[2] R. G. Wilson, 'Transport Dues as Indices of Economic Growth, 1775–1820', *Econ. Hist. Rev.* (2nd ser.), xix(1). 113.

[3] *Seasonable Observations on the present fatal Declension of the General Commerce of England*, p. 11.

[4] In 1696 an Aleppo factor had warned his correspondents in London not to buy 'any Yorkshire or other coarse cloth' which could be got just as cheaply in Aleppo, P.R.O., S.P.110/20, fols. 19, 41.

[5] R. Heath, op. cit., p. 98.

[6] Defoe, *Tour* ii. 610. Although published in 1726 much of the information it contains was collected earlier.

middle of the century, its production of broadcloth (including dozens) nearly doubled between 1727 and 1765.[1] It is improbable that the western industry grew at all between those dates. What figures exist are partial and unsatisfactory,[2] but they show a complete stagnation, or even a decline, up to 1770. After that date they give some reason to think that the twenty years before 1790 saw an increase, sufficient at least to make up past losses.

The fall in exports from 1720 to 1730 took place entirely under the heads of 'long' and 'Spanish' cloth. Exports of 'short' cloth rose gradually to become over three times as great as those of Spanish cloth in 1750. This again raises the question of classification. One cannot expect accuracy of eighteenth-century exporters, and short cloth and Spanish cloth would be easily confused. In fact it is difficult to tell what was the difference between them at this time. Originally 'Spanish cloth' had denoted a medley, but this was not necessarily so by the late seventeenth century.[3] Although the evidence of the Custom House Ledgers about the fall in exports of Spanish cloth is confirmed from other sources, their level is at times suspiciously low when compared with surviving accounts in merchants' papers, particularly with the invoices of cloth sent to Russia by William Heath of London between 1748 and 1751.[4] The quantity exported may not, therefore, have fallen quite so low as the Ledgers suggest; but there is nothing in the general evidence to support the view that the large increase in exports of short cloth after 1756 included any considerable amount of western cloth which could qualify to be entered as 'Spanish'.

A considerable part of the fall in the early twenties was in 'soldiers' cloth' for Russia, and, since this cloth was of the cheapest description, Yorkshire may have suffered more than the west. From 1722 onwards its place was being taken by even

---

[1] See figures for broadcloth stamped, H. Heaton, *The Yorkshire Woollen and Worsted Industries*, p. 278.

[2] See below, p. 53.

[3] See p. xvii, n. 5.

[4] P.R.O., C. 104/143. The account marked 'Our sterling account' shows 52 pieces of Spanish cloth exported to Russia in 1748 when no Spanish and only 4 short cloths appear in the Customs Ledgers, P.R.O., Customs 3/48. There are other discrepancies in 1751.

cheaper cloth from Silesia.[1] Gloucestershire must have felt the decline in finer cloth which had been taken across Russia into Persia but had been superseded by Dutch cloth, because the silk brought by Armenian merchants from Persia by this route was sent to Holland and cloth was purchased there in return. Dutch and German competition was felt in other parts of Europe both by Yorkshire and by western manufacturers;[2] but exports were perhaps even more affected by the growth of native manufactures in several countries, often accompanied by prohibitions or duties on imported material.[3] Reports of English artisans being lured abroad to conduct foreign cloth-making establishments began to alarm the Government from 1718 onwards,[4] although by 1750 some clothiers discounted the harm they might do.[5] Exports of Spanish cloth to central Europe[6] declined steadily from 11,000 pieces in 1714 to an average of under 4,000 between 1720 and 1726 and continued to decline thereafter, until in the fifties the amount never reached 1,000 pieces annually. There was no compensation for this fall in any rise under the heading of short cloth, which remained at under 2,000 pieces except in one or two unusually good years.

Increasing home consumption in the twenties may possibly have balanced the fall in exports, for there were few complaints until the depression of 1726–8.[7] A pamphlet, which appeared in 1727, and is said to have been written by Defoe, on the declining condition of the industry, ascribed it partly to the increase in the number of manufacturers attracted by the

---

[1] P.R.O., S.P.36/30/81. Exports of long cloth to Russia dropped from 6,969 pieces in 1721 to 2,339 in 1722 and were lower still in succeeding years. Those of 'single dozens' from the outports (probably Hull) fell from 6,386 pieces in 1720 to 3,082 in 1721, but rose in 1724. The story of the Russian uniforms made of English cloth which shrank in a storm while the wearers were on parade, though later related of Glos., originated in Yorks. at this time, see Heaton, op. cit., pp. 407–8.

[2] *Gentleman's Magazine* vii. 3–4.

[3] *J.C.T.P.* 1714—18, pp. 150, 437; ibid., 1722/3–27/8, p. 385; P.R.O., S.P.35/65/170 (1), fols. 3, 65.

[4] *J.C.T.P.*, 1714–18, p. 441; ibid., 1718–22/3, p. 213; ibid., 1722/3–27/8, pp. 48, 71, 80; ibid., 1728/9–34, p. 156; P.R.O., S.P.35/48/76; S.P.36/20/147.

[5] See esp. P.R.O., S.P.36/118/286 (Thomas Beavan).

[6] i.e. Holland, Germany, Flanders, and 'East Country' (mainly Poland).

[7] J. de L. Mann, 'Clothiers and Weavers in Wiltshire during the eighteenth Century', *Studies in the Industrial Revolution*, ed. L. S. Pressnell, p. 67.

profits to be obtained in the good years before 1720 and partly to their folly in making lighter materials which competed with broadcloth and were more easily imitated abroad.[1] These lighter goods, made chiefly of a mixture of wool and worsted, challenged the consumption of cheap medleys at 5s. to 8s. a yard, and in 1739 it was suggested that the latter were 'greatly lessened if not quite disused'.[2] They were decreasing too in the export trade,[3] although some were being sent to Hamburg and Lisbon as late as the 1770s.[4] The druggets made in Wiltshire, which were said to be among the materials which were replacing cloth, also became less popular a few years later, though they continued to be made until late in the century.[5]

The greatest threat to exports came from the Levant, where, in the thirties, the quantity of English cloth sent out sank to an average of 13,000 pieces a year. In the next decade it averaged under 10,000. French exports meanwhile went up to over 64,000 pieces in 1738, a quantity which glutted the market and led to temporary restrictions; but even then they greatly exceeded those from England.[6] Furious complaints from clothiers in 1744 and again in 1753, led to a relaxation of the terms on which merchants could join the Company, but no increase in cloth exports followed.[7] After 1760 English trade declined still further, exports in the ten years 1763–72 inclusive only averaging 3,306 pieces annually,[8] while those from France reached over 85,000 pieces.[9] The chief cause of this decline, said the Aleppo factory in 1765, was the distracted state of

[1] *A Brief Deduction of the Original, Progress and Immense Greatness of the British Woollen Manufacture*, pp. 38–41. If this was written by Defoe it must have been commissioned by the clothiers or their factors, for Defoe did not generally discriminate between different kinds of woollen goods.

[2] Smith, op. cit. ii. 315.

[3] 'Essay on the Decline of the Foreign Trade' (1750), repr. J. R. McCulloch, *Scarce and Valuable Tracts on Commerce*, p. 206. Cf. the remark in 1751 that this branch of the trade was 'formerly advantageous', *W.A.S. Rec. Brch*, XIX, p. xxvii.

[4] Ibid., 49–169.

[5] The decline about 1740 may only have been due to the current depression. Druggets were exported to Russia in 1751 and 1753, P.R.O., C.104/141 and 143. German serges from Devizes are found in a draper's stockbook of 1779 (P.R.O., C.114/38), and an advt. of premises in Devizes for making 30 pieces of serge weekly appeared in the *Salisbury Journal* 5 Apr. 1779.

[6] R. Paris, *Le Lévant*, (*Histoire du commerce de Marseille 1660–1789*, v), p. 545, n. 1.

[7] Wood, op. cit., pp. 153, 156.

[8] Averaged from annual figures in Add. MSS. 38, 375, fols. 53–73.

[9] Paris, op. cit., p. 545, n. 1.

Persia,[1] which was plunged into internal strife. Silk, the chief Persian commodity for which cloth was exchanged, could also be obtained from Syria, but Bengal silk was cheaper and gradually took its place. As returns in silk declined, the Company's sales of cloth declined also.[2] These conditions also applied to Smyrna, but not to Constantinople, where French competition seems to have been the main factor. The number of bales sent there from England between 1739 and 1748 was less than half of that received in the previous decade,[3] and this was a loss which particularly affected the west, since Constantinople was a good market for finer cloth. French cloth was of a different type from English, thinner, cheaper, and with livelier colours, loosely woven, and lightly fulled, which made it very pliable. 'They never crack' wrote a contemporary English author, 'and the looseness of the woofe thread rising from time to time keeps them from wearing thread-bare. Our hard cloths are liable to grow bare at the seams; these never do because they are less harsh.'[4] The thick texture of English cloth made it very suitable for the Persian winter, but French cloth was better liked in Constantinople and better adapted for the southern parts of Asia Minor which, in mid-century, offered the largest area for sales from Aleppo.[5] It was said that imitations could not be made at competitive prices[6] and the fine English cloth which was comparable with that from France was far more expensive.[7] The French enjoyed some other advantages. Apart from the fact that from 1740 onwards they had established themselves as prime favourites with the Porte and had secured reduction of customs duties and exemption from other charges on their imports,[8] their cloth was made in establishments which received highly favoured treatment from the Government. The *grandes manufactures* of Languedoc had

---

[1] P.R.O., S.P.105/184, fol. 128.

[2] Heath, op. cit., Chs. 7 and 8.

[3] J. Porter, *Observations on the Religion, Law, Government and Manners of the Turks* (2nd ed. 1771), p. 377.

[4] T. Hale, *A Complete Body of Husbandry* (2nd ed. 1758–9), iii, p. 593. Cf. Porter's description, op. cit., p. 367.

[5] P.R.O., S.P.105/184, fol. 128.

[6] Ibid., fol. 130. There was an attempt to produce imitations in Wales, *J.C.T.P.* 1734–41, p. 395.

[7] Porter, op. cit., p. 419.

[8] Wood, op. cit., p. 143.

been set up by Colbert with bounties and interest-free loans from the State;[1] and this, together with the proximity of Marseilles to the Levant and the alleged lower wages of French workers,[2] was the despair of their English rivals. It was acknowledged that the English were supreme in the dearest and the cheapest cloth, the former for its beauty and the latter for its price;[3] but the market for the former could not be greatly expanded and the latter was largely furnished from Yorkshire. Competition with the French and Dutch was keenest in the middle qualities, and these were just the varieties in which the west was free from Yorkshire's challenge.[4] The situation became serious for Gloucestershire in the later forties and fifties. There were eighteen bankruptcies in the eleven years between 1746 and 1756 inclusive as against seven for the preceding eleven years; and there must also have been a number of clothiers who made private compositions with their creditors. A contemporary estimated that in the five years previous to 1756 £50,000 had been lost by 'bankruptcies, fall of goods, and want of sales'[5] much of which must have been due to the state of the Levant trade. Some finer cloth continued to be exported in the seventies, and in 1779 the trade was said to be worth £50,000 a year to the county;[6] but by the eighties it had almost vanished.[7]

Worcester which made good cloth of the medium type and perhaps some of the best, was even more affected, having no other outlets to turn to. Its trade seems, however, to have succumbed as much to Gloucestershire competition as to the decline in the Levant. Decay began about 1711 and continued steadily, until in 1729 the number of clothiers was said to have fallen from nearly eighty to about twenty and that of looms from about four hundred to one hundred.[8] Worcester cloth was

---

[1] Smith, op. cit. ii. 456–7, Cf. P.R.O., S.P.36/48/19.

[2] See below, p. 107.

[3] Masson, op. cit., pp. 367, 480–1. The decline in sales of English cloth at Smyrna and Aleppo in the thirties was not as great as French reports suggested.

[4] Heath, op. cit., pp. 103–5.

[5] *A State of the Case and a Narration of Facts relating to the late Commotions and Rising of the Weavers in the County of Gloucester* (W. Dallaway), p. 2.

[6] S. Rudder, op. cit., 61.

[7] Annual average 1783–9, 425 cloths.

[8] *C.J.* xxi. 240, 291–3. 80 clothiers may be an exaggeration. Only 47 signed a petition from Worcestershire about the export of white cloth in 1674 (P.R.O., S.P.29/361/236–7).

sold in London immediately after fulling, whereas the 'Worcesters', which had been made in Gloucestershire as early as 1630,[1] were finished (though not dyed) in the country,[2] which made them cheaper. Levant merchants seem to have turned more and more to these imitations, which were more like French cloth (or so their makers averred), in the hope of competing successfully with the latter. Worcester was still supplying high-grade cloth to Levant merchants in the 1750s,[3] but the industry finally died out. Salisbury offers a similar example. Its trade in cloth for the Levant had declined before 1711, in face, it was said, of cheaper French cloth;[4] but in the later eighteenth century the 'Salisburys' exported came from Gloucestershire, where a Painswick clothier, among others, was making them in 1768.[5] Both these cases illustrate the difficulties experienced by urban industries, with at least a tradition of Company control, in competing with the cheaper conditions of the countryside. Salisbury, however, had a substitute in the manufacture of flannels, introduced in the 1680s, which after some vicissitudes, became a very flourishing industry.[6] By the 1780s (and probably much earlier) Salisbury flannels had made their mark in the export trade, especially in Spain and Portugal.[7]

Some compensation for the decline in exports to the Levant was found about the middle of the century in the increased quantity of cloth exported by the East India Company, the greater part of which also came from Gloucestershire. The Company's continued exports of a material which it had the utmost difficulty in selling, even at a loss, is not surprising in view of the continual scrutiny to which it was subjected. The Commissioners of Trade and Plantations kept a consistent eye

---

[1] P.R.O., S.P.16/180/71.

[2] *A Copy of some Reasons formerly offered by the Gloucestershire Clothiers to show the true Cause of the Decay of the Worcester Trade, proper to be presented at the present time* (?1743). It seems likely that this was first issued in 1729 when the Worcester clothiers sent up their first petition to Parliament (see p. 42, n. 8). The one they sent in 1743 was in the same terms as that from Gloucestershire (*C.J.* xxiv. 570), and did not mention the latter county's competition.

[3] Heath, op. cit., p. 105.

[4] 'The British Merchant' in Smith, op. cit. ii. 120, note.

[5] Glouc. C.R.O., D.149, F.114, (Packer Letters).

[6] R. Benson and H. Hatcher, op. cit., p. 579.

[7] P.R.O., B.T.6/114, fol. 101; *Encycl. méth.* 257.

on exports, and if they fell off an official enquiry was sure to follow.[1] Beyond a small quantity of lead, the Company found no produce more likely to sell than woollen goods and prided itself on its patriotic action in exporting them.[2] Between 1700 and 1750 the quantity of cloth did not amount to more than an average of 5,000 to 6,000 pieces annually,[3] but it rose to 20,000 in 1751 and, after a period of wide fluctuation, came to average over 16,000 pieces between 1760 and 1773. A renewed attempt to trade with China (although records are missing until 1774)[4] and more hopeful conditions in Persia which lasted until 1779,[5] may be partly responsible for the rise; but the bulk of it was due to the military operations in which the Company was engaged in the later fifties and sixties. Most cloth sales were still for European consumption, and the increase of soldiery in India, either European or under European command, provided a much larger market than had existed earlier.[6] India was the only country which remained a preserve for West of England cloth throughout the eighteenth century, for the Company did not export for profit and therefore does not appear to have looked for cheaper goods.

In spite of complaints, the west retained a fairly large share of the cloth trade to Portugal until the sixties, although broadcloth did not play a very large part in comparison with the worsteds, bays, and serges which were sent there,[7] and markets were often overstocked.[8] There was keen competition from the French and Dutch as well as from Yorkshire, and complaints about Portuguese neglect of the Methuen Treaty[9] did not restore the balance in favour of English cloth. From the end of the Seven Years' War the Portuguese market contracted, a development which has generally been ascribed to

---

[1] *J.C.T.P.*, 1722/2–27/8, pp. 267, 298; ibid., 1741/2–49, pp. 357, 359; ibid., 1754–8, pp. 219, 225; ibid., 1759–63, pp. 150, 318;

[2] First Rept. on the Export Trade to the East Indies, P.R.O., B.T.6/42 (1) fols. 41–2.

[3] Averaged from figures in C.O. 390/12/3 and from Customs Ledgers.

[4] H. B. Morse, op. cit. i. Ch. XXIX.

[5] Third Rept. on Export Trade, P.R.O., B.T.6/42 (3) section headed 'Persia'.

[6] Ibid., First Rept. (1), fols. 43–4. Cf. the statement that the accoutrements of the Mahratta cavalry had at one time been made of cloth, ibid., fol. 35.

[7] See H. E. S. Fisher, loc. cit., p. 222.

[8] *Gloucester Journal*, 26 May 1752.

[9] M. Postlethwayt, *Dictionary of Commerce* (4th ed. 1774), s.v. 'Portugal'.

Pombal's measures in favour of native manufactures, but was due, to an even greater extent, to the fall in output from the Brazilian mines.[1] No such event affected Spain, but the market there, much interrupted by wars in the early part of the century, was equally open to foreign competition. Although the decline in sales to both countries can be overestimated,[2] the western share in them decreased steeply during the seventies and eighties. By 1786 the interest which western clothiers had always felt in the trade to Portugal had passed completely to Yorkshire,[3] except for the one article of Salisbury flannels.

The rapidly expanding exports to the New World also attracted some western cloth, but not, it would seem, to a very large extent. Trade was reported to be very dead in Chippenham and Devizes in the autumn of 1774, 'chiefly owing to the merchants in Bristol not making their usual provision for America',[4] but there was nothing like the distress which was reported from Leeds just before the outbreak of war.[5] In the autumn of 1775 a petition from Westbury, Warminster, and Trowbridge signed by 138 persons, complaining of the decay of trade since war broke out, was presented by Burke to the House of Commons,[6] but it was indignantly repudiated by nearly all the inhabitants of Warminster and by a number of other clothiers in the county.[7] An examination of the surviving signatures from Warminster and Westbury shows that some were those of persons not connected with the industry at all and that at least a proportion of the remainder were makers of the cheaper kinds of cloth who had been suffering from the general decline in exports for the past ten years.[8] To them the loss of the American market

---

[1] Fisher, loc. cit., 231.

[2] The complaints in 1765 about the trade being halved (D. Macpherson, *Annals of Commerce* iii. 425) can only be due to comparison with the very large exports of 1756–62. Average exports of cloth to Portugal 1763–78 were only down by some 2,000 pieces from those of 1733–9, and exports to Spain increased after 1769.

[3] P.R.O., B.T.6/114, fol. 92.

[4] *Salisbury Journal*, 1774 (W.A.S. Libr. Devizes, Scraps and Cuttings iii. 13).

[5] *Gentleman's Magazine* xlv. (1775), 45. Cf. *Gloucester Journal*, 9 Jan. 1775.

[6] *C.J.* xxxv. 447. The number of signatures is given in *Salisbury Journal*, 20 Nov. 1775.

[7] Ibid., 13, 20, and 27 Nov.; 25 Dec. 1775.

[8] Of 31 clothiers, whose names are printed in the *Salisbury Journal*, 18 Dec. 1775 seven are those of correspondents of James Elderton, 1763–9 or their near relations (see below p. 48), all of whom had felt the decline in the export trade in cheap cloth in the later sixties.

can only have been the last straw. To the great majority of Wiltshire clothiers the war had made no difference and they were participating in the expansion of trade which took place soon after it began.[1]

In the complaints about the general decline in exports much was made of the fall in quality of western cloth, a reproach familiar to every cloth manufacturer under the stress of declining markets. In Constantinople, according to Sir James Porter, the degeneration of English cloth was very marked after 1740;[2] but in the fifties Aleppo factors commented quite as often on the good quality of the cloth sent them as upon its bad making.[3] The French, in the Levant as well as in Lisbon, sometimes attributed their success to the deficiencies of English cloth,[4] but their own could also, on occasion, be accused of many faults in spite of the severe inspection which it was supposed to undergo.[5] The British Factory in Lisbon was accustomed, in the early years of the century, to make routine complaints about the inferiority of English to Dutch cloth;[6] but the success of Yorkshire cloth, which was certainly not better made than western, suggests that it was price more than anything else which turned the scale. The best Dutch cloth was not, in fact, quite so good as the best English,[7] but it was cheaper; and a French report from the Levant said that it satisfied the needs of those buyers (and they must have been the majority) who liked a combination of good quality and low price.[8] Colour was another important element. English medley colours seem to have been the best[9] but in many piece-dyed

---

[1] *Gloucester Journal*, 11 Dec. 1775; Macpherson, op. cit. iii. 589–91.

[2] Porter, op. cit., pp. 393, 422. There is a good deal of evidence from later prices that the 'Salisburys' and 'Worcesters' made in Gloucestershire (which were also exported to India) degenerated considerably towards the end of the century.

[3] Heath, op. cit., p. 127.

[4] Masson, op. cit., pp. 370, 481.

[5] Ibid., pp. 474–5. Cf. *Encycl. méth.* 260, on Languedoc cloth ruined by stretching.

[6] P.R.O., C.O.388/15/1 (2), Lr. of 1 Oct. 1711; S.P.110/89, fol. 37. (1715). The wording of the second complaint is a copy of the former which rather weakens the criticism.

[7] O. Burrish, *Batavia Illustrata* (2nd ed., 1731), pp. 373–4.

[8] Masson, op. cit., p. 376. By the 1780s, however, Dutch cloth was said to be too heavy and too dear to sell outside Holland, *Encycl. méth.* 259.

[9] Burrish, op. cit., p. 374; *Encycl. méth.* 258, quoting Lord Sheffield in the *Courier de l'Europe*, 14 Oct. 1783.

colours, especially black, English cloth fell short of French or Dutch.[1] This was a decisive failing and may explain why in Portugal more is heard of medleys than of the piece-dyed cloth of Gloucestershire, for Spanish and Portuguese buyers wanted black cloth, which at this time (though not later) was always dyed in the piece. Otherwise, the characteristic feature of English cloth was its hardwearing properties, 'but this is not the principal quality which inhabitants of these hot countries desire'.[2]

Quite apart from questions of the type or price of cloth, there may have been some real degeneration in the middle of the century, though probably not so much as critics imagined. The Spanish wool, of a lower quality than that imported to England, which was mixed with the wool of Languedoc to make French cloth for the Levant, afforded a cheaper raw material than Hereford wool which was the finest English kind; and the best sorts of the other short wools, though possibly as cheap as the French mixture, were probably less fine. The reluctance of English clothiers to produce imitations may have been due to that insularity which has often characterized English manufacturers to a greater or less degree, but the cost of doing so seems a more probable reason. One of the points about foreign cloth, noted on many occasions, was its fine spinning;[3] and with their feeling that wages were in any case a heavy expense, western clothiers probably judged that the cost of finer spinning would make their cloth dearer, and so less likely to sell.

From the sixties onwards it was competition from Yorkshire not from abroad which prevented the west from sharing in the expansion of cloth exports which was especially visible between 1775 and 1790.[4] By 1786 the western export trade had become 'comparatively speaking, small';[5] although between 9,000 and

---

[1] *The true State of the Case of the Dyers and Clothworkers etc.* (though this reference is mainly to bays); *C.J.* xx. 791.

[2] *Propositions for improving the Manufactures, Agriculture and Commerce of Great Britain*, p. 34.

[3] Macpherson, op. cit. iii. 240. *Gentleman's Magazine* vii. 3–4 and many other references.

[4] From 24 per cent of the total value of woollen piece goods exported in 1775 to 41 per cent in 1790. See App. I., Table B.

[5] P.R.O., B.T. 6/114, fol. 100.

10,000 pieces of superfines were still sent abroad, including those
from Gloucestershire which went to India and a few still sent
to the Levant.[1] The bulk of the export trade had always been
in the cheaper varieties,[2] and Yorkshire had been taking a
progressively greater share of these ever since the twenties.
Although, by the forties Gloucestershire had recouped some
part of its losses by gaining trade from Worcester,[3] ten years
later the strength of Yorkshire competition was being emphasized by outside observers,[4] and it was recognized in the county
itself that the manufacture of some types of cloth had been
lost.[5] Further inroads in the sixties can be traced in the correspondence of James Elderton, a Blackwell Hall factor, whose
letter book is still in existence.[6] He came of a Frome family and
his mother's kindred, James and Nicholas Cockell, carried on
business as clothiers at Chapmanslade between Frome and
Westbury. Most of his correspondents also came from the
Wiltshire–Somerset border though there were a few from
Gloucestershire. Elderton was apt to magnify both the faults
in the cloth sent him and the gloomy prospects for its sale; but
his letters show that the later sixties saw an almost continuous
contraction in the market for the lower kinds of western cloth,
in the face of cheaper material from Yorkshire. In November
1764 he was telling his cousin of a foreign order, 'I find they
cannot give the price; they want to have them made in Yorkshire'[7] and a month later a small clothier also from Chapmanslade, was informed that if he charged 6s. 3d. a yard for his
cloth instead of 6s., 'the trade must and will go into Yorkshire'.[8]
In 1767 the Bath coatings which had been made for some years
by a Gloucestershire clothier at 7s. a yard were contemptuously
dismissed, 'there are much better sold at 4s. & 4s. 6d. (York-

---

[1] Ibid., fol. 176.
[2] 'The coarse cloths are mostly for the merchants' trade,' Elderton Lr. Book (see
below, n. 6), To Read & Wilkins, 3 Apr. 1766.
[3] See above, p. 42.
[4] J. Tucker, 'Essay on the Advantages and Disadvantages which attend France
and England with regard to Trade' (1753), in *Select Collection of Scarce Tracts on
Commerce*, ed. J. R. McCulloch, p. 356.
[5] *A State of the Case*, p. 17.
[6] Som. C.R.O. DD/X/MSL. No pagination after the first 100 pages. The firm
was Elderton & Hall, 2, Bevois Court, Basinghall St.
[7] To N. Cockell, 15 Nov. 1764.
[8] To M. Withy, 6 Dec. 1764.

shire ones), the town is full of them'.[1] The period from the beginning of 1765 until the end of 1768 was one of depression everywhere.[2] Trade was so bad in Wiltshire in 1765 that a dry-salter's agent wrote that the clothiers 'have little else to do than take the diversion of the Field, and many of them (are) so intent on destroying Partridges that I have met but few of them at home'.[3] Yorkshire was also affected,[4] but in such a situation, cheaper cloth was naturally preferred. It was not that Elderton thought Yorkshire cloth good. 'No better set out than a Yorkshire', 'ill-dressed greasy Yorkshire stuff', 'as coarse as a Yorkshire', and many similar expressions were all opprobrious epithets intended to convince his clothiers how bad their cloth was; but, if they were deserved, the lower price of Yorkshire cloth would necessarily carry the day. Western cloth of 5s. 6d. to 8s. a yard according to colour would still sell abroad in the early seventies and even later, provided that it was good and cheap;[5] but the poorer clothiers, who lived on credit and tried to economize on wool, got the worst workers and made the worst cloth, which in a contracting market was bound to lie on hand.[6] By 1767 Elderton was cursing the coarse trade in which his money was locked up in advances to clothiers;[7] and they were not the only ones who suffered from declining trade in these years. Daniel Packer, a Painswick clothier who had been making cloth for Sir Samuel Fludyer, wrote in 1768 that he had met with so many losses in the cloaking trade that he thought of relinquishing it altogether.[8]

[1] To S. Baylis, 3 Nov. 1767. This reproach must have been due to the quality of the cloth. John Anstie in the same year considered 6s. a yard hardly sufficient for thick Bath coating (Bodington, Notes for *V.C.H. Wilts.* in the possession of the Institute of Hist. Research), and Bath coatings from the west at prices up to 13s. 9d. a yard were being sold in Salisbury in 1779, P.R.O., C.114/38.

[2] Ashton, op. cit., pp. 152–4.

[3] P.R.O., C.109/2, 2, of 12 Sept. 65. The correspondence during 1765–6 is filled with references to the dullness of trade. (I owe this information to Professor A. H. John of the London School of Economics.) It was suggested in 1772 that Glos. had felt the depression so acutely in 1766 that many workers had emigrated, *Bath Chronicle*, 30 Jan. 1772.

[4] See esp. *Bath Journal*, 11, 18, and 25 Apr.; 23 May 1768.

[5] *W.A.S. Rec. Brch.* xix, p. xxv.

[6] 'The Coarse trade . . . has been very bad but . . . if our makers had made their cloths good and dyed the colours they would have had but little stocks on hand.' To M. Withy, 30 Mar. 1769.

[7] To N. Cockell, 3 Sept. 1767.

[8] Glouc. C.R.O. D.149; F.114, To Marsh & Hudson, 31 May 1768.

This account of the western manufacture since 1720 has so
far been one of steadily increasing losses. To accept this
without correction would give a very false picture of the whole
state of the trade. The market was predominantly at home and
it was growing all the time as the population increased and
became richer. In addition to superfines of several grades it
comprised, for Gloucestershire, such cloths as 'seconds, forests,
drabs, naps, and duffils'[1] and many of these were also made in
the medley area,[2] as well as the 'liveries' for which Frome and
Westbury in particular were well known. It was in this branch
of the trade that clothiers prospered and grew rich; and one
must not forget how many rich clothiers there were in all parts
of the region, especially perhaps in Gloucestershire. If their
wealth had originally been derived from the Levant trade, it
was nourished on the expansion of the inland market.[3] It was
largely clothiers who originated and supported the plans for
the Stroudwater canal, from its first abortive beginnings in
1730 through the equally abortive scheme of 1759 to its final
opening in 1779.[4] Communications were less difficult in Wiltshire especially after the Avon was made navigable from Bristol
to Bath, but there was a plan in 1734 and again in 1765 to
extend navigation to Chippenham, though nothing came of
it.[5]

In superfines the west was still unrivalled. The narrow
'cassimeres', patented in 1766 by Francis Yerbury of Bradford,

[1] Rudder, op. cit., p. 61. Forest cloth, probably narrow, often appears in advertisements at *c.* 2s. to 5s. per yard. Drabs were a very heavy and expensive cloth,
naps had a surface twisted into little knots by a napping machine (of which frequent advertisements appear in the *Gloucester Journal* from 1726) and sold at 5s. to
11s. a yard; duffils were a coarse cloth with the wool left long on the surface. Other
cloths made were Bath coatings, also with wool left unshorn, and 'Hunters'
cloth' at *c.* 5s. a yard.

[2] *Salisbury Journal*, 28 June 1779. Salisbury and Wilton were also well known for
a time for the 'marble cloth' produced there, *V.C.H. Wilts.* iv. 160.

[3] Cf. Lr. from Chalford in *Gloucester Journal*, 8 Nov. 1784.

[4] T. Rudge, *History of the County of Gloucester*, pp. xxx–xxxi. About half the commissioners appointed in 1730 were clothiers (3 Geo. ii, c. 13) and the promoter of
the second scheme was the clothier John Dallaway. There was opposition however
by clothiers owning mills along the river and much additional expense was caused
in 1775 by lawsuits, which injured the canal's profits.

[5] *C.J.* xxii. 389, 411; *V.C.H. Wilts.* iv. 272; J. Stratford, *A Plan for extending
the Navigation from Bath to Chippenham* (W.A.S. Lib. Devizes, *Wilts. Tracts*, 73,
no. 13). This, however, was put forward not by clothiers but by Bristol merchants.

formed an important addition. Much thinner and less heavily fulled than broadcloth,[1] they proved an instant success. In 1768 Elderton was prophesying a good profit on them;[2] and by this time he was advising those of his clothiers whom he thought capable of it to make superfines, which he foresaw would be in scarce supply.[3] The failure of the export trade was giving a powerful stimulus to a movement towards making finer cloth with which Yorkshire could not yet compete. In Shepton Mallet the change had begun as early as 1756;[4] but even Frome, noted for its seconds and liveries, was experimenting with superfines in 1770,[5] and it may have been the rush to make them which accounted for the low price at which some of them were sold in that year.[6] Since better wages were made on superfines, the increase in them reacted on the coarser branches of the industry, making it harder to produce 'interfines' at a competitive price.[7] Although the combination of Yorkshire competition and loss of foreign markets probably led to a decline in production over the middle of the century, there seems to have been a recovery later. Rudder, whose history of Gloucestershire was published in 1779, thought that the manufacture had been increasing throughout the century 'though by very unequal steps'.[8] Had he been writing in the forties or fifties his opinion might have been different,[9] but

[1] Patent no. 858. They were woven with a rib which made a stronger fabric. Some are indistinguishable from cloth but in others the rib can be clearly seen. See patterns in P.R.O., C.113/16 (1799). (Hanson & Mills.) When taken up in Yorkshire after 1790 they were generally known as 'kerseymeres', a name which occasionally appears in the west (e.g. *Bath Chronicle*, 30 Jan. 1772) but is not common there. Both names were used in the trade in the nineteenth century and in 1871 the two were distinguished by the fact that 'kerseymeres' were the more heavily fulled, *Off. Rept. of the Int. Exh. of 1871*, ed. Lord Houghton, II Rept. on Woollen and Worsted Fabrics.

[2] To J. Noad, 26 May 1768. They appear in a draper's stock book in 1769, P.R.O., C.104/38. Presumably Yerbury charged a fee for the use of his patent but no difficulties seem to have arisen.

[3] To J. Huntly, 5 Mar. 1767; W. Read & J. Bythesea, 21 Apr. 1768; E. Eyres, 18 Dec. 1768.

[4] *Ev. on Woollen Trade Bill, 1802–3* (H. C. 220), pp. 62, 67.

[5] *W.A.S. Rec. Brch.*, xix. nos. 310, 363, 379.

[6] See below, p. 86.

[7] *W.A.S. Rec. Brch.* xix. loc. cit.; Glouc. C.R.O., D.149, F.114 (Packer letters).

[8] Rudder, op. cit., p. 60.

[9] Ibid., p. 61. Cf. the statements about the decline of trade in G. Bickham, *The British Monarchy* (1748 ed.), p. 72, and in *County Curiosities, or a new Description of Gloucestershire* (1757), p. 3.

there had been good years at the beginning of the seventies and again after the outbreak of the American War, which, incidentally, like the Seven Years' War nearly twenty years earlier, had created a demand for uniform cloth of which Gloucestershire seems to have had its fair share.[1] The figures for the county's production in the late seventeenth century are so vague that it is impossible to tell whether the estimated value of the trade at £600,000 a year, given to Rudder by 'some of the most intelligent clothiers',[2] really shows an increase in quantity over the £500,000 of 1695,[3] seeing that the production of fine cloth had increased and that far more of it was now dyed and finished in the county. It is also doubtful whether the estimate itself, which is made up of the returns of four different branches of the trade, can be wholly justified for the date at which it was published. Figures of £250,000 for the 'inland trade'[4] and of £100,000 for that done with London drapers do not sound improbable and may even be on the low side; and that of £50,000 for what remained of the Levant trade may possibly be justified on the basis of the average exports from 1773 to 1778, assuming that all the fine cloth came from Gloucestershire.[5] But, for reasons given below, it does not seem possible that the East India trade was worth £200,000 to the county at this date, though the figure would have been nearer the truth some ten years earlier.[6]

Whatever may have been the case in Gloucestershire, there is some evidence from the medley-making area further south of an increase in production after 1770. Although in Wiltshire and Somerset the manufacture was dying out in some of the

---

[1] Rudder, op. cit., p. 60.

[2] Ibid., p. 61. But cf. his statement (op. cit., p. 711) that the value of the cloth made in Stroud parish was supposed to amount to very near £200,000 annually. It is doubtful whether Stroud parish, though a very large one, did one-third of the trade of the county; but if it did not and the statement is correct, the annual value would be well over £600,000.

[3] See App. V.

[4] This comprised not only cloth sold in England but also that sold for export if (unlike that sent to Turkey and India) it was of a kind consumed at home.

[5] Exports 1773–8 averaged 2,241 long and 2,107 short cloths per annum. Gloucestershire superfines seem to have averaged about 30 yards long and were worth £20 to £30 per piece according to colour. They would fall under the heading 'short cloth', whereas the coarse cloth, which at this date probably came from Yorks., was 'long'.

[6] See pp. 44, 56.

outlying places,[1] it seems to have been increasing in and immediately round the towns. Figures which survive for production in Somerset,[2] although too fragmentary and perhaps too uncertain to be relied upon very far, show no fall in the production of medley broadcloth between 1727–8 (though this was a very bad year) and the fifties, and a modest rise from the seventies onwards. Even when allowance is made for the quantities given being below the truth, the increase is nothing like that which was taking place in Yorkshire, but it does signify a turn towards greater prosperity.

These figures were recorded in conformity with the Act of 1727,[3] which was primarily concerned with wages and conditions of work, but included a provision that medleys should be measured at the fulling mill by inspectors appointed by the magistrates. They were to receive 2d. per cloth and to report the number of cloths sealed at Easter Sessions every year. Only in Somerset have any figures survived. For 1727–8 they give a total of 12,720 cloths for a period of about nine and a half months—perhaps a little over 15,000 cloths in the year. After 1728, no further return has been preserved until Easter 1753, when salaries were claimed for 15,454 cloths sealed since the previous Easter, a not unlikely total which fits other evidence suggesting that there was no increase in production over the middle of the century. The figure did not begin to rise significantly until 1770 when it reached 17,000 pieces. At Easter 1779 it rose to 18,000 and then, after another fall, to over 19,000 at Easter 1788. The returns also show how the area in which medley cloth was made was contracting, although cloth made in one district might be fulled in another.[4] The inspector for the Bath division reported fitfully, only three times (if that) after 1760. At Twerton the industry continued for another hundred and eighty years, but its extent in the division as a whole must have become so small that it was not worth the inspector's time to make a report. Some mills in the Batcombe

---

[1] e.g. in Malmesbury soon after the middle of the century and in Castle Combe and other villages, especially north of Chippenham, probably because they produced goods for the Levant. For Somerset see below App. V.

[2] See App. V.

[3] 13 Geo. i, c. 23, see below, p. 109.

[4] e.g. some Shepton Mallet clothiers used the mill at Mells, Som. C.R.O., Q. Sess. Min. Book, Easter 1728.

district remained active until 1776 but only that at Stoke Lane is mentioned afterwards. The small division round Harptree, of which nothing is known apart from this source, disappeared after 1774 and when it appears again twenty years later it is impossible to be certain of the area which its inspector covered. The absence of returns does not, of course, mean that production had ceased; it must often have been the case that the inspector through illness, idleness, or some other cause failed to appear at Quarter Sessions and merely kept his receipts. If the Bench did not insist on his appearance (and there is no sign that it did so) he was very likely to remain away. Again when the receipts were small it may not have seemed worth while for anyone to apply for the post when an inspector died or retired.

Such considerations raise the question how far the figures can be trusted. In the later part of the century they are certainly below the real figures, and it seems safe to conclude that a good deal more was produced than appears from them. It must be remembered that the Act covered only medley broadcloth and not the white cloth, narrow cloth, druggets, and serges which were also made. Since there is no reason to think that developments in Wiltshire took a different course from those in Somerset, an increase of at least 20 per cent in the production of medley broadcloth in the period between 1770 and 1790 is probable; and the great popularity of cassimeres, which appeared long after the Act was passed and were not covered by it, suggests a larger one although to some extent they may have taken the place of the druggets and serges which were beginning to disappear.

The figures have another value in showing the absurdity of some contemporary references to the production of Frome. One, given in 1745 by an anonymous author (but possibly derived from Defoe), suggested that Frome and the adjoining villages within a circle of about four miles produced cloth to a value of £700,000 annually. This was calculated from the statement that 'seven waggons have been sent out with cloth weekly for Blackwell Hall . . . and each of these waggons has been known to hold 140 pieces' valued on an average at £14 each.[1] It is improbable but not inconceivable that 980 cloths

---

[1] *The Voyage of Don Manoel Gonzales (late Merchant) of Lisbon to Great Britain*, p. 101.

may have been sent to London in one week in exceptionally busy times. The writer of the London letter in the *Gloucester Journal* remarked in 1742 that such was the depression of trade that only 39 cloths from Frome had come up to Twelfth Market 'whereas ordinarily we have had 500, and, if we are not misinformed, in extraordinary times above 800 from that town and villages adjacent'.[1] Cloths were saved up for fairs and however great a quantity was sent it was unlikely to have been the production of one week; nor can one believe that the value of the cloth made in a small area round Frome was more than that estimated for the whole of Gloucestershire. The figure given in 1791, 'from an accurate inspection lately made', of 160,000 yards per annum (perhaps about 5,300 cloths), of which four-fifths were broadcloth, is much more likely to be correct.[2]

Although production increased after 1770 there were many setbacks. Crises, such as that of 1773 which affected internal consumption, were severely felt.[3] Bristol Fair in September of that year was 'the smallest ever remembered'[4] and Salisbury Spring Fair in 1775 showed little improvement.[5] The effect on superfine cloth may be seen in the books of Messrs. Stevens & Bailward of Bradford,[6] which show a drop from 364 cloths sent to their Blackwell Hall factor in 1771 and only a little less in 1772, to 195 between January 1773 and April 1774. As one would expect, the west took very little part in the successful agitation in 1774 against the imposition of a tax on foreign linen. Yorkshire would have been the chief sufferer from a reciprocal tax on British woollens; and although delegates from Wiltshire and Somerset produced evidence of the rise in the poor rates in various centres of the industry, Gloucestershire took no part at all and the effective representations seem to

---

The voyage purports to have been taken in 1730. The villages mentioned are 'Elm, Mells, Whatley, Nunney etc.' Prof. J. R. Moore believes that the material in this chapter is drawn from an unpublished Tour by Defoe, 'Defoe in the Pillory and other Studies', *Univ. of Indiana Publ., Humanities ser.* no. 1 (1939), pp. 72–103.

[1] *Gloucester Journal*, 13 Jan. 1742.
[2] J. Collinson, *History of Somerset* ii. 186.
[3] *Bath Chronicle*, 25 Feb. 1773, where the starving condition of workers in Glos. is described.
[4] Ibid., 9 Sept. 1773. Cf. Ashton, op. cit., pp. 157–8.
[5] *Salisbury Journal*, 10 Apr. 1775.
[6] Deposited in Bath Central Reference Library.

have come entirely from Yorkshire.[1] Gloucestershire was affected by other factors. After 1773 the East India Company's exports fell to under 10,000 pieces a year and only averaged about 6,500 pieces for the next four years, with two very bad ones in 1776 and 1777. It is this fall which must account for Rudder's report of a decline in trade in Chalford, and perhaps in Horsley,[2] in spite of his belief in a general increase. There was some recovery between 1778 and 1782 and exports to India reached over 13,000 pieces in the latter year, thus partially offsetting the depression which began after the entry into the war of France and Spain, and later Holland.[3] This may be the reason why Gloucestershire seems to have been less affected by it than some other parts of the country;[4] indeed, a reference in 1781 to the 'flourishing and increasing woollen manufacture of Wiltshire, Somerset and Gloucestershire'[5] suggests that the recession was very short.

After the end of the war the combination of a crisis in the autumn of 1783, a severe winter in 1783–4 and another slump in the East India's Company exports produced what, if one could judge by the statements of relief organizations, was the most severe depression that Gloucestershire had experienced for many years. In January 1784, 'owing to the complete disappearance of our trade', relief committees were set up in Stroud and neighbouring places and there were computed to be nearly 15,000 destitute persons, men, women, and children, in the fifteen Stroudwater parishes.[6] The distress did not end

---

[1] J. Bischoff, *Comprehensive History of the Woollen and Worsted Manufactures* i. 177.

[2] Rudder, op. cit., pp. 289, 502.

[3] Cloth sold very low at Bristol Fair in 1779 (*Salisbury Journal*, 20 Sept. 1779), but if one may judge from Bailward's books, (see p. 55, above) the superfine trade does not appear to have suffered much. Bailward had no difficulty in getting his cloth accepted in London throughout the year; in fact, there was competition for it.

[4] Cf. the remarks about the misery of the workers in the industry in *An Answer to Sir J. Dalrymple's Pamphlet . . .* (1782), quoted by Ashton, op. cit., p. 163. The author was rector of a church in Colchester and his account refers to the East Anglian bay industry where the interference with exports to Spain was serious. See also A. Young, on Sudbury, *Annals of Agriculture* ii. 106. The years 1779–81 are said to have been the gloomiest the Yorkshire woollen industry had ever known, R. Wilson, op. cit., p. 114.

[5] Macpherson, op. cit. iii. 703.

[6] *Gloucester Journal*, 12 and 26 Jan; 2, 9, and 16 Feb.; 1 Mar.; 5 Apr. 1784 (advts. of meetings of supporters of the relief fund). Appeals for the poor were also made in Wilts. (*Salisbury Journal*, 9 and 16 Feb. 1784), but the notices give the impression that the hard winter was the only cause of the distress.

with the bad weather,[1] although by the autumn and probably much earlier, the inland trade was prosperous again. Exports to India had fallen to under 8,000 pieces in 1783 and they fell again to a little over 6,000 in 1784. Even if Rudder's suggestion that one-third of the county's trade was done with the Company is an overestimate, this fall represents a cut of nearly two-thirds from the level of the sixties, and the situation was aggravated by the almost complete disappearance of what remained of the Levant trade. There was not much improvement during the last five years of the decade; from 1785 to 1789 average annual exports to India were only a little over 8,000 pieces,[2] and it is not surprising that in 1786 this section of the industry was said to be still in a very distressed state.[3] The decline arose from a variety of causes—the end of the war in India and the dispersal of the armies, renewed disorders in Persia, the distressed state of Bengal and finally the debts of the Company itself, all played a part in the restriction of purchases.[4] Trade with China was not yet large enough to make any significant difference; and there were said to have been 2,826 bales of broadcloth unsold in the Company's warehouses in India in 1783–4 and 2,621 in 1789–90.[5]

In these circumstances it was perhaps natural that the Gloucestershire manufacturers should have been almost the only makers of woollen goods to express doubt about Pitt's abortive attempt, in 1784–5, to remove the restrictions on Irish trade.[6] Few concessions had been made to Ireland over the woollen manufacture and the great majority of those engaged in it took no part in the activities of the Chamber of

---

[1] Lr. from Chalford, *Gloucester Journal*, 8 Nov. 1784.

[2] There is a discrepancy between the Company's figures of exports and those given in the Ledgers, partly but not entirely because the Company reckoned from Michaelmas to Michaelmas and the Ledgers from Xmas to Xmas. On the five years 1785–9 the Company claimed to have exported altogether an average of about 1,000 more pieces a year than the Ledgers show, P.R.O., B.T.6/42 (i), App. 8.

[3] P.R.O., B.T.6/114, fol. 101.

[4] 'Ninth Rept. from the Select Committee on East Indian Affairs' (1783), *Misc. Repts.* vi. 53, 56; P.R.O., B.T.6/42 (i), fol. 27.

[5] B.T.6/42 (i), App. 7.

[6] *C.J.* xl. 847–8. The only other petitions against the Propositions from anyone connected with the industry were from Halifax against Art. 10 (due to fears about export of wool) and from the county of Southampton (due to fears over the import of Irish stuffs), ibid., 923, *L.J.* xxxvii. 316, 331.

Manufacturers in opposing the Propositions;[1] but those of Gloucestershire, though not declaring themselves entirely opposed, wanted further investigation before they became law. The rest of the area was not quite so favourably inclined as appeared at first sight. A meeting in Salisbury of manufacturers from Wiltshire, Somerset, and Dorset decided to approve by a majority which was afterwards disputed, and there was evidently a good deal of opposition, which found public expression in letters to the county press.[2] The whole region considered itself to be suffering from the effects of the Irish non-importation resolution of 1779[3] (although the decline in exports was probably just as much the result of previous over-stocking); and, in general, sentiment seems to have been divided fairly equally between hopes for a resumption of trade at its former level and fears that Irish cloth might compete with English.

The next step towards removing trade barriers, the Commercial Treaty with France in 1786, was also the subject of divided opinion. In this case the Government took great pains to discover the views of manufacturers beforehand, both by consulting London factors who were in touch with the provinces and by hearing evidence from persons deputed by the manufacturers to make known their views.[4] Yorkshire, confident in the spinning machinery now firmly established there, was enthusiastically in favour of the Treaty, provided that both the machinery and the wool could be kept at home.[5] The west, too, was in favour as far as the makers of cloth from English wool were concerned.[6] The superfine makers were less confident. The majority in Gloucestershire were flatly opposed.[7] In Trowbridge, Warminster, and Frome, after a good deal of wavering, the majority came to the conclusion that a freer

[1] Witt Bowden, *Industrial Society in England towards the End of the Eighteenth Century*, p. 175. The export of wool from England remained prohibited and this was the main thing which interested clothiers.

[2] *Salisbury Journal*, 11, 18, and 25 Apr.; 2 and 9 May 1785; *Gloucester Journal*, 18 Apr. and 13 June 1785.

[3] P.R.O., B.T.6/109, fol. 148.

[4] See P.R.O., B.T.6/111 (correspondence) and 114 (evidence). As in the case of the Irish Propositions, Anstie and the Blackwell Hall factor Thomas Everett were the only persons connected with the western industry to give evidence, but letters were received from clothiers in all three counties.

[5] P.R.O., B.T.6/114, fols. 85–92.

[6] i.e. cloth at under 14s. a yard, ibid., fol. 103.

[7] P.R.O., B.T.6/111, no. 27; 6/114, fol. 104.

trade would be no injury;[1] but in Bradford, Chippenham, and Melksham, manufacturers were against, or at least considered that they had not enough evidence to form an opinion.[2] The figures sent them purported to show that English superfine cloth was about 1s. per yard cheaper than French,[3] but this conclusion depended upon factors such as breadth and allowances for measure which had not been stated. Fear of the unknown, combined with the experience they had already had of the competition of French cloth in the Levant, made them very cautious in expressing a firm opinion;[4] and the Wiltshire towns in favour only produced about two-fifths of the whole number of superfines.[5] No one, however, expressed sentiments so pronounced as those uttered by pamphleteers in opposition to the Treaty.[6] French wages might be lower than English, but enlightened opinion, as expressed by John Anstie of Devizes the chairman of the western manufacturers, now considered that an Englishman at 2s. a day might do his work more cheaply than a Frenchman at 1s. 6d.[7] Nor was the alleged advantage in obtaining Spanish wool any danger to the English manufacturer, for the favourable terms of payment offered enabled them to get it cheaper by 3d. per pound.[8] Political views certainly played some part in influencing those who approved of the Treaty. Contrary to the view of Arthur Young, who, following his quarrel with Anstie over the export of wool,[9] was consistently unfair to the west, there was a liberal and progressive spirit among some of the western clothiers not inferior to that found in Birmingham or Manchester.[10] Not only

[1] B.T.6/111, nos. 31, 35, 36, 38.

[2] Ibid., nos. 39, 41.

[3] French cloth sold at the equivalent of 17s. 9d. in France or 18s. 7d., if the difference in breadth was taken into account, while English cloth was at 17s. in England. The French also made a cloth at 19s. a yard superior to any produced in England; the English manufacturers said they did not copy it because they thought they would never get the price, B.T.6/114, fol. 110.

[4] B.T.6/111, nos. 29, 31–35, 39; Everett reported unanimous support from Trowbridge (B.T.6/114, fol. 104), but it is clear that J. Mortimer, who reported on the meeting there, was not himself convinced, B.T.6/111, no. 32. See also no. 33 from J. Cook of Trowbridge.

[5] B.T.6/114, fol. 175.

[6] *J.R., A Woollen Draper's Letter on the French Treaty; A View of the Treaty of Commerce with France.*

[7] B.T.6/114, fol. 98. See also below, pp. 106–7.

[8] Ibid., fols. 96, 107–9.

[9] See below, pp. 270–1.   [10] See W. Bowden, op. cit., p. 195.

was this true of Anstie himself; Walter and William Sheppard wrote from Frome 'for our part, as citizens of the World, we think that the general advantages the kingdom would receive would more than overbalance the disadvantages that any one manufacturer might suffer'.[1] It was perhaps in this spirit that Anstie allowed two French manufacturers to inspect his factory and collect 'the most essential information on the best method of manufacturing his Superfine Cassimeres', a proceeding greatly disapproved of by some of his contemporaries,[2] for liberal sentiments were far from universal. Nevertheless, the confidence of the liberal element forms a striking contrast with the attitude prevalent in the middle of the century and was, no doubt, partly a symptom of English superiority in making some kinds of superfines. In this French opinion agreed. Roland de la Platière, the French Inspector of Manufactures for the Rouen district, quoted with approval Lord Sheffield's statement in 1783 that the French could offer a cloth of equal quality with a superior gloss, but it lacked substance, did not last as long and was more expensive.[3] The first three were the traditional attributes of French cloth, but the disadvantage in price was new. It may justify Anstie's opinion of the efficiency of English workers; but another element in it may well have been the opportunity which English clothiers had of mixing English wool with Spanish up to a quarter of the total weight, without its being easily detectable.[4]

Another element in this new-found confidence must have been the prosperity which was returning to the industry, although there was still a good deal of unemployment.[5] The new fancy cloths were being received with much favour in France, although there was hardly any direct trade except by smuggling.[6] First made, apparently, by Anstie himself, and

---

[1] B.T.6/111, no. 36.

[2] Lr. from a Crediton manufacturer to Lord Sheffield, quoted H. B. Carter, *His Majesty's Spanish Flock*, p. 67.

[3] *Encycl. méth.* 258, quoting Lord Sheffield in the *Courier de l'Europe* of 14 Oct. 1783.

[4] B.T.6/114, fol. 109.

[5] B.T.6/111, fol. 39. Lr. of M. Humphreys of Chippenham, 6 Feb. 1786.

[6] B.T.6/114, fols. 94, 96, 112, 176. Cf. Macpherson, op. cit. iv. 82. The 'petits draps mélangés de diverses couleurs' which Roland says were known as 'Wiltons' (*Encycl. méth.* 256), may have been the 'marble cloth' for which Wilton was noted, Benson and Hatcher, op. cit., p. 579.

often mixed with silk, cotton, or mohair,[1] they were a development of plain cassimeres, the making of which had spread considerably in the eighties after the expiry of Yerbury's patent, although the manufacture was still small in comparison with that of broadcloth. Another market for them was Russia,[2] and their popularity in England was recognized by royal patronage in 1789.[3] The superfine manufacturers still had much cloth in hand in 1786, mainly because of difficulties in Ireland and America, but there had already been signs of improvement. Salisbury Spring Fair in 1785 was expected to be the largest for many years,[4] and from 1784 onwards complaints of the shortage of English wool, together with the great rise in imports of Spanish in 1787 and afterwards, both point to an increase in demand as important for the west as for Yorkshire. The Blackwell Hall factor, Thomas Everett, considered in 1786 that the manufacture of superfine broadcloth had declined, but in saying so he was thinking of the decline in the East India Company's purchases and the loss of the Levant trade.[5] Other evidence suggests that internal consumption was increasing. Superfines in ordinary colours were selling at 17s. a yard in 1786 a rise of 6d. to 1s. over 1770;[6] and although this was due to the increased cost of Spanish wool, the fact that the price was paid points to a continued internal demand, of which there is evidence from other sources. In 1788 a pamphleteer remarked that there was never any period when sales of cloth had been greater, the novelties introduced 'together with the general luxury and fashion of the times induce people to buy more than they can fairly wear; those who formerly bought but one coat in two or three years have now nearly as many in one'.[7] Two years previously, production of superfines in the west had been estimated, again by Everett, at 35,000 pieces a year of which

---

[1] Anstie's stock book for 1793, now apparently lost, shows nine different species mixed with silk, such as silk stripes, silk checks, silk spotted Manilla, and figured silk cloth. In all he was making 31 different kinds or qualities of cloth and cassimeres, Bodington MSS. (see below, p. 69, n. 1).

[2] P. A. Nemnich, *Neueste Reise*, p. 217. The figures for exports of Spanish cloth to Russia rose consistently from 22 pieces in 1777 to 1,534 in 1789.

[3] *V.C.H. Wilts.* iv. 161.

[4] *Salisbury Journal*, 28 Mar. 1785.

[5] B.T.6/114, fols. 113–4.

[6] Ibid., fol. 110.

[7] *While we Live, Let us Live*, p. 10.

24,000 were made in Wiltshire and Somerset.[1] The comparatively small amount of 11,000 pieces assigned to Gloucestershire is surprising, but it must have been much exceeded by the large quantity at lower prices which was produced there. The accounts of William Carruthers of Painswick, for example, show that all the cloth he sent to his London factors in 1788 and 1789 was priced at 7s. 6d. to 15s. a yard, with the bulk of it at 10s. 6d. to 15s. A few of those at 15s. were described as 'superfine' but most were 'super', 'fine', 'Ladies' cloth', or in one case 'uniform cloth'.[2] Far more 'liveries' and other cloths of English wool were made in and round Frome and Westbury than superfine; and much fancy cloth was produced in Devizes and Salisbury as well as in Trowbridge. It seems certain that in Gloucestershire the quantity of the cheaper cloth made was still much greater than that of superfines, and, although any estimate of production can only be conjecture, it does not seem possible that less than 85,000 to 90,000 pieces of broadcloth besides cassimeres and fancy cloth were made in 1787.[3]

To sum up, production of broad cloth in the west seems to have made good the loss it had suffered during the middle of the century; and it is possible that the number of cassimeres, fancy cloths, and flannels may have been greater than that of the druggets and serges which were now disappearing. Moreover most of the goods produced were of finer quality than they had been at the beginning of the century. Yorkshire's production, taking broad and narrow cloth together, was almost three times as much, not to mention the worsteds and half worsteds made there in increasing quantities; but the west was still making quite a good showing and was about to make a better one with the installation of spinning machinery.

[1] B.T.6/114, fol. 175.
[2] Palling Papers. See p. 60, n. 4. Carruthers had married the heiress of this branch of the Palling family.
[3] See App. V.

III

MARKETING

ALTHOUGH London was the chief market for cloth in early Stuart times, a good deal was sold elsewhere. It is true that the outports, especially Bristol and Southampton, which had exported much cloth in the fifteenth and sixteenth centuries, now exported very little;[1] but much of what was dyed and finished in the country was sold at fairs, of which most of the larger market towns had one or two a year. The improved red cloth, introduced by the Stroudwater clothiers soon after the beginning of the century, was all disposed of in this way at first; and not until it was well known in the country was it sent up for sale in London.[2] Bartholomew Fair in London[3] and certain of the provincial fairs such as those of Bristol and Salisbury, had special significance for cloth; and those of Bristol were attended by London merchants[4] and were important enough to attract cloth which would otherwise have gone to the London market at Blackwell Hall in Basinghall Street.[5] Nor was all the cloth which came to London sold in this Hall, in spite of repeated efforts to confine it there. Much was disposed of by private contract and there were constant complaints that cloth was carried straight to merchants' houses without having first been deposited in the Hall, thus defrauding Christ's Hospital of the hallage payable on each cloth and making it impossible to verify whether aulnage had been paid.[6] Informations were laid against several Wiltshire clothiers for this offence in 1610,[7]

[1] Friis, op. cit., pp. 65–8.   [2] P.R.O., S.P.16/287/77.
[3] A.P.C. 1599–1600, 606.
[4] H.M.C. Sackville Papers, vol. I, Cranfield Papers, ed. A. P. Newton, i. 10; C.S.P.D. 1636/7, 18; Analytical Index to the Remembrancia of the City of London, p. 345.
[5] C.S.P.D. 1640, 521.
[6] Ibid. 1619–23, 401 (1622); A.P.C. 1615/16, 122–3; P.R.O., P.C.2/49, fol. 59 (1638); Remembrancia, 72 (1610), 76 (1638). In 1625, however, clothiers were ordered to sell by private contract for fear of plague, A.P.C. 1625/6, 211.
[7] 'Tradesmen in early Stuart Wiltshire,' ed. N. J. Williams, W.A.S. Recd. Brch. xv. 60, 61, 63.

but without any effect in altering the practice. In the later thirties, James Ashe was sending by far the greater part of his Spanish cloth direct to his son Edward in London, and much of it was sold through a shop in which the family had an interest and probably the sole control. He also sold smaller quantities direct to other London merchants, as well as to two in Bristol, and one each in Salisbury, Blandford, and Dorchester; and there is no indication that any went to Blackwell Hall.[1] Nevertheless, the Hall was the chief market where the majority of clothiers met their customers; and in the early part of the century it was still the general custom in the west for them to take up their own cloth for sale. Before the end of it this direct relationship between clothier and merchant had been largely superseded by the intervention of the Blackwell Hall factors, who arranged for the selling of the cloth and eventually came to provide much of the clothier's raw materials. As middlemen they were naturally unpopular; but the main charge against them was the long credit which they exacted from the clothier and the resulting elimination from the industry of those whose capital was too small to enable them to wait for payment.[2]

Factors were in existence as early as 1611 and complaints that clothiers were being ruined by them were made at intervals throughout the early Stuart and Commonwealth periods,[3] but the City never succeeded in suppressing them. On one of these occasions, in 1623, they were defended by the Clothworkers' Company, from whose ranks many of them sprang, in a statement which, although well known, is worth quoting again because it describes so exactly the functions which made the factors useful and contributed to the increase in their numbers in spite of all complaints:

In theis people very great trust is committed both by the Clothier (and) Marchant for the clothier sendeth upp his Clothes to the Hall where he payes his duetyes himself and cannot stay untill the markett serveth him but leaveth his clothes to the care and order of these Clothworkers, who have in their charge some tymes 6 moneths or

---

[1] P.R.O., C.107/20, Cloth Book of James Ashe, 1631–41. See also C.107/17 which contains lists of cloth sent to the firm of Ashe in London from a number of clothiers (including Paul Methuen) from 1656 to 1663.

[2] For a complete account of the clothiers' grievances see E. Lipson, *The Economic History of England* ii. 27–30.

[3] Ramsay, op. cit., pp. 133–4.

12 moneths for a markett five hundred or a thousand Clothes (the Clothier wholly depending upon these Clothworkers) . . . and the Marchant giveth order to him likewise to cause the Clothier . . . to dye such and such collours, advising the Clothier what marchants he hath that are ready to take what he doth advise for. Also if the clothier at any tyme want money, the Clothworker is the Instrument to furnish him, (and) if the marchant be unknown to the Clothier and would have credit the Clothworker[1] doth advise him of his sufficiency. And the Clothier and Marchant find him so upright as good content is given to either party, as it cannot be proved that they have at any time fayned betweene the Clothier and the Marchant, which if the clothworker did faine would presently be discovered, for generally the Marchant payeth the Clothier himselfe or giveth his bill if it be for tyme, so that theis people gett only for their work and have no other trade but this. . . . Upon theis Clothworkers the Suffolk men, Stroudwater and all other that bring their Clothes to London which have their full manufacture do depend.[2]

It is clear from this passage that factors were not much, if at all, concerned in the transactions between the clothier and the Merchant Adventurers for the sale of unfinished cloth; and some of the grievances against them in the later part of the century must have been the result of the increasing sales of coloured cloth. But there is also a very significant difference between the situation depicted in this passage and that which existed at the end of the century. By 1690 the merchant no longer paid the clothier direct and often did not know who he was,[3] but made the factor his intermediary; and the latter passed on the money after deduction of the various charges of factorage, hallage, porterage, and insurance. This change seems to have taken place during the Civil War and may have been caused by it. During the Commonwealth some factors were acting a useful part in transmitting public money to and from London. Thus, when the Mayor of Salisbury, who happened to be a clothier, wanted money for the keep of Dutch prisoners in 1653, he drew a bill payable to his factor in

---

[1] In the original this word is 'Clothier' which is obviously an error.

[2] P.R.O., S.P.14/133/36, partially quoted G. Unwin, *Industrial Organisation in the Sixteenth and Seventeenth Centuries*, pp. 112–13.

[3] *Cobbett's Collection of State Trials* xi. 443 (Henry Cornish 1680) where a merchant said he was indebted to Cornish 'for whom it is I cannot tell'.

London;[1] and in 1657 Thomas Salmon of Wells, Receiver of the Assessments for Somerset, was accustomed to employ 'Richard Burt, factor in London, to receive many thousand pounds thereof by way of return from clothiers'.[2] It is typical of some of the complaints made later that Burt had absconded, after lading goods to the value of £8,000 on an Amsterdam ship which had been detained at Gravesend.

In spite of such incidents and other occasional complaints, such as one from the clothiers of Worcester in 1647,[3] clothiers in general seem to have felt no particular resentment against the Blackwell Hall factors for some years after the Restoration. Antagonism to them came from the City, which resented them as non-freemen who interposed themselves between buyer and seller and usurped the functions of the merchants who were free of the City.[4] The Civil War had increased the opportunities for packers, clothworkers, and others connected with the industry to undertake the custody and disposal of cloth and they seem to have established themselves in so strong a position that the City had to abandon the attempts to proscribe them. Instead it endeavoured to control them. The question of new regulations for Blackwell Hall was under consideration at intervals from 1651 onwards;[5] but it was not until 1658 that the Court of Common Council passed a new and comprehensive Act[6] which, however, owing to the events leading up to the Restoration, never came into force. It was re-enacted with rather more detail in December 1661.[7] Among other provisions, the Act increased charges, forbade even freemen to act as agents for strangers, and provided that no one should act as a Blackwell Hall factor unless he had been approved by the Lord Mayor and Aldermen and had entered into recognizances of £200 not to buy or sell cloth either in his own name or in that of any other person. This measure was imposed with a view to preserving the privileges of citizens and was not intended for the defence of the clothiers, among whom the increase in

---

[1] *C.S.P.D. 1652–3*, 252.

[2] Ibid., *1657–8*, 209.

[3] City of London Repertories, 59, fol. 19.

[4] Complaints had been made of them in 1612, 1619, and 1645, City of London Journals, 28, fol. 348v.; 31, fol. 122; 40, fol. 146.

[5] Repertories, 61, fol. 122; 62, fol. 160v; 63, fol. 395.

[6] Journals, 41, fols. 195–199.   [7] Ibid., 45, fols. 152v–157v.

charges and the provision that cloth must remain in the Hall for a certain period aroused much opposition. In 1663, in response to petitions from clothiers and factors together,[1] the House of Commons appointed a Committee which reported in strong terms against the City's action;[2] but the situation remained the same and the question came up again the following year, on the receipt of a further petition.[3] In December 1664 a bill condemning the City was brought in and had its second reading,[4] but was dropped owing to the desire for an accommodation expressed by some of the members for the clothmaking districts.[5] The factors had, meanwhile, begun a suit in the Court of Common Pleas against the City's demand for recognizances,[6] on the ground that they were the clothiers' servants and thus not liable to be treated as independent brokers, over whom the City had exercised control from the Middle Ages onwards. The result of the suit (if any) is unknown, but in June 1665 the Act of Common Council was withdrawn in favour of a new and less stringent one.[7] It still included a provision for the registration of factors, but the majority avoided compliance. The names of twenty-six appear in the City Books as having been admitted in 1662 or later;[8] but about fifty are known from other sources to have existed in the period between 1660 and 1680[9] and only four or five of them can be identified with those who gave recognizances.[10] Many Blackwell Hall factors were freemen[11]

---

[1] *C.J.* viii. 448. A petition was also sent to the Privy Council, P.R.O., P.C.2/56, fol. 316.

[2] *C.J.* viii. 492–3, 526. For the City's protests see Repertories, 69, fols. 86v–87, 101v.

[3] *C.S.P.D. 1663–4*, 535; *C.J.* viii. 526.

[4] *C.J.* viii. 572–3.   [5] Journals, 46, fol. 68v.

[6] *Remembrancia*, 77.   [7] Journals, 46, fols. 72–76.

[8] Repertories, 68, fol. 173v; 80, fol. 275; 81, fol. 113v–114; 82, fol. 75v; 83, fol. 62.

[9] There are 40 names in the *Directory* of 1677, and Turner's Waste Book, 1677–85 (P.R.O., C.104/44) gives ten more. One or two come from other sources. Not all were active at the same time but there were certainly more in 1692 than the 30 mentioned in *The Clothier's Complaint*, p. 4, though possibly only 30 dealt in West of England cloth.

[10] John Diamond (P.R.O., C.107/20); Edward Bickley (*London Gazette*, no. 2216); George Woodford (Directory and C.104/44); John Tucker (Arch. H.L. 1699, 13 Mar. no. 1402); and possibly Osgood Cornish (Ashe books 1657–60, C.107/18, though the Christian name is not given).

[11] This was recognized by the Act of 1678, Journals, vol. 48, fol. 386v. Henry Cornish was one. Among those who gave recognizances only one, John Tucker in 1676, is stated to be a freeman, Repertories, vol. 82, fol. 75v.

and it was probably impossible to interfere with them. When the City passed a new Act in 1678,[1] still with the object of preventing 'foreign buying', this requirement was omitted, and the City took precautions to safeguard its provisions from objections by clothiers.[2] This Act may be regarded as a victory for the factors, since it permitted them, if freemen, to buy cloth for themselves, provided that it was of a kind in which they did not normally deal and that it was for export on their own account; which no doubt merely legalized a practice already carried on.

The friction between the City and the factors made them a convenient scapegoat in the dispute with the clothiers over increased hallage charges. The latter were told that the City was only consulting their best interests and that the factors were the 'vile instruments' who 'labour to make a difference where none is or can be if rightly understood'.[3] Nearly all the familiar charges about the factors jostling the clothiers out of the market or ruining them by delaying the sale of their cloth in order to lower the price may be found either in the pamphlet quoted above or in the Act of Common Council of 1665. These documents formed a convenient quarry from which later adversaries of the factors could draw their arguments; but the arguments themselves originated with the City and not with the clothiers, and at a much earlier date than is generally supposed. It was not until 1677 that the clothiers' grievances began to be publicized. They were no doubt connected with the growth in the influence of factors during the four years which had elapsed between the destruction of Blackwell Hall in the Fire of London and its rebuilding, and still more with the financial troubles caused by the Dutch war and the Stop of the Exchequer in 1672, which made money difficult to obtain. The following letters, the first so far discovered from a factor to a clothier, illustrate some of the complaints:[4]

To Edward Palling, Painswick   London, Feb. 13, 1673/4

. . . The reason why I did not right to you sooner was because I could not give you any incouridgement. You know you did leave

---

[1] Journals, vol. 48, fols. 385v–398.   [2] Repertories, vol. 83, fol. 131.
[3] D.S., *To all the Clothiers of England*. (Dated 1662 with a query in the B.M. catalogue, but it refers to the clothiers' petition of 11 Mar. 1662/3, *C.J.* viii. 448.)
[4] Palling Papers. I am indebted to Mrs. Smith of Wick Street Farm, Painswick, for allowing me to see these papers.

with me tenn one hed[1] reds . . . your prize of them was £9 5s. per cloth in redy mony. I haveing a chapman that did want sum reds about that prize did sell your eight full cullers to him for £9 5s. per cloth as you ordered me . . . (it) is now becum dew within a few days. I was the unwillinger to right to you because I gave a little time with them at your lowest redy mony prize, but I thought if the war did continue it was better for me to doe soe than to keepe them; but now there is a peace I hope cloth will fetch a better price . . . Thomas Wh(iting?).[2]

I hope this bad markitt that is past will not discouridge you as to me, now I have hopes of a better.

It may have done so, for the next letter, a few years later, is from another factor:

To the same   London, July 11, 1678

I am sorry that you have made so many Jorneys to Glos[r] about your mony; had your Mony been at my Command you should not have been failed of it, but being in another Man's hands, And he disappointed of mony have failed me, and that have occasioned me to faile you; but you need not question or doubt of your Money, for it is As good a man as any within the walls of London that have bought your Cloth, but he have not yet Rec'd a penny of money; and therefore do desier a Littel forbearance which will not be Longe but it shall be paid you. Other men doe forbeare as have not had soe much hand as you had. I shall take care to get it in and to pay it in speedily for you. John Taylor.[3]

It is not difficult to imagine the effect of such letters on the recipient and the volume of grumbling must have grown steadily.[4] Pamphleteers who declaimed against the factors wrote as if in former times the clothier had always been able to get cash for his cloth; but in fact credit was nothing new in the trade, having been common in the previous century and, indeed, much earlier. On the other hand, purchases by the Merchant Adventurers are said to have been made for cash in

---

[1] The coarser cloth sent to the Levant and India is always designated by the number of 'heads', from one to eight, but the meaning of the term has not been discovered. The numbers do not correspond with any range of prices.

[2] Most of the name has been torn off, but there was a Blackwell Hall factor named Whiting (no Christian name given) in Coleman St., *Directory* of 1677.

[3] Of Basinghall St., ibid.

[4] Cf. Stephens in 1693, B.M. Loan Colln. 29/187, 'The long credits in sale of cloth introduced by (the factors) is a great grievance.' (See p. 105.)

the early part of the seventeenth century[1] and so were many of those made by other merchants. The books of Edward Ashe from 1640–3,[2] which were difficult years, show a good proportion of sales and purchases for ready money (paid within a month or six weeks). Even just after the Restoration, when the business seems to have been carried on by his younger brother Jonathan, accounts were seldom outstanding for more than a month.[3] The business of their father, James the clothier, was mainly conducted on short credit. He kept running accounts with his customers who paid off substantial sums at intervals while ordering more cloth at the same time. Such payments were always made in money, sums of £200 or even £500 being brought from London by an employee, or from Bristol by the common carrier. Cash was also handed over personally at fairs and other meeting places.[4] After the Civil War had begun, some debts were outstanding for as much as four years, but this was unusual and must have been due to war conditions.[5] The Ashe family dealt in a kind of cloth which was worn only by the well-to-do and their books may give too favourable an impression. Other clothiers did not always receive their money when due;[6] and many must have suffered delays in payment from merchants in much the same manner as they did later from factors.

Cash purchases or short credit persisted, however, until well after the Restoration. 'The London trade was on long credit, now in ready money', said Josiah Child in 1669,[7] reminding us that there was no steady progression from cash to credit buying but rather an oscillation between them according to the prosperity or otherwise of the times. The books of the Levant merchant, Jacob Turner, from 1677 to 1691 show a large number of transactions for cash or at not over four months'

---

[1] Supple, op. cit., pp. 40–1, quoting MS. Lansd. 152, fol. 284, and Misselden, *Circle of Commerce*. In the mid-sixteenth century however, purchases had been made half for cash and half on three to five months credit or more, R. Ehrenberg, *Hamburg und England im Zeitalter der Königin Elizabeth*, p. 276.

[2] P.R.O., C.107/20, 'Groot Boeck'.

[3] C.107/18, Book with marbled paper cover.

[4] C.107/20, Cloth Book of James Ashe.

[5] C.107/18, Notebook of debts owing to Grace Ashe, 1646.

[6] P.R.O., S.P.18/25/23, Lr. from Thomas Woodward 21 Oct. 1652.

[7] *H.M.C. 8th Rept.* (*H. of L. MSS.*), 134a. He was not referring specifically to the trade in woollen goods.

credit.[1] Longer periods became more common after 1680. 67 cloths ordered from John Blanch of Eastington in November 1680 were to be paid for one-third in February, one-third in June, and one-third the following October. Another contract with the same clothier made before 24 June 1684, for 70 cloths to be delivered by September, was struck on credit for nine months and then to pay £100 a month, and a similar one in 1687 allowed a year for complete payment. In 1689 85 cloths bought from a factor were to be paid for at £55 a month.[2] No doubt this longer credit was the result of the depressed condition of the Levant trade, and Turner appears to have been in debt by the end of the eighties. In 1692, however, there were still many merchants and drapers 'that now buy cloth and make good payment'[3] but whether cash was obtained quickly or not depended on the market for which the cloth was destined as well as on the financial stability of the buyer. When the East India Company became a large buyer of cloth in 1693, an advance had to be made to the clothiers on the delivery of their goods;[4] but bonds carrying interest for six months were given for the remainder and these were still outstanding a year later, without further interest.[5] Long credit was certainly not, as was alleged, a device of the factors; but the fact that direct communication between merchant and clothier was getting rarer (and this is noticeable in Turner's books during the eighties) made it inevitable that factors should be blamed for it. Insurance against non-payment by the merchant had been introduced by factors by the end of the century,[6] perhaps as a result of the Blackwell Hall Act,[7] but the clothier was inclined to regard the premium as one more device of the factor to get hold of his money.

The sudden outburst of criticism in 1677 was, in all probability, a reply to the landowners' complaints about the low price of wool.[8] If clothiers were reproached for not paying more,

---

[1] P.R.O., C.104/44, Waste Book.

[2] Ibid., fols. 95, 174, 13 (new pagination from 12 Jan. 1685/6).

[3] *Clothier's Complaint*, p. 9.   [4] E.I. Co.'s Court Book, 36, fol. 211.

[5] J. Blanch, *Abstract of the Grievances of Trade*, p. 12.

[6] In an agreement made by Thomas Long of Melksham with his factor in 1703 insurance was charged at 10s. per cloth (including factorage) but in 1720 it was reckoned at 2 per cent. Wilts. C.R.O., 947.

[7] See below, p. 77.

[8] For the reasons for the fall in price see below, pp. 260–1.

they had a ready-made excuse to hand in the plea that the Blackwell Hall factors detained their money. The number of pamphlets appearing in the years 1677 to 1681 in which the price of wool and the abuses practised by the factors figured largely,[1] was, no doubt, connected with the fact that Parliament was discussing the state of the industry. Discontent with the factors was a West-of-England phenomenon, and at least two of the pamphleteers came from thence. Andrew Yarranton knew Salisbury well, having surveyed the Avon when it was proposed to make it navigable, and the clothier who voices his grievances is represented as coming from that city.[2] *A Treatise of Wool and Cattel* appears to have been written by a small landowner, George Clark of Swainswick near Bath,[3] who evidently had hopes of some action being taken; but 'the business of the Popish Plot then breaking out, all things of that nature were then put off'. It was he who was behind the presentation of the Grand Jury at Bruton in January 1685, which named as grievances the illicit export of wool and the abuses of the factors; and he reprinted his pamphlet, with some alterations and a stronger condemnation of them, in the following year to accompany a petition he sent up to the Privy Council.[4] The Revolution of 1688 intervened, and it was not until 1691 that another petition was presented to Parliament, this time by Gloucestershire clothiers, ascribing the decay of their trade partly to the practices of woolbroggers and partly to those of the Blackwell Hall factors.[5] The emphasis in this petition was laid, not on long credit or other artifices of factors,

---

[1] For portions of three of them, much abridged, see Smith, op. cit. i. 311–26. There were several others.

[2] A, Yarranton, *England's Improvement by Sea and Land*, pp. 97 ff.

[3] A copy of the re-issue of this pamphlet (see below, n. 4) is bound with Aubrey MSS. 2 (fol. 124), with a note by Aubrey 'Ex dono auctoris Geo. Clark arm'. An adverse opinion by Francis Lodwick, a London merchant, follows. Clark was probably the 'G. Clark of Swannick' who was appointed a magistrate in 1680 when the Bench was purged of Whigs; he is included among those by whose names the words 'of very small estate and no good repute' have been written, presumably by a later Whig hand, *H.M.C. 11th Rept.* (*H. of L. MSS.*), 188. The identification with Swainswick is rendered probable by the fact that a George Clark was churchwarden there in 1664 and his wife and daughter were buried in 1670 and 1690 respectively, J. Collinson, *History of Somerset* i. 154–5.

[4] P.R.O., P.C.2/72, fol. 464. The new edition was *A Treatise of Wool and the Manufacture of it*. The above quotation comes from the preface, p. 5.

[5] *C.J.* x. 590. The pamphlet, *Reasons of the Decay of the Clothing Trade humbly offered to Parliament*, seems to have been written in support of this petition.

but solely on their alleged combination with the engrossers of wool to make the clothiers buy it of them, and it asked for the total suppression of both classes of middlemen. Clark was now able to bring up the Grand Jury's presentment,[1] but from this point onwards it was the Gloucestershire clothiers who sustained the agitation. Their action may probably be explained by the state of the Levant trade and the rising price of English wool[2]— a situation in direct contrast to that which had existed at the time of the earlier complaints.

A bill in the sense of the Gloucestershire petition was introduced into Parliament early in 1692 by Sir John Guise,[3] one of the members for the county, but it did not get beyond the Committee stage before Parliament adjourned. Another in the next session, which avoided the question of woolbroggers and concentrated on the banishment of factors from Blackwell Hall and the confinement of sales there, and made provision for the marking and length of cloth, also failed to become law.[4] Others were introduced in every succeeding session, by Sir John until his death in 1695 and then by Sir George Hungerford one of the members for Wiltshire; but none got beyond the Committee stage until 1697.[5] The bill which then passed[6] was a much watered-down version, which did not get anywhere near suppressing the factors and made no mention of broggers. It merely confined sales to Blackwell Hall on appointed days, required the Clerk to keep a register of sales with names of the buyer, seller, and factor, and obliged the latter to take a note from the buyer with particulars of the cloth sold, which was to be given to the seller within eight days. These provisions, though answering many of the objections which had been raised by pamphleteers, were very different from those envisaged

[1] *C.J.* x. 611.

[2] See below, p. 262. The fact that some Gloucestershire clothiers were petitioning in 1694 against the Hamburg Company's monopoly, on the ground that a free trade would raise the price of wool (*C.J.* xi. 79), does not invalidate this statement; such an argument was a natural one to use in addressing a Parliament of landowners, however much the clothiers might privately have resented a rise.

[3] *C.J.* x. 644.

[4] *The Clothier's Complaint*, pp. 1–2. The second bill, brought in on 19 Nov. 1692, must be that described in this pamphlet.

[5] *C.J.* xi. 78, 90, 147, 189, 475, 636, 724, 729.

[6] 8 and 9 Wm. iii. c. 9.

in the original Gloucestershire petition; and they seem to have been carried unanimously, perhaps because the factors considered that they were innocuous. Opinion, even in Gloucestershire, was divided.[1] The anti-factor party was supported by the depressed areas of Reading and Newbury,[2] but clothiers of Oxfordshire and those of Wiltshire and Somerset petitioned in their favour.[3]

The passage of the bill did not settle the question. In the following year, against a background of high prices for wool and dyestuffs, there were renewed petitions against woolbroggers;[4] and in the bill for improvement of the woollen manufacture discussed in Parliament in April 1698 a clause forbidding factors to sell wool and dyestuffs was offered but withdrawn.[5] In February 1698/9, a new bill was introduced by another Wiltshire member[6] to enforce the previous Act by raising the penalties for not giving notes of sale, to which merchants and drapers strongly objected.[7] During its passage through the House a clause was adopted forbidding factors to sell any cloth except by order of the maker and the bill was passed; but following disputes between Lords and Commons it was delayed so that it had not become law when Parliament was prorogued.[8] The same fate awaited another bill introduced in the next session;[9] and there was one more attempt in 1701,[10] which seems never to have reached the stage of becoming a bill. In 1714 unsuccessful attempts were made to tack clauses on to the bill for measuring medleys,[11] again prescribing that all cloth should be brought to Blackwell Hall and setting a higher penalty on refusal to give notes;[12] but the only result was a

---

[1] See the two Gloucestershire petitions in 1694, one from clothiers against the obligation to sell in Blackwell Hall (*C.J.* xi. 139) and the other from gentlemen and clothiers in favour of maintaining the market there (ibid., 181).

[2] Ibid., 211.   [3] Ibid., 132; x. 731.

[4] See below, p. 262.   [5] *C.J.* xii. 203.

[6] Ibid., 520. The member was Mr. Eyre, who may have been either Robert Eyre, M.P. for Salisbury, or John Eyre, who represented Downton. The interests of Salisbury and Glos. in the Levant trade were the same. In the bill ordered in November 1699 the two members for Glos. were associated with him, *C.J.* xiii. 5.

[7] *C.J.* xii. 524, 530.   [8] Ibid., 553, 558, 650, 652, 675.

[9] *C.J.* xiii. 5, 39–40, 52, 106–7.   [10] Ibid., 350.

[11] *C.J.* xvii. 637.

[12] *The Clothiers' Reasons . . . for adding a Clause to oblige all Buyers of Cloth upon Credit to give notes. . . .* Cf. Blanch, *The Beau Merchant.*

provision making it illegal for anyone but a clothier to sue the factor for not demanding them.[1]

The voluminous body of literature which surrounds these proceedings has probably given them an importance in the eyes of historians which they do not appear to have had for contemporaries. No doubt the clothiers grumbled, but it needed more than grumbling for action to be taken in a cause so long drawn out and attended, in all probability, with so much lobbying and expense. According to the factors 'some Gloucestershire rich designing clothiers'[2] were the chief promoters of the bill, and the attempts to prevent them from selling wool were got up by a small group whose spokesman was 'one Blanch formerly a clothier but now setting up to sell Spanish wool'.[3] John Blanch came of a family at Eastington which had been in the industry for several generations.[4] Such of his many writings as have survived[5] show him as an extreme conservative, attacking not only middlemen of all kinds, but the East India Company and the wearing of printed calicoes, alien merchants and the removal of alien's duty, all forms of credit instruments and, after 1713, the South Sea Company. He retired from the industry in 1694 at the age of forty-four[6] and seems to have become both a Spanish merchant and a member of the Hamburg Company, for which he passionately campaigned.[7] He gave evidence against woolbroggers before the Parliamentary Committee in 1698,[8] and was himself M.P. for Gloucester from 1710 to 1714.[9] He was thus excellently qualified by wealth and temperament to lead the conservative element in the industry against innovations. It is difficult to

---

[1] 1 Geo. i. c. 15, § 13.

[2] *Reasons for a general Liberty to all Clothiers to sell their Cloth when, where and as they please.*

[3] *The Blackwell Hall Factors' Case.*

[4] *Glos. Inq. P.M., 1625-42*, 13. In 1712 he had an estate at Wootton Barton just outside Gloucester, Atkyns, op. cit., p. 586.

[5] *Swords into Anchors*, gives a list of eighteen publications. Four are in the British Museum and the above with another play (so-called) is in Gloucester City Library.

[6] *C.J.* xiii. 849. In the preface of *Swords into Anchors* (1725), he speaks of himself as in his 75th year.

[7] *Gloucester Journal*, 8 June 1724. His attack on the South Sea Company for ruining the trade to Cadiz supports the factors' allegation that he was a Spanish merchant.

[8] *C.J.* xii. 277.

[9] W. R. Williams, *The Parliamentary History of the County of Gloucestershire*, p. 207.

ascertain how large this element was. No originals survive of the petitions to Parliament before the passage of the bill of 1697; but there are two, one on each side, addressed to the House of Lords on the occasion of the supplementary bill of 1699,[1] which show 57 clothiers in favour of it and 24 against. By this time clothiers may have been tiring of the subject, but the number of those in favour is far lower than the 98 who had supported the East India Company two years earlier,[2] although this may be a tribute to the thoroughness with which the factors who served that Company organized their clothiers.

If Blanch was the spearhead of the agitation, it is unlikely that his motives were disinterested. Passages in *The Clothier's Complaint* point out that, when a shipping was imminent, factors would rush to order cloth from small clothiers and so obtain it cheaply; and the Levant Company was accused of deferring its ships in order to obtain cloth at its own price.[3] In 1689 the Company had returned, after an interval of five years, to the custom of sending out general ships and forbidding goods to be sent by any other form of transport.[4] If on this occasion the regular Levant clothiers, of whom Blanch was one, had had to meet competition of the kind suggested above, it would have been quite sufficient, together with the rising price of wool, to set in motion an attack which could take advantage of the general grievances against factors.[5] Although the Levant Company bought little between 1692 and 1695, the advent of the East India Company as a large buyer in 1693 prolonged the situation, for it operated as far as possible through packers who gave orders through factors for the cloth needed. If the above interpretation is correct, it would appear that the whole agitation was not, as has been suggested, 'the work of the older less specialized trades',[6] but rather falls into line with the

---

[1] Arch. H.L. 1698/9, 13 Mar., no. 1402. The second petition is not said to have come from Glos. but several Gloucestershire names are recognizable.

[2] Ibid., 1696/7, 19 Feb., no. 1121a. Petition dated 22 Feb. 1696/7. Only two names in the Blackwell Hall petitions, one for and one against, coincide with those in this one.

[3] *The Clothier's Complaint*, pp. 7, 10, 22. Cf. *Reasons for preserving the Public Market at Blackwell Hall and restraining the Levant Company. . . .*

[4] *An Account of the Number of Woollen Cloths exported. . . .*

[5] Cf. the insistence on the 'bondage by the conjunct interest of the Turkey merchants and Packers', *The Reply of the Country to the kind reasons of the Great City*.

[6] G. N. Clark, *The Later Stuarts*, p. 48.

earlier efforts of wealthy clothiers to suppress middlemen and preserve to themselves the privilege of dealing with principals in selling as well as in buying.

The Blackwell Hall Act was, of course, perfectly ineffectual as a legal measure. Conditions did not return to what they had been in the early part of the century and notes of sale were seldom, if ever, given, although the factors said that they had agreed to demand them.[1] In a pamphlet published in 1705 it is stated that when clothiers insured their cloth with the factor it became the latter's business to sue the buyer in case of non-payment, and it seems probable that factors favoured insurance to avoid the necessity of insisting on notes.[2] If so, it did not fully answer the same purpose and involved the clothier in additional expense. Most factors seem to have rented shops and possibly storage space in Blackwell Hall, but most of the sales were effected by sending out cloth to merchants' houses and drapers' shops. In the opinion of the conservatives this was wholly to the bad, 'Cloth is sold up and down in holes and corners . . . whereby the buyers have been countenanced in taking exorbitant measure . . . and the clothier put to great charge as well as damage by having more cloth sent out than is bargained for, by its being opened and when the best is cull'd out the rest returned without just cause of complaint.'[3] John Haynes, himself a Gloucestershire man and at one time a Blackwell Hall factor,[4] who wrote this in 1706, appears to have agreed with the clothiers in placing the blame on the increase of factors, 'or rather such as officiously intrude into that employment'; but the real reason was the multiplicity of the sorts made, the variation in their quality and the extent of the merchants' and drapers' requirements. The remark about exorbitant measure, however, seems to have some justification, and it led to a struggle between clothiers and drapers which aroused more excitement in the Spanish cloth-making districts than even the proposed commercial clauses of the Treaty of Utrecht.

---

[1] *The Blackwell Hall Factors' Case.*
[2] *A Hint to the Blackwell Hall Factors.*
[3] J. Haynes, *A View of the Present State of the Clothing Trade in England*, p. 89.
[4] Haynes's name appears in a petition by Blackwell Hall factors in 1674 against the export of white cloth, (P.R.O., S.P.29/361/227), but he appears to have suffered losses in business (*C.J.* xiii. 159) and had been employed for some years as a Commissioner for preventing the export of wool, *C.S.P.D. 1699–1700*, 165–6.

This agitation began in the country with petitions in February 1711 from Wotton-under-Edge, and Frome,[1] praying that the straining of medleys might be forbidden and that they might be measured in water at the fulling mill, which was only what the ancient statutes had provided for.[2] Worcester followed with a petition against the merchants' practice of putting cloths into water to measure them again when sold.[3] Behind these petitions lay a history of overmeasure demanded by the drapers to compensate them for the shrinkage which affected over-strained cloths.[4] Parliament quickly responded with an Act,[5] concerned only with medleys, which put the owner or occupier of every fulling mill in the place of the searchers who had now vanished from the scene.[6] The buyer was to pay by the seal; but, as might have been expected, this measure was no more successful than earlier attempts to control the manufacture. Two years later the drapers were petitioning for its repeal.[7] A Committee of the House of Commons found their allegation that cloths were often under the stated length to be fully proved,[8] and a bill was introduced[9] which aroused the most passionate feelings in the medley-making districts. Petitions had never been more numerously signed,[10] and Samuel Brewer, son of the great clothier William Brewer of Trowbridge who had died in 1707, was sent up to campaign for the clothiers and was assaulted by a draper in the Court of

---

[1] *C.J.* xvii. 68, 118.

[2] A clause for sealing cloth at the mill had been offered for this purpose in 1700 to one of the abortive Blackwell Hall bills, but negatived.

[3] *C.J.* xvii. 140.

[4] For straining see below, pp. 296–7. It was said that the overmeasure had been sometimes four to six yards, *Reasons humbly offered against the Bill for explaining and amending the Act of 10 Anne relating to Medley Broadcloth*. The books of Thomas Long of Melksham (see above, p. 71, n. 6) covering the period 1700–30, show that in the early part of the century he was sometimes made to give an allowance of three yards.

[5] 10 Anne, c. 16. A similar measure had recently been passed for Yorks.

[6] The last mention of a searcher appears to have been in 1669 when the Somerset Quarter Sessions desired Justices to present two or four persons at the next General Sessions to be triers of cloth, Somerset Quarter Sessions Records, 1666–77, *Som. Rec. Soc.*, vol. 34, p. 55. They do not appear to have done so.

[7] *C.J.* xvii. 558; xviii. 67.

[8] *C.J.* xvii. 562.

[9] See *The Drapers' Bill . . . with the Clothiers' objections.*

[10] *C.J.* xvii. 637, 639, 641, 672, 674. *C.J.* xviii. 161, 164–5. Those in the House of Lords from Trowbridge, Westbury, Bradford, and adjacent districts have, in all, 518 signatures, Arch. H.L. 1714, 2 July, no. 75.

Requests.[1] The final result in 1714 was a compromise which allowed any buyer to have the cloth put into water and measured in Blackwell Hall, after giving two days' notice to the clothier.[2] The clothiers secured the mode of measurement they desired and the right to nominate one of the measurers, but it is doubtful whether any use was made of these concessions. The question was to come up again in 1727 when searchers were once more appointed to measure cloth at the mills;[3] but overstraining continued and, with it, constant grumbling from clothiers. Throughout the eighteenth century drapers were regularly wetting and re-measuring the fine cloth they bought, in spite of the statutory allowance of one yard in twenty—a proceeding which, according to a later Blackwell Hall factor in 1766, the clothiers had brought upon themselves: 'If clothiers had been honest this would never have been, but the drapers will not trust them now.'[4] As late as 1796 another firm of factors, Messrs. Hanson & Mills, were writing that cloth was not saleable without damping and pressing, 'but the mode of its being done by the manufacturers in the country is to damp it for no other purpose than to stretch it out to the longest length the fabric ... will bear ... we have the privilege of again putting it in water to try if it has been improperly stretch'd and to bring it back to a proper substance.'[5]

Ineffectual though the Blackwell Hall Act was, relations between clothiers and factors appear to have become more regularized after it. The agreement made between Thomas Long and Samuel Vanderplank in 1720 is noticeably less rigorous than that which Long had made with Charles Slaughter in 1703.[6] It gradually became regarded as inadmissible for the factor to lower the price without consulting the clothier[7] (though there was another outburst about this in 1743),[8] and a case where the factor had sold by auction without

---

[1] *L.J.* xix. 752; *H.M.C. Portland* v. 471; Arch. H.L. 1714, 7 July; 1715, 11 June.
[2] 1 Geo. i. c. 15, § 4. See *C.J.* xviii. 140.
[3] 13 Geo. i. c. 23. See below, App. V.
[4] Som. C.R.O., Elderton Lr. Book, To Read & Wilkins, 3 Apr. 1766.
[5] P.R.O., C.113/18, Large Lr. Book, fol. 137.   [6] See above, p. 71, n. 6.
[7] Several letters in the Palling Papers from the Blackwell Hall factor Thomas Gryffin, from 1714 to 1718, inquire whether cloth may be sold at a lower price than invoiced.
[8] 'The Causes of the Declension of the Woollen Trade,' *Gentleman's Magazine* xii. 87.

obtaining the clothier's consent was decided in favour of the latter in 1777.[1] In the 1720s Messrs. Usher & Jeffries of Trowbridge had been settling their accounts at regular intervals of eight months and were aggrieved when the factors insisted, in the depression of 1727, on a longer period which seems to have been a year.[2] Such periodical settlements did not mean that cash was not available in the meantime. The increased use of inland bills towards the end of the seventeenth century had greatly facilitated the transfer of money. Although they were not legally negotiable until 1698,[3] they were almost universally used long before that date; and they offered a means whereby a clothier could draw on his factor at any time irrespective of whether the account was balanced or not. Defoe, who knew the trade well, blamed the clothiers for drawing bills on their factors almost as soon as they sent up their goods;[4] but the practice was well established from an earlier date than one would suppose. Factors could object. In 1681 Edward Palling, who then had an account with yet a third factor, was told in December to draw no more till March, 'our Trade now groes to an end';[5] but in actual practice, the factor was unlikely to refuse accepting such bills, except after repeated warnings.[6] In the case of Usher & Jeffries, it is clear that bills drawn before the date of settlement were treated as accommodation bills on which interest was chargeable, and the partners, though they protested against the factor's charge for the service, always promised to supply cash before the date of payment. Other factors seem to have been less particular, but they took their profit in other ways; and their dealings may partly account for the continuing criticism of the whole body during the eighteenth century, a criticism which was not lessened by the fact that many, and probably the majority, were members of clothiers' families and had close relationships with some of their clients in the country.[7] Apart from valid causes of complaint, they

---

[1] *Salisbury Journal,* 10 Mar. 1777 and 6 Apr. 1778.

[2] *W.A.S. Rec. Brch.* xix, nos. 86, 87. See Pressnell, op. cit., p. 82.

[3] 9 and 10 Wm. iii. c. 17. See J. M. Holden, *The History of Negotiable Instruments in English Law,* Ch. iii.

[4] D. Defoe, *Complete English Tradesman* (3rd ed. 1732), i. 353 ff.

[5] Palling Papers, Lr. of 14 Dec. 1681 from Joel Andrews.

[6] See below, pp. 82–3.

[7] *V.C.H. Wilts.* iv. 164, n. 1. There were at least an equal number from Glos.

were far too valuable as scapegoats to be immune. It was easy and satisfying to pass on the blame for lowering wages or paying in truck by explaining that it was all due to long credit;[1] and the London end of the trade had certainly always professed indifference to problems of wages and unemployment.[2]

Where impecunious clothiers were sustained in business by loans from factors, differences were bound to occur. Elderton's letter book, already quoted, illustrates most of the criticisms made of factors, but at the same time, it shows how useful clothiers might find the credit he unwillingly gave them, even if they chafed at his conditions. His usual charges were $2\frac{1}{2}$ per cent commission on sales, $2\frac{1}{2}$ per cent on wool supplied, and $2\frac{1}{2}$ per cent insurance,[4] the latter showing an increase over the 2 per cent paid by Thomas Long of Melksham in 1720.[5] Insurance was voluntary, but recalcitrant clothiers were apt to be reminded that there had been many bankruptcies lately, or even that 'there is a draper that is bankrupt and of whom you are creditor, but if you insure notwithstanding shall take the debt on myself.'[6] Some remained recalcitrant but most seem to have agreed; and the terms for payment of insured debts, one month after the debt was due,[7] seem reasonable if they were adhered to.

When anxious to obtain new clients Elderton was very willing to offer credit. 'If a man has £1,000 or £1,500 I would advance him £1,000' he wrote in 1763, in asking one of his clothiers to inquire at Salisbury Fair for a superfine maker who would engage with him.[8] Most of his agreements did not involve such large sums—£200 or £300 to a young man, or to the poorest not more than £100. With George Walker of Rode,

---

[1] *Gentleman's Magazine* ix. 89–90, 126, see Pressnell, op. cit., p. 82.

[2] *Two Letters sent from Amsterdam. Lr. 2 to John Beauchamp* (1642); Elderton Lr. Book, to G. Walker 11 July 1765, 'If they won't spin (at a lower price) let them go without, they will be glad to spin by Christmas.' Defoe remarked that the factor had no obligation to consider the spinners and weavers, *Complete English Tradesman* (3rd ed. 1732), i. 356.

[4] To J. Hooper, 7 June 1764. Occasionally for friends the percentage for insurance was reduced to 2 per cent. By the end of the century factors seem to have ceased to charge commission on sales, C. Gill, 'Blackwell Hall Factors, 1795–1799', *Econ. Hist. Rev.* (2nd ser.) vi(3). 274.

[5] See p. 71, n. 6.

[6] Elderton Lr. Book, fol. 45, to E. Eyres.

[7] fol. 56, to the same.

[8] fol. 1, To B. Peach.

a young man who seems to have had little money of his own, the arrangement was 'to make two cloths per week . . . which . . . I agreed to take at 14s. 6d. per yard to be paid in ready money and half for wool, and . . . if he wanted a hundred pounds at any time he should have it without any interest'.[1] George drew far more than this, and in 1764 Elderton was complaining that 'we are £469 4s. advanced more than we have got any cloth'. 'We are not against being £100 advanced at any time' he remarked a week later, 'but so large a one at present cannot be';[2] and he inquired eagerly into George's matrimonial intentions and the amount of money the lady was likely to bring in. Other agreements were made on the basis of allowing the clothier to draw a certain sum, from £6 to £10 per cloth, leaving the remainder to be paid in wool as required.[3] The obligation to buy Spanish wool and pay commission on it was frequently evaded, even by George Walker; and by 1769 Elderton had despaired of making his clothiers comply and was allowing them to buy it where they liked and charging them an extra 1 or $1\frac{1}{2}$ per cent on sales of cloth instead.[4] Nor was he very successful in making them send him all the cloth they produced, even when it was made with his money.[5] 'For a clothier to employ two factors is not the thing' he told one of them,[6] but he was unable to prevent some of his clients from doing so, or from sending cloth to the great Sir Samuel Fludyer, whose position in the market is indicated by the fact that three out of the four clothiers of the fifties and sixties whose accounts or correspondence have survived dealt with him as well as with other factors.[7] Moreover Elderton found that in the depression of 1765–9 the lavish promises of 1763 were difficult to fulfil. Those who drew bills in excess of sales were repeatedly adjured to forbear—not that they did so, for their need of money was even greater than their factor's; and in spite of being told again and again that this was the last bill which would be honoured,

[1] fol. 42, to J. Walker.
[2] fols. 100, 103, to G. Walker.
[3] To J. Banks, 9 Oct. 1766; to W. Tree, 6 Oct. 1768.
[4] To G. Walker, 23 Feb. 1769; S. Perry, 14 and 26 Mar. 1769.
[5] To T. Bythesea, 23 Feb. and 23 Mar. 1769; S. Perry, 30 Mar. 1769.
[6] To T. Hill, 25 June 1767.
[7] These were George Wansey of Warminster, John Clark of Trowbridge, and Daniel Packer of Painswick.

some continued to draw even without sending up cloth. Only
when this had gone on for some time did it lead to the ending
of the connection.[1]

Though he expected honourable dealings from his clothiers,
Elderton was not a particularly honourable man himself. He
had no compunction about deceiving buyers if he thought he
could do so safely. 'No. 2323 I wish was in grain, it's a pretty
colour, if I say it's out of grain I shall never sell it, and if I can
sell it for a grain colour I may lose a good customer' he reported to the maker on one occasion.[2] 'Use very little, if any,
English wool for these are for samples. I think you had better
use all Spanish' he wrote to another in 1763,[3] and to the
partners Read & Wilkins of Trowbridge, 'We would have you
mark your cloth Read & Co.—as people in town may think
you succeeded the late Mr. Read the Clothier.'[4] There were
few of his clients with whom he did not have disputes, and one
cannot entirely trust his remarks about the defects in their
cloth; for after several lines of denigration he would add that
he hoped to sell it after all. He may be taken as an example of
the less desirable type of Blackwell Hall factor; but his correspondence is paralleled in a remarkable way by that of Messrs.
Hanson & Mills, one of the foremost firms in the trade at the
end of the century.[5] Selling to others cloth made of wool
supplied by the factor, drawing bills without sending up cloth
to pay for them, advances far beyond those stipulated in their
agreements, and the production of poor quality cloth which
would not fetch the price set on it were practices which were
not confined to the men who dealt with Elderton. Hanson &
Mills dealt with some well-known western clothiers, but even
they were sometimes informed that their cloth was not of their
usual standard. With the smaller ones the correspondence was

---

[1] To J. Banks, 18 Feb. and 12 May 1768; C. Sparks, 1 and 22 Nov. 1764, 11 and
25 Apr. 1765, 16 Jan. 1766, 21 Mar., and 2 Apr. 1767.

[2] To S. Perry, 21 Apr. 1768. A 'grain' colour in the eighteenth century denoted
cochineal, not the original 'grain' dye. Neither would fade.

[3] To J. Huntly, fol. 18.

[4] To Read & Wilkins, fol. 105.

[5] P.R.O., C.113/16–18. See Conrad Gill, op. cit., pp. 268 ff. They were
the successors of Everett & Hanson whose standing in the trade may be seen from
the fact that Thomas Everett was the factor chosen to give evidence both on the
Irish Propositions and the Commercial Treaty with France in the eighties. See
above, p. 58, n. 4.

conducted with less irritability than that of Elderton, but the complaints were substantially the same.

In fact, by the middle of the eighteenth century clothiers had many outlets for their cloth. A few sold directly to individual consumers[1] and others, probably in increasing numbers, by-passed the factors and sold direct to the draper or merchant.[2] The factors were still resisting this tendency in the last decade of the century. 'As for buyers' names', wrote Hanson & Mills in 1798, 'we never give them nor ever will, the clothiers find means readily enough after selling cloth to the factor of selling to the very persons who are to buy said cloth.'[3] This practice could work both ways. Occasionally it was not in the interest of the clothier to have his name known; and in a case in 1754 when certain cloth supplied to the East India Company was not up to sample, the factors strenuously resisted the Company's demand for the makers' names though they had to give way in the end.[4] Concealment of names may have been a practice which increased with the years, for the account sent by his factor to the executors of Anthony Methuen in 1717 included them.[5] As time went on, some large firms of clothiers established their own warehouses in London. Cam, Read & Co. of Bradford had one as early as 1757.[6]

More widespread in the early part of the century though declining towards the end of it, were sales at the great fairs which most clothiers attended at one time or another.[7] From about 1720 or even earlier[8] this had led to the growing custom

---

[1] In 1727 John Hewlett, a drugget maker of Knook near Warminster was advertising his druggets wholesale or retail and was evidently accustomed to selling short lengths to individual customers and matching patterns sent to him, *Gloucester Journal*, 4 Apr. 1727.

[2] *W.A.S. Rec. Brch.* xix. nos. 18, 31, 33–4, 36, 70, 80. See also P.R.O., C.114/138 which appears to be a draper's stock book referring to both London and Salisbury, dated 1769–79. Goods are frequently entered as coming direct from clothiers. Elderton wrote to G. Walker in 1763, 'Desire you will never sell any more cloth to any draper', Lr. Bk. fol. 8.

[3] P.R.O., C.113/18, Lr. Bk. fol. 498.

[4] L. S. Sutherland, *A London Merchant 1695–1774*, App. I.

[5] Corsham Papers, no. 3263.   [6] *Salisbury Journal*, 13 June 1757.

[7] *W.A.S. Rec. Brch.* xix. nos. 19, 22, 35–6, 39, 51, 64, 96–7, 148. Woodbury Hill fair in Dorset was declining by 1770 (*Salisbury Journal*, 17 Sept. 1770) but those at Bristol and Salisbury maintained some importance for cloth until 1790, if not longer. Cf. note in *Gloucester Journal*, 12 Mar. 1792 on the decline of fairs.

[8] Cf. the statement, probably exaggerated, that in 1715 more was sold in the country than in London, above, p. 32, n. 1.

of keeping up a relationship with the buyers who had been originally met there. The improvement in communications during the first twenty years of the eighteenth century meant that, for the first time, correspondence with country customers was readily possible. From the thirties many clothiers sold their whole production in the country.[1] By the third quarter of the century the richer ones had their riders-out who covered large areas[2] while others might entrust their patterns to a traveller who acted as agent for other manufacturers of different commodities.[3] The chief hazard which they had to face was that of bad debts, for country tradesmen were anything but reliable customers. William Westley of Shepton Mallet, who did all his business by correspondence with individual buyers, inherited from his father in 1750 bad debts of over £300, some of which dated back to 1731; and he acquired another £500 or so before 1764, nearly all in small sums.[4] Westley sold cloth from Cornwall in the west to Rochester in the east and as far north as Birmingham and Chester;[5] like another clothier, the third George Wansey of Warminster,[6] he tried a venture to America which turned out badly owing to the death of the friend who took out the goods. Indeed, the few surviving instances where clothiers themselves undertook responsibility for the marketing of their cloth abroad seldom came to a successful conclusion. John Webb of the Iron Mills, Minchinhampton, who in 1756 made an agreement with a Russia merchant to send out 75 long cloths to St. Petersburgh in partnership with him, was grievously disappointed with the result. He had drawn bills for £300 against them, but since the cloth arrived during a glut 'the merchant was at last forced to barter them against Hogs bristles and linens with a great advance of money', and

[1] *W.A.S. Rec. Brch.* xix, pp. xix, 153.

[2] Rudder, op. cit., p. 61. Ambrose Reddall of Stonehouse was sending out a rider in 1765 and he was certainly not the only one to do so. P.R.O., C.109/5, R inland. (I owe this reference to Professor A. H. John.)

[3] *Gloucester Journal*, 17 Apr. 1786. The advertiser, who travelled in hardware, nails, and men's hats, wanted a connection with 'a respectable house in the clothing trade'.

[4] P.R.O., C.110/119. (Large Bk. in box.) No debt was over £100. Several are entered in more than one place and the total is not certain. Moreover he possibly expected a dividend on some of them.

[5] Cf. Paul Newman of Melksham who was trading to the north and Scotland in 1765, P.R.O., C.109/1N (also from Professor John).

[6] Wilts. C.R.O. 314/2/1, Ledger of the third George Wansey.

Mrs. Webb (her husband having died in the meantime) found herself faced with a debit balance of 3,877 roubles.[1] Only very well-to-do men, like John Anstie of Devizes or Thomas Tippetts of Dursley, were able to carry on trade for themselves on the Continent before the last decade of the century. Even so, Tippetts was bankrupt in 1789 and one reason why Anstie could not get over his difficulties in 1793 was probably the impossibility of getting returns from France during the Revolutionary period.[2]

In times of depression cloth was often sold at much under the figure set upon it by its makers. A running battle in 1770 between several manufacturers in Wiltshire and Somerset and Keale's warehouse in Salisbury, which was advertising superfine cloth at 14s. 6d. a yard when they maintained that they never sold under 16s., appears to have ended in favour of Keale; for, as he pointed out, 'it may be true that clothiers do not sell under 16s. but is there not a discount of five per cent and 21 yards for twenty; if so they don't receive nearly 14s. 6d.'[3]. Clothiers, in fact, had very little success either in resisting falling prices or in combinations to raise them. Attempts at the latter in 1764 and 1767 never got beyond the planning stage and Elderton remarked of the second one that the clothiers would never abide by their agreements in any matter which affected price.[4] That this inability to combine persisted is illustrated by Playne's remark in 1839 that forty years earlier the Gloucestershire clothiers had met to regulate the selling price of cloth made from English wool and in less than a month the agreement had been broken by one of the largest manufacturers in the county.[5]

In the later eighteenth century the one remaining department in which clothiers felt themselves victimized was that of sales to the East India Company, in connection with which all

---

[1] P.R.O., C.104/141, Bundle labelled 'Mr. Webb's Affairs'.

[2] See below, p. 133. Anstie had cloth on commission in the hands of persons in Paris, Hamburg, Frankfurt, Limoges, and Lisbon in 1793, Bodington MS., see p. 49, n. 1. One source gives its value as £100,000, W. E. Brown, 'Long's Stores, Devizes', *W.A.M.* lv, 142. Thomas Tippetts of Dursley, who was bankrupt in 1789, also had debts owing to him abroad, *Gloucester Journal*, 14 Mar. 1791.

[3] *Salisbury Journal*, 3 Sept., 22 Oct., and 3 Dec. 1770. Some of the cloth was bankrupt stock, but he denied that all was. Ibid., 27 May and 3 June 1771.

[4] To J. Noad, 31 May 1764, 22 Jan. 1767, 9 June 1768.

[5] *Repts. Asst. Commrs. Hdloom Weavers 1840*, Pt. V (H.C. 220), 470.

the old complaints which had been made of the Blackwell Hall factors were repeated.[1] They came to the fore when the Company's purchases began to fall off in the seventies and eighties. By the middle of the eighteenth century, and probably much earlier, it bought by sample direct through certain factors of whom, in 1799, there were said to be only four or five in the coarse branch of the trade. The Company generally paid ready money, seldom made deductions (though it could take stern measures when cloths were not up to sample)[2] and prided itself on buying regularly, sometimes weekly, throughout the season.[3] But there was always too much cloth on offer; and current opinion in Gloucestershire ascribed this to the factors' cunning in getting persons with little knowledge or credit to make cloth on borrowed money and then striving to undersell each other. A letter in the *Gloucester Journal* in 1784 puts the situation in a slightly different light.[4] 'No factor is allowed to offer for any more cloths than he has ready to deliver immediately, therefore the whole quantity that are usually sent to Blackwell Hall for the Company's sales are made entirely upon speculation.' That this statement is correct is shown by an experience of Messrs. Hanson & Mills in 1796, when, after the factors who were responsible for the supply of Devonshire long ells had offered more than double the number they could deliver, the Committee of Buying at East India House sent to all the factors supplying them with cloth to count the quantity in stock in order to compare it with the tenders. It was possible to deceive them and Hanson & Mills did so, possibly with the aid of 'a small compliment to the examiners';[5] but it is not surprising that the factors encouraged speculation in the making of cloth for the Company since they had no idea how much would be bought. As the cloth was not very suitable for any other market,[6] 10,000 to 15,000 pieces were said to lie unsold from year to

---

[1] Rudder, op. cit. .pp. 61–3.

[2] Above, p. 84.

[3] Second Report of the Committee to consider the Export Trade to the East Indies, P.R.O., B.T.6/42 (II), 51.

[4] *Gloucester Journal*, 8 Nov. 1784.

[5] Like the long ell factors, they had offered more than they had received and advised one clothier to exaggerate the number he was sending. In the end the Company only took one-third of the superfines and one tenth of the supers on offer, P.R.O., C.113/18, Lr. Bk. fols. 180, 183, 188.

[6] Though not quite unsaleable, see *W.A.S. Rec. Brch.* xix, no. 573.

year. Although this was certainly an exaggeration, clothiers had a legitimate grievance, which was unquestionably one of the reasons for the difficulties in which a part of the Gloucestershire trade found itself in the 1780s, since the fact that their capital was locked up in a stock of unsaleable cloth made it impossible for its owners to turn to manufacturing for the rapidly expanding branch which served the inland trade. The situation also affected many others connected with the industry. In 1770 a meeting of woolstaplers, yarn dealers, and others who had dealings with clothiers trading with the Company was advertised 'to consult on measures for rendering their property less precarious than under the present method of trade',[1] though it does not appear that they found any. The remedy suggested by the writer in the *Gloucester Journal* was a contract system by which each factor knew how many cloths he was to supply; but it took many years for the Company to change its methods and adopt something like this procedure.[2]

[1] *Salisbury Journal,* 10 Dec. 1770.
[2] See below, p. 152.

IV

CAPITAL AND LABOUR

By the beginning of the seventeenth century the western cloth
industry had long been a field in which large capitals were
employed; but clothiers of every degree of wealth were to be
found, as well as men who called themselves weavers but were
as well-to-do as many clothiers. Although the large capitalists
dominated the industry, the small clothiers formed a large
element in it, even if we must regard as exaggerated the statement, made in 1615, that half the western cloth came from men
who bought their wool or yarn from broggers, who gave them
credit from one market day to the next.[1] The only county for
which we have any statistics is Gloucestershire, where the figures
derived from Smyth's muster roll of 1608, if taken only for the
area with which we are concerned (south of Gloucester and
running from Cirencester on the east to the river Severn on the
west), give a ratio of a little under seven weavers to one clothier.[2]
Smyth himself estimated that a quarter of those who should
have appeared did not do so, and weaving attracted many
disabled or sickly persons who would not be required to attend
at musters; but the total figure of 1,786 weavers (which is
reduced to 1,519 if only the clothing area proper is included) is
far too small to produce the quantity of cloth which must have
been made. Broadcloth, which was the characteristic product
of the county, needed two weavers to the loom,[3] and if there

[1] P.R.O., S.P.14/80/13, printed Bland, Brown, and Tawney, *English Economic
History, Select Documents*, p. 355. As the statement was made on behalf of the
broggers it no doubt made the most of their services.

[2] See p. xvi, n. 3. The ratio is lower than that given by Professor and Mrs.
Tawney and has been reached by excluding districts west of the Severn, the
Kiftsgate Hundred, and all places east of Cirencester, where the weavers are
scattered one or two to a village and appear to be 'customer weavers'. It is very
near that given by Perry (*B.G.A.S.* 66. 83–92) for a rather more restricted area.

[3] It looks as if no significant difference was intended by the terms 'weaver' and
'broadweaver' attached to the names in the Muster Roll. Only 233 persons
described themselves as broadweavers, far too few to weave the amount of Gloucestershire cloth exported in 1606 by the Merchant Adventurers.

were at least 1,500 looms in 1622 when the depression in the industry was at its worst,[1] there may well have been more in 1608. In fact, there can be no doubt that cloth was also woven by men who owned or leased small patches of land and called themselves yeomen or husbandmen.[2]

Nine of Smyth's weavers were assessed for subsidy (as against forty-one clothiers) and others no doubt maintained an independent status; but there must have been many villages like Kingswood (a Wiltshire enclave in the middle of Gloucestershire) where, in 1597, 100 householders out of a total of 170 had only gardens insufficient to maintain their families and so were forced to spin and weave for clothiers.[3] It is clear that many of the latter must have employed more than seven looms, although they did not keep weavers in their houses to any significant extent. Only twenty-one in Smyth's list, some of whom were fullers, had two or more servants. Evidence of the extent of their dealings in 1608 is lacking, but in 1626 Richard Wood of Woodchester kept twenty looms at work[4] and Toby Chapman of Tetbury, who did not employ a servant in 1608, could sell 100 cloths at once ten years later and was described as 'a great trader in clothing and sets many on work'.[5] There were many others of similar standing.[6] On the other hand, the largest sum lost by any clothier in 1645 when a consignment for London was captured by Royalist troops under the Earl of Northampton, was £200,[7] but, in view of the risks, the quantity sent up may have been kept to a lower figure than would ordinarily have been the case.

As we come south into Wiltshire and Somerset we find at least an equal number of producers on a large scale. Thomas Hawkins of Chippenham was said to be worth £10,000 when he died in 1638.[8] Christopher Potticary of Stockton, a maker of white cloth, claimed to employ nearly 1,000 persons which, if

[1] See p. 34.

[2] Cf. *Glouc. N. and Q.* v. 100, 331.

[3] *A.P.C.* xxvii. 221.

[4] E.134/14, 2 Car. I, Easter 1626, no. 19. I owe this reference to Mr. J. P. Cooper.

[5] *A.P.C. 1618–19*, 52, 67–8.

[6] Cf. the 'very wealthy' clothiers who would not take the trouble to prevent the export of corn from the county in 1609, *Glouc. N. and Q.* i. 203.

[7] Arch. H.L. 1647, 8 July.

[8] *C.S.P.D. 1637–8*, 447.

it were true, might mean nearly seventy looms.[1] The two
Brewers, from the Frome valley, gave the number of their
employees as about 400.[2] Perhaps a more usual level was represented by Isaac Selfe of Lacock who, in pleading poverty
as an excuse for not furnishing a man and armour at musters,
said that his income was not above £300 a year and that he
employed nearly 100 persons,[3] which might mean about seven
looms. The pioneers of Spanish cloth were richer than any of
these. James Ashe was thought by his neighbours in Batcombe
to be worth not less than £15,000 in 1637.[4] He sent away,
mainly to his son Edward in London, from 300 to 400 cloths a
year between 1638 and 1642,[5] and his son John of Freshford,
who was said in 1656 to have £3,000 per annum and to be
worth £60,000,[6] sent up to his brother between April 1640 and
April 1641, 682 cloths valued at £12,400, and in the following
year 761 valued at £13,407;[7] and this may not have been the
whole of his production. Even so, it was probably not so high
as that of some Suffolk clothiers, who in 1618 might make 20
cloths a week;[8] but the best Spanish cloth cost more to make
than the variety of dyed and finished cloth produced in Suffolk
and this may account for a lower level of production.

The Ashe family were the giants of the industry. It might
have been impossible for many clothiers making white cloth to
turn to the much more expensive business of producing it fully
dyed and dressed if it had not been for the market spinners who
seem, in a large measure, to have taken over this branch of the
industry in the late twenties and thirties, much to the disgust
of those wealthy clothiers who could finance the whole process
themselves.[9] This system, however, which might have developed

[1] Ibid. *1629–31*, 505, taking 14 persons to a loom, see App. III. The claim may
be exaggerated, see *C.S.P.D. 1631–33*, 45–6, where he said that seven makers,
including himself, employed 1,500 people.

[2] *C.S.P.D. 1640*, 357.

[3] Ibid. *1639–40*, 228. This again may not be true, for he had bought much land
at an earlier date, Corsham Papers, nos. 4833, 5824, 5794.

[4] *C.S.P.D. 1637*, 117.

[5] P.R.O., C.107/20, Cloth Book of James Ashe.

[6] *Diary of Thomas Burton*, ed. J. T. Rutt, i. 127.

[7] P.R.O., C.107/20, 'Groot Boeck', fols. 22, 45, 72, 92. The period for 1641–2
includes an extra month.

[8] G. Unwin, *Studies in Economic History*, p. 280.

[9] P.R.O., S.P.16/243/23, S.P.16/180/71 where it is said that market spinners
were spinning two-thirds of the yarn.

into a vertical division of the industry like that which existed
in worsted between combing on the one hand and spinning and
weaving on the other, disappeared after 1650. Market spinners
still existed and the smaller clothiers, especially those making
coarse cloth for export, bought yarn from them as they had
always done;[1] but they seem to have supplied only white yarn.
The medley clothiers, possibly because of the importance of
blending their own colours, organized their own spinning,
although they often put out their wool for dyeing.[2]

It was the fact that no great amount of fixed capital was
necessary which made it possible for small clothiers and
independent weavers to exist side by side with large capitalists.
So long as a man had sufficient money or could get credit to
buy his wool or yarn on market day and live until he could sell
his cloth, he might maintain his independence. Such an existence depended largely on the possession of some land; and the
village freeholder or copyholder who was also a clothier or a
weaver was still much in evidence in the seventeenth century.[3]
The difficulties which faced these men were, one would suppose,
those of getting their cloth fulled and of selling it without an
expensive journey to Blackwell Hall. The position in regard to
fulling mills differed to some extent in Gloucestershire from
that in Wiltshire and Somerset. In the latter counties, although
there are a few traces of independent fullers,[4] in the early
seventeenth century nearly all the mills were owned or leased
by the well-to-do clothiers,[5] in spite of legislation forbidding it.
In Gloucestershire, where the swift streams supported more
mills than the more sluggish ones further south, it looks as if
far more independent fullers existed.[6] Many mills were, of
course, owned by large clothiers; but Mr. Perry's analysis of
Smyth's figures[7] shows that in the Stroudwater region there
were over 2½ fullers to every clothier, while on the Little Avon

---

[1] See below, pp. 264–6.

[2] Bath Cent. Ref. Libr., Dyebook of Wallbridge Mill, Frome, which contains
many accounts for dyeing wool belonging to Wiltshire clothiers.

[3] Everett, Wiltshire Wills (W.A.S. Libr., Devizes), vii. 33; xi. 3; *Glouc. N. and Q.*
v. 185, 331–2, 350, 368.

[4] e.g. Everett, op. cit. iv. 69; Somerset Quarter Sessions Records 1607–1625,
Som. Rec. Soc., vol. 23, 95; Wilts. C.R.O., Will of Thomas Whelply.

[5] Ramsay, op. cit., p. 19.

[6] For one in 1639, Wm. Rowles of Aveniss, see Rudd, op. cit., p. 288.

[7] See above, p. xvi, n. 3.

and round Dursley, where the escarpment falls away to the vale, the ratio was only about $1\frac{1}{3}$: 1. This difference supports a statement of 1632 that Worcester cloth was sent to Stroudwater to be fulled;[1] and there would be nothing improbable in supposing that many Stroudwater mills were owned or leased by independent fullers. But after the Civil War the positions appear to have been reversed. In Wiltshire there are far more instances of independent fullers who took cloth to full on commission, while several of the urban clothiers, even well-to-do ones, never occupied a mill at all.[2] These independent fullers sometimes held much the same position as a weaver. Such was that of the fuller of Allom mill in Batcombe who in 1685 took cloths for fulling from the master in Shepton Mallet whom he usually worked for,[3] but obviously did not consider himself permanently employed by anyone; or the journeyman fuller at Twerton, Thomas Hayman, who had rented a mill at Westbury for £15 a year at some time before 1765 but did not make it succeed.[4] With others, such as the Tanner family which owned Shearwater mill from before 1700 until 1748,[5] or, much later, Samuel Perkins, who bought Freshford mill from the Methuens in 1794 after having been a tenant,[6] fulling seems to have been a not unremunerative family business. In Gloucestershire, on the other hand, independent fullers are much more difficult to find, though mills were occasionally leased to a fuller when the owner had abandoned clothmaking.[7] Nevertheless, no difficulty seems ever to have been found by clothiers who did not own a mill in getting their cloth fulled by those who

[1] P.R.O., S.P.16/221/28.

[2] e.g. the Clark family, see 'The Trowbridge Woollen Industry 1804–24', ed. R. P. Beckinsale, *W.A.S. Rec. Brch.* vi. p. xx. George Wansey, about 1700, was sending all his cloth to be fulled by the Tanners (below, n. 5). See also *V.C.H. Wilts.* iv. 158.

[3] Som. C.R.O., Sess. Rolls 162/8.

[4] *Bath Chronicle*, 28 Dec. 1937, Art. by R. G. Naish.

[5] *Econ. Hist. Rev.* (2nd ser.), ix(2). 245. Edward Tanner was advertising Shearwater mill for sale in 1748, *Salisbury Journal*, 9 May 1748. Cf. will of Wm. Davison of Rode, fuller, Som. C.R.O. DD/PL 33.

[6] From documents in the possession of the Paradin Rubber Co., kindly communicated to me by Mr. H. W. Porter of Bath. The property also included a grist mill and it looks as if this combination was common. For another case of leasing a mill at Colerne in 1668 see *W.A.S. Rec. Brch.* xiii. 56.

[7] E. Moir, 'The Gentlemen Clothiers', *Gloucestershire Studies*, ed. H. P. R. Finberg, p. 244.

did;[1] and no complaint about the disappearance of the small clothier ever mentions such difficulties.

The other problem which faced the small maker was that of selling his cloth. Whatever pamphleteers at the end of the seventeenth century may have said,[2] it seems incredible that the kind of clothier who bought his wool or yarn on market day and depended on a quick sale to buy more can have made the journey to Blackwell Hall very often. There are instances of cloth being sent up in case of neighbours[3] and no doubt small clothiers sold at fairs which were attended by wholesale merchants who furnished the inland trade; but this implies the power to hold a stock for some time. The market towns probably afforded opportunities of sale at the weekly markets; indeed this must have been the case with the men who made cloth on the broggers' credit. The Charter granted to the Devizes Guild of Merchants in 1614 allowed persons from outside the town to sell retail cloth made by themselves.[4] It may be that there were enough buyers in normal times to take the small clothier's stock off his hands; but in general the only solution seems to be that such men occupied enough land to give them the power to wait for a market. Most clothiers in the early seventeenth century had sprung from the farmers and yeomen of the countryside; and some of the largest producers had evolved in two or three generations from ancestors who had begun as small farmer-weavers. Only a few at this period can be identified as coming from other walks of life, mainly from the Church. The Methuens[5] and Awdrys[6] of Wiltshire and the Pauls of Gloucestershire[7] were all descended from clergy. A group of wealthy clothiers in the Shepton Mallet area may possibly have been members of old-established

[1] In advts. of cloth stolen from tenters in the *Gloucester Journal* during the eighteenth century the owner of the cloth is frequently not the owner of the tenter.

[2] e.g. *The Clothier's Complaint*, p. 21.

[3] Ramsay, op. cit., p. 25. Cf. the taking of a cloth by a neighbour to Bristol fair in 1693, Som. C.R.O., Sess. Rolls, 191/1.

[4] E. Kite, 'The Guild of Merchants in Devizes', *W.A.M.* iv. 167.

[5] Pedigree in Jones and Jackson, op. cit., p. 208.

[6] Several members of this family, which derived from John Awdry, Vicar of Melksham in 1603, were clothiers in Melksham and Seend in the seventeenth and early eighteenth centuries.

[7] Pedigree in *B.G.A.S.* 51, p. 160.

gentry families;[1] but most of those who obtained recognition at the Visitations of the later sixteenth and early seventeenth centuries had reached that status by their own or their ancestors' efforts, and in the bad years of the 1620s several abandoned their claims to be ranked as gentry.

It is probably the difference between the comparatively flat, rich pastures of Wiltshire and east Somerset and the steeply indented valleys of much of the clothing region of Gloucestershire, which accounts for the contrast between the dense population of well-to-do clothiers in these valleys, handing on their business from father to son for many generations, and the predominantly urban industry further south, where clothiers tended to concentrate in towns and often left the industry as soon as they made money. The contrast must not be overstressed, for there were country clothiers in Wiltshire also. Some Gloucestershire clothiers left the industry to become landowners and some Wiltshire families remained in it for generations; yet the difference between the two regions must strike anyone who compares them. 'A little Commonwealth of Cloathiers and Cloathworkers—not the like in the Nation,' was Aubrey's description of Stroudwater;[2] but Baskerville writing at about the same time recognized a type of community which might be reproduced in other places under similar conditions:

Here at this town (Painswick) you begin to enter the land of clothiers, who in these bourns building fair houses because of the conveniency of water so useful for their trade, do extend their country some miles, for they delight to live like the merry rooks and daws chattering and prating together, and if a man be able to purchase so much ground as will keep a horse or two yearly you shall have a house built there to spend £500 p.a. . . . and he that shall take a prospect of Wootton-under-Edge, Croscombe in Somersetshire and other places where clothiers live, shall find the sides of the hills and country full of little grounds and paddocks.[3]

[1] The Strodes of Shepton Mallet are said to have been a branch of the family of that name at Parnham, Dorset, J. Hutchins, *History of Dorset* ii. 130–1, note U. A rather unsatisfactory connection with the Esse family of Devon has been made out for James Ashe, through Ashe of S. Petherton, *Som. and Dorset N. and Q.* ii. 283; iii. 179. Members of the family sometimes appear as 'Aish alias Mercer', e.g. in Somerset Quarter Sessions Records, 1625–29, *Som. Rec. Soc.* 24. 204 (where it is written 'Mercet'), and in Corsham Papers nos. 1608, 1609, 2740, 2741.

[2] Bodl. Libr. MSS. Aubrey, 2, fol. 141.

[3] *H.M.C. Portland* ii. 304. The date is probably about 1680.

Conditions for the small manufacturer had been exceptionally favourable in the early sixteenth century, but they became progressively less so in the seventeenth. This was not only a question of the diminishing export of white cloth, for, as we have seen, the market for it did not contract as much as might have been expected. Moreover, dyeing and finishing could be done on commission and, although the production of finer cloth with more expensive raw material was increasing throughout the century, there was still a large market for the coarser. Nor, in spite of complaints, was long credit the only, or even the chief factor in the small clothier's decline. The pamphleteer who wrote in 1692 that £300 was now necessary to keep one loom employed whereas in former days it had only needed £100, or £50 if the yarn was bought in the market,[1] was guilty of some exaggeration. Just a year later a Gloucestershire squire Richard Stephens, in a letter already quoted gives a lower figure: 'A loom cannot be kept a year about under £100 and formerly £50 was sufficient to manage it.'[2] Another condition which must be taken into account was the growing complexity of farming, which made it more profitable for the farmer to concentrate upon it rather than to engage in two occupations at once, and this probably accounts for the diminution in the number of clothiers in the Vale of Severn, as well as in the Wiltshire countryside. Some 'farmer-clothiers' or 'farmer-sergemakers' lasted well into the eighteenth century in Wiltshire,[3] but there do not appear to have been many of them; and in the high land of Gloucestershire it looks as if all the agricultural activities carried on by clothiers were subsidiary to the industry.

In places where conditions were favourable a number of land-owning weavers and other workers in the industry also survived. Thus at Freshford a weaver bought two acres of arable in 1703 for £39 and another, in 1712, leased meadows

[1] *The Clothier's Complaint*, p. 9.

[2] See below, p. 105, n. 3. Sir Matthew Hale remarked that if cloth could be sold as soon as made £24 would be sufficient, *A Discourse touching Provision for the Poor*, pp. 50–1, see below, p. 102–3.

[3] See *Wilts. N. and Q.* iii. 65–6, for one who died 1738. For a 'farmer and sergemaker' see Isaac Taylor, *Historical Memoirs of the Baptist Church Meeting in Castle St., Calne* (Wilts. Tracts iii. no. 10, in W.A.S. Libr., Devizes).

at a rent of £8 a year.[1] Robert Payne, a weaver of Woolverton in Somerset, rented five acres in Tellisford in 1676 and James Paine, narrow weaver of North Bradley near Trowbridge, owned land and an additional house at Faulkland in 1741.[2] In Corsley a will of 1796 shows a weaver owning at least six acres of land and he may well have been typical of others.[3] In Gloucestershire, Richard Osborn of Horsley, who called himself a yeoman and owned four acres of land, an orchard, and garden, had two looms in his house when he died in 1705. Samuel Clutterbuck, weaver of Stanley St. Leonards, left an 'estate' on long leasehold in 1713,[4] and there are several other examples.[5] There was no rigid dividing line between the small clothier and other workers in the industry; clothiers who went poaching in the company of cordwainers, shearmen, bakers, victuallers, and glaziers[6] must be classed with the small tradesmen of the places they lived in, much as a prosperous weaver would be. Clothiers in a very small way of business continued to exist throughout the eighteenth century,[7] though it is improbable that they were the sons and grandsons of the men who were in this position at the end of the seventeenth. Even in the nineteenth century there were clothiers who had begun life as weavers or who 'manufactured in their own families'.[8] Shopkeepers, too, often combined a little clothmaking with their own line of business. The books of one of them, Joseph Udall, a grocer of Melksham, show that he sent 16 cloths to a Blackwell Hall factor between September 1759 and the end of January 1760, and he also dealt with a Bristol clothier.[9]

Other small capitalists abounded. It cost under £100 to set up as a master clothworker[10] and much less to become a burler

---

[1] Corsham Papers, 2760, 2783.

[2] Som. C.R.O., DD/PL 33.

[3] M. F. Davies, *Life in an English Village, Corsley*, pp. 43–4.

[4] Wills, G.C.L., For others who seem to have been comfortably off see wills of John Barnefield, Horsley, 1689; Samuel Webb, Bisley, 1712; Thomas Blanch, Miserden, 1712; Daniel Pegler, King's Stanley, 1729.

[5] e.g. Rudd, op. cit., pp. 200, 268, 270.

[6] Som. C.R.O., Sess. Rolls, 164/11 (Rode, 1686); 190/3 (Shepton Mallet, 1692).

[7] See *V.C.H. Wilts.* iv, 153, and Pressnell, op. cit., p. 83.

[8] *Ev. on Woollen Trade Bill 1803* (H. C. 95), pp. 6, 31, 206, and see p. 131.

[9] I am indebted to the late Mr. Stratton of Melksham for allowing me to see this book which was discovered when Messrs. Stratton's premises were demolished to make way for Woolworths stores. See also M. F. Davies, op. cit., pp. 47–8.

[10] *Econ. Hist. Rev.* (2nd ser.), ix(2). 243–4.

or a drawer,[1] employing women at a wage which was presumably comparable to that which a spinner could earn. Warp spinning for superfine cloth seems generally to have been entrusted to men who employed specialised spinners.[2] But while some such men might rise in the world to become substantial clothiers, the majority lacking the will, the opportunity, or the ability to rise, fell victims to depressions, sold or mortgaged their holdings, and lapsed into the proletariat.[3] The men who rose did not, however, become superfine clothiers, at any rate to begin with; for the most part they made the cheaper cloth for sale at fairs, the medleys at 5s. to 7s. a yard which went via Spain and Portugal to South America, or the unfinished cloth which was dyed elsewhere and went to India and the Levant. For a clothier using Spanish wool £300 or a little more seems to have been thought sufficient capital to begin with in the mid-seventeenth century,[4] but a hundred years later it was more like £500, though a beginner who belonged to a family established in the industry, like the third George Wansey, might manage with much less.[5]

If the very small producer was gradually disappearing, the man with slightly greater resources found new assistance in the credit extended by the Blackwell Hall factors. By the later seventeenth century apprenticeship had not been enforced for many years[6] and the industry was open to anyone who wished to enter it. The existence of such impecunious clothiers was a constant irritant to those who were already established. Small clothiers tended to undersell them and were, no doubt, often

---

[1] Ibid. 245. Burling was claimed not to be a 'prentice trade' in 1658 (*H.M.C. Var.* i. 135) but there are instances of girls being apprenticed to burlers by the parish in the eighteenth century, F. H. Hinton, 'Notes on The Administration of the Relief of the Poor at Lacock, 1583 to 1834', *W.A.M.* xlix. 186.

[2] Both Thomas Long (1700–30) and Usher and Jeffries (1721–7) had their warp spinning done in this way. Cf. the mention of Thomas Cooke 'spinner' in the will of Wm. Moore of Synwell, Glos. in 1701. In one case a girl was employed as a warp spinner by a scribbler of Trowbridge at 1s. 6d. a week and her keep, Wilts. C.R.O., Sess. Rolls, Michaelmas 1756.

[3] Rudd, op. cit., pp. 335, 343; Corsham Papers 2112, 2766, 2768, 2949; Som. C.R.O., DD/PL 23.

[4] Paul Methuen instructed his executors to allow both his nephew and his servant to borrow this sum from his estate at 5 per cent if they desired to set up as clothiers, P.C.C. Carr, 95.

[5] *W.A.S. Rec. Brch.* xix. xiii.

[6] J. Haynes, *A View*, p. 83.

tempted to skimp on raw materials, to pay in truck and to make faulty cloth which brought discredit on the industry,[1] though none of these practices was confined to them alone. Many of the larger clothiers had established their marks as pledges of good quality which were accepted abroad;[2] but marks could be counterfeited and often were, and there was a constant demand for some kind of organization which would prevent this and keep up the standard of the product.[3] Clothiers had bitterly resented the activities of searchers in the early part of the seventeenth century, but those who were well-to-do were by no means averse to a measure of control if they could have a say in its management.[4] In 1640 the Privy Council Committee on Clothing had recommended the establishment of a series of corporations based on certain towns to oversee the manufacture in their neighbourhoods;[5] and schemes on these lines began to be propounded soon after the Restoration. In 1667, 1668,[6] 1678,[7] and 1689[8] attempts to get legislation in this sense with more or less detailed provisions were either rejected outright or failed to get through the House of Lords in time to become law. Similar efforts, often involving only inspection or the

[1] *C.J.* xii. 525.

[2] *The Golden Fleece defended; The Proverb Crossed*, p. 21.

[3] Cf. W. Smith, *An Essay for the Recovery of Trade*, p. 4; 'A Narrative of the whole Proceedings of the two last Sessions of Parliament ending July 15, 1678, concerning the Transportation of Wool' (printed on the back of *Some Considerations . . . upon a Bill . . . about Transportation of Wool*) and many other pamphlets.

[4] Cf. H. Heaton, *The Yorkshire Woollen and Worsted Industries*, pp. 230 ff. on the incorporation of the Leeds clothiers in 1654, and John Ashe's support of this measure, *Diary of Thomas Burton* i. 127. See also G. D. Ramsay, 'Industrial Laisser Faire and the Policy of Cromwell', *Econ. Hist. Rev.* xvi(2). 93 ff.

[5] G. D. Ramsay, 'The Report of the Royal Commission on Clothing', *E.H.R.* lvii. 485–93.

[6] *L.J.* xii. 132, 226, 231; *C.J.* ix. 17. Cf. *H.M.C. 8th Rept.* (H. of L. MSS.), 113b. Texts of bills are in Arch H. L. 1667, 8 Nov., no. 106 and 1668, 20 Apl., no. 182.

[7] *C.J.* ix. 444, 484, 504; *L.J.* xiii. 259, 275, 282. See 'A Narrative of the whole Proceedings. . . .' (above, n. 3).

[8] *Reasons for the Bill for Improvement of the Woollen Manufacture*, which was evidently intended as propaganda for the bill for encouraging the woollen manufacture introduced on May 7 and passed by the H. of C. on 13 Aug. 1689, *C.J.* x. 123, 198, 227, 264–5. Although the only indication of its nature in the *Journals* is that it was intended to prevent the export of wool, to prescribe the wear of woollen goods at certain times of the year and to abolish privileges for exporting cloth (see petitions, ibid. 243, 245–6, 258), the pamphlet shows that originally it was intended to contain provisions for inspection at various stages of manufacture, assessment of wages and regulation of the price of wool.

enforcement of apprenticeship, continued up to 1741;[1] but success was only obtained on one point, the institution, as already mentioned, of inspection of medley broadcloth at the fulling mills.[2] In the case of single towns, where the incorporation of clothiers and weavers did not need Parliamentary sanction, it was sometimes obtained from the Privy Council, as at Wilton in 1699 and Witney in 1711;[3] but when bills covering a larger area were brought into Parliament nothing came of them. There is no record of any organized opposition, but the strong tendency towards *laissez faire* which is apparent in Parliament after 1700 had much to do with the failure of the later attempts. 'The Parliament have been always against regulations' said a Blackwell Hall factor in 1715,[4] though he himself thought them desirable. This was not the opinion of all factors, at any rate with regard to small incorporations. Five years earlier one had suggested that it might not be for the benefit of Witney, 'they might then monopolise that trade and keep up the price of their blankets so high that it would put people upon finding out some other manufacture to serve in lieu thereof'.[5] Incorporation of clothiers over a wide area would have presented the factors, in theory at any rate, with a body which could negotiate as a whole and deprive them of the opportunity of getting some clothiers to undercut others. Judging by the state of long established Companies in provincial towns, this is unlikely to have occurred in practice, for in nearly all of them the rules were unobserved. Salisbury still set a water seal on its cloth in 1700,[6] but by 1719 it was not insisting that everyone should join the Company.[7] In Worcester,

---

[1] See below, p. 111, n. 2 for a project in 1726. In 1741 the agitation took the form of a petition for the enforcement of apprenticeship, *C.J.* xxiv. 117.

[2] Above, p. 53.

[3] *V.C.H. Wilts.* iv. 159; A. Plummer, op. cit., pp. 12–15.

[4] *J.C.T.P. 1714–18*, p. 96. Cf. the report of a Committee of the H. of C. in 1702 over the question of enforcing apprenticeship in Taunton. The Committee found the allegations true 'but yet are of opinion that the said trade ought to be free and not restrained', *C.J.* xiii. 783. It reversed this decision later in the year but the House negatived the resolution and ordered the statutes affecting apprenticeship to be repealed, though this was not done, ibid. xiv. 67–8, 70.

[5] *J.C.T.P. 1709–14*, p. 154. This was alleged to have happened at Kidderminster following an Act to keep up standards.

[6] *C.J.* xiii. 106. It looks as if this statutory obligation had been forgotten in other places.

[7] *C.J.* xix. 61.

which before the Civil War had made an allowance to searchers and thereby kept up the quality of its cloth,[1] clothiers were bringing in workers from outside the city by 1693 in order to employ them at cheaper rates.[2] The Company in Devizes seems to have abandoned almost all its functions by the early eighteenth century, although in the bad year of 1740 the Mayor and burgesses renewed the prohibition on outsiders selling cloth by retail in the town unless it had been made by themselves.[3] This impatience with regulation would, no doubt, have quickly penetrated any corporation formed on a larger scale; but the freedom which the industry enjoyed formed a remarkable contrast with conditions in France and Holland, where minute regulation, enforced by municipal authority or Government inspectors, was the ordinary rule. It did not always result in the production of better cloth, at any rate in France,[4] and may also have had the result of creating a more static industry; but Colbert's rules for the use of dyestuffs did play an important part in securing the superior colours of French piece-dyed cloth, which were frequently mentioned as a reason for preferring it to English.[5]

In fact, wealthy clothiers had no desire to exclude well-to-do newcomers who looked upon the industry as a good investment for their capital. In 1723 a house in Trowbridge was advertised as very suitable for the business on the authority of the well-known clothier Samuel Brewer, with the additional advantage that should the buyer be unacquainted with it he would be instructed by his neighbour.[6] It was only the small intruders who were resented, especially when sustained by the factors' credit; and, although the attempts to exclude them were long over by the end of the eighteenth century, the division

---

[1] P.R.O., S.P.16/180/71, Reading and Newbury did the same.

[2] M. Beloff, *Public Order and Popular Disturbances, 1660–1714*, p. 61.

[3] B. H. Cunnington, *Some Annals of the Borough of Devizes, 1555–1791*, p. 210.

[4] See above, p. 46.

[5] Cf. the remarks of J. Savary on the bad dyeing of French cloth sent to the Levant in the seventeenth century (*Le Parfait Négociant* (1679), ed. 1749, Pt. II, pp. 402, 445) as compared with the excellent colours of the eighteenth. It was only for one or two difficult colours that French clothiers making for the Levant were allowed to use the lesser, non-fast dyes, and not the whole range, as might be inferred from S. Fairlie, 'Dyestuffs in the eighteenth century', *Econ. Hist. Rev.* (2nd ser.) xvii(3). 489, n. 6.

[6] *Gloucester Journal*, 16 July 1723.

between those who called themselves 'the respectable clothiers' (or, in the more countrified region of Gloucestershire, 'the gentlemen clothiers') and the 'inferior' ones became more and more marked.

Although the industry offered abundant opportunities to men who had inherited or could accumulate a little capital, the bulk of the workers had no other resources but their labour. Most weavers were people with no land or with so little that it amounted to no more than a garden. Many of them had originally settled on commons and had a prescriptive right to their tenements.[1] Others owned their houses in the towns,[2] but many, especially the town workers of Wiltshire and Somerset, were rentpayers and often the tenants of the clothiers. In the late Tudor and early Stuart period wages had certainly been inadequate; and clothiers had often failed to pay the prices agreed upon in Wiltshire by a committee of clothiers and weavers in Trowbridge and confirmed by the magistrates in 1602 and 1605.[3] Although the weaver considered himself superior to the mere agricultural labourer, he was much more subject to unemployment; and in depressions, especially that of 1620 to 1622, he had come very near starvation.[4] So too he did in some years in the 1690s[5] and at later periods in the eighteenth century when work was scarce or prices high. In 1655 the Wiltshire magistrates again rated wages with rather higher payments for some processes,[6] but they were rated on traditional lines for white cloth and tell us nothing about the rising production of medleys. Here the only evidence we have comes from a pamphlet written by Lord Chief Justice Sir Matthew Hale (who came of a family, originally clothiers, settled at Alderley near Wotton-under-Edge). It was published in 1683 seven years after his death,[7] and the date of its composition is un-

---

[1] Cf. R. Bigland, *Gloucestershire Collections* i. 191 (Bisley); Rev. J. Wilkinson, *History of Broughton Gifford*, p. 90 (Wilts. Tracts vii. W.A.S. Libr. Devizes); P.R.O., S.P.14/144/24 (Frome).

[2] Several of those who came to Bradford in the 1670s owned houses at home, Wilts. C.R.O. 73/23 (Bradford Poor Law Papers, Settlement Certs.).

[3] *H.M.C. Var.* i. 162, 168.

[4] *C.S.P.D. 1619–23*, 358.

[5] J. Blanch, *Abstract of the Grievances of Trade*, p. 1; *Econ. Hist. Rev.* (2nd ser.), ix(2). 252.

[6] See App. iv.　　　　　[7] *A Discourse touching Provision for the Poor.*

known. Eden placed it in 1659,[1] but it may well be connected with Hale's views on the poor of Kingswood as expressed shortly before his death in 1676 to John Smyth of Nibley.[2] Hale gives the rate for spinning weft of dyed wool as 2½d. per pound, which shows little rise over that assessed for undyed wool in Wiltshire in 1605 and was much below the 4d. rated by the Somerset Justices for spinning dyed English wool in 1677.[3] The price for weaving a piece of coarse Gloucestershire medley is £1. 1s. 3d. for three weeks' work, or 7s. 1d. a week. This was a gross wage from which the weaver would have to find the expenses attached to the loom such as harness, size, and candles, but not loom rent, for it was only in exceptional circumstances that he did not own his loom.[4] He would also have to pay a journeyman and a boy to wind his quills, unless, as is most probable, he employed his children or apprentices for both. If he did, his earnings may have been adequate, for a net 6s. a week was a relatively high wage for the woollen industry in the last quarter of the seventeenth century, earned only by shearmen, though they sometimes wanted more.[5]

The only information we have for the early eighteenth century refers to the men who worked in the superfine medley industry of west Wiltshire, owing to the preservation of two cloth books covering the period from 1700 to 1730.[6] In 1738 it was said that a weaver could complete a cloth of this kind in three weeks[7] and the books show that occasionally a man did so; but none ever wove 17 cloths in a year and very few completed 10. Certainty about earnings is impossible to reach

[1] Sir F. M. Eden, *The State of the Poor* i. 214–15, mainly on the ground that Hale would have been too much occupied with legal business later, but also because of the absence of any mention of the Act of Settlement.

[2] *H.M.C. Var.* i. 154.

[3] See App. iv.

[4] Weavers sometimes sold or pawned their looms; for a case of the former see *Econ. Hist. Rev.* (2nd ser.), ix(2). 250. In Trowbridge in 1749 a spinning wheel and other implements forfeited in distraint for rent was sold to the Parish which immediately lent it to the man from whom it had been taken, Wilts. C.R.O. 206/95. In 1743 a parish loom was lent to a pauper in Bradford, ibid. 77/249.

[5] *H.M.C. Var.* i. 155. Although only 'men' are mentioned in this entry, it seems certain that they were shearmen. G. Wansey paid his shearmen 1d. an hour about 1700. For comparable wages outside the industry see E. W. Gilboy, *Wages in eighteenth century England*, Ch. III.

[6] Those of Thomas Long of Melksham (see p. 71, n. 6) and of Usher & Jeffries of Trowbridge, Wilts. C.R.O. 947 and 927 respectively.

[7] See App. iv.

since we can never be sure whether a weaver had more than
one loom or whether, in the gaps which often appear between
the dates when he took warps, he was not working for another
master. But in a few cases, where employment seems to have
been continuous, we find among those who worked for Thomas
Long of Melksham one, with 10 cloths finished in approximately
a year from June 1704, earning £17. 11s. 4d. and in the same
period in 1718, with 8 cloths at a partially higher rate, £17. 2s.;
another in 1707 with 11 cloths earning £21. 1s. 8d., and a third
in 1719 with 10 cloths earning £19. 12s. 2½d. These earnings
meant that the weaver made an average of 6s. 9d. to 8s. 2d. a
week gross, and in all the cases (except that of the man who
earned £17. 2s.) it does not look as if there would have been
time for him to weave another cloth in the period between the
dates of taking one warp and the next. The weavers employed
by Usher & Jeffries of Trowbridge made from 7s. 10d. to
12s. 6d. a week in 1725–6.[1] This rather higher figure comes not
from higher rates of payment but from the fact that they
completed more cloths in the time. Perhaps we may take it
that, in the early eighteenth century, weavers who were
constantly employed might expect a gross return of about £20
a year, which would put them not among the artisans and
handicraftmen but among the 364,000 'labouring people and
out-servants' at £15 a year net in Gregory King's estimate of
1696. In the middle of the eighteenth century a few, but
probably very few, made considerably more, 16s. to 18s. a
week, according to evidence given by weavers themselves
to a Parliamentary Committee in 1757.[2] Whether, as they
averred, any industrious and skilful weaver could earn this
amount may be doubted; apart from the fact that many were
not skilful, constantly recurring unemployment would have
made such continuous earnings impossible for a large number.
But the sum on which the weaver's family lived was, of course,
a composite one, and Hale expected family earnings, with the
wife's spinning and something made by two children, to reach
10s. a week, enough to keep them and another two children
too young to contribute. In fact, apart from unemployment,
the adequacy of weavers' earnings depended on two conditions,
firstly whether they could employ members of their own families

[1] Pressnell, op. cit., p. 91.   [2] *C.J.* xxvii. 731.

or unpaid apprentices and secondly on the price of provisions. That of bread, which was their staple food, could fluctuate very quickly over a wide range.[1]

Weavers might have enjoyed a rather higher wage if their numbers had not been continually increasing. In 1693 Sir John Guise, one of the Members for Gloucestershire, brought in a bill to repeal that part of the Statute of Artificers which made it illegal for anyone to be apprenticed to a weaver unless his parents held land to the value of £3 a year, a clause which had long been ignored.[2] Richard Stephens of Chavenage, who had been asked for his opinion by his cousin Sir Edward Harley, M.P., wrote, in a letter which has already been quoted, that the clothiers in his neighbourhood did not approve of the repeal:[3]

Tis probable at the time of the making of the Act . . . and many years since (as I have heard) a Weaver was esteemed a good Trade, but now one of the poorest, it being now commonly practised by Parishes to bind out their poor boyes to weavers, which may perhaps be one Reason why the Sessions hath discouraged the prosecution of them for taking Apprentices not qualified according to the sd. Act . . . The Practice of the Clothiers to turn off their workemen upon any deadness of Trade and paying them in comodities above the market price is a great mischief to the countrey, tho' many of their workemen are to be blamed who in cheap times when work is plenty will not work above two or three days in a week.

Weavers made considerably by apprentices taken with a premium of perhaps £5 or even without one. At the cost of another mouth to feed, they gained a servant who could be useful at least after the first six months, if not earlier. Parish apprentices were not always well treated and, like their successors in the factories, they had no friends to stand by them in case of ill usage. Cases of their being beaten to death by drunken or violent masters appear from time to time in the Sessions Rolls and the local newspapers; and in 1770, and again in 1787, the *Salisbury Journal* printed an advertisement warning overseers not to apprentice children in or round Wilton as

[1] Cf. Salisbury City Books, 244/3 where an assize of bread for 1672–3 shows that the penny loaf, which contained nearly 23 oz. in December 1672, had dwindled to 15 oz. in August 1673.
[2] *C.J.* xi. 9, 106. This bill did not pass.
[3] B. M. Loan Coll. 29/187, fol. 208. See p. 34.

several had been cruelly treated and one, in 1787, had died as a result.[1]

The complaint that weavers, like other domestic workers, would not work the whole week through was very common in the later seventeenth and early eighteenth centuries.[2] When wheat was at 5s. per bushel or under (and it was more often under than over that price between 1700 and 1750)[3] many weavers were not disposed to spend twelve hours a day in the loom for six days a week if they could achieve their normal standard of life with less.[4] A perusal of any country newspaper of the earlier eighteenth century will show the number of races, prize fights, cockfights, backsword playing, fairs, and other jollifications spread throughout the week which served to distract the minds of the workers from their often monotonous jobs. Attendance at some of these, combined with that 'tippling in the alehouse' so much reprobated by otherwise sympathetic observers, took up a good deal of the time which might have been spent in earning more money. One can only sympathize with this desire for variety, but it had one important and unfortunate consequence; it fortified the clothiers in their belief that low wages and high prices were the best conditions for getting their work done. Constantly aware of foreign competition and believing that French wages were only two-thirds, or even half, of those paid in England,[5] they were only too ready to welcome a rise in the cost of living and had strong arguments against raising wages to meet it. 'No country in Europe manufactures all kinds of goods so dear' said Davenant in 1697[6] and the sentiment was constantly repeated. Although Defoe and others might argue that the English workman justi-

---

[1] *Salisbury Journal*, 26 Feb. 1770; 16 Apr. 1787. The latter was especially addressed to the Parish Officers of Southampton.

[2] See, among many other authorities, E. S. Furniss, *The Position of the Labourer in a system of Nationalism*, pp. 117 ff.

[3] The price of wheat at Michaelmas was over 5s. a bushel in only 17 yr. between 1700 and 1750, Ashton, op. cit., p. 181 (Table I). These are Windsor prices; in Gloucester, as given in the *Gloucester Journal* from 1722, they were often lower.

[4] A few worked very long hours. Joseph White of Randwick, born 1745, later Regius Professor of Arabic in the University of Oxford, worked with his father at an early age from 4 a.m. to 9 p.m. learning Latin as he did so, J. Stratford, *Gloucestershire Biographical Notes*, pp. 153 ff.

[5] Arch. H.L. 1713, 4 June, no. 3010 (3) clothiers' petition; *H.M.C., H. of L. MSS.* (N.S.) x. 142.

[6] *Works*, ed. Sir C. Whitworth, i. 100.

fied his higher wage by doing more work in the time,[1] the clothiers remained sceptical and one must admit that, as far as their weavers were concerned, they had some reason for being so. This attitude did not exclude benevolence in other relationships. In times of real dearth there were frequent subscriptions to provide bread at lower rates;[2] but this was a temporary expense which never covered more than a fraction of the need and could be retracted at will, not a permanent rise in cost of production the results of which the clothiers believed they could foresee only too clearly.[3]

The difference between English and foreign wages was probably exaggerated, but there was some justification for the belief that it existed. John Munn, who wrote under the pseudonym of 'A Manufacturer of Northants', seems to have known a good deal about conditions in northern France, Flanders, and Holland, and his statement in 1738 that wages in Abbeville, where the Van Robais had their great manufactory for fine cloth, were more than one-third lower than in England carries conviction. In Leiden he found them higher but still below the English level.[4] Some later writers were inclined to minimize the gap by stressing Defoe's point that an Englishman did more work in a given time[5] and in 1788 the Blackwell Hall factor Thomas Speidel found that in Louviers, where fine Spanish wool was used, wages were about the same as in England though in other parts of northern France they were much lower.[6]

---

[1] *Mercator*, no. 67; *A Plan of the English Commerce*, 1728 ed., pp. 37, 40–2. See also Furniss, op. cit., pp. 125 ff.

[2] Pressnell, op. cit., p. 80; *W.A.S. Rec. Brch.* xix. no. 194, *Bath Journal*, 18 Jan. 1760. For other instances see *Glouc. N. and Q.* iv. 14; *Gloucester Journal*, 27 Jan. 1730. Joseph White (above, p. 106, n. 4) was educated at the expense of Joseph Ellis, a wealthy clothier of Ebley.

[3] Cf. *Bath Advertiser*, 10 Dec. 1757 'To raise the price of wages would be such a clog to trade as must drive many useful manufacturers out of the kingdom and compel them to fly to our enemies and rivals in trade'.

[4] *Observations on British Wool* (1739 ed.), pp. 21, 47. The author was said to have been sent by the Government to investigate the woollen manufacture abroad, 'Essay on the Decline of the Foreign Trade', McCulloch, *Scarce Tracts on Commerce*, p. 257. He gave evidence in 1731 about the English wool he had seen in Holland in 1726, *C.J.* xxi. 691.

[5] *Propositions for improving the Manufactures, Agriculture and Commerce of Great Britain*, pp. 29–32. This author is too much inclined to minimize the difference. He wanted to regain the export trade by setting up manufactures in Cornwall.

[6] *C.J.* xliii. 284.

In the question of wage levels, therefore, the clothiers had some arguments on their side, but the prevalence of truck, a very ancient abuse, could only be excused by a real shortage of coin. Although silver was overvalued and therefore constantly disappearing in the eighteenth century, the form of truck to which Stephens had objected was independent of any difficulty in coming by it. Complaint was made of it in the medley branch in 1714,[1] and the obligation to deal at shops owned by clothiers was not uncommon later. Delays in payment were also usual; indeed a clothier who was in debt might not be able to help himself. 'There is no person who pays their people so soon as you do ... you must not pay your people so soon' wrote Elderton to William Tree of Beckington in 1768.[2] Lengthening the warp by two or three yards while paying the same price for weaving the piece, and using weights of eighteen ounces to the pound in weighing out wool for spinning were also common in the industry before 1720.[3] The depression of 1718–21, especially in the medley branch of the industry, coming after several years of prosperity which had drawn many newcomers into the trade, probably caused an increase of such practices as well as a hardening attitude towards the poor. 'The poor people ... are ... much increased in numbers since my time', wrote Thomas Smith of Melksham in 1722, 'and much misery I fear is among them.' Although he believed that much of it was due to their 'laziness and vicious lives' he had thought some of them hardly dealt with at an earlier Vestry.[4]

On the whole, it is surprising that no disturbances occurred until 1726. Further west, in the serge-making districts of Devon and Somerset, weavers' clubs had existed early in the century and there had been several riots;[5] but neither in Gloucestershire nor in Wiltshire was there any disorder, in spite of the vicissitudes of the trade. The riots in Wiltshire and east Somerset in 1726–7, in Wiltshire in 1738 and in Gloucestershire in 1727 and 1756 are well known, and it is unnecessary to

[1] *The Drapers' Bill ... with the Clothiers' Objections*, p. 6.
[2] Som. C.R.O., Elderton Lr. Book. To W. Tree, 6 and 13 Oct. 1768.
[3] Pressnell, op. cit., p. 68.
[4] Diary of Thomas Smith of Shaw House, Melksham, *W.A.M.* xi. 314, 211.
[5] *C.J.* xv. 312; W. G. Hoskins, *Industry, Trade and People in Exeter, 1688–1700*, pp. 58–9. The combination of employers mentioned in 1696 seems also to have taken place in Devonshire, P.R.O., P.C.2/76, fol. 442.

recapitulate them in detail.[1] All were concerned either with the level of wages or with unfair practices which had the effect of lowering earnings; and the cumulative effect of the evidence is to suggest that up to the middle of the century there was an almost continuous decline in rates for weaving.[2] We hear little of other workers in the trade. Spinners' earnings fluctuated enormously and could rise very high when clothiers were busy;[3] but when they fell, the widely dispersed body of female labour had no machinery by which they could call attention to their troubles. Clothworkers, at any rate in Wiltshire and Somerset, appear to have concentrated on keeping the number of apprentices low. By the end of the eighteenth century they were imposing high entry fees on journeymen from elsewhere so that their earnings, in Wiltshire at least, had almost doubled.[4]

Briefly, the riots of 1726–7 in Wiltshire and Somerset, with which country gentlemen and some clothiers felt much sympathy, led to the passing of an Act[5] in which the only clause consistently observed was the obligation to pay weavers by the yard; but this was only the case in the superfine branch of the Wiltshire industry.[6] No such remedial action was taken in face of the second Wiltshire riot in 1738 and some of the ringleaders were hanged; but the 'Essay on Riots', printed in the *Gloucester Journal*, parts of which were reprinted in the *Gentleman's Magazine*,[7] publicized the weavers' grievances in a way which was not counteracted by the replies made on behalf of the clothiers. Its author, now revealed as Thomas Andrews of

---

[1] For those in Wilts. see Pressnell, op. cit., pp. 66 ff. The events in Glos. in 1756–7 have been described by J. L. and Barbara Hammond, *The Skilled Labourer*, pp. 157–9; and some of the petitions on both sides have been printed by W. E. Minchinton, 'The Petitions of the Weavers and Clothiers of Gloucestershire in 1756 *B.G.A.S.* 73, 216 ff.

[2] See below, App. iv.

[3] *W.A.S. Rec. Brch.* xix. nos. 203, 439; Som. C.R.O., Elderton Lr. Bk., fols. 12, 37, 54, 56 (all 1763), to J. Watts, 13 Nov. 1764. See App. iv.

[4] *W.A.S. Rec. Brch.* xix. no. 172; *V.C.H. Wilts.* iv. 166. In 1790 high entry fees were being imposed by Shepton Mallet clothworkers (*Salisbury Journal*, 3 May 1790) and the following year the same attempt was made at Bradford, *Gloucester Journal*, 9 May 1791. Whether the clothiers' determination to stop this practice was effective is unknown.

[5] 13. Geo. i. c. 23.

[6] For evidence that weaving of cheaper goods was paid by the piece in the area round Frome see Lord St. Aldwyn's MSS., BC/2, Lr. from J. Harding of Mere to Amsinck & Co. of Oporto, 4 Aug. 1757.

[7] *Gentleman's Magazine* ix. 7 ff.

Seend, a village between Trowbridge and Devizes,[1] was a stern moralist who paid high poor rates and, perhaps in consequence, was alive to any signs of extravagance among working people; but he rightly placed the causes of their misery not primarily upon their tippling habits but on the unfair practices of the clothiers. His eloquence made an impression throughout the country and has helped to create the widespread but quite untrue belief that the Wiltshire industry was already moribund.[2] In Gloucestershire both disturbances took place during efforts to obtain the rating of wages, and in 1756 Parliament actually passed an Act directing the Justices to do so; but it was repealed the following year.[3] Rating of wages was the unanimous desire of weavers throughout the region.[4] Agricultural wages were still being rated in Gloucestershire in 1732[5] even if, as is probable, no attention was paid to the rates laid down; and the memory that rates in the woollen industry had once been included was persistent.

The most noticeable point about the whole series of disturbances (with the possible exception of the Melksham riot in 1738)[6] is, on the one hand, the anxiety of the weavers to act in a legal manner to get what they believed to be their legal rights and, on the other, the clothiers' disregard of any legal obligations. In 1726 the Wiltshire weavers had approached several of their friends among the gentry for advice about how

---

[1] *Country Commonsense* by a Gentleman of Wilts., pp. 155–7. There were two men of this name, father and son, the former in Holy Orders but without a cure. *Country Commonsense*, p. 156, and *The Miseries of the Miserable*, p. 21, both imply that the 'supposed author of the Essay' was the son, who died in the same year; but it so much resembles an earlier pamphlet, *An Enquiry into the Causes of the Encrease and Miseries of the Poor of England*, that this is difficult to believe. *An Enquiry* seems certainly to have been written by the father, according to the list of previous publications which it contains. The family lived at Seend Row House and much information about land owned by them is in the Wadham Lock papers, Wilts. C.R.O., 477.

[2] Cf. A. Young, *Annals of Agriculture* vii. 163. The attack on truck was referred to with great approval in the *Champion*, 3 Mar. 1743, *Gentleman's Magazine* xiii. 140.

[3] 29 Geo. ii. c. 33, repealed by 30 Geo. ii. c. 12. See *C.J.* xxvii. 468, 503, 730–32, 741, 785, 787.

[4] *The Miseries of the Miserable*, p. 28.

[5] *Glouc. N. and Q.* iii. 283–4.

[6] If the story that an attorney had been summoned to London on the charge of fomenting the riot (*Gloucester Journal*, 26 Dec. 1738) had any basis, it may be that the weavers had tried to take legal advice, but there is no other evidence of their having done so.

to proceed; and two of the latter appear to have asked some better qualified authority about the possibility of obtaining an Act of Parliament to remedy their grievances. The answer they obtained was that it was vain to hope that Parliament would ever meddle with wages, although on general grounds the adviser was sympathetic, pointing out that the clothiers' habit of beginning an action at common law for damages against the weaver, whenever the judgement of the Bench went against them, was a piece of great barbarity which should be remedied by law. He also recommended the enforcement of apprenticeship both for clothiers and weavers; and it may have been the resentment felt by the latter at this advice (which if strictly enforced would have prevented a weaver from ever becoming a clothier) which started the riot.[1] There were already rumours of a design on the part of the clothiers to obtain an incorporation separately from the weavers,[2] which would have had the same effect; and such an opinion, coming from those whom they thought their friends, would have been quite sufficient to induce a violent reaction. As soon as there was a prospect of a petition to Parliament being organized they behaved in a most orderly manner.[3]

In Gloucestershire a few months later the weavers first applied to Quarter Sessions and, on being advised to settle a rate with their masters for the Bench to confirm, they advertised in the *Gloucester Journal*[4] desiring the clothiers to meet them and warning them that in default they would submit a scheme of their own. There was a certain amount of disorder but when the clothiers failed to appear, the Bench, after a further inquiry, confirmed the weavers' table of rates by the yard,[5] which gave them, as they said later, wages on which 'we could

---

[1] See letter in *Gloucester Journal*, 11 Apr. 1727 signed T. A. and addressed to Messrs. Long and Wilson (of Trowbridge) two of the gentry in whom the weavers put most trust (P.R.O., S.P. 35/63/94, fol. 240) 'which has been impudently imputed to be the chief cause of their late Tumults'.

[2] P.R.O., S.P.35/63/95, fol. 252(2). This rumour may have some connection with an undated memo. of the period, S.P.35/65, Pt. II (2) 170, 368v–370, which proposes, among other things, that deputies for all the clothiers of England should draw up a list of goods to be made regulating lengths etc., and that inferior pieces should be forfeited to hospitals and the poor.

[3] P.R.O., S.P.35/64/9, fol. 17.

[4] *Gloucester Journal*, 25 July 1727.

[5] Glouc. C.R.O., Q. Sess. Min. Book, Michaelmas, 1727; Easter, 1728.

subsist ourselves and families by our honest labour'.[1] These rates were never observed; but when, at the end of another depression in 1755,[2] the weavers again took action, the same regard for legal forms was evident. The application to Parliament was preceded first by an appeal to an individual magistrate, on whose advice a table of possible rates, lower than those confirmed in 1728, was drawn up;[3] and then by a week of meetings held daily in different centres so that all weavers might know what was happening.[4] After the Act was passed they again took legal advice about the individual wage agreements which clothiers were asking their weavers to sign. It was the opinion they received that, unless these private contracts were suppressed, the Act of Parliament would be of no avail that prompted the first outbreak of disorder.[5]

The clothiers' behaviour was very different. They took no notice of the provision in the Act of 1727 which made the Justices' decision final, but continued to carry disputes to a higher court where the weavers lacked means to defend them. This was not because they were ignorant of the Act which was well publicized in Gloucestershire.[6] Their only recorded reaction to the possibility that weaving prices might be rated is a document by which thirty of them bound themselves not to raise them during the following twelve months unless they were advanced by 'Parliament or other legal means';[7] and when the Bench acted it is clear that they threw doubt on whether it had the legal right to do so. Again in 1756 they took little notice of the weavers' petition to Parliament, being assured that 'nothing more was intended but to amuse the weavers';[8] and they were surprised and horrified when the Act empowering the magistrates to make wage rates was passed and the Bench proceeded to take it seriously. No doubt they had considerable justification for their disbelief in rating, if not for their attitude

---

[1] Weavers' petition to Giles Gardner J.P., 23 July 1755, Glouc. C.R.O., D.149, B.8.

[2] Ashton, op. cit., pp. 171–2. In 1755, when trade was improving elsewhere, exports both to Turkey and India were markedly lower than they had been for several years, which had serious consequences for Gloucestershire.

[3] Weavers' second petition, 22 Aug. 1755, Glouc. C.R.O., D.149, B.8. See App. IV.

[4] *Gloucester Journal*, 13 Jan. 1756.

[5] *A State of the Case*, p. 7.   [6] *Gloucester Journal*, 25 Apr. and 2 May 1727.

[7] Glouc. C.R.O., D.149, B.7, 18 July 1727.   [8] *A State of the Case*, p. 5.

towards authority. It had never been very effective, even under the much simpler conditions of the seventeenth century, and was totally impossible in the eighteenth with the increased variety of materials made and the lack of any means for joint discussion. It would have required powerful organizations on both sides, such as were only in process of development a hundred years later, to produce anything like the agreed price list which operated in the cotton industry in the later nineteenth century. The clothiers were also right in arguing that high rates were not a test of high earnings or vice versa. With the best will in the world a weaver might have a bad warp or a rotten weft which would result in his taking twice as long as another to finish his piece.[1] In fact, clothiers were on firm ground in arguing against wage regulation; and the repeal of the previous year's Act was logical, though disappointing to the weavers and their supporters. One need not suppose that those weavers who gave evidence of satisfactory earnings were either intimidated or cajoled to do so, although they aroused the anger of their neighbours.[2] Between them and those who signed the petition to the Justices who, according to their own statement, could not make 'above 6d. or 6½d. each in the course of fifteen to sixteen hours'[3] there must have been a wide range of weavers receiving sums which might suffice to keep them when bread was cheap but not in the high priced year of 1757. The wretched state of the people commented upon by Wolfe, whose regiment was sent to keep order in Gloucestershire,[4] was probably far more typical at that time than the comfortable living of the few who were more or less continuously employed and able to earn satisfactory wages. In many cases it may be that the habits of the poorer ones were at fault, but their serious and premeditated actions during the long-drawn-out struggle to get redress give the lie to the idea that they were nothing but a drunken and disorderly mob of idle people.

Whatever justification the clothiers may have had, the

[1] Cf. *Repts. Asst. Commrs. Hdloom Weavers 1840*, Pt. V (H.C. 220), pp. 382–3.

[2] *Gloucester Journal*, 1 Mar. 1757, which contains an account of an attack on the house of Lazarus Brown of Horsley while he was giving evidence in London.

[3] Glouc. C.R.O., D. 149, B.8, Petition of 23 July 1755.

[4] See E. Moir, 'The Gentlemen Clothiers', *Gloucestershire Studies*, ed. H. P. R. Finberg, p. 250.

struggle did not promote good relations between employers and employed. The increase in the practice among spinners and weavers of defrauding their masters in new ways not employed, apparently, earlier in the century, prompted the Gloucestershire clothiers in 1774 to ask for renewed legislation with higher penalties.[1] The Act which followed had little effect and ten years later it was the custom of the Minchinhampton clothiers to send all their wool to be spun at a distance, because 'our poor spoil their yarn by dirtyness, bad spinning, damping and frequently putting several masters' yarn together and many other frauds'.[2] This retaliation on the part of the clothiers, together with the unemployment created by the decay of the export trade, had resulted in a mass of poverty and misery in the places affected; and the account of Minchinhampton in the autumn of 1784, even allowing for some exaggeration on the part of charitable persons about the situation they were trying to relieve, suggests a continuous want of employment which had gradually driven the workers to sell or pawn everything which could raise money to keep them alive.[3] This crisis coincided with the rise of the Sunday School movement and the *Gloucester Journal* was full of reports of its beneficial effects in the clothing villages. That the interest of benevolent well-to-do people did indeed produce a measure of social reform is indisputable, even if, as was inevitable in that age, it was accompanied by a great deal of social patronage and authoritarianism; but it did nothing to reconcile the workers to their lot or to produce a more acquiescent attitude towards their masters.

Less information is available about Wiltshire and Somerset, but clothiers there seem to have suffered less from frauds,[4]

---

[1] *C.J.* xxxiv. 414, 451–2, 568, 594; 14 Geo. iii, c. 25. The embezzlement of odds and ends of yarn had, of course, always been common, and numerous prosecutions of the men who collected and sold them are recorded.

[2] *Gloucester Journal*, 9 Feb. 1784.

[3] Ibid., 8 Nov. 1784. After charitable activities since the early spring, which had provided food and clothing, there were in November many families 'who have no other bed than straw; not a blanket nor rug'. Yet the inhabitants of Minchinhampton, which had suffered exceptional mortality from fever that summer, were said to have been preserved 'from that extreme distress experienced in many parts of the county'.

[4] Wiltshire and Somerset clothiers joined in petitioning for the Act of 1774 but provided no evidence.

and thefts from tenters were not quite so common (or, at least, were not so often advertised) as they were in Gloucestershire. It was not unemployment but the grouping of narrow looms in shops which agitated a section of Wiltshire weavers. The popularity of fancy cassimeres after 1780 made it desirable to keep the pattern under the master's eye; and Anstie's large factory at Devizes, begun in 1783, may have been designed for this purpose, since in his heyday he employed 300 looms.[1] There was no trouble in Devizes, but the spread of the practice to Trowbridge, combined with the inclusion of plain cassimeres among the fabrics woven in shops, occasioned serious riots in 1787. Curiously enough, the first of these took place in Bradford, where the Trowbridge narrow weavers tried to get Bradford weavers to join them; but since narrow weaving had never been extensively taken up in Bradford (in spite of the fact that it was a Bradford clothier who had invented cassimeres), it is not surprising that they had no success. An unsuccessful attempt by the magistrates to arbitrate was followed by another riot in Trowbridge, but the ringleaders escaped with relatively light penalties and it looks as if the masters were not anxious to exasperate their men. This seems to have been the first instance of the weavers' repugnance to weaving shops being openly displayed; according to Anstie, some of them were even willing to accept a reduction of a penny a yard in wages on condition that no more should be put up.[2]

Whether or not weavers in the medley section of the industry were rather better off than those in the Stroudwater region (and the impression that they were may simply be due to lack of evidence), the contrast between their position and that of their counterparts in Yorkshire, made familiar by Tucker's well-known description,[3] was widely recognized and frequently

---

[1] MS. Diary of George Sloper, fol. 178 (W.A.S. Libr., Devizes) entry of 4 Apr. 1788. See W. E. Brown, 'Long's Stores, Devizes', *W.A.M.* lv. 139 ff. Mr. Brown believes Anstie to have been a silk manufacturer and to have installed silk throwing machinery there. He was in fact making fancy cloth in which some silk was used and he may have had some machinery for producing it (there was certainly some there later); but the absence of any reference to silk throwing in Devizes at this time makes it more probable that the greater part of the building was intended for looms.

[2] *Bath Chronicle*, 1, 8, and 22 Feb. and 1 and 22 Mar. 1787. Much of the information comes from advts. inserted by Anstie as chairman of the clothiers' Ctee.

[3] J. Tucker, *Instructions to Travellers*, pp. 37–9.

used by the landowners in their controversy with the clothiers over the export of wool.[1] By 1788 the fact that the more independent Yorkshire weavers were less wasteful of materials and more economical housekeepers, content with a smaller return because they spent less in the alehouse, was recognized to be due to the fact that they had an interest in producing cloth which they could sell whereas the western weavers had none. (Curiously enough, no one raised the point that they had what was, conventionally at least, a lower standard of life, living on oatmeal when wheaten bread, of a sort, was consumed in the west.) Anstie was open-minded enough to wonder whether the Yorkshire system could not be imported, at least partially, into some branches of the western industry;[2] but it was far too late to alter methods of marketing and to revise the process by which most of the capital had become accumulated in the hands of large employers. Superfine cloth, with its expensive raw material, could not have been produced under the Yorkshire system; but Anstie's suggestion that, for the production of coarser cloth, capital was less economically used in the west than in the north, may well be true because its wide dispersion there gave the workers an interest in production which the meagre wages paid by the western clothiers could never do.

There were several differences between the position of clothiers in Gloucestershire and that of their counterparts further south. Wiltshire had had clothiers on the Bench since the later seventeenth century. The first appointment had been that of William Brewer who had come in as a Tory in 1680 when the Whigs were turned out after the Rye House Plot.[3] He found no difficulty in accepting William III,[4] and retained his position until the end of his life. By 1726 there were at least four clothiers on the Wiltshire Bench,[5] perhaps because the western corner of the county was somewhat deficient in suitable gentry.[6]

---

[1] See below, pp. 270–2.

[2] J. Anstie, *A General View of the Bill . . . for preventing the illicit Exportation of British Wool and Sheep*, pp. 81—4.

[3] *H.M.C. 11th Rept.* (H. of L. MSS.), 191.

[4] He signed the Association of 1696, *Wilts. N. and Q.* vi. 349.

[5] John Cooper of Trowbridge, Thomas Methuen of Bradford, and the brothers John and Thomas Phipps of Westbury.

[6] *C.S.P.D. 1702–3*, 142.

Clothiers continued to be appointed as magistrates throughout the eighteenth century, and, although in 1726 there was one champion of the workers among them in John Cooper of Trowbridge, he was not typical. A Steeple Ashton lawyer writing to the Duke of Bolton in the early 1750s deplored the want of Justices in the neighbourhood, but begged him to use his influence to see that 'Gentlemen only and not Tradesmen' were put into the next Commission, since the poor were complaining of truck by the clothiers 'who kill beef and sheep every week and put it off at their own price to the poor scribblers, weavers and spinners'.[1] Gloucestershire, on the other hand, seems to have had no clothier on the Bench until the later eighteenth century, and Somerset not even then. The Gloucestershire clothing district was rich in gentry, but although some were descended from families which had made their money in the trade, their sentiments were those of their class and not those of the clothiers. In fact, the rift between clothiers and gentry tended to widen as the century progressed and the two subjects dividing them, the burden of the poor rates and the prohibition of the export of wool, came more and more to the fore. Both the rise in poor rates, of which the agricultural interest was thought to pay more than its fair share, and the renewed agitation in the eighties over the illicit export of wool were a constant reminder that the industry was favoured at the landowner's expense; and if the gentry somewhat over-estimated their injuries, they had an arguable case on both counts.

The presence of clothiers on the Wiltshire Bench may be the reason why it was the only one to ignore the Act of 1756. The Somerset Bench tried to make rates for weaving but, like their brethren in Gloucestershire at first, were defeated by the complexity of the subject.[2] In Gloucestershire magisterial sentiment seems to have been solidly on the side of the workers with some individual magistrates taking an active part in advising them, whereas in Wiltshire opinion was frequently divided. On the other hand the clothiers were a greater political force in Gloucestershire than they were elsewhere. Since many were

---

[1] Wilts C.R.O., 730/300. The date is determined by the mention of Alderman Fludyer. Samuel Fludyer became an alderman in 1751 and was knighted in 1754. I owe this reference to Mr. K. H. Rogers.

[2] See *V.C.H. Wilts.* iv. 166.

freeholders, they had a vote in county elections and there were enough of them to make their influence felt. They were being courted as early as 1660,[1] and in 1695 the young John Guise attributed his defeat partly to the fact that the clothing interest, represented by the Sheriff Thomas Ridler, had swung against him.[2] By 1750 they were 'an opulent and significant body of men' whom it was desirable for the Government to conciliate;[3] and it can only have been their complete disbelief that Parliament would do anything so out of character as to direct the magistrates to rate wages which allowed the Act of 1756 to pass without representations from them. No such political importance attached to clothiers in Wiltshire and Somerset, except perhaps in some boroughs.[4] Many of the urban clothiers outside the boroughs (and they included all who lived in Bradford, Trowbridge, and Frome) were not freeholders, and those who were were swamped by the mass of voters who had no connection with the industry. This, rather than the larger scale of the industry in Gloucestershire, may be the reason why clothiers there frequently took the lead in petitioning Parliament and furnishing evidence about topics on which they wanted legislation.

The gentlemen clothiers of Gloucestershire have certainly received more publicity, and were more numerous and perhaps rather more wealthy than their counterparts in Wiltshire and Somerset. Yet there were one or two in Wiltshire who surpassed any from the neighbouring counties in enterprise, especially John Anstie of Devizes, whose position in the industry was marked by his election as chairman of all the western clothiers in their efforts from 1784 to 1788 to procure a new bill against the smuggling of wool,[5] and his selection to give evidence

---

[1] Smyth MSS. II, fol. 100 (G.C.L., no. 16525).

[2] Memoirs of the Family of Guise of Elmore, *Camden Soc.* (3rd ser.), 28, 139.

[3] B. M., Add. MSS. 32, 906, fol. 399, Lr. from N. Calvert to the Duke of Newcastle, 31 May 1760.

[4] The election of the Blackwell Hall factor, Josiah Diston, for Devizes in 1705 seems to have been the result of Whig influence (or bribery) rather than of that of the clothiers. That of Sir S. Fludyer for Chippenham in 1754 was achieved by buying up burgage houses; but Fludyer and his successors, who belonged to the same firm, took care to promote the clothiers' interests, see *V.C.H. Wilts.* iv. 159. In Wilton a candidate in 1710 promised the town 'the clothing of one or two regiments' if he were elected, *C.J.* xvi. 559.

[5] See below, pp. 270-2.

on behalf of the western industry on the Irish Propositions and the Commercial Treaty with France. The dispute with Arthur Young in which his advocacy of anti-smuggling measures involved him has not only reflected on the Wiltshire industry as a whole, about which Young's jibes have too often been accepted as correct,[1] but has also served to obscure Anstie's place in it. Following Francis Yerbury of Bradford who had invented the manufacture of cassimeres, it was he who, by introducing fancy cloth, made the second of the only two innovations in the production of cloth up to 1790. Although both were taken up in Yorkshire after that date, the fact remains that it was western and not Yorkshire enterprise which had introduced them.[2] His bankruptcy in 1793 put an end to his activity though not to his interest in the industry; but, as any reader of his works must recognize, he was certainly the most forward-looking and one of the most liberal among the western clothiers. The greater liberality of sentiment on economic policy in Wiltshire and Somerset in the age just before spinning machinery was introduced, which has already been mentioned,[3] may have been due to greater prosperity; but another factor may well have been the greater extent to which non-conformity prevailed among the urban clothiers.

Whatever their political or religious views, the general impression made by the clothiers of the whole region at the beginning of the machine age is of a far better educated and more tolerant community than had existed sixty years earlier. It might be equally insistent on the subordination of the workers, but it was genuinely anxious to suppress abuses and to gain their cooperation in the modernization of the industry. That it did not wholly succeed was due not only to the legacy of bad feeling from the past but to the organization of the industry, which made it difficult to convince the workers that the introduction of machinery could be to their benefit as well as to that of their employers.

---

[1] *Annals of Agriculture*, ix. 361; vii 163–5.
[2] Anstie, *A General View of the Bill*, pp. 78–9.
[3] See above, pp. 59–60.

PART II

1790 to 1880

V

THE ADVENT OF SPINNING AND FINISHING MACHINERY, 1790–1814

In their first attempt at introducing spinning machinery the western clothiers were not far behind those of the north. The carding engine and spinning jenny were acclimatized in Yorkshire during the seventies.[1] They did not arrive in the Holmfirth district on the borders of Lancashire until 1776[2] and it was this year which saw the well-known attempt to introduce them to the west. A group of twelve Shepton Mallet clothiers united to set up an experimental machine in the workhouse, after having made a compact with their weavers not to oppose it.[3] The inducement for the men was probably the agreement, signed before a magistrate in Wells that year, by which the clothiers bound themselves to restore the rate of 1s. 3d. a yard for weaving superfine cloth which had been originally fixed twenty years earlier.[4] It was a mob outside the town, mainly from Frome and Warminster, which destroyed the machine, outwitting the magistrates, who had had prior warning, by waiting until they had dispersed in the belief that no violence would take place that night.

Six weeks later clothiers from all three counties met at Bristol Fair and issued two statements.[5] The first, signed by fifty 'principal Manufacturers', contained a recommendation that experimental machines should be provided and worked in the various places where the manufacture was carried on. The signatories promised to hold meetings in their several neighbourhoods and to report local reactions to a general meeting in Bath a month later. The second statement thanked the Shepton clothiers for their 'spirited conduct' and was signed

[1] *Ev. to Ctee on State of Woollen Manufacture*, 1806 (H.C. 268), p. 113.
[2] W. B. Crump and G. Ghorbal, *History of the Huddersfield Woollen Industry*, p. 64.
[3] *Bath Chronicle*, 18 July and 1 Aug. 1776.
[4] *Ev. on Woollen Trade Bill*, 1803 (H.C. 95), p. 62.
[5] *Gloucester Journal*, 9 and 16 Sept. 1776.

by 101 clothiers including many who were not at the meeting. Of these thirty-four cannot be identified with certainty. Fifty-three of the remainder came from Wiltshire and Somerset and only eight from Gloucestershire, which suggests that Gloucestershire clothiers may not have been quite so enthusiastic about machinery as their neighbours.[1]

Those who attended the next meeting held in Bath in October issued a statement declaring themselves fully determined to encourage the use of machinery and refuting reports that workers would be deprived of their livelihood and become burdensome to their parishes. Should jennies be found prejudicial to the poor it was promised that they would be discontinued.[2] On the workers' side a petition against machinery was presented to Parliament from Frome, Shepton Mallet, and other Somerset towns, but was rejected.[3] There must, however, have been some private efforts, probably through one of the county members, to induce the men to try its value, for three weeks later the *Bath Chronicle* printed as an advertisement a statement, which, in spite of its odd grammar, deserves reproduction as the only one of its kind.[4] Addressed to the Gentlemen Clothiers of Shepton Mallet, it referred to the statement issued after the Bath meeting and continued:

On this declaration, in consequence of a petition to Parliament, and on particular advice from the Hon. House of Commons, at a meeting of the principal workmen in the several branches of (the) Woollen Manufacture, it was humbly resolved:—That we the principal workpeople, do consent and agree, that YOU the Clothiers who are now concerned in the use and working of the Machines, which are now employed in your workhouses only, for the space of two months from the day of the date hereof, by way of trial; provided you will work the Machines in their full capacity, by the most able workmen you can get, and to work them openly, subject to the inspection of two proper persons appointed by us, in order to give a creditable account of its utility which you have asserted, or the dangerous consequences which WE have apprehended, may evidently appear.

[1] P. H. Fisher in his *Notes and Recollections of Stroud*, p. 292 reports the breaking up of a spinning machine in 1776 but there is no mention of any riot in Gloucestershire in contemporary sources. Probably he was referring to the Shepton Mallet case. Fisher himself was not born until 1779 or 1780.

[2] *Gloucester Journal*, 14 Nov. 1776.

[3] *C.J.* xxxvi. 7.

[4] *Bath Chronicle*, 28 Nov. 1776

The trial appears to have been satisfactory if reliance can be placed on a statement in the *Bath Chronicle* in 1781, according to which they were still employed 'with most useful effects'.[1]

Elsewhere it seems to have been only on the fringes of the industrial area that machinery was set up. In Salisbury jennies were reported to be 'introducing with the greatest success' in April 1777; and in August they were in use at Sturminster Newton for the coarse cloth known as swanskins.[2] The experiments at Chard are mentioned below. From the autumn of 1776 an enterprising bellfounder, T. Pyke of Bridgwater, was advertising jennies with a lighter barrel than those made in Yorkshire, to run more easily.[3] After August 1777 both advertisements and information come to an end. There was great opposition, not only from the workers but from the general public. Henry Wansey, who had recently become a clothier in Salisbury, wrote to his brother in Warminster in November 1776 urging clothiers to take vigorous action against a petition to Parliament which was being got up against the machines,[4] but nothing seems to have been done. In Yorkshire the jenny and the carding engine had been introduced by the domestic clothiers who, in an expanding industry, had no fear of being unable to find work for unemployed spinners; but even so their use had created some apprehension.[5] The organization of the western industry was much less favourable to anything which involved the employment of fewer hands in spinning, for it occupied women over a very wide area in what were otherwise purely agricultural districts. Nor did the depressed state of the trade between 1779 and 1783 encourage innovation. This was certainly one of the reasons why other places did not follow the example set by the Shepton clothiers. As far as we know, the only place to do so (apart from the towns mentioned above) was Frome, where at least one jenny and carding engine had been set up by the spring of 1781, when a Whit-Monday mob destroyed them.[6] No other riots are recorded, but the fear of

---

[1] Ibid., 13 June 1781.   [2] *Salisbury Journal*, 21 Apr. and 14 Aug. 1777.
[3] *Bath Chronicle*, 30 Oct. 1776; *Gloucester Journal*, 13 Jan. and 3 and 10 Mar. 1777.
[4] Wilts. C.R.O., 314/4/1, Lr. of 23 Nov. 1776. As the county member mentioned was a Mr. Phillips who was a Somerset M.P. this may refer to the petition mentioned above, though it had been already presented on 1 Nov.
[5] *Ev. on State of Woollen Manuf.*, 1806, pp. 73, 403.
[6] *Bath Chronicle*, 13 June 1781.

them was a potent influence on the clothiers' attitude. 'If we in this part of the kingdom attempt to introduce (machinery),' wrote Matthew Humphreys of Chippenham in 1786, 'it must be with the risk of our lives and fortunes', and he wondered what would become of those who would lose their work in consequence.[1] There were already too many unemployed in the county and, like many others, he was unable to envisage the growth in demand which more confident supporters of machinery predicted as bound to follow its introduction.

Another reason for failure to persist was the fact that the machines as they stood were something of a disappointment. This was brought to the notice of the newly founded Bath and West of England Society in 1777 by a letter from a man named John Cook at Thorncombe near Chard.[2] After pointing out that clothiers had for some time found difficulty in completing their orders for want of spinning, he added:

> To remove this obstacle they have introduced the machines called Jennys but these on Tryal are found not fully to answer the expected end. This disappointment has excited several persons to try newly-invented improvements in the Spinning and Carding way, which at present are kept secret. If the Society should adopt some Method to call forth plans of their Machines with Specimens of their Work, it will soon turn to public advantage.

Though Cook was not a disinterested witness, since he was trying to improve the machines himself and was anxious to receive a reward for doing so,[3] his statement appears to have been well founded. Almost immediately the Society's Committee of Manufacturers proposed a premium of five guineas 'to the person who shall make such improvements in the Machines called Spinning Jennys as to render them equally fit for the making of fine as well as coarse cloths'.[4] This offer

---

[1] P.R.O., B.T.6/111, no. 39. Cf. H. Fox, *Quaker Homespun*, p. 51.

[2] Arch. B. and W. i, fol. 3, Lr. of 1 Sept. 1777. There were three clothiers in Thorncombe at this time. (Information from Asst. Archivist, Devon C.R.O., Thorncombe, now in Dorset, having been in Devon in the eighteenth century.) There were also several at Chard a few miles away in Somerset. In the 1790s a manufacture of fine cloth was set up there by some Wiltshire manufacturers, (J. Billingsley, *General View of the Agriculture of Somerset*, p. 260), but there is no other information about it.

[3] Arch. B. and W. i, fols. 56–7, Lr. of 23 Feb. 1778. For a description of Cook's machine see below, p. 288.

[4] Ibid. xi. Ctee of Manufacturers, minutes of 19 Nov. 1777, Item 5.

cannot have been the result of misinformation, for there were several prominent Wiltshire and Somerset clothiers on the committee, which also included the well-known John Billingsley who seems to have been the moving spirit in the introduction of the jenny to Shepton Mallet.[1] The premium was never claimed, and Cook, who spoke of himself as old and infirm, may have died before he could send in his model; but the incident suggests that, as far as the fine clothiers were concerned, there was not enough advantage to be gained from using the machines in the contemporary state of their development to balance the dangers of introducing them.

Renewed interest in machinery did not begin to appear until after the end of the American war, when improvements in the jenny and the appearance of the slubbing billy had probably made the spinning of fine yarn possible and economical.[2] In 1784 a man from the west was arrested at Leeds with a sackful of miniature machines which he was not allowed to keep.[3] Some machines were exhibited in Exeter in November 1785[4] and towards the end of the decade spinning machinery is again heard of in the area. The earliest reference comes from Twerton, just outside Bath, where spinning machines were among the effects to be disposed of when the mill lately in possession of Samuel Heaven was advertised for sale in January 1787.[5] These were presumably bought by its purchaser, Paul Bamford, who in the nineties had by far the most complete assortment of machinery in the whole district. The position of this mill in a small manufacturing neighbourhood some miles from the main clothing area[6] no doubt facilitated its introduction. No other mention occurs until the following year. In September 1788 the effects of Thomas Turner of Ebley in Gloucestershire, advertised for sale after his bankruptcy,

---

[1] He was represented as the only clothier to do so, but the others affirmed that the decision was theirs also, *Bath Chronicle*, 1 Aug. 1776. Billingsley was afterwards more celebrated as an agriculturalist, but for his early life as a clothier see his obituary in *Letters and Papers of the Bath and West Society* xiii. pt. 1 (1813), p. 90.

[2] See below, p. 288.

[3] W. B. Crump, *The Leeds Woollen Industry*, p. 10.

[4] P.R.O., B.T.6/111, no. 39. Arkwright's machinery is mentioned but other models may have been included.

[5] *Bath Chronicle*, 4 Jan. 1787.

[6] In 1801 there were three factories on the Avon at Twerton and another on the Weston side, R. Warner, *History of Bath*, pp. 215, 217.

included several spinning machines;[1] while Thomas Tippetts of New Mills, Dursley, bankrupt at the beginning of 1789, had 'one spinning machine complete'.[2] Both had small quantities of 'slooping'[3] which suggests that the pronunciation had been imported from Yorkshire with the billy.

Machinery appeared in Wiltshire about the same time,[4] and by 1790 jennies were being introduced over a wide area. There were machine-makers at Westbury, Melksham, and Frome,[5] although the last named soon found it more convenient and perhaps safer to remove to Bath.[6] How much of the current demand they supplied is uncertain; the Bath machine-maker's stock was sold up in 1793[7] and in the only case for which we have evidence, that of Messrs. Were, the Wellington serge-makers, in 1790–1, the machinery was brought down from the north with rather unsatisfactory results.[8] Trade steadily improved from 1787 onwards and by 1790 some manufacturers had orders they could not fulfil,[9] a potent motive for taking the plunge. The only resistance recorded was at Keynsham, where the Kingswood colliers and their wives endeavoured in 1790 to destroy the machines which would render the women's labour unnecessary;[10] and, although they were pacified at first, violence broke out again three months later and dragoons were sent to deal with the rioters.[11] Colliers, however, were a turbulent body of men; agricultural labourers, whose wives and children throughout the country were the chief sufferers, were

---

[1] *Gloucester Journal*, 8 Sept. 1788.

[2] G.C.L., R.115.118. Catalogue of stock at New Mills, Dursley, 16 Mar. 1789.

[3] Also spelt 'slobbing'.

[4] *V.C.H. Wilts.* iv. 167.

[5] *Salisbury Journal*, 4 Oct. 1790, 18 July and 12 Sept. 1791. J. Ogden of Melksham in 1791, had been a partner of J. Salisbury at Westbury Leigh in 1790. There was also a machine maker in Bristol in 1792, ibid., 11 June 1792.

[6] Ibid., 5 Dec. 1791.

[7] Ibid., 16 Dec. 1793.

[8] H. Fox, *Quaker Homespun*, pp. 52–5.

[9] H. Wansey, *Wool encouraged without Exportation*, p. 68.

[10] See P.R.O., H.O.42/16 quoted by J. and B. Hammond, *The Skilled Labourer*, p. 149. But the notice in the *Salisbury Journal* (below, n. 11) mentions disturbances elsewhere.

[11] *Salisbury Journal*, 7 June 1790. The earlier riot had taken place in March. Possibly these disturbances ended the industry in Keynsham since Collinson, a year later, says that the formerly considerable manufacture had entirely ceased though many of the poor were still spinning for Bradford, Trowbridge, and Shepton clothiers. *History of Somerset* ii. 400.

less likely to take violent action. In Gloucestershire a writer, recalling in the nineteenth century the events of his youth, said that jennies had been 'hailed with delight by masters and weavers' who had often been frustrated when yarn was not returned from villages at a distance when they expected it.[1]

Up to 1791 the production of yarn by machinery was still limited by the necessity of scribbling by hand. In Yorkshire the carding engine had been adapted for this purpose before 1780; and although it had caused at least one riot[2] it was firmly installed there long before 1790. It was probably the threatening attitude of the scribblers in the west which prevented its immediate adoption. Francis Hill, who moved from Bradford to Malmesbury, where the industry had been extinct for about twenty years, in order to install machinery in an atmosphere free from opposition, had arranged for the purchase of the mill by the bridge (then a corn mill) from the heir of the last clothier there as early as 1790,[3] some time before rioters destroyed the scribbling machine set up by Joseph Phelps in Bradford in 1791.[4] Scribbling by machinery went ahead none the less, and when a similar riot took place at Woodchester in April 1792, the workpeople stood by their master and the rioters found them 'universally convinced of the advantages the machines rendered the trade of the country and how entirely it owed its flourishing state to their introduction.'[5] This did not prevent a petition being sent to Parliament from Gloucestershire in 1794 for the limitation of scribbling engines 'so as to have enough work for others';[6] but this was probably

[1] *Stroud Journal*, 4 July 1868. Anonymous article on the cloth trade of the borough of Stroud, past and present, extending over three issues of the paper. The author wrote of his own knowledge and spoke of his grandfather having been a clothier; it seems possible that he may have been P. H. Fisher who finished his *Notes and Recollections of Stroud* in 1871, in his 92nd year.

[2] Crump, op. cit., pp. 12, 315–6.

[3] *Wilts. N. and Q.* viii. 438. Joseph Cullerne who sold the mill was presumably the heir of William Cullerne, clothier of Melksham late of Malmesbury, who died 1772, *Bath Chronicle*, 26 Mar. 1772.

[4] W. H. Jones and J. E. Jackson, *History of Bradford-on-Avon*, ed. J. Beddoe, pp. 65–6.

[5] *Gloucester Journal*, 30 Apr. 1792. By 1803 there were public scribbling mills for the small manufacturer in Gloucestershire, just as in Yorkshire, *Ev. on Woollen Trade Bill*, 1803, p. 308.

[6] *C.J.* xliv. 599–600. In the petition scribbling machinery was combined with gigmills.

motivated by the depression of 1793 from which the county had not wholly recovered. In the same year Shepton Mallet, which, after its pioneer effort in 1776, seems to have lost all its initiative, had also to face a riot when introducing the machine and applied for military aid;[1] but there was no trouble over it afterwards.

For reasons given below Wiltshire and Somerset were now much more hostile to machinery than Gloucestershire. Anstie regretted that the Wiltshire magistrates had taken no action on a memorandum presented to them in 1791 'to recommend the adoption of precautionary measures, not only for the protection of the clothiers, but also for satisfying the minds of the workpeople';[2] but, in fact, it is very improbable that the gentry as a whole would have taken any steps in this direction. Decreasing earnings from spinning affected the poor rates in every rural parish; and even if the use of machinery ultimately increased employment in the towns, it was bound to remove a source of income from the agricultural labourers' families at a time when, with rising prices, they needed it most.[3] Only a few places benefited by the establishment of spinning mills located where there was a fall of water.[4] The country gentlemen had not forgotten the controversy of 1788 about the export of wool and by 1793 they were dismissing the plea that the use of machines had been forced upon the industry by Yorkshire competition and were again accusing clothiers of thinking of nothing but their own profit.[5] Both Phelps in 1791 and Francis Naish of Trowbridge, whose mills there and at Littleton were burnt down during a wages dispute in the troubled year of 1802, obtained damages from the places in which their mills were situated for the failure of the inhabitants to come to

---

[1] *An Account of the Proceedings of the Merchants*, pp. 153–4. This work includes some evidence omitted from the *Ev. relating to Wool* attached to the *Resolutions of the two Houses of Parliament of Ireland respecting a Union . . .* in *B.P.P. 1799–1800* cix.

[2] J. Anstie, *Observations on the Importance and Necessity of introducing improved Machinery into the Woollen Manufactory*, pp. 5–6, 20–21.

[3] Cf. T. Davis, *General View of the Agriculture of Wilts.*, p. 215, for the disastrous effects of the loss of spinning on the agricultural labourer's standard of life.

[4] See J. L. and B. Hammond, op. cit., p. 148. Water to turn machines was eagerly sought for in Glos. (*Stroud Journal*, 4 July 1868, see p. 129, n. 1), but in Wilts. according to Britton *Beauties of Wilts.* i. 16, machinery had caused the manufacture to be concentrated in towns, see below, p. 133, n. 4.

[5] *A Letter to the Landholders of the County of Wilts. on the alarming State of the Poor*, pp. 6–8 (W.A.S. Libr., Devizes, Wilts. Tracts. XVI).

their assistance,[1] which must have made them even more un-popular.

The mills which began to appear after 1790 were not, in most cases, the imposing piles familiar to a later generation, but small buildings, often converted tenements,[2] which would hold scribbling and carding machines, billies, and sometimes jennies. Only the scribbling and carding were done by power, and fulling mills with lofts over and gearing to drive machinery were often advertised. There were also many instances of horse-drawn machines which could be set up in any building large enough to allow a horse to walk round a shaft; and a trained horse seems to have been a valuable animal to judge from one Gloucestershire advertisement which printed the words 'machine horse' in capital letters.[3] Failing everything else the machines could even be turned by hand, . . . 'slow and laborious work' according to one Gloucestershire account,[4] . . . and one well known Trowbridge firm was said to have started in this way.[5] The whole range of spinning machinery might be in the same building; but jennies were often worked by independent operators in small workshops. Some must have bought their slubbings since they possessed nothing in the way of machinery except jennies.[6] In fact, the introduction of spinning machinery provided an unrivalled opportunity for the man with unlimited ambition and small, or almost no capital to set up for himself. The preservation of two memoirs, written by men who attained wealth in the nineteenth century[7] makes this

[1] *Salisbury Journal*, 12 Mar. 1792; 14 Mar. 1803. Phelps got £250 from the inhabitants of Bradford. Naish was awarded damages expected to be about £4,000 from the hundred of Whorwellsdown but it is not known whether this was paid. He took over the Twerton mill after Bamford's bankruptcy in 1802, see articles by R. G. Naish (no relation) in *Bath Chronicle*, 5 and 13 Aug. 1938.

[2] See the many advertisements of tenements suitable for conversion in all the newspapers of the region, e.g. *Gloucester Journal*, 11 June 1792.

[3] Ibid., 31 Oct. 1808.

[4] Art. in *Stroud Journal*, 4 July 1868 (see p. 129, n. 1).

[5] Reminiscences of W. Walker born in 1840, the son of a shearman who, on being superseded by machinery, learnt to spin and built up a business. See below, n. 7.

[6] e.g. S. & S. Sparrow of Stonehouse in 1806, G.C.L., R.R.289.1. They were primarily farmers.

[7] 'Reminiscences of Departed Years' by George Tucker who started life in the counting house of a Trowbridge mill in 1827 and became a very successful cloth merchant; and the reminiscences of W. Walker referred to above (n. 5). Walker began life as a travelling salesman of cloth and flock and ultimately

particularly clear in the case of Trowbridge, where such opportunities were still being taken up to the middle of the nineteenth century. As late as 1862 a house in Hilperton was advertised to let 'convenient for two jennies and reels'; and a week earlier gigs, carding engines, and cutters belonging to a man who had given up business and taken an inn were advertised to be sold.[1] In Gloucestershire many ex-shearmen, if they were 'steady and laborious', were said to have done well in other occupations and to have reached high positions in Stroud, though these were not specifically stated to have been in the cloth industry.[2] There were also several yarnmakers in Gloucestershire not all of whom did so well; one was bankrupt in 1811.[3]

The economies made by introducing spinning machinery were undoubtedly great. Henry Wansey, making flannels in Salisbury in 1791, estimated that his expenses in labour for making up 3,200 lb. of wool were reduced from £455 to £380 at a cost of about £30 for machinery, a net saving of nearly 10 per cent.[4] It was an additional reproach to the clothiers that such economies were not passed on to the consumer.[5] Their defence was to point to the rising price of wool. In 1792 Gloucestershire clothiers even made an agreement to add sums varying from 3d. to 6d. per yard to the price of cloth made with English wool,[6] and in 1793 a majority of those who attended a meeting in Bath resolved that, on account of the high price of Spanish wool, no clothier using it could keep up the quality of his cloth unless the price rose by 1s. 6d. a yard.[7] If

owned five mills in Wiltshire including those of Messrs. Salter. I am indebted to Mr. Ponting for knowledge of his MS. and to the late Major Mackay of Wick House, Trowbridge, for the loan of that written by Tucker.

[1] *Trowbridge Advertiser*, 11 and 18 Oct. 1862.

[2] See Art. in *Stroud Journal*, 18 July 1868 (p. 129, n. 1).

[3] *Gloucester Journal*, 6 and 13 May 1811.

[4] H. Wansey, *Wool encouraged without Exportation*, p. 68. The table drawn up by the Commr. for Handloom Weavers for the S.W. in 1839 shows a much greater saving, from £3. 13s. 6d. to £1. 6s. 3¾d. on 75 lb. of wool, or about 64 per cent; but he has omitted the costs of the machinery and the wages of the men in charge of the scribblers and carders. *Repts. of Asst. Commrs. Handloom Weavers*, 1840, Pt. II (H.C. 43 I), pp. 439–40.

[5] *A Letter to the Landholders of the County of Wilts . . .*, p. 8.

[6] Glouc. C.R.O., Pamphlets C, I. 5. Copy of a document dated 16 Mar. 1792 in the possession of Messrs. Marling & Evans, Stanley Mills. For the price of wool at this time see below, p. 271.

[7] *Bath Chronicle*, 10 Jan. and 17 Jan. 1793. A few dissented.

they obtained this rise it did not last long,[1] but all the same it must have been largely from profits made in the early years of the nineties that they accumulated enough capital to build their large mills, though these did not become common until after 1800. The number of persons who entered the industry in the nineties as an investment for capital does not appear to have been larger than usual;[2] nor does it look as if clothiers depended at all upon advances from country banks, though many of them ended their careers as partners in such establishments. The large number of failures among these banks in 1793 was not followed by an unusual number of bankruptcies among clothiers. The only important one was that of John Anstie of Devizes, and he had been in difficulties since 1789 'owing to the failure of a house in town'.[3]

Water power was easily obtainable in Gloucestershire, but in Wiltshire and Somerset those who did not already possess suitable premises sometimes found it difficult to obtain them. Lord Lansdown refused to let a mill to a Bradford clothier in 1792, although he approved of the installation of machinery and foresaw its beneficent effect in increasing trade and encouraging business activity. 'Rather than attempt anything so arbitrary and absurd as to stop the progress of the Machinery,' he wrote, 'I am very clear it would be better to come to a general rise of Wages, especially if every Person was compell'd at the same time to belong to some amicable Society.' But his love of quiet and the feeling that he could defend the use of machines more forcibly if he did not benefit from them, led him to refuse the offer;[4] and it is probable that his attitude was

[1] In 1795 the Blackwell Hall factors, Hanson & Mills, were scouting the idea of cloth selling at 17s. even on long credit, which had at one time been the regular figure (P.R.O., C.113/18 Letter Book, fol. 80, To Cross & Co. 15 Oct. 1795.), but it was said to be 19s. in 1803, *Ev. on Woollen Trade Bill,* 1803, p. 207.

[2] By far the greater number of the Gloucestershire clothiers who contributed to the cost of petitioning for the repeal of the woollen statutes in 1802 bore names which had been familiar in the industry for many years. Rather more of the Wiltshire clothiers were newcomers, Jones and Edridge for example, but most of these had been in business before 1789.

[3] P.R.O., H.O.42/95, Lr. from Anstie to Lord Hawkesbury asking for employment, 4 Feb. 1808.

[4] Lr. in University of London Libr., A.L.327. It is signed J. Cross but gives Lord Lansdown's opinion 'in his own words'. I owe knowledge of this letter and permission to quote from it to Dr. Pafford, late Goldsmith's Librarian. A similar attitude among other landowners may have been the reason for the concentration of the industry in towns in Wilts., see above, p. 130, n. 4.

more or less typical of that of the more enlightened residents who had no connection with the industry.

Some early mills can still be traced. One of the first was that of Francis Hill at Malmesbury, built about 1793 and now owned by an antique dealer.[1] Another was Dunkirk mill at Freshford (now in ruins) erected by Moggridge & Joyce of Bradford in 1795.[2] The mill at Twerton belonging to Bamford, Cooke & Co. must also have been in existence in the nineties to accommodate the mass of machinery which Bamford accumulated there.[3] Besides the usual scribbling and carding machines, billies and jennies, he was using Arkwright's spinning frame for making worsted yarn which he sold to Exeter sergemakers,[4] and in 1793 he introduced Cartwright's combing machine.[5] In 1797 he was introducing the gigmill and probably the shearing frame;[6] and many Wiltshire clothiers had sent cloth to him to be gigged before his bankruptcy at the end of 1801. He and one other clothier in Twerton are the only ones in the three counties known to have employed parish apprentices, many of whom also came from Exeter.[7] When the mill was advertised for sale in 1802 it consisted of two large six-storey buildings and an apprentice house.[8]

Evidence for Gloucestershire mills is more difficult to obtain. One building at Bowbridge dated from 1795.[9] Various dates

[1] J. T. Bird, *History of Malmesbury*, pp. 203–4.

[2] A medallion with the initials M and J showing a picture of the mill and the date 1795 is still in existence.

[3] See arts. by R. G. Naish, *Bath Chronicle*, 5 to 25 Aug. 1938. There is some confusion over the Twerton mills. The Upper mill, recently pulled down, was said in 1833 to have been in use 'about 40 years ago', i.e. 1793. Later owners acquired both the Upper and the Lower mills; the latter was enlarged 'when first used as a cloth factory' in 1800, according to its owner in 1833. *Suppl. Rept. of Factory Inq. Com. 1834* ii, *Answers to Queries* (H.C.167), B.1., 54, but it must have been used as a factory earlier for there were three mills in Twerton in the 1790s. See below, n. 4.

[4] R. Warner, *History of Bath*, pp. 215–16.

[5] *C.J.* xlix. 322.

[6] P.R.O. H.O.42/41, Lr. from J. F. Bowen J.P., 20 Dec. 1797 describing a riot against machinery. He does not specify the machine but the mob began by destroying £30 worth of shears belonging to Bamford in the house of a sheargrinder at Nunney which suggests that a shearing frame may have been involved. When the mill was advertised in 1802 there were 18 of them, *Bath Chronicle*, 8 July 1802.

[7] Warner, op. cit., p. 216; Hoskins, op. cit., p. 146. The name of the other clothier is not given. See also art. by Naish in *Bath Chronicle*, 5 Aug. 1938.

[8] Ibid., 8 July 1802.

[9] *Suppl. Rept. Fact. Inq. Com. 1834* ii. *Answers to Queries*, B.1., 35.

are given for Dunkirk mill at Nailsworth the earliest being 1795, and Woodchester mill is said to have been erected by Sir Samuel Wathen in 1799. Two mills at Nailsworth were put up in 1800[1] and in 1801 the Austins had a mill outside Wotton-under-Edge which employed 195 persons.[2] Other pre-1800 dates given to the Factory Commissioners in 1833 seem only to refer to small additions to fulling mills. Mills were sometimes built for letting[3] and in one instance at least an enterprising millwright appears to have done so as a speculation.[4] In the next decade the cost of a moderate-sized mill, without including machinery, appears to have been rather more than £3,000.[5]

It was the great increase in demand, especially strong in the early nineties, which induced manufacturers to lay aside their fears and workpeople, or most of them, to acquiesce in the use of spinning machinery. Exports of cloth of all kinds increased from 89,620 pieces in 1786 to 214,489 in 1791; and although they fell in 1792 and were only a little over 133,000 pieces in 1793, this was still a great advance on any year before 1788. By far the larger part, of course, came from Yorkshire, but the west had its share. In 1791 a letter to the *Gloucester Journal* in support of machinery pointed out the contrast between the current state of affairs and the depressed years of the mid-sixties when unemployment was rife, 'whereas now all the manufacturers (are) fully employed even to the children'.[6] From 1794 to 1796 exports continued to expand, though it is impossible to say how much of the mounting totals of long and short cloth came from the west. There was a distinct fall in the small quantity entered as Spanish cloth, perhaps because of the ending of the trade in cassimeres to France, which had

---

[1] All these dates were given by Charles Playne in 1871, *Stroud Journal*, 25 Feb. 1871. *V.C.H. Glos.* gives 1798 for Dunkirk mill, on what authority is not stated, and Messrs. Playne and Smith who occupied it in 1833 told the Factory Commission that it was built in 1800, *Suppl. Rept. Fact. Inq. Com. 1834, Answers to Queries*, B.1., 14.

[2] Warner, *Excursions from Bath*, p. 332. It was called New Mill but cannot have been Alderley New Mill which was then in the occupation of the Lartons.

[3] e.g. Frigg's mill, Woodchester, 'newly created' next to a grist mill, *Gloucester Journal*, 8 June 1812; Well Head mill, Westbury, with a reservoir, *Salisbury Journal*, 21 Sept. 1807.

[4] At Lullington, Som., built by a millwright of Rode in 1799, ibid., 26 Sept. 1803.

[5] Wilts. C.R.O., 540, List of Westbury mills.

[6] *Gloucester Journal*, 22 Aug. 1791.

checked the manufacture of them in Frome by 1795.[1] After that
year, however, exports of the two kinds of cloth specially
associated with the west, Spanish cloth and cassimeres, small
as they were in comparison with those of long and short cloth,
rose from a combined value of over £61,000 in 1796 to over
£300,000 in 1800[2] without any check in the depressed year of
1797; whereas those of long cloth fell slightly and those of
short cloth heavily. It was under the latter head that much
of Gloucestershire's production must have been entered, and its
clothiers joined the many other petitioners for peace, instancing
the closing of foreign ports to English exports, the reduction of
consumption at home and the scarcity of money, all of which
had created much unemployment and misery.[3] The correspondence of the Blackwell Hall factors, Hanson & Mills, well
illustrates the shortage of money from the middle of 1796 up
to the suspension of cash payments in February 1797, and the
latter led them to sarcastic but despairing comments on the
financial operations of the 'heaven-born Pitt'.[4] A year later
the home market was still dull, 'old coats are the fashion this
spring',[5] but recovery began soon afterwards. The rise in
exports was unaffected by the political events of 1798 to 1801,
beginning with the rebellion in Ireland and continuing with
the defection of Russia and the Northern Confederacy in 1799,[6]
though more than one manufacturer said in 1803 that trade
had been very flat at the beginning of this period.[7] All the same,
in spite of Russia's change of sides, Spanish cloth continued to
reach her in increasing quantities throughout 1800 and 1801;
and this trade was substantial enough to figure in the petition
which the Gloucestershire clothiers sent up in 1802 protesting

[1] Sir F. M. Eden, *State of the Poor.* ii. 644. J. Billingsley, *General View of the Agriculture of Somerset*, p. 161 (1798 ed. but written 1795), speaks of 'the present check
on exports'.

[2] Schumpeter, op. cit., Table XIII. (Computed value for Spanish cloth.)
Cassimeres were first entered separately in 1796 but the rise must be estimated by
value because the quantity (at first entered by the yard) is not given after 1797.

[3] *C.J.* lii. 463.

[4] P.R.O., C.113/18, Lr. Book, fols. 205, 253, 302–3, 308. They had reported a
scarcity of money as early as July 1795. Ibid., 37.

[5] Ibid., fol. 463.

[6] An apparent heavy fall under the headings of long and short cloth in 1799 is
more than compensated by the vast quantities under the new heading 'coloured
cloth' introduced that year.

[7] *Ev. on Woollen Trade Bill*, 1803, p. 317, 369.

against the proposal to levy import and export duties.[1] Some of the cloth exported found its way through Russia to China,[2] and several Gloucestershire manufacturers, including Edward Sheppard, the Austins, and the Coopers of Woodchester were extensively concerned in this trade.[3]

Gloucestershire was now getting ahead of Wiltshire and Somerset for a number of reasons. The manufacture of cassimeres had been introduced before 1788 and was proving very successful.[4] Black cloth had been much improved with the assistance of a French refugee, so that it could take the place of the fine French blacks from Sedan which had previously been regarded as the best in Europe.[5] The outbreak of war meant a demand for uniform cloth which was drawn from Gloucestershire as well as from Yorkshire[6]—indeed from Wiltshire and Somerset too, but not, it would appear, in so great quantity. The East India Company's exports, at 10,000 to 12,000 pieces a year in the early 1790s, were back at the level of the years before 1773; and at the turn of the century they rose from 14,000 pieces in 1798–9 to 21,500 in 1802–3 and averaged over 18,000 in the next eleven seasons up to 1813–14.[7] About half of this cloth was destined for India itself, where the wars were increasing the number of Europeans in the country; but the market in China was growing and was to become increasingly important as time went on.[8] Most important of all, perhaps,

---

[1] G.C.L., J.F. 13.8, n.d. but apparently of 1802.

[2] *First Rept. on Affairs of E.I. Co.*, 1830 (H.C. 644), pp. 193, 199.

[3] R. Cooper visited Russia in 1802, *Ev. on State of Woollen Manuf.*, 1806, p. 434. For the Austins' Russian trade see *Ev. on Woollen Trade Bill*, 1803, pp. 275 ff, 347, 350, and *First Rept. on the Affairs of the East India Company*, 1830 (H.C. 644), p. 199.

[4] The dates given in 1803 were 1789 to 1793 ('ten to fourteen years ago', *Ev. on Woollen Trade Bill*, 1803, p. 94) but John Wallington of Dursley was proposing to make them in April 1788 and his factor feared he might be undersold by two other Gloucestershire makers, Glouc. C.R.O., D.149 F.161, Lr. from John Cowley to J.W., 17 April 1788.

[5] P. Nemnich, *Beschreibung einer im Sommer 1799 von Hamburg nach und durch England geschehenen Reise*, p. 371. On his next visit, however, he remarked that they did not yet equal French blacks, *Neueste Reise*, p. 224. In 1798–9 William Phelps of Dursley was making 'French cloth', some marked, or in imitation of, 'Furneaux et Fils de Sedan', P.R.O., C.113/18, Lr. Book II, fol. 10 and C.113/17 Lr. Bk., fol. 45 ('French black').

[6] *Ev. on Woollen Trade Bill*, 1803, p. 102, and Nemnich, *Beschreibung*, loc. cit.

[7] P.R.O., B.T.6/43. The figures are given by seasons and do not correspond with those in the Custom House Ledgers.

[8] See A/c of cloth exported to China 1793–1810. *4th Rept. on East India Affairs*, 1812 (H.C. 148), p. 463.

was the fact that the better finish obtained in fine cloth by the use of the gig-mill, first introduced for this purpose in 1793 or 1794,[1] was beginning to draw the superfine trade away from Wiltshire. All these advantages had contributed to increasing, one witness said doubling, the size of the Gloucestershire trade in the ten years before 1803,[2] and a visitor in 1801 remarked that Stroud flourished 'with a vigour unknown to the manufactories of Wiltshire', though he believed this to be due to the abundant supplies of water power.[3] Evidence given in 1803 suggested that any loss of the coarse trade was not due to Yorkshire competition but was owing to the fact that the fine section was so prosperous that weavers for coarse cloth could not be found.[4] There may have been some truth in this as far as the 'lower region'—the strip along the foot of the Cotswolds from Dursley to Kingswood—was concerned. The coarse trade had been flourishing in 1794 when the fine was depressed,[5] and several manufacturers in Uley and Dursley had been making cloth for the East India Company;[6] but the normal home of this branch of the trade was in Chalford,[7] and to some extent in Painswick and Nailsworth;[8] and it continued there in considerable volume for the next thirty years.

The industry in Wiltshire and Somerset also increased, though not to so great an extent.[9] The check which had been noticeable in Frome in 1795 had vanished by 1801. When Warner visited it in that year he was told that 200 pieces of 28 yards apiece were being made every week.[10] If production had been constant, this would have resulted in a total of 291,000

---

[1] See below, pp. 141–2.

[2] *Ev. on Woollen Trade Bill*, 1803, p. 265.

[3] Warner, *Excursions from Bath*, p. 325.

[4] *Ev. on Woollen Trade Bill*, 1803, pp. 251, 280, 327.

[5] G. Turner, *General View of the Agriculture of the County of Gloucester*, p. 31.

[6] Phelps of Dursley was making both uniform cloth and cloth for the E.I. Co. in 1796 (P.R.O., C.113/18, fols. 189, 219), see above Ch. IV.

[7] *Gloucester Journal*, 7 Sept. 1807, where a mill at Brimscombe Port is advertised as being in an eligible situation 'between the coarse and the fine trade'.

[8] See sales of English wool to Painswick clothiers by J. and T. Beavan of Holt and Thomas Colfox of Bridport up to 1818–23, below, p. 276, n. 6. The Playnes of Longfords and Nailsworth also made goods for the Company.

[9] *Ev. on Woollen Trade Bill*, 1803, pp. 362–3 (Calne and Chippenham); J. Britton, *Beauties of Wilts.* ii. 49 (Warminster); *Ev. on State of Woollen Manuf.* 1806, p. 309 (Bradford).

[10] R. Warner, *Excursions from Bath*, p. 39.

yards a year, nearly twice Billingsley's estimate of 150,000 in 1795[1] (which was under the amount given for 1791);[2] but no doubt it varied considerably, and the annual total must have been much less. All the same, the estimate shows that a great advance must have taken place in Frome in the later nineties. Its neighbour Shepton Mallet, however, had begun a decline which was to be permanent; since, in addition to losing trade to Yorkshire, it was finding that its exports to Ireland were being superseded by goods made in that country, because it was easier to install machinery there.[3] All those western clothiers who made goods of English wool were extremely open to Yorkshire competition, and the Blackwell Hall factors, Hanson & Mills, like Elderton at an earlier date, warned their correspondents more than once that any rise in price would immediately result in the order being placed in the north.[4] Yet in 1796 the agricultural writer, William Marshall, could compare Frome and Trowbridge very advantageously with northern towns. 'The manufacturing areas of Lancashire and Yorkshire, more especially those of the woollen manufactures, are marked by their dirt and misery; companions, however, which it would appear in travelling through Somerset and Wiltshire are not essentially necessary to the woollen manufacture.'[5] This was perhaps a superficial judgement (especially as later descriptions make both towns appear as anything but salubrious), and other observers did not always agree;[6] but at least the passage shows that symptoms of decline were not yet present.

Considerable gloom was generated, however, among the superfine manufacturers of Wiltshire about 1800 over the partial loss of the trade to Gloucestershire;[7] and there was certainly more unemployment in the two southern counties. This made the introduction of any new device such as the fly-shuttle, which depended upon the co-operation of the weavers themselves, a much more difficult task. In the Yorkshire woollen

---

[1] Billingsley, op. cit., p. 160.
[2] See above, p. 55.
[3] *An Account of the Proceedings of the Merchants*, pp. 145 ff.
[4] P.R.O., C.113/118 Lr. Bk. fols. 11, 144.
[5] W. Marshall, *Rural Economy of the West of England* ii. 218–19, also 209, 212.
[6] Eden, op. cit. ii. 644 gives an entirely opposite view of Frome.
[7] J. Anstie, *Observations on the Importance and Necessity of introducing improved Machinery*, pp. 7, 18; *Ev. on Woollen Trade Bill*, 1803, pp. 55, 212.

industry it had been adopted very slowly after its first appearance about 1763,[1] and it had at first been regarded with
much the same aversion as was shown to it in the west;[2] but
it had been completely accepted by the eighties. It is sometimes
said to have been partially adopted in Gloucestershire by 1757,
but this statement derives from a misinterpretation of the term
'bobbing shuttle' in Dallaway's statement of the clothiers' case
after the riots of that year.[3] In 1892, when the misinterpretation first occurred,[4] it was natural to translate this phrase into
the fly-shuttle; but the discovery of the suits in Chancery which
Kay brought against Lancashire weavers proves that 'bobbing'
refers to the bobbin which was substituted for the quill upon
which the yarn was wound inside the shuttle,[5] a device which
placed less strain upon the yarn and was said to save one day
in eight in weaving a piece. The fly-shuttle proper is first heard
of at Trowbridge in 1792, when a riot followed an attempt to
introduce it.[6] There is no information to connect earlier riots
with efforts to use it, and the fact that when Henry Wansey of
Salisbury visited the United States in 1794 he noted that one
cotton mill was using 'the new-invented spring shuttle'[7] shows
that it cannot have been at all widely known. Between 1793 and
1795 much alarm was felt among Gloucestershire weavers
when a Stonehouse clothier named Watts tried to bring it in;
but other clothiers persuaded him to withdraw it, fearing disturbances.[8] Some were sold to weavers and one in 1803 said
that he had had it for nine or ten years;[9] but it was not until
the growth of the trade and enlistment in the army had led to
a real shortage of weavers, about 1798, that it was adopted by
the majority of the men.[10] By 1803 its use in the broad loom

---

[1] *Ev. on State of Woollen Manuf.* 1806, p. 166.

[2] There was a riot against it in Leeds in 1770, R. G. Wilson, 'Leeds Merchants,
1700–1830', p. 126 (unpublished thesis in the Brotherton Library, Leeds). It must
have been the prosperity of 1771–2 which induced weavers to accept it.

[3] *A State of the Case . . .*, p. 23.

[4] E. A. S. Hewins, *English Trade and Finance*, pp. 122–3.

[5] A. P. Wadsworth and J. de L. Mann, *The Cotton Trade and Industrial Lancashire,
1600–1780*, pp. 452–3. See below, p. 292.

[6] *V.C.H. Wilts.* iv. 167.

[7] H. Wansey, *Journal of an Excursion to the U.S.A.*, p. 83.

[8] *Ev. on Woollen Trade Bill*, 1803, p. 15.

[9] Ibid., p. 9.

[10] Ibid., pp. 299–300.

was widespread though not universal in Gloucestershire.[1]
Elsewhere it was hardly known. Efforts to introduce it into
Chippenham may have led to riots in 1801–3 and there were
certainly election riots in 1802 in which the use of 'machinery'
was said to have figured.[2] A few examples were in use there in
1803 but it certainly was not common. In most parts of Wiltshire it was 'not allowed',[3] and in 1800 a weaver who, having
used it in the north tried to do so at Freshford, was forced by a
mob to give it up.[4]

Up to 1793 the innovations were only concerned with spinning and weaving. The introduction of machinery for finishing
was far more strenuously resisted in Wiltshire and Somerset, as
in parts of Yorkshire, than any other process. In Gloucestershire the use of the gigmill for raising the nap upon coarse
undyed cloth before shearing it had been practised for many
years; and when it was extended first to finer white cloth and
then to fine medleys, which were more tender than any other
variety, there had been very little protest. Gloucestershire clothworkers petitioned against the extension in 1794[5] and about
the same time an inconclusive action was brought against a
Wiltshire clothier who had tried to introduce it, on the ground
that it was the machine prohibited by an Act of Edward VI.[6]
The Gloucestershire petitioners had not invoked this Act because they were told that if they did so 'common informers

[1] Ibid., pp. 6, 7, 262, 358. It was hardly known in cassimere weaving, no doubt
because the presence of more than two treadles made the work already more com-
plex. Ibid., p. 282.

[2] An account of persistent rioting in Chippenham in 1801–3 is given by J.
Daniell, *History of Chippenham*, p. 91, and in the case of the election riots of 1802
it was suggested (but denied) that the cries for the respective candidates were
'Maitland and Machinery' and 'Brooke and Freedom', *Ev. on Woollen Trade Bill*,
1803, p. 189. See also G.C.L., J.F.13.27, fol. 14, 'Questions to be asked of Mr.
Brooke'.

[3] *Ev. on Woollen Trade Bill*, 1803, pp. 81, 83.

[4] *C.J.* lviii. 885, Ev. of T. Joyce.

[5] *C.J.* xlix. 599.

[6] P.R.O., H.O.42/83. Lr. from J. Read, 19 Feb. 1805. He gave the date as twelve
years ago (1793) but in a later note in the same file he said ten years ago (1795) at
Salisbury Assizes. The only entry in the Assize Min. Book for the Western Circuit
(P.R.O., Assizes 2/4) which seems at all likely to be this case is that of Roberts v.
Saunders, which was heard and compromised at Salisbury in March 1794. If this
is so, Saunders would presumably have been Joseph Saunders the Bradford clothier.
But the case was not reported in the local Press, which is odd if, as Read stated,
the affair caused great interest.

would proceed to destroy the gigmills entirely', and they had no wish to interfere with the long established practice of using them to finish 'army and coarse cloth, since they are not injured by it and it is cheaper'. In the subsequent debate much was made by the clothiers of the possible difference between the gigmill they were using and that described in the Statute. In fact, the two must have been substantially the same.[1] The gigmill can never have been disused in Gloucestershire. The last occasion on which it was forbidden was in 1633, and even then the prohibition had had to be limited to the setting up of new machines.[2] It is mentioned in documents of 1652 and 1678,[3] and in 1707 coarse cloth for export was being finished by it before being sent to London.[4] From this time onwards there is plenty of evidence of its use for this purpose. In the eighteenth century it is unusual to find an advertisement of a fulling mill which does not include a gigmill on the premises. On the other hand, its use did not extend beyond the area in Gloucestershire and north Wiltshire[5] which made cloth for India and the Levant; when William Everett at Horningsham, south of Warminster, tried to introduce one in 1767, it was attacked and destroyed.[6] Thus, while the antipathy of Gloucestershire clothworkers to the extension of its use to fine cloth was easily overcome, that of their counterparts in Wiltshire and Somerset, who had never known it in connection with coarse cloth, was constant and unyielding. Even though its illegality had been left undecided by the Salisbury trial, no clothier in Wiltshire or Somerset, with the exception of those on the outskirts of Bath, introduced it in the nineties, no doubt because they were intimidated by the hostility of the clothworkers. It was not until 1801, when they found themselves losing trade to Gloucestershire because of the better finish obtained by its use, that its introduction appeared to be imperative. It was unfortunate for them that the depression of the winter of 1801–2 and the return of men from the army had led to more unemployment than usual.[7] Men 'sent

---

[1] See below, p. 300.   [2] See B. Supple, op. cit., p. 146.
[3] Glouc. C.R.O., D.822, T.53, T.68.   [4] *C.J.* xv. 456.
[5] Only two have so far been discovered in Wilts., at Bulkington mill in 1730 (*V.C.H. Wilts.* viii. p. 258) and at Widenham mill, Colerne, in 1752, *Gloucester Journal*, 7 July 1752. But cf. Anstie, *Observations on the Importance . . .*, p. 69.
[6] *Bath Chronicle*, 6 Aug. 1767. See below, p. 302.
[7] *Ev. on Woollen Trade Bill*, 1803, pp. 99, 187 (Wilts. and Som.); pp. 11, 16, 35, 89, 91 (Glos.).

home to starve',[1] with their military experience behind them, were probably the instigators of most of the attacks on mills and other possessions of clothiers in the summer of 1802.

At the same time the Gloucestershire weavers had started a movement of their own to prosecute clothiers who transgressed against another statute of Edward VI by employing weavers who had not been apprenticed. Most of them had not been formally apprenticed themselves, and, as they stated again and again, they did not wish to interfere with men who had worked at the trade under supervision for seven years, whether or not they had been bound by indenture.[2] The object of the movement was simply to make it impossible for masters to set up loom shops in which they could employ men without experience under a foreman who knew the trade. The riots which had resulted from this practice in Wiltshire as far back as 1787 have already been described;[3] and there had been one in Gloucestershire in 1792 when a mob, which had begun by attacking a weaver for working, as they believed, under price, had gone on to threaten the loomship of his master in Uley.[4] It is difficult to estimate how far such shops had spread in Gloucestershire. Where broadlooms were concerned there were very few.[5] The motive for establishing them was to prevent the embezzlement almost universally practised by weavers who worked in their own homes, but some clothiers thought they were uneconomic because of the size of the buildings required.[6] Cassimeres woven on the narrow loom were a different proposition, and the greatest concentration of weaving shops for this species appears to have been on the Cotswold slopes and around Dursley, where several clothiers had set them up, although one at least said that he only kept his men until they had learned the new technique and was glad to let them go.[7] There were very few round Stroud, where clothiers had not taken up

---

[1] P.R.O., H.O.42/65, Lr. of Bradford shearmen to B. Hobhouse, M.P., July 1802.

[2] Clothiers' Brief to Counsel on Bill of 1803, citing the weavers' case, G.C.L., J.F.13.5; *Gloucester Journal*, 13 Dec. 1802.

[3] Above, p. 115.

[4] G.C.L., R.V.319.6 (1–52). Account of riot 8 June 1792, esp. ev. of Wm. Webb.

[5] Larton had 20 at Alderley and there were a few elsewhere, *Ev. on State of the Woollen Manuf.*, 1806, pp. 332, 334–5; *Ev. on Woollen Trade Bill*, 1803, p. 16.

[6] Ibid., pp. 250, 298, 344; *C.J.* lviii. 886.

[7] *Ev. on Woollen Trade Bill*, 1803, p. 266.

cassimeres with the same enthusiasm as those in the Dursley
area. It was the fear that the practice would spread, rather than
its actual extent, which prompted the institution of prosecutions.[1] The Gloucestershire weavers found ready allies in the
other counties, where there were probably more cassimere
weaving shops, although those for broad looms were exceedingly
rare.[2] It was, however, quite usual there for weavers and others
to keep several looms in their houses and to take work in bulk
which they sublet to others, either on their own premises or in
the weavers' own houses;[3] and weavers considered that three
broad or six narrow looms should be the limit of the number
allowed in one shop. Nevertheless, the movement against un-
apprenticed weavers was always primarily a Gloucestershire
affair, just as that against the gigmill was the preserve of Wiltshire and Somerset. Here Gloucestershire sympathizers could
not give much assistance, though they provided some evidence
from men who had worked on the gigmill and had subsequently moved elsewhere.

The two movements became entwined in the autumn of
1802 when Gloucestershire clothiers, who were facing prosecutions for employing unapprenticed weavers, met in Bath those
from Wiltshire and Somerset who had already formed a fund
to prosecute the authors of the outrages committed in the past
summer.[4] The combined body resolved to petition Parliament
for the repeal of all the restrictive statutes. Yorkshire employers
were drawn in a good deal later, although the shearmen, much
to the dismay of the Government, already had sympathizers
there. It is difficult to decide in which area the struggle against
the gigmill began. Just as Gloucestershire had shown no great
opposition to it, so in Yorkshire clothiers in the Huddersfield
district had been able to use a few on fine cloth without difficulty.[5] The machine had been known for sixty years,[6] and it

[1] Ev. of Joseph Bailey, echoed by John Phillis of Shepton Mallet, ibid., pp. 58, 63.
[2] Ibid., pp. 98, 338, 369; *C.J.* lviii. 887. The only known loomshop for broad
looms in Wilts. is that of Hill at Malmesbury, *Ev. on Woollen Trade Bill*, 1803, p. 78.
[3] Ibid., pp. 59, 75. Cf. the practice of J. & T. Clark at Trowbridge of putting
out most of their weaving to one or two men, 'The Trowbridge Woollen Industry',
ed. R. P. Beckinsale, *W.A.S., Rec. Brch.* vol. vi, pp. xix, xx.
[4] Min. Bk. of the Joint Ctee., 1 Nov. 1802, G.C.L., J.F.13.25.
[5] Crump, op. cit., p. 46.
[6] *Ev. on Woollen Trade Bill*, 1803, pp. 247, 373. There had been an agitation
against it in 1747 in Lancashire, Wadsworth and Mann, op. cit., p. 353.

seems probable that, as in Gloucestershire, it was a survival from the seventeenth century. It was thought in the west that the shearmen's headquarters were in Yorkshire,[1] but a Yorkshire witness in 1806 believed that the whole movement had been inspired from the west;[2] and, on the whole, this seems to be more probable.[3]

The ensuing struggle has often been described, notably by the Hammonds,[4] and Professor Aspinall has published many of the documents.[5] Parliament was unable to make up its mind. The first repeal bill in 1803 was stopped in the House of Lords, and from that time the question came up every year without the House of Commons ever having time to give its full attention to it. In spite of two full-scale Parliamentary inquiries in 1803 and 1806, it was not until 1809 that repeal finally took place. Meanwhile the laws were suspended year by year. The manufacturers, who had thought that they had an unassailable case, were thoroughly disillusioned.[6] They did not include by any means all the clothiers in the area. Eighty-three signed the Gloucestershire petition for repeal and it was said that only one of the 'respectable' clothiers had refused,[7] but there were many in a small way of business who were ignored. Even so, only seventy-eight of the eighty-three appear to have contributed to expenses and a few of these defaulted before the end.[8] In the other counties it is more difficult to ascertain who the supporters were, since no list of those who attended the early Bath meetings is in existence and later proceedings were carried on by a Committee of five, John Jones of Staverton, A. L. Edridge of Chippenham, Thomas Joyce of Freshford, Henry Wansey Jr.

[1] A. Aspinall, *The Early English Trade Unions*, no. 55.

[2] *Ev. on state of Woollen Manuf.*, 1806, pp. 191–2.

[3] Cf. Speech of Mr. Dickinson in the House of Commons, 6 Apr. 1803, *Parl. Reg.* vol. 82, p. 594.

[4] J. L. and B. Hammond, *The Skilled Labourer*, pp. 167–90.

[5] See n. 1 above.

[6] Minute Bk. of Joint Ctee., 23 Nov. 1803, G.C.L., J.F.13.25.

[7] There are several lists of signatories in varying numbers in G.C.L., J.F.13.6 and 13.25, but the main one is in J.F.13.27, fol. 35 which contains the 83 names to the petition itself, as stated by the clothiers, *Ev. on Woollen Trade Bill*, 1803, p. 250. An incomplete list containing only 74 names has been printed by J. Tann, *Gloucestershire Woollen Mills*, pp. 44–6. A 'respectable' clothier was one who employed about thirty looms according to one witness in 1803, *Ev. on Woollen Trade Bill*, 1803, p. 37.

[8] G.C.L., J.F.13.27, fols. 36–40, 91.

of Warminster, and William Sheppard Jr. of Frome.[1] These, with the exception of Sheppard, seem to have been the main users of the gigmill in this area,[2] although eighteen clothiers of Wiltshire and Somerset were said to have signed a petition for the repeal of the statute concerning it.[3] It would appear that many who had contributed to the fund for the prosecution of those who had committed outrages were not consulted about the petition for repeal or the use of the remainder of the fund to pay expenses, and would not have consented if they had been.[4] The smaller clothiers were not anxious to participate in a movement which gave an advantage to the men who could afford new machinery and it was believed that many of the independent clothworkers were actively supporting the shearmen.[5]

The expenses on the manufacturers' side were at first mainly borne by the western petitioners, three-fifths by the fund already established by the Wiltshire and Somerset clothiers, and the remaining two-fifths by those of Gloucestershire.[6] In the latter county the 78 firms contributing were divided into three classes, of which the 11 placed in the first class contributed £20 each, 22 in the second £12 each, and 43 in the third £6 each. There was a second call in May 1803 and a double one in November to which a few contributors did not respond.[7] By 1804 Wiltshire and Somerset clothiers were heartily sick of the expense and Gloucestershire could not obtain co-operation from them for a new statement of their case, 'as the very declining and impoverished state of the manufacture in those counties have (sic) rendered individuals unable to subscribe . . . and indifferent even to the existence of the trade'.[8] In 1805 the

---

[1] J.F.13.25, Minute Bk 1 Nov. 1802.

[2] There were some others in Chippenham, *Ev. on Woollen Trade Bill*, 1803, pp. 110, 142, 146, 362. Wm. Sheppard of Frome (brother of Edward of Uley) was sending his cloth to be gigged in Gloucestershire. A Bradford clothworker knew of no gigmills at Trowbridge or any except that of Jones at Staverton, ibid., p. 181.

[3] G.C.L., J.F.13.5, fol. 75, Brief to Counsel in support of the bill of 1803. This petition is not entered in the *Journals*.

[4] *Ev. on Woollen Trade Bill*, 1803, pp. 133, 149, 187, 199, 201, 205, 365. Jones certainly exaggerated in saying that those who approved did seven-eighths of the trade, ibid., pp. 339, 345. A petition against repeal was signed by 13 Chippenham clothiers, ibid., pp. 154, 182.

[5] Aspinall, op. cit., no. 61.

[6] G.C.L., J.F.13.25, Min. of meeting 1 Nov. 1802.

[7] J.F.13.27, fols. 91, 149.   [8] Ibid., fol. 113.

total expenses had amounted to £6,557 14s.[1] of which Yorkshire had only contributed £240 10s. in spite of a resolution by the merchants and manufacturers of Huddersfield in December 1803 to pay a proportionate share.[2] When the Western Joint Committee met to settle accounts, it was ordered that no further expense whatsoever should be undertaken without the written consent of the two chairmen.[3] The solicitors had found such difficulty in extracting payment for their services that one of them was driven to write that 'neither of us can speak with satisfaction of the conduct we have experienced, . . . but it will be a good lesson'.[4] At the end of 1806 Wiltshire and Somerset were disputing with Gloucestershire over a sum of £203 which was said to be owing from the former, and Joyce was still arguing about his share in 1807.[5] It is for this reason that the witnesses on the manufacturers' side at the Parliamentary Committee of 1806 came almost wholly from Yorkshire. The Gloucestershire Committee still had some funds[6] and it may have paid the expenses of the two Gloucestershire clothiers who spoke in favour of the gigmill, but it seems probable that they were called by the solicitors for the Yorkshire manufacturers, for at the end of 1806 Jones, having recovered from the gloom of 1804, was accusing Gloucestershire of refusing to co-operate in the last session of Parliament and declaring his intention to go on to the end.[7]

The men also continued to the end,[8] but whether they were ever able to pay their lawyers in full is very doubtful. Their expenses in connection with the 1803 Committee amounted to upwards of £3,000 according to the solicitor for the Wiltshire and Somerset men, but the Gloucestershire solicitor, Mr. Jessop,

---

[1] Ibid., fol. 94.

[2] J.F.13.19. Sixteen Blackwell Hall factors contributed £50 each (*Gloucester Journal*, 11 Oct. 1802) but this does not appear in the accounts.

[3] J.F.13.25, Min. Bk 22 Jan. 1805. The Gloucestershire chairman was Edward Sheppard.

[4] J.F.13.27, fol. 103.

[5] Ibid., fols. 152–3.

[6] At a meeting in Aug. 1805 there had been a balance of £378. 16s. No further meeting was held until 1812 when the balance was £300. 17s. 5d. which the Ctee resolved should remain at interest to be used for the benefit of the trade. *Gloucester Journal*, 13 Apr. 1812.

[7] J.F.13.27, fol. 151. He seems to have acted alone.

[8] The last petitions were sent up on 2 May and 26 May 1809, praying for a hearing which was not granted, *C.J.* lxiv. 268, 349.

through whose hands the bills passed, gave the figure for these as only £1,500.[1] Jessop has received rather less than the credit due to him. A Cheltenham solicitor (whose firm is still in existence and whose family in due course produced the famous cricketer G. L. Jessop) he played a highly responsible part in the proceedings of the Gloucestershire weavers up to the end of 1803, drawing up their rules and taking the chair at their meetings. It was probably owing to his influence that the judge who presided at the only trial of a clothier for employing un-apprenticed weavers was able to compliment the prosecutors on their peaceable behaviour.[2] This case was not pressed to a verdict, but the judge expressed himself strongly in favour of apprenticeship,[3] as had also the chairman of the Gloucestershire Quarter Sessions earlier in the year.[4] The aspersions cast by the manufacturers on Jessop's motives and character were totally unfounded.[5] He had received nothing for himself by 1806 and there was about £70 due to him for fees he had paid.[6] The weavers, as their Counsel pointed out in 1806,[7] were only copying the manufacturers in combining for a legal purpose and they had firmly disassociated themselves from all other movements in defence of the statutes, though in 1804 they did support an abortive bill brought in on behalf of the domestic clothiers of Yorkshire, to permit a greater number of looms to be kept in private houses but to forbid the establishment of weaving shops.[8] The men could not lobby as the employers did[9] (not that lobbying had assisted their cause as much as they had expected), and their active supporters were few and not very effective.[10] But it was only after the Committee of 1806,

---

[1] *Ev. on State of Woollen Manuf.*, 1806, p. 350. This did not include any remuneration for himself.

[2] *Gloucester Journal*, 6 Sept. 1802.   [3] Ibid., 9 Aug. 1802.

[4] Ibid., 3 May 1802.   [5] *Ev. on Woollen Trade Bill*, 1803, pp. 47 ff.

[6] *Ev. on State of Woollen Manuf.*, 1806, pp. 350–1. The bills of the clothiers' solicitors amounted to over £3,000 in all.

[7] Speech of E. Wigley on behalf of the woollen weavers, 1806, p. 37, G.C.L., 36–3,165. Cf. *Gloucester Journal*, 25 Oct. 1802.

[8] *The Case of the Woollen Weavers in Gloucestershire and Wilts.* G.C.L., J.F.13.9(2); *C.J.* lix. 226, 245, 322, 337.

[9] Many details of their activities in this direction are to be found in the Minutes of the Joint Ctee in London, J.F.13.26.

[10] Charles Brooke, whom the Hammonds call the men's champion, had been elected M.P. for Chippenham but was unseated on petition. He sat just long enough to give evidence to the first H. of C. Ctee, *C.J.* lviii. 889. He was returned

with its emphasis on Yorkshire, that the conversion of Wilberforce to the view that the abolition of apprenticeship would not injure the domestic clothiers there led eventually to repeal.

In Wiltshire and Somerset where the struggle was primarily against finishing machinery, both weavers and clothworkers were far less peaceable. There was obviously some intimidation of workers,[1] and much rumour and exaggeration of the manufacturers' intentions,[2] just as the latter exaggerated the revolutionary attitude of the men.[3] Everything suggests that the active agitators were comparatively few, but the whole body of workers was deeply suspicious and resentful, especially after the execution of a young man named Hilleker for arson in connection with the burning of Littleton mill, a crime of which he was believed to be innocent. The appearance at Freshford, in January 1803, of a poster declaring it to be the wish of the community that the shearmen should bid defiance to the military by force of arms and asking all men who had arms and ammunition to give in their names[4] must have stimulated fears of renewed violence. The determined resistance to the gigmill appears to have been due to the belief that its use was only the first step to the introduction of the shearing frame[5] which, as the Government agent foresaw, would in time 'entirely cut out the artists in that branch of the trade'.[6] It is possible that this was Jones's intention at Staverton,[7] but most manufacturers do not appear to have contemplated such a step. The few who did use it only did so when the men's refusal to work after the gigmill made it impossible to get cloth finished in any other way.[8]

The shearing machine in question had been invented by an

again for Ilminster in 1805. He had his own reasons for hostility to the clothiers (see below, p. 267) but he did not press the men's case with any insistence, see *Parl. Reg.* vol. 89, p. 360. Peter Moore, the Member for Coventry, was a much more strenuous advocate.

[1] Aspinall, op. cit., nos. 45, 52; *Ev. on Woollen Trade Bill*, 1803, p. 370.

[2] Ibid., p. 58; Anstie, *Observations on the Importance* . . ., p. 87.

[3] G.C.L., J.F.13.5, fol. 78, Brief to Counsel in support of Bill of 1803.

[4] *Gloucester Journal*, 31 Jan. 1803. The wording clearly indicates that it emanated from returned soldiers.

[5] Clothworkers' petition, cited in Clothiers' Brief to Counsel, J.F.13.5, fol. 78.

[6] Aspinall, op. cit., no. 61.

[7] Cf. Britton, *Beauties of Wilts*. ii. 308, written in 1801 when Staverton mill was being built.

[8] Aspinall, op. cit., no. 61.

Independent minister in Sheffield, John Harmer, who took out his first patent in 1787 and a second improved one in 1794.[1] It had, of course, appeared far too late for any statutory prohibition, and it was therefore not mentioned in the petition for the repeal of the statutes. References to it by witnesses in 1803 were disallowed,[2] so that we know less than we otherwise might of the extent to which it was employed at this date. It was said to do the work more evenly than any but the best shearmen but there was not much economy in time to be made by using it.[3] Apart from the mills at Twerton,[4] we know of no instance of its use in Wiltshire and Somerset except for Jones's machine at Staverton and possibly one or more at Warminster;[5] but in Gloucestershire a few may have been installed in the last years of the century.[6] Paul Wathen had one at Woodchester in 1801[7] and it earned him a threatening letter in the following year,[8] apparently the only instance of such a document in Gloucestershire at this time. No violence followed. One reason for the apparent apathy displayed by Gloucestershire shearmen was given many years later by the anonymous writer already quoted who said that they had welcomed the earlier machinery for scribbling and carding and had even consented to be enrolled as special constables to guard against any disturbance by the scribblers; so that when they themselves came to be displaced (which they had thought would never happen) they could hardly complain, for the scribblers would have shown them up and they would have been ridiculed ever after.[9]

Finishing machinery remained rare in Wiltshire and Somer-

[1] Patents 1595 and 1982. I am indebted to the Sheffield City Librarian for such information as exists about Harmer. See below, p. 302.

[2] *Ev. on Woollen Trade Bill*, 1803, p. 118. In 1806 they were allowed.

[3] *Ev. on State of Woollen Manuf.*, 1806, p. 427.

[4] See above, p. 134, n. 6.

[5] Aspinall, loc. cit.

[6] *Ev. on Woollen Trade Bill*, 1803, pp. 174–5. A witness in 1806 said they had not been in use in Glos. more than ten years. *Ev. on State of Woollen Manufacture*, 1806, p. 325. But Wathen in 1800 said they were not in use, *Account of the Proceedings of the Merchants*, p. 161.

[7] R. Warner, *Excursions from Bath*, p. 323. Warner says he invented it, but the description suggests that it was Harmer's machine.

[8] D. M. Hunter, *The West of England Woollen Industry under Protection and Free Trade*, p. 21.

[9] Art. in *Stroud Journal*, 18 July 1868.

set, except in some country places, until the end of the war. Even the fly-shuttle was only used here and there, whereas in Gloucestershire both that and the gigmill were universal by 1806 and the shearing frame had been adopted by some of the larger firms.[1] This difference between the two areas was no doubt assisted by the greater prosperity of Gloucestershire, but that is not to say that Wiltshire and Somerset were not prosperous also. Whatever truth there may have been in the statement about the languishing state of the industry there in 1804,[2] conditions soon improved. John and Thomas Clark, hardworking young men in Trowbridge who had recently begun trade and whose capital at the end of 1804 amounted to just over £1,700, made a profit of 30 per cent in 1805.[3] The years from 1808 onwards were not propitious to the industry anywhere in England, but although western manufacturers said that the Orders in Council had done them much harm, they appear to have suffered less than Yorkshire both from their direct effect and from the various periods of non-intercourse with the United States ending with the war of 1812–13. No petition against them reached Parliament from the west in 1808 or 1812, though Yorkshire sent one up in the latter year.[4] This was probably due to the fact that production for export was not so important for them as for Yorkshire. Where they did depend upon it the picture was different. Those who traded with Russia, which they regarded as one of their best markets,[5] suffered considerably from her declaration of war in 1807. If we may assume, as seems likely, that all the Spanish cloth and cassimeres exported there came from the west, its loss would have meant well over £160,000 per annum.[6] One firm for which

[1] Trowbridge is a partial exception for the use of the fly-shuttle, see below, p. 160. Nemnich (*Neueste Reise*, p. 225) gives the impression that shearing frames were very widely used in Gloucestershire by 1805–6, but no doubt he saw only a few large establishments.

[2] See above, p. 146.

[3] *W.A.S., Rec. Brch.* xix., p. 20. (The figure of £1,634 given on p. xxxi as 'money in trade' would appear by reference to p. 20 to be a mistake for £1,762.)

[4] *C.J.* lxvii. 266.

[5] See G.C.L., J.F.13.27, fol. 118. Petition to Lord Bathurst on the conclusion of peace in 1814.

[6] Average exports per annum to Russia of Spanish cloth and cassimeres for the 7 years 1801–7 inclusive amounted to a computed value of about £167,000 (P.R.O., Customs 17/23–29), far more than to any other destination. There are no details of exports for 1808–11.

this was serious was that of H. & G. Austin of Wotton-under-Edge. An account book belonging to George Austin shows that, while his share of profits in 1805 had been £6,975, nothing was drawn in 1807 and profits remained low until 1811–12 when he drew £15,918 for the two years.[1] The loss caused by the interruption of access to the American market is more difficult to assess. One Trowbridge clothier said long afterwards that when the war had closed the market with France his business had been half kept on by American orders,[2] but the Spanish cloth and cassimeres exported to the United States in 1807 were valued at some £62,000 and the whole of the short cloth sent there amounted only to 3,786 pieces.[3]

To offset such losses Gloucestershire seems to have had almost the sole custom of the East India Company.[4] Their purchases provided a regular source of income to those manufacturers who did not make fine cloth (and to some of those who did); and, together with the demand for uniform cloth, did much to prevent the severe unemployment which had prevailed in some years of the eighteenth century. About 1807 the Company altered its practice of buying through factors to one of dealing directly by contract with the makers, a change which seems to have been prompted by complaints from the manufacturers of the serges known as 'long ells', and particularly by Thomas Fox of Wellington.[5] The new method had the advantage of preventing the locking up of capital in unsaleable goods; and although factors still had to be employed as representatives in London, the manufacturer knew at the beginning how much cloth he was liable for. Most Gloucestershire makers, however, would have preferred freedom to export through private merchants. Several in the west of the county, who had been making cloth for the Company about 1790, opposed the retention of

---

[1] Glouc. C.R.O., Austin Papers, D.2078. Bound book containing accounts from 1805. The decline had begun in 1806 when he recorded only £700 'from trade' though exports to Russia rose slightly both in 1806 and 1807, but payment no doubt took at least a year and possibly more. See also p. 183, notes 1 and 2.

[2] *Bath Chronicle*, 13 Jan. 1842, Samuel Salter.

[3] P.R.O., Customs 17/29.

[4] The Company gave Glos. 'a decided preference', see petition from its clothiers in 1812, *C.J.* lxvii. 378. For the quantity involved see above, p. 137.

[5] H. Fox, op. cit., pp. 109–10. In 1808 the Company was advertising for tenders for six qualities of cloth, *Gloucester Journal*, 5 Sept. 1808.

its monopoly when its Charter came up for renewal in 1812.[1] On the other hand the Company's regular makers in the Stroud-water region were just as anxious for its continuance.[2] When the Charter was finally renewed with the loss of the Company's monopoly of trade to India but the retention of it with China, exports fell for a time, but from 1813–15 trade to other markets was improving.

There were, of course, several casualties from war conditions. By 1812 at least six of the seventy-eight Gloucestershire clothiers who had contributed to the cost of repealing the restrictive statutes, as well as several lesser ones, had gone bankrupt and two others had sold their mills, houses, and furniture and left the county.[3] In Wiltshire John Jones of Staverton was bankrupt in 1812[4] but the other promoters of repeal remained in business. The Clarks made a profit of under 6 per cent in 1808, but they did better in 1809 and reached between 17 and 21 per cent in the years up to 1812, when they rose to 33 per cent. Early in that year the Dorset woolstapler, Thomas Colfox, was writing of the 'very large quantity of fine cloth which have (sic) been and continue to be manufactured (of Spanish wool) especially in Somerset, Wiltshire, and Gloucester-shire'.[5] Trowbridge and Bradford were fairly well-to-do throughout, and so, in spite of complaints, was that part of Gloucestershire which had taken the lead in making cassimeres and Spanish cloth, the area surrounding the rivers Cam and Little Avon under the scarp of the Cotswolds from Dursley to Kingswood. The figures of early censuses are known to be defective and there were, no doubt, more men in the army in 1811

---

[1] *C.J.* lxvii. 321; *Gloucester Journal*, 13 and 20 Apr. 1812. The petition is in G.C.L., J.F.13.21. The leaders of the anti-Company movement were Sheppard, Austin, Wallington, R. Cooper, and D. Lloyd. Sheppard & Wallington had been making cloth for it in 1790, see Glos. C.R.O., D.149, F.161, Lr. from J. Cowley to J. Wallington, 19 Mar. 1790; *Ev. on Woollen Trade Bill*, 1803, p. 323.

[2] *C.J.* lxvii. 378; *Gloucester Journal*, 27 Apr. and 4 May 1812. The leaders were S. Wathen, W. and P. Playne, J. Innell, C. Ballenger, N. Wathen, W. Bayliss, S. Wood, W. Gardiner, J. Iles, and D. Cox. All who can be identified came from the Stroudwater region.

[3] 25 Gloucestershire clothiers were bankrupt in the seven years from 1806–12 and several others made arrangements with their creditors. Those who left the county were T. Larton of Alderley and J. Remmington of Horsley, both in 1808. *Gloucester Journal*, 16 and 28 May and 1 Aug. 1808.

[4] *Bath Chronicle*, 24 Dec. 1812.

[5] Dorset C.R.O., Colfox Letters, Lr. of 8 Feb. 1812.

than in 1801; but, for what it is worth, a comparison of the Census returns for these two years shows that, while the population of the region as a whole increased by 5½ per cent, the parishes in the Stroudwater basin and its tributaries, from Chalford down to Eastington, showed a rise of only 3 per cent (provided almost entirely by Bisley, Stonehouse, King's Stanley, and Eastington) while those adjacent to the Cam and Little Avon, the 'Lower Region', increased by 11 per cent.[1] Similarly in Wiltshire and Somerset the towns of Chippenham, Calne, and Devizes showed small decreases and the area round Shepton Mallet one of some 8 per cent; but Bradford, Trowbridge, and Frome with their surrounding villages received an over-all increase of between 7 and 8 per cent, only four of the villages showing small declines.[2]

The rise in exports after the withdrawal of the Orders in Council in 1812 was considerable; and anticipations of peace, which was finally achieved in 1814, in Europe in March and in America in December, led to rising prosperity in 1813–14, although manufacturers who made goods for the United States suffered as long as the war continued. Exports in 1814 were rather higher than two years previously and those for 1815 much higher[3] in spite of the Napoleonic interlude. The Clarks made a profit of over 50 per cent in 1814 and a year earlier George Austin had recorded £8,821 'from trade'.[4] In Trowbridge there was a rush to acquire land along the river bank, the Biss having suddenly gained a reputation for piece-dyeing.[5] It must have been about this time that 'a good weaver was scarcer than a jewel'[6] and the scarcity may have assisted the adoption of the fly-shuttle, at least in Trowbridge. Steam engines were also coming in, though slowly. Gloucestershire and Wiltshire

[1] Many places in the Stroudwater region showed decreases including Stroud itself, while the only one in the Lower Region which did so was the tiny parish of Owlpen.

[2] Hilperton, Freshford, Tellisford, and Berkley. The total loss in these places only amounted to 72 persons.

[3] No figures are available for 1813 owing to the fire at the Custom House. For 1814 see *Account of the Quantity of Woollen Goods and Yarn exported in the yrs. ending 5 Jan. 1813 and 5 Jan. 1815* (1814–15, H.C. 467).

[4] However he made an unexplained loss in 1814, due perhaps to the 'imprudence' which led to his being insolvent when he died in 1815, see below, p. 183.

[5] Bodman, *History of Trowbridge*, p. 13.

[6] 'Thirty Years ago' in 1839, *Repts. of Asst. Commrs. for Hdloom Weavers*, 1840, Pt. II, p. 441 n.

could each show one in 1805,[1] but by 1815 Wiltshire and Somerset had a considerable lead. At that time only four can be traced in Gloucestershire,[2] where most manufacturers seem to have shared the opinion expressed by a Yorkshire counterpart in 1800 that steam was not necessary where there was a good fall of water.[3] In Wiltshire and Somerset, where good falls were scarcer, the opening of the Somerset Coal Canal in 1811, with its promise of cheaper fuel, hastened their installation in Trowbridge and Bradford. Frome, which was not served by the canal but was not far from the Somerset coalfield, had one engine of 4 h.p. before 1810;[4] and William Sheppard put one into his Spring Gardens mill in 1811.[5] Others had been erected by 1812 at Salisbury and Bradford (but the proprietors of these soon became bankrupt possibly as a result of the expense).[6] Coal at the pithead in the southern section of the Mendip coalfield was only 3¾d. per bushel in 1795 or (assuming that the large Somerset bushel equalled one hundredweight) about 6s. 3d. per ton; but the cost of transport by hilly roads to Frome raised this to a much higher figure. The retail price in Midsomer Norton, which was much nearer to the pithead than Frome, was 8½d. to 9d. per bushel between 1808 and 1817, or 14s. 2d. to 15s. per ton;[7] but when the Clarks installed a steam engine in 1815 they paid 24s. 6d.[8] This must be contrasted with the 6s. 8d. per ton paid by Benjamin Gott in Leeds in 1800, though Saddleworth on the Lancashire border was paying 14s. to 15s.[9] In Gloucestershire

[1] *Trowbridge Advertiser*, 11 Apr. 1857. The Gloucestershire one was installed by Sheppard at Uley, J. Tann, op. cit., p. 135.

[2] The others were at Steep Mill, Wotton-under-Edge, before 1811, where there was no water on the site (see articles of partnership between George and Edward Austin, 1 Jan. 1811, Glos. C.R.O., D.2078); Strange's mill also at Wotton by 1812 (Tann, op. cit., p. 105) and possibly at Longfords mill, A. T. Playne, *Minchinhampton and Avening*, p. 153.

[3] *An Account of the Proceedings of the Merchants*, p. 113. This remark, made by John Ratcliffe of Saddleworth, is omitted from the *Ev. relating to Wool*, 1800 (see p. 130, n. 1).

[4] *Salisbury Journal*, 7 May 1810.

[5] Som. C.R.O., DD/LW/244, Scrap Book of E. A. Singer.

[6] *Bath Chronicle*, 30 Apr. (Salisbury), 28 May (Bradford), 5 Nov. (Woolley nr. Bradford), all 1812.

[7] J. A. Bulley, 'To Mendip for Coal', *Proc. Som. Arch. Soc.* xcvii. 46 ff. All the details of Mendip coal are taken from this article.

[8] *W.A.S., Rec. Brch.* vi, xxvi.

[9] *Ev. relating to Wool*, 1800 (see above, n. 3), p. 21, but small coal was 4s. to 5s. a ton cheaper, *Account of the Proceedings of the Merchants*, p. 117.

in the same year the cost was 18s. to 21s. per ton.[1] Trow-bridge, which was not very well situated for water power, prob-ably used more steam in 1815 than any other western centre. When the Clarks were proposing to insure the mill in which they intended to place a steam engine, they enumerated eight other mills similar to their own on which the premium was 7s. 6d. per £100 insured;[2] presumably therefore all eight had steam engines already.

[1] *Account of the Proceedings of the Merchants*, p. 162.
[2] Wilts. C.R.O., 927, Clark Papers, Book marked 'Insurance'.

VI

'STAGNATION AND DECLINE',
1815–1842

'In 1815 . . . the trade began to stagnate. Since 1820 it has retrograded', wrote Anthony Austin, the Commissioner investigating the condition of handloom weavers in the south-west of England in 1839.[1] He was not referring to Gloucester-shire on which a different Commissioner, W. A. Miles, reported; but by 1840 the decline was as evident there as it was further south. In the early years after the peace the Gloucestershire industry seems to have weathered the post-war depression better than that of Yorkshire, perhaps because its manufac-turers, serving predominantly the home market, were less subject to the aftermath of the over-speculation which had taken place in 1814. This is not to say that there was no distress. Apart from the general depression in trade, the change from war to peace meant a great drop in the demand for uniform cloth which caused much unemployment in Bisley and Chal-ford, as well as in some parts of Wiltshire and Somerset. It was in Warminster that a vivid memory was retained by the Wansey family of cloth commissioned for the Austrian Army which was thrown on the manufacturer's hands and made the drawing-room curtains and the daughters' dresses for many years.[2] The loss after 1812 of the East India Company's monopoly of trade with India meant a heavy fall in its exports of cloth between the seasons of 1814–15 and 1818–19 inclusive,[3] although the Company did not altogether cease sending cloth

---

[1] *Repts. Asst. Commrs. Hdloom. Weavers*, 1840, Pt. II on S. W. England by A. Austin, p. 438 n. Both this and the report from W. Miles on Glos. in Pt. V are dated early in 1839, though not published until 1840.

[2] Recollections of Miss Ellen Wansey, kindly communicated by Mrs. Hare of Frome Vauchurch.

[3] From an average of over 19,000 pieces in the previous three seasons to one of 12,753 for the five in question, P.R.O., B.T.6/43.

to India until 1824–5.[1] The total exported was much greater than before, but all the evidence goes to show that individual merchants tended to buy their cloth more cheaply in Yorkshire, so that the Gloucestershire makers had little to balance the fall in the Company's orders. It was not until 1819 that its exports to China made up, and finally surpassed, the earlier figures.

Nevertheless there appears to have been less distress, and certainly less agitation, during the gloomy years of 1816 and 1819 than in most other districts of England, although it was alleged in 1819 that half the workers in Gloucestershire were unemployed.[2] There was some emigration,[3] and rather more bankrupts than usual in that year;[4] and the Austins at Wotton-under-Edge made a loss of over £15,000 in 1819 and over £22,000 in 1820.[5] Whether these staggering figures were paralleled by other manufacturers we do not know; but the only bankrupt of note in Gloucestershire seems to have been Edward Jackson of Uley who is said to have been the first manufacturer in Gloucestershire to light his factory by gas.[6] In general an air of confidence and prosperity seems to have prevailed there in the early twenties. This impression is reinforced by the Census figures, though they were still inaccurate. Some of the growth in population between 1811 and 1821 must have been due to the return of men from the army but an increase of nearly 29 per cent for the lower region of Gloucestershire and one of 28 per cent for the Stroudwater basin is well above the county average; and in Stroud and Kingswood attention was called to the fact that the increase was due to the flourishing state of the industry.[7] The next decade was to show a far lower increase, only between 8 and 9 per cent for the whole area; but in view of the severe depression of 1826 what growth there was must have been con-

---

[1] *Ev. on E. India Co.'s Affairs* ii., *Finance and Accounts—Trade*, 1831–2 (H.C. 735, ii.), p. 77.

[2] G.C.L., J.F.13.27, fol. 119. Petition against Wool Tax.

[3] See 'A Gloucestershire Mill in South Africa', *Industrial Archaeology*, 4. 3 (1967), 226–31.

[4] Six in Glos. and seven in Som.

[5] Pencilled note in Account Bk. It is not clear whether these sums were the total losses or only those of Mrs. Austin who had a half share, see below, pp. 183–4.

[6] *Gloucester Journal*, 26 Feb. 1816. He had been in Cl. 2 for contributions in 1803.

[7] *Census, 1821: Abstr. of Answers and Returns* (H.C. 502), p. 105, note k; p. 357, note d.

centrated in the first five years. Up to 1825 the population round Dursley, Cam, and Uley was growing fast, 'an immense increase having taken place since the last census' according to a local magistrate in 1826,[1] but this was partially wiped out during the last five years of the decade.[2]

Most of the manufacturing towns in Wiltshire and Somerset suffered more heavily. Much of the diminution in the number of manufacturers was due to concentration into larger units encouraged by the use of machinery; but in Chippenham, Calne, and Melksham it seems certain that production declined as well. Calne, Melksham, and Warminster raised subscriptions for their poor in 1816[3] and at the beginning of 1818, when trade was reviving elsewhere, Thomas Moore and his wife, settled at Sloperton Cottage between Melksham and Calne, found that in Bromham 'there never was such wretchedness in any place where we have been'.[4] There was renewed trouble with weavers in Chippenham in 1816, probably over another attempt to make them use the fly-shuttle.[5] The town's extremely low growth rate, only 3 per cent between 1811 and 1821, shows a state of depression worse than that of any other connected with the industry in Wiltshire, though Salisbury with 6 per cent and Wilton with 4 per cent (against a general growth rate for the county of 16 per cent) were not much better. Salisbury's manufacture of flannel and linsey-woolsey was suffering from the competition of cotton[6] and of flannels made in Lancashire, and from the decrease in exports to Portugal for which many of them had been made.[7] It was never prosperous again. In

[1] P.R.O., H.O.40/19 no. 17, Lr. from P. B. Purnell to Duke of Beaufort, 31 Jan. 1826.

[2] Increase for lower region 1821–31, 5 per cent; for Stroudwater, 10 per cent.

[3] *Simpson's Salisbury Gazette*, 19 and 26 Dec. 1816.

[4] *Memoirs, Journals and Correspondence of Thomas Moore*, ed. and abr. by Lord John Russell (1860 ed.), p. 152.

[5] *Bath Chronicle*, 20 June 1816.

[6] *Repts. Asst. Commrs. Hdloom Weavers*, 1840, Pt. II, pp. 411, 444 note.

[7] Exports of flannel sank from 7 million yd. in 1815 to under 3 million in 1820. They averaged 3½ million from 1820–4 and just under 2½ million 1825–9, sinking further thereafter, J. Bischoff, op. cit., ii. Table VII. Users of this Table should note that exports are given for the years ending 5 Jan., so that the figures appearing in the line against each year refer to the previous year. This will be clear if the table is compared with that for 1820–32 in *B.P.P.* xxxiii. 1833 (H.C. 526). The annual returns of woollen exports, from 1816–19 at least (e.g. *B.P.P. 1820* xii. H.C. 92), do not correspond at all with the figures given later and are presumably uncorrected totals.

Wilton at the beginning of 1817 'the real extent of want and misery has to be seen to be believed',[1] and its industry shared the fate of Salisbury's with the exception of carpet-making; but even this declined, employing only twenty-five to thirty weavers in 1840.[2] Devizes had never recovered from Anstie's bankruptcy, but cloth manufacture continued until about 1830, though silk-throwing had been gradually superseding it.[3] Francis Hill's factory at Malmesbury was idle for some years before his death in 1828, since he was 'unable to accommodate himself to the rapid changes then passing over the cloth trade'; but in 1833 it was sold to another firm and carried on for a number of years.[4] A Gloucestershire manufacturer, William Playne, remarked at a later date that such isolated factories never succeeded,[5] but the success of the Twerton mills, one of the best-known and most successful establishments in the whole district, belies this statement.[6]

The chief towns in this region, Trowbridge, Bradford, and Frome, though faced with considerable disturbances when they began in earnest to introduce the machinery which they had postponed during the war,[7] obtained varying degrees of success, greatest of all in Trowbridge where the population increased by 57 per cent between 1811 and 1821 (3 per cent more than that of Leeds).[8] No trouble over the fly-shuttle is recorded there and it seems to have been adopted well before the end of the war. There were prolonged disturbances over finishing machinery in 1816[9] and some further threats in connection with the elections of 1818 and 1819.[10] Neither gigmills nor shearing

---

[1] *Salisbury Gazette*, 16 Jan. 1817.

[2] *Repts. Asst. Commrs. Hdloom Weavers*, Pt. II, p. 445.

[3] H. G. Barrey, Reminiscences of Devizes (from *Devizes and Wiltshire Gazette*, 1894), W.A.S. Scraps and Cuttings, vol. 5, p. 151; Cf. J. Waylen, *History of Devizes*, p. 398; W. E. Brown, 'Long's Stores, Devizes', *W.A.M.* lv. 139–45.

[4] *Wilts N. and Q*. viii. 439.

[5] *Repts. Asst. Commrs. Hdloom Weavers*, Pt. V, p. 449.

[6] See articles by R. G. Naish, *Bath Chronicle*, 22 and 25 Aug. 1928. C. Wilkins, already manufacturing at Twerton, took over the second mill there after Naish's bankruptcy in 1822 and was succeeded by the Carrs in 1847, under whom the factory continued for another hundred years.

[7] There was, however, some finishing machinery in country mills, *V.C.H. Wilts*. iv. 169, n. 65.

[8] *Report on Manufacturers' Employment*, 1830 (H.C. 590), p. 2.

[9] P.R.O., H.O.41/1, fols. 148, 189.

[10] Not much damage was done but the magistrates were much frightened, see below, p. 232, n. 7, p. 233, n. 2.

machinery completely superseded the older methods of finishing before the forties,[1] long after both were universally used in Gloucestershire; but they may have been less important in the finishing of cassimeres, the Trowbridge speciality, than for broadcloth, where Wiltshire manufactures must have found it hard to compete with Gloucestershire without using them. Trowbridge was certainly the most prosperous centre of the industry in Wiltshire and Somerset, with no very large factories[2] but a number of medium capitalists, many of whom were self-made men who were not tempted to neglect their business for other occupations.[3] Bradford grew by only 27 per cent in these ten years. It suffered from combinations to prevent the use of the fly-shuttle in 1816 and 1822,[4] though by the latter year it looks as if a number of weavers, perhaps the majority, were using it. The Frome region grew by over 22 per cent and, rather surprisingly, managed to maintain its position up to the early twenties without seriously tackling this problem.[5] In 1822, in what seems to have been a double-pronged attempt to enforce the use of the fly-shuttle and to economize in costs, its manufacturers lowered rates for weaving, which led to widespread riots extending as far as Warminster and Heytesbury.[6] Messrs. Sheppard, the leading manufacturers, refused to give out work to weavers who used the double loom, and by the following year the fly-shuttle was in use, though it is doubtful whether it was ever fully adopted in the surrounding villages. The position with regard to finishing machinery is equally doubtful. The Frome clothworkers had joined those of Leeds and Trowbridge in petitioning against it in 1816[7] and were said to have collected

[1] Notes by Bodington, Inst. of Hist. Research. This is corroborated by the Reminiscences of W. Walker (see p. 131, n. 5) who recalled that gigs and cutters 'were invented' about the time of his birth in 1840. As a small boy he saw the last pair of shears worked in Trowbridge.

[2] Only two of the seven factories listed in Trowbridge in 1816 had over 100 employees and there is no reason to think that the few others had more.

[3] See p. 131, notes 5 and 7. Walker gives several examples of contemporaries who, like his father, had risen from being shearmen or weavers to running businesses as manufacturers.

[4] *Bath Chronicle*, 20 June 1816; *Salisbury Journal*, 28 Jan. 1822.

[5] Nemnich in 1805–6 had found it here and there and was assured that it would become more common, but this does not appear to have happened, *Neueste Reise*, p. 222.

[6] See below, pp. 234–5.

[7] *C.J.* lxxi. 431, 517, 523.

800 or 900 signatures.[1] As in Leeds itself, there may have been very little in use before the early twenties.

Where competition with Yorkshire was strong, as in the medium types of cloth, western manufacturers had little chance of surviving. The decline of Shepton Mallet, begun by 1800, had resulted in extreme depression by 1830, although the Directory (possibly inaccurately) still listed the names of ten clothiers.[2] In 1833 the Factory Commissioners mentioned only silk,[3] but there was one woollen mill in 1837–8 employing only six people.[4] Frome felt Yorkshire competition most severely in the mid-twenties. Twelve clothiers went into the bankruptcy court in 1823–4 and many others must have made compositions with their creditors. This catastrophe was due to the mistake of continuing to use English wool for second and livery cloth at a time when Yorkshire had discovered that foreign wool, alone or mixed with English, produced a much better material.[5] Frome did not follow suit until after 1824.[6] It was by far the most depressed of the three towns and ten years later there was said to be hardly one small clothier left.[7] Assisted emigration began in 1819 when twenty-five families were sent by the parish to the Cape of Good Hope,[8] and many more emigrated to other destinations later. Those manufacturers who remained, mainly those making superfine cloth, faced a more stable situation afterwards and they enjoyed a measure of prosperity in the thirties, though the town itself was overburdened with poor rates for the support of those thrown out of work earlier.[9]

The disappearance (except in Trowbridge) of the small clothier was balanced by the establishment of factories, some of which were among the largest of their kind. A list, by no means

[1] *Salisbury Gazette*, 4 July 1816.

[2] Pigot's Directory 1830. One of the clothiers mentioned had been bankrupt in 1827 and another was in the same predicament in Dec. 1830.

[3] *First Rept. Fact. Com.* 1833 (H.C. 450), B.1, p. 70.

[4] *Return of Mills and Factories*, 1839 (H.C. 41), for yr. ended 6 June 1838.

[5] C. J. Francis of Messrs. Everett and Francis of Heytesbury produced conclusive evidence of this in 1828, *Rept. on British Wool Trade*, 1828 (H.L. 515), pp. 265–6.

[6] Ibid. pp. 293–4, 299.

[7] T. Bunn, *A Letter relative to the Affairs of the Poor of Frome Selwood* (orig. written to the Poor Law Commrs. in 1834, repr. 1851), p. 18. But see below, p. 240.

[8] Som. C.R.O., DD/LW 49, Extracts from Frome Vestry Books, Sept. 1819.

[9] Bunn, loc. cit.

exhaustive, of 'the principal woollen establishments' in Wilt-shire and Somerset, drawn up in 1816,[1] shows most of them to have been in the area between Trowbridge, Bradford, Frome, and Westbury; but there were notable exceptions. Out of thirty-three listed two were at Chippenham, one at Calne, two at Heytesbury and one at Twerton and five of these six were among the larger employers, having 100 or more, and in one case, at Heytesbury, over 200 people in the mill. The largest of all was the factory of Saunders, Farmer and Co. at Bradford, employing 321 people; one other at Bradford, one at Staverton, and one at Frome, besides that at Heytesbury mentioned above, employed over 200, and of the rest seven had 100 or more and ten between 50 and 100. The remaining ten may have operated only spinning machinery; the Clarks of Trowbridge, who came lowest on the list with only 35 people in the mill, introduced finishing machinery in this year and it may not have been in operation when the list was drawn up. Those mills where large numbers were employed may have had weaving shops on the premises; but the outside weaver working in his own home was still the characteristic feature of all the western clothing districts.

No similar statistics have come to light for Gloucestershire, but the number of mills was, of course, much larger. Building both of new factories and of extensions to older ones went on vigorously between 1815 and 1825[2] and it is evident that the wealthier manufacturers in all three counties were confident of the future of the industry. Hardly any evidence of profits can be obtained; but the Clarks, who took very little cash out of the firm, showed profits of between 16 and 32 per cent in the eleven years from 1815 to 1825 inclusive (with the exception of 1823 when a large debt remained unpaid). The average, at nearly 22 per cent per annum for these eleven years, was under 3 per cent below that of the previous decade.[3] Larger firms, which paid overseers to do what the Clarks did themselves, may not have reached these figures; it may be noted that Benjamin Gott the great Leeds manufacturer, who also made superfine

---

[1] *Ev. on State of Children employed in Manufactures*, 1816 (H.C. 397), pp. 546–7.

[2] Of 34 mills in Glos. about which information on building dates can be obtained in or before 1834, 25 were either built or enlarged between 1810 and 1825.

[3] Av. from table in *W.A.M., Rec. Brch.* vi., p. xxxi. By reference to p. 32 it will be seen that there is a misprint under 'Money in Trade' for 1806, which should read £2,323.

cloth, only showed a profit of 18 per cent in 1818 against nearly 33 per cent made by the Clarks in the same year, but his capital was almost ten times as large.[1]

Up to 1830 exports of cloth were declining though there was a great rise in those of worsteds. Merchants had begun the peace with great expectations and had exported over 600,000 pieces of cloth alone in 1815;[2] but, with some fluctuations, the quantity fell progressively thereafter. A five-year average from and including 1816 clearly shows the decline:

Average exports per annum for periods of five years, 1816–1830[3]

	cloth (pieces)	cassimere (kerseymere) (pieces)
1816–20	404,149	85,946
1821–5	388,468	103,213
1826–30	357,041	72,158

The European cloth manufactures were growing and their products were protected by high tariffs. They had equal access to foreign wool, which was becoming a necessity for all but the coarsest cloth; and the tax on it which Parliament imposed in 1819[4] made it more difficult for English goods to compete. This tax bore more heavily on Yorkshire than on the west, partly because exports formed two-thirds of its production against under one-third in Gloucestershire[5] and probably less in the other two counties, but also because, being a fixed sum, it was more severely felt by makers of cheaper cloth. Western manufacturers complained that the shilling or fifteen pence per yard which the tax added to their costs was a serious hindrance

---

[1] 'The Yorkshire Woollen and Worsted Industry, 1800–1850' (Unpublished Thesis by Dr. R. M. Hartwell in Bodl. Lib.), p. 748. 1818 is the only year after 1808 when Gott's profits can be calculated and it is done in exactly the same way as those of the Clarks.

[2] Bischoff, op. cit. II, Table VII (p. 159, n. 7).

[3] Averaged from above table. Bischoff's figures differ slightly from those given in official returns in *B.P.P. 1821*, XVII (H.C. 443) and *1833*, XXXIII (H.C. 526), but the differences are not serious.

[4] See below, p. 276.

[5] Bischoff, op. cit. I.466. One-third of the cloth made of foreign wool in Glos. was believed to be exported, *Privy Council Ctee on Wool Tax*, 1820 (H.C. 56), p. 1.

in competing with European cloth abroad;[1] but in the Americas
at least they appear not to have lost as much as they feared, and
when the tax was removed in 1823 they soon made it up.[2]
Lower wages in Europe and the reputation which the French
had gained from their earlier use of Saxony wool[3] were obviously
factors to be reckoned with; but the degree of competition to be
met with in America was greatly exaggerated. Cloth from
Sedan or Verviers may have been as good as English cloth[4]
but it could not be made so cheaply. One of the Sheppards said
in 1819 that English manufacturers had an advantage over the
the French of $7\frac{1}{2}$ per cent,[5] which still left a margin after the
tax was imposed; and when it was removed, fine foreign cloth,
though narrower, was no cheaper than English.[6] In 1824 when
Huskisson reduced the duty on imports of fine cloth from the
50 per cent at which it had stood throughout the war, manufacturers claimed that a minimum duty of 20 per cent was
necessary to compensate for the higher wages payable owing to
the existence of the Corn Laws;[7] but when it was fixed at 15
per cent no influx of foreign cloth seems to have followed.

On the other hand the tax may have been the deciding factor
in the decay of the southern European market after 1820.[8] Up
to 1819 a considerable trade was still done there[9] but it got
gradually smaller in the next decade and, as far as western
cloth was concerned, it seems to have faded away altogether.[10]
The same was true (though not altogether for the same reasons)
of Russia, which had been an expanding market up to 1807.
Gloucestershire manufacturers had high hopes of a return to it
at the end of the war, when they petitioned unsuccessfully for
a commercial treaty which would allow free entry to English

---

[1] Ibid., pp. 4–5; *Rept. on British Wool Trade*, 1828, p. 294.

[2] Ibid., p. 42. The factor, H. Hughes, even said that exports of finer cloth did
not decrease while the duty was in force.

[3] Ibid., p. 44.

[4] In general foreign cloth was said not to be so well dressed, loc. cit.

[5] *Privy Council Ctee on Wool Tax*, 1820, p. 3. Bischoff (op. cit. ii. 6) supplies the
surname; the witness may have been the Blackwell Hall factor, Thomas Sheppard,
or his brother Edward of Uley.

[6] *Rept. on British Wool Trade*, 1828, p. 44.

[7] Bischoff, *The Wool Question considered*, p. 107. The western manufacturers, or
their factors, had originally said 25 to 30 per cent. Ibid., p. 103.

[8] Bischoff, *Comprehensive History* ii. 70.

[9] *Privy Council Ctee on Wool Tax*, 1820, p. 4.

[10] *Rept. on British Wool Trade*, 1828, pp. 43–4.

cloth.[1] The large quantity sent out immediately after the peace (most of which must have come from Yorkshire, since it was the result of an agreement to pay certain sums in cloth for the Russian army)[2] did not continue; but as late as 1821 over 13,000 pieces of cloth, of which one-fifth was said to be fine, as well as nearly 10,000 pieces of cassimere were still being exported. In 1820 the Austins had goods to the value of £12,744 in the hands of agents in St. Petersburg.[3] The heavy fall in the succeeding years was said to be mainly due to the way in which the duties were levied, which favoured cloth from Prussia. The transit trade to China had also been made very difficult for English goods,[4] but one cannot exclude the possibility that the tax again provided the deciding factor. When it was removed, however, the trade did not recover[5] and those who continued in it did not always secure returns. One Somerset manufacturer, T. W. Ledyard of Rode, left his family impoverished for this reason when he died in 1835.[6]

The place of lost markets in Europe was taken by Latin America, 'a wonderful market' according to a Blackwell Hall factor in 1828,[7] but apt to be an uncertain one. Total consignments of cloth there from 1823 to 1840 varied between 44,000 and 89,000 pieces a year, with another 2,000 to 18,000 pieces of cassimeres. Of this the proportion of fine cloth was about one-third.[8] The United States, the largest of all markets, exports to which varied in the same period from under 100,000 to nearly 370,000 pieces of cloth and cassimere together, took from one-third to one half of its supplies in fine cloth,[9] and although Yorkshire provided the greater part[10] the west had a

---

[1] G.C.L., J.F.13.27, fol. 118, Mem. of Gloucestershire manufacturers to Lord Bathurst. Cf. p. 137, n. 3.

[2] Lord Sheffield (1820), quoted by Bischoff, *Comprehensive History* i. 475.

[3] Glouc. C.R.O., D.2078, Balance sheet of 1821.

[4] *3rd Rept. on Foreign Trade* (*E. Indies and China*) 1821 (H.C. 746), pp. 207–8, 217, 338; *1st Rept. on Affairs of the E. India Co.*, 1830, p. 199.

[5] Average annual exports 1822–30 inclusive, 3,958 pieces of cloth and 3,187 cassimeres. There was no increase, but a heavy decrease in cassimeres in the next decade.

[6] Som. C.R.O., DD/LW 52, Extracts from Diary of Miss E. H. Sheppard, *c.* 1858. Ledyard had married into the Sheppard family.

[7] *Rept. on British Wool Trade*, 1828, p. 297.

[8] *Privy Council Ctee on Wool Tax*, 1820, p. 4.

[9] Ibid.

[10] For the Yorkshire fine cloth trade see *Rept. on British Wool Trade*, 1828, p. 285.

considerable share. The instability of both these markets in the later twenties and thirties was an important factor in the failure of many western clothiers.

Finally, up to 1833 the East India Company was still taking for China a large proportion of Gloucestershire's production, an annual average (though with great fluctuations) for the thirteen years from 1820 to 1832 inclusive of over 11,000 pieces of 'stripes' (so-called from their striped list).[1] It also bought in the county some of the coarser cloth for its army uniforms.[2] Yorkshire was said to have made inroads into this trade in the later twenties,[3] but if the figures supplied to the Commissioner for Handloom Weavers in 1839 were correct,[4] its share was never a large one as far as stripes were concerned, though probably much greater in the case of the cheaper uniform cloth.

The year 1824 and the early months of 1825 were a boom period all over the country, with a great deal of speculation, especially in 1825. With this prosperity came a multitude of strikes, mainly the result of the repeal of the Combination Acts in 1824. In the west cloth had been improved by being more closely woven, but this meant that weavers had to put more weft into it, in most cases without any increase in their pay for the piece. They had good reason to follow the fashion by striking in May 1825;[5] but after a quick victory in the lower region, where Sheppard acceded to most of their demands and persuaded other manufacturers to follow suit, the strike dragged on until the autumn on Stroudwater with the result, according to another manufacturer thirteen years later, that the spring trade was stopped and the stock in hand had to be sold in the autumn at very low prices.[6] A downturn from the peak of the boom began in the latter half of the year and as early as August trade was bad in Warminster, where work had proceeded as

---

[1] Averaged from table in *Repts. Asst. Commrs. Hdloom Weavers*, 1840, Pt. V, see App. V, Table R. Stripes were often called 'superfine' but were not comparable with other superfine cloth, being very flimsy though made of Spanish wool, Playne, op. cit., p. 149.

[2] Some contracts for this cloth were being advertised in Glos. as late as 1841, *Gloucester Journal*, 23 Jan. and 22 May 1841.

[3] *Rept. on Manufactures, Commerce and Shipping*, 1833 (H.C. 690), p. 67.

[4] See Table R.

[5] See below, Ch. VIII.

[6] *Repts. Asst. Commrs. Hdloom Weavers*, 1840, Pt. V, p. 450.

usual.[1] Then in December came 'the panic', the failure of numerous country banks and the sudden plunge into deep depression. In addition, the increase in the United States' tariff and the collapse of the South American market owing to the ending of loans to the new republican Governments added to the manufacturers' difficulties.[2]

The year 1826 was the great dividing line of the period. There was severe distress all over the country but it seems to have lasted longer in the west than in many other districts, right up to the end of the year when things were improving in Yorkshire.[3] In Trowbridge employment dropped to one-third of the normal amount, but at first the masters shared it out evenly so that only a few were wholly unemployed.[4] The position gradually got worse and by September about half the working population in Trowbridge, Melksham, and Frome were idle.[5] In Chippenham the trade seems to have ceased altogether for a time and the Parliamentary candidate gained popularity by buying a large mill which he was said to intend keeping constantly employed; but it did not last long.[6] In Gloucestershire sixteen firms went bankrupt and at least four others were insolvent, as against only seven bankruptcies in Wiltshire and Somerset; but this may be a fairly accurate reflection of the relative size of the industry in the two areas. The lower region of Gloucestershire suffered more than Stroudwater,[7] but Bisley, where over 2,000 were wholly unemployed and another 450 in half work out of a population of about 6,000, was also very badly hit.[8] It got some help from the London Committee for distressed manufacturers and Uley obtained £100 from a similar committee in Bristol. How much else was received in Gloucestershire is unknown, but a Benevolent Committee at Wotton-under-Edge gave a

[1] Nottingham Univ. Lib. Papers of Henry Wansey, Jr., Lr. to his father, 5 Aug. 1825.

[2] *Rept. on British Wool Trade*, 1828, p. 285. Cf. *Gloucester Journal*, 29 July 1826.

[3] See *Gloucester Journal*, 5 Aug. and 9 Sept. 1826 on the improved demand at Leeds.

[4] *Salisbury Journal*, 15 May 1826.

[5] Ibid., 23 Sept. 1826; *Devizes and Wilts. Gazette*, 21 and 28 Sept. 1826.

[6] *Salisbury Journal*, 12 June 1826; *Devizes and Wilts. Gazette*, 8 June and 2 Aug. 1826.

[7] Nine of the bankrupts and three of the insolvents came from the lower region, mainly from Uley and Wotton-under-Edge.

[8] Glouc. C.R.O., P.47ª M.I, 1. Answers from Bisley to questionnaire of London Ctee.

distressing account of destitution there in December.[1] Wiltshire and Somerset obtained at least £1,000 from the committees in London and Bristol, a large part of it for Bradford and the surrounding villages.[2]

The crisis ushered in a steep decline in prices. In Gloucestershire the drop was about 30 per cent for fine cloth and 50 per cent for 'stripes' (but part of this was due to a fall in the price of wool).[3] 'My father made as much profit on one cloth as I do on twenty,' said J. F. Lewis of the Oil Mills, Ebley, in 1833; but the more sober estimate of Messrs. Millman of Kingswood and Long of Charfield in 1839 that there was formerly more profit on five ends of cloth than now on fifteen, is probably nearer the truth.[4] Yorkshire was similarly affected, but there the manufacturers who survived made up their losses by enlarging their businesses and accepting low profits on a much larger turnover. Some western manufacturers did so too, but the majority did not attempt it. The fine cloth trade did not, of course, offer the same opportunities for expansion as that in medium and low-priced cloth, but there was certainly a field for adventure of which more could have been made. Instead, many manufacturers behaved like the old-established Leeds merchants, who, as a recent historian of them has written, preferred 'to return a reasonably large profit on a relatively small capital' rather than to 'secure a small profit on a large turnover'.[5] 'The sweeping reductions that have been made in profits and wages incline us not to overwork ourselves,' said

---

[1] *Gloucester Journal*, 16 Dec. 1826.

[2] *Salisbury Journal*, 5 June 1826; *Devizes and Wiltshire Gazette*, 7 and 21 Sept. 1826. The London Ctee sent £700 to Bradford and surrounding villages but it is not clear whether this included the £200 sent earlier.

[3] Prices dropped from 30s. and 35s. a yd. in 1820 (*Privy Council Ctee on Wool Tax*, 1820, p. 4) to 24s. and 28s. for the best superfines, *Rept. on Manuf., Commerce and Shipping*, 1833, p. 68. In 1831 'stripes' for China were bought at £10 per piece instead of £20, *Ev. on East India Co.'s Affairs* ii. *Finance and Accounts—Trade*, 1831–2, p. 77. The average price of Spanish and German wool fell about 25 per cent between 1823 and 1828 (*Rept. on British Wool Trade*, 1828, p. 328) but this is no guide to the price for the qualities of which the best superfines were made, for which there was no regular criterion. They were however lower in 1829, see E. M. Onslow, *Some early Records of the MacArthurs of Camden*, pp. 412, 423–4.

[4] *Suppl. Rept. Fact. Com., 1834* ii, *Answers to Queries* (H. C. 167), B.1, 40; *Repts. Asst. Commrs. Hdloom Weavers*, 1840, Pt. V, p. 367.

[5] R. G. Wilson, 'The Leeds Merchants, 1700–1830'. Unpublished thesis in Brotherton Libr. Leeds.

J. F. Lewis in 1833,[1] and this seems to have been a very prevalent attitude. The dilemma which faced woollen manufacturers everywhere is clearly seen in a statement by a wealthy Yorkshire manufacturer, John Brooke, in the same year. He would not, he said, think of investing his large capital in the industry if it were not already there, nor could he expect to get the value of his mill if he sold it on retirement, since a man with enough capital to work it to advantage would not undertake such a business. On the other hand, he considered that a man with a little capital might embark on the trade with every prospect of success.[2] Men who were willing to build up a business on hard work and low profits were more numerous in Yorkshire 'where there is more capital and more speculation' than they were in the west, where, at any rate in Gloucestershire, 'expensive establishments and improvident expenditure' were sometimes blamed for failures.[3] Nevertheless some did exist and it was with them that the future of the industry rested.

An improvement took place after 1826 and by 1828, which was a year of considerable activity, trade was fairly well established again;[4] but the west was feeling Yorkshire competition more keenly than ever[5] and the sudden depression in the second half of 1829 seems to have hit it with exceptional force. While an improvement in the Leeds trade was reported in November, and in January 1830 it was steady with London buyers again in the market,[6] the west remained in depression at least until the spring and in some places longer. Manufacturers there 'were in a very wretched state three or four years ago' said the Blackwell Hall factor Henry Hughes in 1833;[7] and in the autumn of 1829 several local newspapers printed a statement that 'at this moment there are no less than seventy mills in the wool business in the West of England to be let'.[8] It may have referred to a larger area than that depicted

---

[1] Suppl. Rept. Fact. Com., 1834 ii, Answers to Queries, B.1, 40.

[2] Rept. on Manuf., Commerce and Shipping, 1833, p. 117. Cf. the remarks of L. Loyd, a banker who had connections with the W. of England, ibid., p. 31.

[3] Repts. Asst. Commrs. Hdloom Weavers, 1840, Pt. V, p. 362.

[4] Rept. on British Wool Trade, 1828, pp. 100, 296.

[5] Ibid., p. 299.

[6] Gloucester Journal, 7 and 14 Nov. 1829 and 30 Jan. 1830.

[7] Rept. on Manuf., Commerce and Shipping, 1833, p. 67.

[8] Salisbury Journal, 19 Oct. 1829. The statement also appeared in the Gloucester Journal, 17 Oct. 1829 as quoted from the Bath Gazette.

in this book, for Devon and Somerset were also in the west and the serge trade was not very prosperous; but a large proportion must have been cloth mills. There was great distress in the Stroud area that winter and extreme destitution in villages such as Coaley where there were no wealthy inhabitants and the lesser ones were overwhelmed by the poor rates.[1] In Frome there were said to be 5,000 out of work and the poor, both men and women, were daily drawing twenty to thirty hand trucks nine miles from the pits to make a little money by selling coal in the town.[2] In Trowbridge as late as August 1830 it was 'hardly possible to imagine the extent of the distress'.[3] In London it was believed to be only partial. R. Hart Davis, M.P. for Bristol, assured the House of Commons in February 1830 that one Gloucestershire manufacturer had told him that he could accept no more orders for the next six months;[4] but the existence of any such person was hotly denied and a meeting at Dursley with Edward Sheppard in the chair resolved that it was necessary to remove any such impression from the minds of ministers, since the distress was universal and not confined to particular districts.[5] All the same, it was admitted that one Wiltshire village was an exception to the general lack of employment, and it is probable that Gloucestershire manufacturers were not all in the same depressed state. Some managed to make money throughout this difficult period. William Marling of Ham mills, Stroud, who already had two sons established in their own businesses,[6] took his son Thomas into partnership in 1825, when the firm's capital was £6,000 all furnished by William. In 1832 when another son, S. S. Marling, was taken in, the

---

[1] *Gloucester Journal*, 13 and 20 Feb. 1830.

[2] Ibid., 27 Feb. 1830.

[3] *Salisbury Journal*, 16 Aug. 1830.

[4] W. Smart, *Economic Annals* ii. 525. It seems probable that this manufacturer was Donald Maclean of Stanley Mills. He was a director of the abortive London and Bristol Railroad Co. formed in 1825, of which Hart Davis was chairman, E. T. MacDermot, *History of the G. W. Railway* i. 1. R. Hart Davis, Son & Co. appear as London Wool Merchants in 1821 in the books of Rawlings & Co. of Frome.

[5] *Gloucester Journal*, 6 Mar. 1830.

[6] N.S. Marling rented Freame's mill, Avening and Pitt's mill, Inchbrook in 1820, Glouc. C.R.O., D.873 (B) T. J. F. Marling appears to have been a partner in Westley and Marling at Lightpill mill, which was described in 1834 as having been built and lately occupied by them. *Gloucester Journal*, 15 Feb. 1834. He went to Ebley in 1833.

capital had grown to £22,000 and a second mill was being
operated. Of this amount Thomas' share was £9,000 built up
from nothing in 1825.[1] The Marlings, like the Clarks, took very
little cash out of the business at this period.[2] The position of the
established and wealthy manufacturers was different. It is
significant that the meeting mentioned above was held in the
lower region of Gloucestershire, for it was there that the largest
number of rich manufacturers was to be found and it was
much more severely affected than the upper region. When the
Factory Commissioners visited Uley, Dursley, and Wotton-
under-Edge in 1833 they commented upon the large number of
mills which had ceased production and found that twelve of the
nineteen manufacturers whose names they had been given had
either failed or retired in the past three years.[3] Only two of them,
and those small ones, had been through the bankruptcy court,
though at least one other firm, the Austins, had made a composition with its creditors.[4] It was the risks they ran which had
decided most of them to retire while they remained comparatively well-to-do.[5] This tendency to give up in the face of
adverse circumstances, which had been noticeable ever since
the end of the war, was accelerated by the crisis of 1826 and
played an even greater part than the failures in the decline of
the industry. In Bradford, too, half the manufacturers were said
to have gone out of business in the ten years before 1826.[6]
Where there had been twenty in 1820 there were fourteen six
years later and by 1833 the number had been reduced to five;
but only ten had been bankrupt since 1815. One can hardly
blame them for retiring, for they might otherwise have shared
the fate of men like R. S. Collicott of Weston Mills near Bath,
who advertised his mill for sale in 1819[7] and, having failed to
sell it, was bankrupt in 1825.

It seems possible that the length of this depression, in Trow-

[1] Deeds of partnership, 1825 and 1832, Glouc. C.R.O., D.873 (B) Business
Contracts. The second mill was Frome Hall.

[2] By the terms of the deed of 1825 neither partner was to take out more than
£100 in each of the first three years of the partnership and not more than £200 in
each of the last four years, without the consent of the other.

[3] 1st Rept. of Fact. Com., 1833, B.I, 52.

[4] See below, pp. 183–4.

[5] Cf. Repts. Asst. Commrs. Hdloom Weavers, 1840, Pt. V, p. 434.

[6] Devizes and Wilts. Gazette, 21 Sept. 1826.

[7] Bath Chronicle, 12 Apr. 1819.

bridge and Frome at least, and possibly in the lower region of Gloucestershire, may be connected with the fall in the export of cassimeres. Trowbridge depended heavily on sales of them to the United States[1] and many were also made in Frome,[2] Uley, and Dursley. At the end of 1828 the American tariff was again raised to heights which were represented as prohibitive,[3] and it seems to have operated more severely against cassimeres than against broadcloth,[4] for exports of the former dropped from over 15,000 pieces in 1827 to a little over 2,000 in 1830, while the loss of cloth exports was almost confined to 1829 and even then was only 10 per cent. In fact, there was a general shrinkage in cassimere exports after 1828 of which that to the United States was only a part; and any manufacturer producing them must have suffered considerably unless he could switch over his production and his markets very quickly.

In the next three years the west succeeded in winning back some of the trade it had lost earlier. It had certain advantages in that its cloth was considered more durable than that of Yorkshire and some of its colours were better, though Yorkshire could still gain by the cheapness of steam power and by its ability to make cloth of inferior wool look almost as good as that made of the best.[5] Trade was 'never better than it is now' in the opinion of one Bradford manufacturer in 1833, and mills were 'pretty well employed' all over the western area;[6] but this opinion must be qualified by the many references to earlier periods, when trade had been brisker and longer hours had been worked, which were made by Gloucestershire manufacturers to the Factory Commissioners in the same year.[7] In comparison with the immediate past it was, no doubt, correct. J. W. Partridge, a Gloucestershire dyer and manufacturer, giving evidence to the Central Board on Children's Employment in June 1833, said that the number of unemployed had

[1] *Salisbury Journal*, 15 May 1826.

[2] *Supp. Rept. Fact. Com. 1834, II Answers to Queries*, B.1, 48, 50.

[3] Smart, op. cit. II, 461.

[4] Owing to the way in which the duties were levied this could easily have been the case, see F. W. Taussig, *The Tariff History of the United States*, 8th ed., pp. 80–1.

[5] *Rept. on Manuf. Commerce and Shipping*, 1833, p. 68.

[6] Ibid., pp. 30, 67.

[7] *1st Rept. Fact. Com.*, 1833, B.1, 46, 50, 53, 54; *Suppl. Rept. ii. Answers to Queries*, B.1, 5, 34, 40, 42.

13—C.I.

been fewer during the last three years than for a long time before,[1] but this did not prevent pockets of destitution in weaving villages such as Randwick in which, like Coaley, no employers and few well-to-do people resided.[2] Yet more cloth was produced in Gloucestershire in 1832 than in any year after 1823,[3] and it is obvious that many manufacturers must have extended their operations to balance the loss from those who had given up. Wiltshire and Somerset seem to have been doing at least as well. Mills in Trowbridge were working longer hours than most Gloucestershire ones,[4] and employers were exerting themselves to a greater extent; it was a Trowbridge manufacturer, John Stancombe, who remarked (in contrast with the opinion of J. F. Lewis quoted above) that with profits so much reduced a factory would not answer unless it was worked a proper number of hours.[5] Such an attitude may account for the surprising recovery of Trowbridge from the depths of the 1830 depression—surprising because it was still making cassimeres and exports of this material to the United States did not look up until 1835, by which time the tariff was 47 per cent *ad valorem* with further reductions to come.[6] Yet not only Trowbridge but what was left of the industry in Frome seems to have been doing well in 1833.

From 1832 to 1836 the woollen industry, in common with others, shared in the general improvement in the economic state of the country in spite of a minor depression in the first half of 1834.[7] Cloth for China continued to be made for sale to private traders. In July 1834 Chalford manufacturers engaged in making it were reported to have been tolerably busy;[8] but a demand for an increase in the miserably low rates paid to the weavers led William Playne of Longfords mill, Avening, probably the largest stripe manufacturer in the county, to give up making them after his weavers had struck for an extra 10s. per

[1] *1st Rept. Fact. Com.*, E.10.

[2] G.C.L., R.Q. 246.1 *Facts submitted . . . in behalf of the distressed weavers at Randwick* (1832).

[3] See App. V., Table Q.

[4] *1st Rept. Fact. Com.*, B.1, 90.

[5] *Suppl. Rept. Fact. Com.* ii, *Answers to Queries*, B.1, 104.

[6] *Ann. Reg.* 1833, Hist. Sect., 298. See Taussig, op. cit., pp. 105–6 for the system of reductions introduced in 1833.

[7] *Repts. Insp. Fact.*, 1834 (H.C. 596), p. 23.

[8] *Gloucester Journal*, 5 July 1834.

piece.[1] Immediately afterwards the general body of stripe manufacturers refused an advance on the grounds that the price in London was so low and the advices from China so discouraging.[2] They were now exposed to the full force of Yorkshire competition from which they had been partially protected earlier, since the Yorkshire manufacturers had disliked the conditions imposed by the Company and preferred to supply American traders, who had been demonstrating ever since 1817 that there was a wider and more profitable market in China than the Company had been able to find.[3] Chalford suffered heavily and by 1839 only fifteen of its forty-one mills were still in use as woollen factories.[4] Some trade with China continued. One Chalford maker was exporting there on his own account in 1839 and receiving tea in return;[5] and T. & S. S. Marling now of Ebley had sent out cloth to Canton in 1841 for which they expected to receive goods worth £9,000.[6] This trade was a casualty of the Opium War which began that year; but after peace had been made in the autumn of 1842 there was said to be an increased demand for cloth for China in Bisley and Nailsworth;[7] and reports on the China market appeared in the *Gloucester Journal* as late as 1848.[8]

The year 1832 had been an exceptional one, when over two million yards of cloth had been made, mainly owing to large orders from the Company for its last year of monopoly. The loss of them meant a drop in production of some 700,000 yards in 1833, but the fact that in 1834 and 1836 the quantity produced rose to over 1,900,000 yards and was very little less in 1835 shows a surprising capacity for growth. A comparison of the seven years from 1830 to 1836 inclusive with the previous seven, 1823–9, shows that average annual production in the later period was greater by over 220,000 yards a year than in the earlier.[9] The industry was shifting its location away from the

[1] Ibid., 8 Mar. 1834. Playne once had a contract for 10,000 pieces and put out part of such large orders to other manufacturers, Playne, op. cit., p. 151.

[2] *Gloucester Journal*, 22 Mar. 1834.

[3] *1st Rept. on Affairs of the E. India Co.*, 1830 (*China Trade*), pp. 194, 197.

[4] *Repts. Asst. Commrs. Hdloom Weavers*, 1840, Pt. V, p. 363.

[5] Ibid., p. 364.

[6] Deed for dissolution of partnership between T. & S. Marling, 1842, see p. 172, n. 1.

[7] *Gloucester Journal*, 17 Dec. 1842.

[8] Ibid., 8 Jan. and 29 Jan. 1848.   [9] See App. V, Table Q.

upper Stroudwater valley and from the region below the Cotswolds to become more concentrated round Stroud and in the Nailsworth valley. The increased efficiency of the manufacturers left in business after 1830 and the lower prices of their goods must have been the main cause of this revival. In 1835 Thomas Marling, giving evidence before the Parliamentary Committee on the Bristol–Birmingham Railway Bill, was confident about the prosperous condition of the trade in Stroud, believing that there had never been greater capital employed and firmly denying, perhaps for propaganda purposes, that cheap coal in Yorkshire gave manufacturers there an advantage, 'sometimes we have the advantage of the north of England and sometimes they of us'.[1] Others bore him out. Charles Stephens of Stanley Mills said at the inquiry about the Cheltenham and Great Western Union Railway in 1836 that Gloucestershire had proved its supremacy over Yorkshire in fine cloth, and like Marling he believed that trade was increasing.[2] This confidence was not confined to Gloucestershire. So buoyant were the towns of west Wiltshire that a witness at another railway inquiry in 1835 claimed that Trowbridge and Bradford were doing better than Gloucestershire.[3] Both towns were building up an Irish trade and were anxious for a direct communication with Bristol and London, believing that Irish buyers would stop on their journey and buy what they wanted locally rather than pay commission on purchases through London factors.[4]

Profits were believed to be low. It was a Yorkshire manufacturer who said in 1840 that in the woollen industry it was extremely difficult, even in good times, to make the average profits of the country,[5] and no doubt this was true of the west as

[1] Arch. H.L., *Min. of Ev. taken before the Lords' Ctee on the Bristol–Birmingham Rly. with branches to Bradford and Trowbridge*, 1835, pp. 67–8.

[2] *Min. of Ev. before the Parl. Ctee on the Cheltenham and Gt. Western Union Rly. Bill*, 1836, pp. 9, 18. (H. of L. Sess. Papers, 1836 xxxi.)

[3] Arch. H.L., MS. Ev. before the Parl. Ctee on the Gt. Western Rly. Bill, 1835, esp. that of J. Bleeck, 13 Apr. 1835; *Min. of Ev. before the Lords' Ctee on the Bristol–Birm. Rly.*, 1835, pp. 735, 744.

[4] Parl. Ctee on G.W. Rly. Bill, 1835, Ev. of J. Bleeck. Benjamin Cooper of Staverton told another Ctee that the bulk of his firm's output went to Bristol for Liverpool and Ireland. Charles Wilkins of Twerton sent most of his to London, *Min. of Ev. on Bristol–Birm. Rly.*, p. 29.

[5] *6th Rept. on Regulation of Mills & Factories*, 1840 (H.C. 504), p. 60 (J. Nussey).

well. Some Gloucestershire manufacturers, however, must have done better if one can trust an advertisement in the *Gloucester Journal* in 1837. Looking for a partner who could bring £4,000 to £5,000 into 'a small but truly respectable woollen manufactory', the advertiser assured any prospective investor that the capital employed 'has netted full twenty per cent per annum since the establishment of the concern and in no year less than that sum'.[1] It is difficult to take this at its face value in view of the fact that two years later, admittedly during a severe depression, another manufacturer was speaking of profits of 5 to 7 per cent,[2] and this probably includes interest. Nevertheless, the Marlings had doubled their capital by 1840 when Thomas and Samuel made a new partnership agreement and Samuel's share, one-third of the whole made in the previous eight years, was £17,868 built up from nothing in 1832.[3] There were of course great differences between one maker and another. 'Six or seven men in the west', said a Blackwell Hall factor in 1828, 'will make very good cloth from the self-same wool that by an inferior manufacturer will make a cloth more than one shilling a yard worse.'[4] It is such men whom one would expect to survive when others foundered; but, in fact, two of the largest firms, most noted for the excellence of their cloth, failed in the mid-thirties, the Hicks of Eastington in March 1835 and Edward Sheppard of Uley in January 1837.[5] It looks as if Sheppard had been in difficulties for some time. There was a mortgage on his mill[6] which he had only been working for eight hours a day from 1830 to 1833,[7] and he had had to face a strike when he tried to reduce wages in 1834.[8] Perhaps it was true that over-trading in 1832 lay at the root of these failures,[9] but to the manufacturers who talked to Miles in 1839 they were prominent examples of the practice of taking too much capital out of the industry to support a high level of consumption.

The prosperity of 1836 was checked at the end of the year

---

[1] *Gloucester Journal*, 12 Aug. 1837. Only the advertiser's initials (W.S.P.) are given and they do not correspond with those of any known manufacturer.

[2] *Repts. Asst. Commrs. Hdloom Weavers*, 1840, Pt. V, p. 516.

[3] Partnership Deed, 1840, see p. 172, n. 1.

[4] *Rept. on British Wool Trade*, 1828, p. 297.

[5] Both failures came too early to have been affected by the depression of 1837, as is sometimes thought.

[6] *Gloucester Journal*, 20 June 1840.   [7] *1st Rept. Fact. Com.*, 1833, B.1, 53.

[8] *Repts. Asst. Commrs. Hdloom Weavers*, 1840, Pt. V, p. 453.   [9] Ibid., p. 367.

when the 'American panic' aggravated a fall in prices which had begun in the late autumn.[1] Production fell by 167,000 yards in Gloucestershire that year and again, by a slightly smaller amount, in 1838. A small increase in activity in 1839 only preceded a downturn of great severity; and at the end of the year T. J. Howell, the Factory Inspector in charge of nearly all the western cloth area,[2] found greater depression than he had ever known.[3] It lasted all over the country until the end of 1842. In the autumn of 1841 came the failure of the banking house of Hobhouse & Co. of Bath, mainly brought about by the state of the industry, since the bank had ruined itself by supporting the two large factories of the Coopers at Staverton and Saunders & Co. at Bradford for the past five years.[4]

The distress turned the attention of the workers to Chartism and that of the manufacturers to Free Trade. They had been against the Corn Laws ever since 1815,[5] but now their inability to sell in America gave a new impulse to the agitation. At an anti-Corn Law meeting in Bath at the beginning of 1842, attended by cloth manufacturers from all over the west, the condition to which the whole area had been reduced was vividly depicted.[6] The almost complete cessation of exports emphasized by Samuel Salter of Trowbridge, the decline in the number of manufacturers everywhere and the decrease in the quantity of cloth produced (by 2,500 pieces a year in Westbury alone between 1839 and 1841), the extent of unemployment often up to 50 per cent, the decline in population (one-sixth of the houses vacant in Frome) and the fall in the value of mill property were all set out at length. From Gloucestershire Charles Hooper, who had succeeded the Hicks at Eastington, said that in the first three months of 1841 three hundred persons had applied to him for work which he could not give them. According to S. S. Marling production in Gloucestershire had decreased to 1,151,280 yards in 1841, only 53 per

[1] See Gayer, Rostow and Schwarz, *Growth and Fluctuation of the British Economy* i. 248–9, 251–2.

[2] Mills in Salisbury and Wilton were in Saunders's district at this time but there were only three left.

[3] *Fact. Insp. Rept.* 31 Dec. 1839 (H.C. 218), p. 18.

[4] *Bath Chronicle*, 13 and 20 Jan. 1842.

[5] G.C.L., J.V.13.2 (10) Resolutions passed at a meeting of woollen manufacturers of Glos. against the Corn Laws, 8 Mar. 1815.

[6] *Bath Chronicle*, 13 Jan. 1842.

cent of what it had been in the peak year of 1832. Fifty manufacturers had failed in the same period and the number in
business had fallen from about eighty to forty-two.[1] A week
later, at another anti-Corn Law meeting in Stroud, the
chairman, John Ferrabee, an iron-founder and machine
maker with close associations with the cloth industry, remarked
that an apparent rise in the export figures was an illusion. To
his knowledge manufacturers in need of ready money, who did
not wish to endanger their credit at home by betraying their
situation, had obtained advances of up to 50 per cent on
consignments sent on speculation to foreign markets, even if
they sold there at a loss.[2] No doubt at anti-Corn Law meetings
speakers had every reason to draw a gloomy picture; but in
reporting the first one the *Bath Chronicle*, whose politics were
not those of the Free Traders, did not deny the position; it
only remarked that the cause did not lie in the Corn Laws but
in trade having gone to the north; 'and this used to be the
reason given by the western manufacturers until two or three
years ago'.[3]

The depression is reflected in the population returns. The
Gloucestershire cloth-making region, which had gained
between 8 and 9 per cent overall between 1821 and 1831, lost
it all in the next decade. Uley lost over 900 people and Wotton-
under-Edge 780. The lower region as a whole lost 16 per cent;
Stroudwater only lost 5 per cent with appreciable gains at
Stonehouse and Eastington. Frome and the villages round it
had been showing a continuous decrease since 1821 which now
amounted to 7 per cent, but this was less in proportion over
twenty years than Gloucestershire had lost in ten. The population of the west Wiltshire towns, on the other hand, showed a
small increase since 1831 of over 2 per cent, but, surprisingly,
it was greater in Bradford and Westbury than in Trowbridge,
which with its surrounding villages, was almost stationary.
This does not bear out the remark of the *Bath Chronicle* in 1842
that Trowbridge had gone up as fast as Bradford had gone
down,[4] although this was certainly true of an earlier period.

There are two unofficial sets of figures showing the decline

[1] *Gloucester Journal*, 15 Jan. 1842. Report of same meeting.
[2] Ibid., 22 Jan. 1842.
[3] *Bath Chronicle*, 13 Jan. 1842.   [4] Ibid.

in the number of mills at work in Gloucestershire, one compiled by Miles in 1839[1] and the other by S. S. Marling in connection with the anti-Corn Law meeting of 1842.[2] With them may be compared the official returns for 1835, 1836, and 1838.[3] In the following table Miles's figures are in brackets and those in italics come from Marling. The official figures are in roman type.

Mills at work in Gloucestershire

c. 1820	1831	1835	1836	Year ended June, 1838	March 1839	1841
(137)	*133*	118	118	96 (plus 29 unoccupied)	(79)	77

(The official figures do not include the Kingswood mills which were in Wiltshire; whether the others do so is unknown. Five mills, plus one which was not working in 1838, should therefore be added to the official figures and possibly to the others.)

Although not strictly comparable, these figures are probably sufficiently accurate to show that the two main periods when mills closed down were immediately after 1832 when the East India Company's orders were lost and during the depression from 1837 to 1841. It must be remembered that not all mills were fully organized factories. Some contained only fulling and finishing machinery while others provided for nothing but spinning. Many manufacturers occupied two or more mills, so that one failure might put several out of commission.

No such table can be drawn up for Wiltshire or Somerset. The official figures, deducting the Kingswood mills, show a decrease from 54 to 45 mills over the greater part of Wiltshire between 1835 and 1838 and only one unoccupied in the latter year;[4] but there had been a much greater shrinkage than in Gloucestershire at an earlier date. The only comparable figures for the relevant part of Somerset are of 28 mills working

[1] *Repts. Asst. Commrs. Hdloom Weavers*, 1840, Pt. V, p. 363.

[2] *Gloucester Journal*, 15 Jan. 1842. These figures are also given by Bischoff, *Comprehensive History* ii. 436.

[3] *Returns of Mills and Factories*, 1836 (H.C. 138); 1837 (H.C. 122); 1839 (H.C. 41).

[4] Three mills at Salisbury and Harnham which were in Saunders's district are not included, as they were omitted in 1835.

in 1835 declining to 22 at work and one empty in 1838.[1] Some
were very small; in 1838 only 10 employed over 50 persons
each.

In this decline the exhaustion of capital by 'large establishments and expensive habits of living'[2] played a smaller part
than is often thought. There is little evidence of it in Wiltshire
and Somerset. Retirements had, of course, been many and the
only capital left in the industry by most retired manufacturers
seems to have been limited to the ownership of mills which they
could not sell and of which the value had in most cases greatly
deteriorated. The bankruptcies were certainly numerous. In
Wiltshire there had been 38 from and including 1816, in
Somerset 46, and in Gloucestershire 85.[3] Many other manufacturers must have made compositions with their creditors if
Marling's estimate of 50 failures in Gloucestershire between
1831 and 1841 is correct, for the bankruptcies only account for
just over half that number. Many of the failures were, of course,
those of men in a very small way of business, but six or seven in
Gloucestershire were among the greatest of the 'gentlemen
clothiers' and account for nearly half the firms which had been
placed in the first class of contributors in 1803.[4] That notorious
character, Sir Paul Baghott, who changed his name from
Wathen to that of the previous owner of Lypiatt Park which
he bought in 1802,[5] failed three times, in 1821 as a banker, in
1826 as a merchant, and in 1837 as a clothier, and was involved
in a case of fraud in between.[6] Osborn Yeats of Monks' mill,
who was not bankrupt but retired in 1826 having apparently
lost heavily, no doubt thought more of his shooting at Llanover
than of his business.[7] Edward Sheppard lived in great splendour
near Uley. Nathaniel Lloyd, bankrupt in 1826, had had a farm

[1] Wellington and the district round Chard are excluded.

[2] *Repts. Asst. Commrs. Hdloom Weavers*, 1840, Pt. V, p. 455. Lr. from S. Sevill.

[3] A few of these were dyers or fullers.

[4] Of the eleven manufacturers in the first class three (or four if the Hicks, who
had been Sheppard's partners in 1803, are counted separately) were bankrupt, one
(the Austins) was insolvent, and one (Yeats) lost money and retired. Three retired,
apparently without great loss, and the fate of the other three is unknown.

[5] See E. Moir, 'The Gentlemen Clothiers', *Gloucestershire Studies*, ed. H. P. R.
Finberg, p. 243.

[6] *Gloucester Journal*, 4 July 1829.

[7] Ibid., 27 July 1812. See also E. S. Lindley, *Wotton-under-Edge*, p. 276; *B.G.A.S.*
68. 85.

near Tetbury where he experimented with merino sheep (as did Sheppard) but he sold it as early as the bad year of 1809.[1] The Hicks consorted with the country gentry and employed Charles Hooper as manager of their business, but to judge from the latter's success when he took it over, no part of their failure can have been due to him. It is these men whose misfortunes have given the impression that Gloucestershire manufacturers took too much capital out of the business, but they formed a very small proportion of the whole number.[2] Those who generalized from their example were men like the Marlings and the Playnes who were in process of building up businesses by hard work and economy and had every reason to dislike people such as Sheppard and Hicks who were not only thought to have been behind most strikes but sometimes adopted a very superior attitude in regard to fears aroused by workers in revolt.[3] Miles may have been right in thinking that production might have been more regular in Gloucestershire if manu- facturers had had more capital to tide over bad times,[4] but it was retirement owing to dislike of risking capital rather than its exhaustion in other pursuits which denuded the industry of it.

Another and probably fairly common cause of failure was inefficient management, which might not be surprising among small manufacturers but is startling when exhibited by the larger ones. When J. F. Marling of Ebley Mills (the only unsuccessful member of the family) failed in 1837, the Elders of the Rodborough Tabernacle (of which he was Treasurer), in whose eyes bankruptcy was nearly equivalent to fraud, called him to account; but after examining his books they came to the conclusion that it was only 'oversight and want of investigation of his affairs' combined with the difficulty of the times which had led to his failure.[5] When a member of such a rising family could neglect his accounts one cannot wonder that lesser men were constantly feeling the penalties of doing so. An even more

---

[1] *Gloucester Journal,* 14 Aug. 1809; 30 July 1810.

[2] *1st Rept. of Fact. Com.,* 1833, B.1, 46.

[3] *Repts. Asst. Commrs. Hdloom Weavers,* 1840, Pt. V, pp. 448, 471; Cf. ibid., Pt. II, p. 450. For Hicks's attitude over the strike of 1829 see below, p. 239.

[4] Miles got this opinion from Stanton another large manufacturer, ibid., Pt. V, p. 415.

[5] *Stroud News and Journal,* 22 Mar. 1963, quoting the books of Rodborough Tabernacle.

striking example of lack of foresight is that of the Austins of
Wotton-under-Edge to whom reference has already been
made.[1] The firm of H & G. Austin dissolved partnership in
1811 when Humphrey retired; and George formed another
with a cousin, Edward Austin, a merchant in London, and his
two sons Edward and Anthony (not to be confused with the
Commissioner for Handloom Weavers in the Southwest in spite
of the identity of name). George died insolvent in 1815 owing
over £54,000, which included £30,000 to his cousin and £9,500
to his late partner and uncle by marriage, Humphrey.[2] The
partnership continued with his widow until the end of its term
in 1820, when a Bristol accountant was called in to draw up a
balance sheet. The nominal capital of the partners was then
£88,000 and the debts of £189,278 exceeded the assets by
£45,879. Some of these were the result of the practice of acting
as bankers to people in the neighbourhood; and nearly
£26,000 was shown on the debit side in cash accounts, accep-
tances, and outstanding notes, as well as some large sums which
seem to have been deposited by local residents, almost certainly
at interest. Whether it was usual among the substantial clothiers
to undertake this kind of miniature banking business is unknown, but the custom of issuing small notes appears to have
been widespread before it was forbidden in 1826.[3] The Austins
made no division between banking and trade debts and it
looks as if money deposited was simply used as capital in the
business, though the large deposits, especially those from the
Austin family, were probably made with this in mind. Bad
debts due to the firm totalled £8,973 and those classed as doubtful made another £14,650 which were valued at only £3,640.
Another £4,502 was allowed for discounts and cost of collection, so that, in all, over 61 per cent of the deficit was due to
these causes. A capital of over £15,000 was locked up in stocks
consigned to foreign centres, mainly to Russia; and cloth and

[1] Glouc. C.R.O., D.2078, Balance sheet of 1821; and D.654 II/4, B.1, Assigna-
tion to creditors, 1832.

[2] Glouc. C.R.O., D.2078, Min. of agreement between Mrs. Austin, E. Austin Sr.
and Jr., and A. Austin, 1820. He had overdrawn his own account by £11,703
possibly for purchase of land though there is not much evidence of this.

[3] P.R.O., H.O.40/19, fol. 263. Lr. from P. B. Purnell, 24 Apr. 1826, 'Distress . . .
will be much increased when the large manufacturers are prevented from issuing
their small bank notes.'

wool to the value of over £32,000 was in hand. Inability to sell was presumably the reason for what looks like heavy overstocking, but one of the main reasons for the deficit was the custom of selling to country tailors and shopkeepers, 139 of whom had become bankrupt since 1812, the majority in the last two years. The banking business was a dangerous activity but it looks as if the firm could not have carried on without the flow of cash which it brought in.

The secret of the deficit remained in the family for another ten years, during the latter part of which the firm contracted its business, relinquishing three of its five mills and reducing its notes and cash deposits. In 1830 it was forced to make an agreement with its creditors[1] by which, in consideration of paying 4s. 6d. in the pound at once, it was allowed to carry on its business and dispose of its assets under the control of trustees. Two years later, having only achieved a total dividend of 7s. 6d., the partners conveyed all their partnership estate to two of the trustees for the benefit of their creditors. The debts then totalled just over £60,000 ranging from the £17,059 due to Miss M. Austin and sisters and the £13,444 to Major Adey, down to sums of one or two pounds. It is impossible to tell how the 110 creditors were divided between banking and trade, but the sum owing on notes and cheques was only £244. 10s. Against these debts the monetary assets appear to have been only £6,040 with another £1,708 to come from trade debts considered good. Those considered bad amounted to £13,827, nearly half of which was represented by a sum of £6,166, owing by an agent in New York, who had partly satisfied it by a grant of land in America. £5,798 was owing from forty-nine insolvent debtors, all apparently shopkeepers in different parts of the country, mainly in Scotland. The final dividend brought up the total to 9s. 4½d. in the pound.

The Austins may have been peculiarly unfortunate in their customers and it is obvious that they never recovered from George's insolvency. The difficulties in the Russian trade must have hit them hard; but they seem to have gone on in the hope of better times without changing their methods of marketing, even when the uncertainties of payment by country shopkeepers had been so clearly demonstrated. One would have

[1] Glouc. C.R.O., D.654 II/4, B1.

thought that a clear look at their position would have convinced
them that a change was necessary.

Any comparison with Yorkshire is impossible until 1838,
just after the start of the depression (see Table overleaf), since
the figures for 1835 are unreliable.[1] The west had over 22
per cent of the total number of workers in woollen factories
throughout the kingdom against 54 per cent in Yorkshire. On
average the western mills were larger, though none were as
large as the biggest Yorkshire factories,[2] and they employed
over 20 per cent of the power in use against 55 per cent in
Yorkshire. Gloucestershire was about as economical as Yorkshire in its use of power, but Wiltshire and Somerset were not,
probably because of the number of cases in which finishing by
hand was still carried out in the mills.[3] Another point which
emerges is the depth of the depression in the west, as measured
by the proportion of power actually in use as compared both
with that in Yorkshire and in the whole industry. The most
surprising fact, however, lies in the amount produced in
Gloucestershire as compared with that in Yorkshire. The
quantity of cloth made there in 1838 was 1,593,594 yards.[4]
Yorkshire, which had nearly four and a half times the power
in use must have produced at least nine or ten times as much
and probably more.[5] A much larger production of coarse and
medium cloth from the same resources is, of course, to be expected; but it is surprising to find it of this order.

Comparison with the past is difficult because of uncertainty
about the length of the piece in the eighteenth century. The
greatest quantity made in one year in Gloucestershire between
1821 and 1838 was a little over two million yards in 1832.
Wiltshire and Somerset together produced about half as much
according to Charles Wilkins of Twerton in 1836,[6] so that the
total annual production of the west in the thirties cannot have

---

[1] See *Repts. Insp. of Facts.*, 31 Oct. 1856 (H.C. 2153), p. 11.
[2] See unpublished thesis by Dr. R. M. Hartwell (p. 164, n. 1), p. 338, n. 2.
[3] See above, pp. 160–1.   [4] See App. V, Table Q.
[5] The production of Yorks. in 1820 (the last year before the repeal of the Stamp-
ing Acts) was over 9 million yd. of broadcloth alone without including narrow
cloth and kerseymere. Bad times may have diminished production there as well as
in the west, but the export figures of cloth for 1838 were much larger than those for
1821. See Bischoff, op. cit. ii. Tables IV and VII.
[6] Arch. H.L., *Min. of Ev. before H. of L. Ctee on the Bristol–Birm. Rly.*, 1835, p. 31.
He excepted his own mill which made 70 pieces a week.

Mills, persons employed, and h.p. available and in use, 1838[1]

	mills	number employed	number per mill	h.p. available				h.p. in use		number of workers per h.p. in use
				steam	percentage of total	water	total available		percentage of total	
Glos.	101	5,740	57	873½	34	1,720½	2,594	2,053½	79·1	2·8
Wilts.	48	2,993	62	688	68	320	1,008	841	83·4	3·6
Som.	30	2,133	71	260	41	372	632	545	86·2	3·9
total West	179	10,866	61	1,821½	43	2,412½	4,234	3,439½	81·2	3·1
Yorks. W. Rid.	543	26,180	48	7,492	78	2,067	9,559	9,302	97·3	2·8
total Engl. and Wales	1,179	48,511	41	10,844	60	7,371½	18,215½	16,857¼	92·5	2·9

[1] *Return of Mills and Factories for yr. ending 30 June, 1838.* There is a discrepancy in the figures for the number employed in Kent's superintendency in Wilts. which is given on different pages as 596, 606, and 616. The figure taken here is 606.

The 5 Kingswood mills have been added to Gloucestershire's total with a corresponding diminution in the Wiltshire figures; but 3 small mills at Harnham and Wilton in Saunders's district have been added to the number given for Howell's district. The Somerset mills include 3 making serges at Wellington employing 298 people and 5 in and around Chard employing 126. These are omitted from the figures on p. 180 but are included here for comparison with later figures which cover the whole county, and also because there is no separate account by mills of h.p. in use. The West Riding figures do not include Saddleworth which fell in Horner's district.

been much more than three million yards of all kinds of cloth. The 85,000 to 90,000 broadcloths already suggested as a possible figure for 1788[1] might have meant something between two and a half and three million yards,[2] but this does not include the narrow cloth which might have amounted to 4–500,000 yards. If this is so, most of the increase due to the introduction of spinning machinery must have been lost, as Yorkshire progressively took over the manufacture of all but the best cloth.

This raises the question of the 'backwardness' which is generally assumed to have been the state of the west as compared with the advanced technology of Yorkshire.[3] In fact, the whole industry was backward as compared with cotton or worsted and the west is often criticized with these industries in mind. No doubt it was partly due to the dislike of change exhibited by all those entrenched in the practices of a traditional industry. Worsted had been conquered for Yorkshire from other parts of the country by a number of determined men who, having begun with innovations, showed no hesitation in continuing them. Yet something must be allowed for the fact that the manufacture of carding wool, with its more tenuous thread, was less easy to mechanize than that of worsted or cotton. After the rapid adoption of the carding machine and spinning jenny in the north there was a long gap before further machinery was introduced. Had manufacturers in Frome and Shepton Mallet persisted with their experiments after 1776–81 their history might have been very different, for they, of all the western centres, were nearest to a supply of coal though it was not such good coal as that of Yorkshire. Here the west was truly backward and by 1830 it had paid the price in the loss of almost all its manufacture of the cheaper kinds of cloth. Backwardness in later inventions was less marked, at any rate in Gloucestershire. The mule made no great headway in Leeds until 1830, though a few were in existence earlier.[4] The first were installed

---

[1] See above, p. 62.

[2] Most of the cloth made by Carruthers in 1787 (see above, p. 62) was *c.* 30 yd. long. Cassimeres were shorter, but such long cloth as was still made was 40 yd. or more. Taking 30 yd. as an average, 90,000 pieces would make 2,700,000 yd.

[3] J. H. Clapham, *Economic History of Modern Britain* i. 144.

[4] Crump, *Leeds Woollen Industry*, p. 25. 'Mule jennys' had been in use at Saddleworth for a few years before 1824, *5th Rept. on Artisans and Machinery*, 1824 (H.C. 51), p. 388.

in the west about 1828[1] and the strikes of 1829 hastened their introduction.[2] They did not entirely drive out the jenny for a long time. Advertisements and catalogues of machinery for sale in Gloucestershire up to 1842[3] show only jennies in several cases, though it is perhaps unfair to judge an industry by those members of it who got into difficulties. In Trowbridge, too, the elimination of the jenny was by no means complete in 1840.[4] But nor was it in Yorkshire. Ure, writing in 1835, speaks of wool being spun by either method[5] and it was only in 1841 that the mule was said to be rapidly coming into use.[6]

Again with the powerloom, the west was not remarkably backward. The factory at Twerton had installed a species of powerloom before 1836 but the shuttle was thrown by hand and no labour was displaced.[7] The mechanized loom was only being slowly introduced into Yorkshire in the thirties.[8] The handloom was still the chief means of weaving in 1841.[9] What powerlooms did exist were mainly used for the coarser cloth, since in 1838 the finest was still better made on the handloom.[10] By this time there were 101 power looms in Gloucestershire where the first four had been introduced by W. H. Stanton in 1836.[11] They were divided between eleven manufacturers in varying numbers, from the forty-three owned by T. & S. Marling to the single examples possessed by three other manufacturers who were evidently beginning to experiment.[12] Their use might save two

---

[1] *Repts. Asst. Commrs. Hdloom Weavers*, 1840, Pt. V, p. 370; ibid., Pt. II, p. 441.

[2] Ibid., Pt. II, p. 459.

[3] *Gloucester Journal*, 30 Jan. 1841 (Shepscombe mills); 22 May 1841 (Capel's mill); 13 Nov. 1841 (Holywell mill, Wotton-under-Edge); 5 Feb. 1842 (Walk mill, Kingswood, and Rock mill, Stroud); 14 May 1842 (Alderley New Mills).

[4] *V.C.H. Wilts.* iv. 172 and see below, pp. 288–9.

[5] A. Ure, *Philosophy of Manufactures* (3rd ed. 1847), p. 183.

[6] *Encyclopedia Britannica*, 1841, quoted by Bischoff, *Comprehensive History* ii. 396.

[7] *Return of Powerlooms in Factories* 1836 (H.C. 24), p. 9 n. It seems probable that these 71 looms, the location of which is not given, were identical with (though rather more than) the 67 mentioned at Twerton in 1838 as 'not on the modern improved plan', *Repts. Asst. Commrs. Hdloom Weavers*, Pt. II, p. 412.

[8] There were 272 in 1835 (but this does not include Huddersfield) and another 226 which could be used either for woollen or worsted. *Return of Powerlooms* 1836, pp. 6–7.

[9] Bischoff, op. cit. ii. 396.

[10] *Repts. Asst. Commrs. Hdloom Weavers*, 1840, Pt. III (H.C. 43 II), p. 587. (Rept. of Chapman on W. Riding.)

[11] Ibid., Pt. V, p. 435.

[12] Ibid., pp. 376–7.

to three days in weaving a piece, but they were thought by some manufacturers not to be worth the cost of installation unless wages rose.[1] Wiltshire and Somerset were not so forward. There were three in Somerset, apart from those at Twerton, in 1835,[2] and eight at Heytesbury four years later.[3] The Staverton factory also installed them in 1839[4] but its subsequent bankruptcy probably did not encourage others to use them. The Commissioner for Handloom Weavers in Wiltshire certainly had some justification for his opinion that the county was far behind Yorkshire;[5] but it is still true that by 1842 the powerloom was only just establishing itself as a machine for weaving the finest cloth. For second and lower qualities, however, it had proved itself efficient, and it looks as if significant savings might have been made in the west by an earlier and more widespread adoption of it.

In finishing the position was reversed, at least in Gloucestershire, which was the only place where the gigmill and shearing frame had been introduced for fine cloth without disturbance. The rotary shearing engine, of which the type most frequently used was patented by a Gloucestershire manufacturer,[6] had almost superseded the older methods there by the mid-thirties.[7] It was used in Yorkshire too, but Ure's account of finishing processes in 1835[8] suggests that many of the older machines and even the hand shears survived, as they did in Trowbridge. Another important process, which was later said to have introduced a new era in the industry by preventing cloth from spotting after rain,[9] was the practice of immersing it in hot water which was variously known as 'roll boiling' or 'patenting in hot water'. This was the product of a Wiltshire inventor, J. C. Daniell, and was worked out by him in conjunction with Charles Wilkins of Twerton in the middle twenties.[10]

---

[1] Ibid., pp. 368, 434–6.

[2] *Return of Powerlooms*, 1836, Saunders's district. These come under the denomination 'Woollen or worsted' and may have been at Wellington.

[3] *V.C.H. Wilts.* iv. 173, n. 16.   [4] Ibid.

[5] *Repts. Asst. Commrs. Hdloom Weavers*, 1840, Pt. II, p. 467.

[6] See below, pp. 303–5.

[7] It is unusual to find an advertisement of a mill and machinery for sale in Glos. in the thirties which does not include rotary cutters of one kind or another.

[8] *Philosophy of Manufactures* (1847 ed.), p. 203.

[9] *Reports by the Jurors appointed . . . for the Exhibition of 1851*, p. 350.

[10] See below, pp. 306–7.

The proportion of steam to total power in the west was very considerably below the average for the whole country except in the case of Wiltshire where it was greater. Even here it was much below the Yorkshire figure. Steam engines began to increase in Gloucestershire about 1819[1] but they remained far fewer than in Wiltshire. In a town like Trowbridge, where the river has little fall, steam was a necessity if spinning and finishing were to be done on the premises. Bradford was better situated for water power, but the seven mills of which particulars are available in or before 1831 all had steam engines, though they were sometimes only used when water was short. The returns to the Factory Commission in 1833 mention only one water mill in Wiltshire as against 24 driven by steam, while in Gloucestershire, out of a total of 51 mills for which information is available by that date, only 23, or 45 per cent, had steam engines.[2] This is not the impression given by a witness to the Committee on Manufactures in 1833, according to whom there was hardly one mill in the Stroud valley where two-thirds of the power was not provided by steam;[3] but other evidence shows this to have been an exaggeration. It was the crises of 1826 and 1829 which convinced the Gloucestershire manufacturers that they must have some means of enabling them to meet delivery dates rather than trusting to the uncertain functioning of water power; but the cost of coal, a problem everywhere in the west, was generally said to be double what Yorkshire manufacturers paid.[4] In fact, if evidence at a railway inquiry in 1839 can be trusted, the average price in the Stroud neighbourhood was 12s. per ton[5] against a maximum of 5s. and often less in Yorkshire. The natural source for it was the Forest of Dean, from whence the coal was carried by private tramways to the Severn

[1] e.g. *Gloucester Journal*, 6 Sept. 1819 (Ebley); 15 Nov. 1819 (Kingswood). A dyehouse was advertised as suitable for a clothing manufactory by the addition of a steam engine, ibid., 8 Mar. 1819.

[2] Figures mainly from the *Suppl. Rept. Fact. Com.* 1834, II, *Answers to Queries*, B.1, 3–45, but some additional mills have been added from advertisements. Obviously many mills failed to answer and many country ones in Wiltshire and Somerset were water-driven, but that at Farleigh Hungerford, occupied by James Fussell of Mells, had a steam engine installed between 1821 and 1823, Som. C.R.O., DD/LW 41, Papers of an Insurance Agent.

[3] *Rept. on Manuf., Commerce and Shipping*, 1833, p. 68.

[4] *Repts. Asst. Commrs. Hdloom Weavers*, 1840, Pt. V, p. 455. Cf. *Gloucester Journal*, 12 Feb. 1831.

[5] Arch. H.L., *Ev. on the Bristol and Gloucester Rly. Bill*, 1839, pp. 101 ff.

and thence by barge up the Stroudwater canal. As early as 1824 Gloucestershire manufacturers had been considering a railroad from the Severn to run parallel with the canal to Brimscombe Port with a branch up the Nailsworth valley; but this scheme seems to have been an attempt to frighten the canal authorities into reducing their charges and was dropped when, after the intervention of several landowners on the route, they consented to do so.[1] Even so, the cost of Forest of Dean coal in 1831 was so high that much came from Newport or even Staffordshire, an anomaly which the manufacturers ascribed entirely to 'the notorious monopoly which prevails among the coalmasters of the Forest and the high rates of charge which their railways exact'.[2] It shows the difficulty of communications that no use could be made of coal from the Bristol coalfield which was so much better than Dean coal that 4 tons were said to produce the same effect as $5\frac{1}{2}$ of the latter.[3] In 1837 much was expected of an extension to Stonehouse of the tramroad from Coalpit Heath to the Severn opened in 1835, which would provide a new source of supply at cheaper rates;[4] but the line from Westerleigh to Standish was not in fact opened until 1844.

In spite of the completion of the Kennet and Avon canal in 1811 the main Wiltshire towns seem to have paid as much for their coal as Gloucestershire did; the small coal used by the Clarks in Trowbridge after 1818 cost 12s. 9d. per ton including carriage from the wharf,[5] as against the 12s. paid in Gloucestershire. Frome, though not far from the Somerset coalfield, suffered from transport costs as high as 5s. per ton, since the branch of the Somerset coal canal projected in 1796 in the direction of Frome was never finished owing to engineering difficulties.[6] Even so the use of coal was economic. In 1833, a

[1] G.C.L., J.F.13.106, nos. 8 and 9; J.F.14.106, nos. 4, 5, 7, 10.
[2] Report of a meeting called to consider a petition to Parliament in favour of the projected steam carriage road from the Forest of Dean to the R. Severn, *Gloucester Journal*, 12 Feb. 1831.
[3] See p. 190, n. 5.
[4] G.C.L., J.F.14/99, no. 5, Petition from Dursley. Two years later some Dursley residents had changed their minds owing to the decay of the cloth industry, Stroud P. L., Clippings iii. 98. For the line see E. T. MacDermot, *History of the G.W. Rly.* i. 208–9.
[5] *W.A.S. Rec. Brch.* vi, p. xxvi.
[6] J. H. Bulley, 'To Mendip for Coal', *Proc. Som. Arch. and N. H. Soc.* xcvii. 56–7. Coal was sold retail in Frome in 1830 at 10d. per cwt. (see p. 171, n. 2).

manufacturer at Hapsford, a mile or two nearer the pits than Frome, found that after installing a steam engine his costs were less and he used less labour.[1]

To sum up, the verdict on the decay of the west must take account of many factors. It was not only the low price of coal but better facilities for transport which made for cheaper production in Yorkshire. Leeds and Huddersfield had easy access by canal to the port of Hull; and Liverpool 'the best port in England for exports'[2] was not so far away. Communication with London was cheaper for Yorkshire manufacturers because of their proximity to Hull, and the Thames and Severn canal was of no use to Gloucestershire, for goods sent that way had been known to take four months to arrive. Manufacturers there complained that for bulky goods such as oil they were confined to Bristol merchants who took advantage of the lack of competition to charge higher prices,[3] and freight charges were extremely heavy.[4] Wiltshire and Somerset were situated in a flatter country where communications were easier, but transport on the canal was too slow for anything but coal. Railways were eagerly looked for, especially when there was a prospect that Leeds would get one before Stroud. In 1835 when the route of the Great Western was under discussion, Stroud ardently desired that it should pass through Swindon because of the opportunity afforded for a branch line; and manufacturers in Trowbridge, Bradford, and Frome were equally anxious for the southern route affording them direct access to Bristol and London. The fact that this route would put Gloucestershire manufacturers at a disadvantage in competing in the London market was rumoured to be an additional reason for desiring it[5] but in any case, access to a railway was about to be an important factor in keeping an industry competitive. If other places had one and Stroud had not, said Charles Stephens in

[1] *Suppl. Rept. Fact. Com.* 1834 ii, *Answers to Queries*, B.1, 52 (G. M. George, Hapsford).

[2] *H. of L. Ctee on Cheltenham and G. W. Union Rly. Bill*, 1836, p. 29, Ev. of E. Barnard.

[3] Ibid., pp. 9–12, 28, 33. See also *Gloucester Journal*, 28 Jan. 1837.

[4] In 1839 freight on heavy goods by trow from Bristol was 10s. to 12s. per ton, and insurance 7s. per cent, Arch. H.L., *Ev. on Bristol and Gloucester Rly. Bill*, p. 132.

[5] G.C.L., J.F.14.105, no. 23, Lr. from R. Osborne reporting on second reading of G.W.R. Bill.

1836, 'I think our destruction is sealed'.[1] The depression postponed the construction of the Stroud branch which was not opened until 1845. Bradford and Trowbridge never got their direct lines. The latter had to wait until 1848 for its branch and Bradford station was not opened until 1857.[2]

These adverse natural circumstances were not countered until too late by exceptional energy among manufacturers. Up to the period of severe competition which set in after the crisis of 1826, they were far too easy-going; 'their knowledge did not keep pace with the improvements of the times'.[3] This was altered in the thirties, but they then remained faithful for too long to the older types of cloth. Some diversification was, it is true, already apparent by 1840. Fancy stripes and tweeds were being made at Trowbridge and Westbury,[4] and 'Venetians' a development from cassimeres with a twill on the face of the material had been introduced.[5] In Gloucestershire rateens, patent twill and doeskins (also developed from cassimeres) were made, the latter new in the late thirties.[6] These helped to maintain what was left of the industry in the forties; but an earlier adoption of them, especially of the very popular tweeds which first appeared in Scotland in 1827, might have kept more of it in being.

---

[1] *H. of L. Ctee on Cheltenham and G. W. Rly. Bill*, p. 9.

[2] MacDermot, op. cit. i. 286, 414.

[3] *Repts. Asst. Commrs. Hdloom Weavers*, 1840, Pt. V, p. 362.

[4] Ibid., Pt. II, p. 409. Cf. G. Tucker, op. cit., who was selling tweeds made by J. P. Stancombe of Trowbridge in Bristol, 2 Nov. 1841, and Saunders's report on their great popularity, *Fact. Insp. Repts.*, 30 June 1843 (H.C. 523), p. 40.

[5] Messrs. Sheppard of Frome claimed to have been the first to introduce them, C. Tomlinson, *Cyclopaedia of Useful Arts* ii. 1036.

[6] *Repts. Asst. Commrs. Hdloom Weavers*, 1840, Pt. V, p. 367.

VII

'THE PALMY DAYS' AND THE BEGINNINGS OF THE FINAL DECLINE, 1843–1880

THROUGHOUT 1842 the industry was at a very low ebb. According to S. S. Marling, whose figures for the drop in production have already been quoted, the number of handlooms in Gloucestershire had been reduced by 1841 to 1,303, less than half those which had existed ten years earlier; and the powerlooms so far installed could not have made up much of the difference in productive capacity.[1] Certainly he somewhat underestimated the number of manufacturers in business. Instead of the 42, 47 names are listed in a directory for 1842 and one or two more can be traced from other sources,[2] but even this shows a loss of nearly 40 from 1830. There had also been a great change in personnel. Of the 83 clothiers who had signed the petition for the repeal of the restrictive statutes in 1802 only five or six firms were still represented by men of the same name. Three others among those who were prominent in 1842 are known to have been in business at the beginning of the century.[3] Most of the remainder bore new names, though some at least were related to the older families in the industry. Wiltshire and Somerset exhibit a similar pattern. About 13 firms survived from the 1790s, though in some cases the survival of the name may conceal a change of partners. Failures had accounted for at least 24 of the 83 Gloucestershire signatories and for a minimum of 100 other manufacturers in the county. 138 firms had gone bankrupt in Wiltshire and

[1] Speech at Free Trade Meeting, Bath, Jan. 1842, see p. 178. The Census of 1841 gave an even lower figure of only 1,069 weavers in the county, *Abst. of Answers and Returns under the Pop. Act. 1844* (H.C. 587), County of Glos.

[2] e.g. Monks' Mill, Alderley, which worked until late in the century, was consistently omitted from all Directories. C. Hooper at Eastington was also omitted in 1842, though he appears in 1856.

[3] Apperley, Marling, and J. Palling of Painswick.

Somerset without including fullers and dyers; and in neither case do these figures include those who had made compositions with their creditors without going through the bankruptcy court. The same picture, of course, could be drawn for the textile manufacture all over the country;[1] but whereas new names appeared in the north in greater numbers than those which had disappeared,[2] in the west the latter greatly exceeded the former. An estimate of the number of manufacturers in business at the beginning of 1843 gives 49 or so in Gloucestershire, 41 in Wiltshire and 17 in Frome and the villages round it, though these figures are, inevitably, not completely accurate.

'Without Corn Laws or with Corn Laws,' declared the Commissioners for Handloom Weavers in 1841, the south of England clothiers 'must yield to the superior local advantages of the North.'[3] They had already yielded a great deal, but the Commissioners did not foresee how long it would take to yield the rest, nor that it was not so much the superior advantages of the north as the prosperity of the west in its diminished field of production up to the late sixties, which in the end led to its further decline. There were, it is true, some bad years to go through before prosperity was reached. The depression began to lift in the west in the summer of 1843[4] and the next two years were active and profitable. The Clarks, whose records again become available in 1843, made a profit of 14 per cent in 1844 and $11\frac{1}{2}$ per cent in 1845. The railway arrived at Stroud in the latter year and everywhere in Howell's inspectorate, which included all the area we are dealing with, new buildings were springing up and old ones were being extended.[5] In 1846 the number of persons employed in Gloucestershire factories showed a decline of over 400 from that of 1838, but there had been a rise in Wiltshire and Somerset, leaving the over-all

[1] Cf. the estimate of 1836 that 9 out of 10 concerns in Lancashire had changed hands since 1819, *3rd Rept. from Select Ctee on Agricultural Distress*, 1836 (H.C. 465), p. 365; and also that of the Yorkshire Factory Insp. R. Baker, in 1846, that only 127 firms out of 318 survived from 1836 to 1846, *Repts. Insp. Facts.*, 31 Oct. 1846 (H.C. 779), p. 30. Bankruptcy and voluntary retirement had accounted for the remainder.
[2] loc. cit. There were 173 woollen mills in the W. Riding in 1846 as against 148 in 1836.
[3] *Rept. Commrs. Hdloom Weavers*, 1841 (H.C. 296), p. 64.
[4] *Repts. Insp. Facts.*, 30 June 1843 (H.C. 523), p. 39; 31 Dec. 1843 (H.C. 524), p. 6.
[5] *Repts. Insp. Facts.*, 31 Oct. 1845 (H.C. 681), p. 17.

decrease at just over 100.[1] There had obviously been considerable extensions to existing mills, the very small ones going gradually out of use and the larger ones taking in additional workpeople.

This recovery was checked in 1847–8 by the depression and shortage of money consequent upon the collapse of the 'railway mania' and the high price of grain. The machinery at Staverton mill near Bradford was up for auction again as the owners were quitting business,[2] but apparently it was not sold. The largest firm at Westbury, Overbury & Matravers, had been obliged to give up one of their mills in 1845, perhaps as a delayed result of the earlier depression; and they defaulted on the mortgage interest for the other in 1847–8.[3] Bankruptcies also occurred in Frome and Trowbridge. Gloucestershire seems to have been less affected, though A. T. Playne records a gradual diminution of profits for the whole period from 1836 to 1848.[4] The next two years, however, presented a more cheering spectacle, and in 1850 Howell again remarked on the universal prosperity prevailing among the West of England woollen mills.[5] The process of concentration was still going on, with a decrease of 32 mills from those at work in 1838;[6] but the number of persons employed was slowly rising. An overall increase of 229 in the twelve years between 1838 and 1850 conceals a small fall in Wiltshire, which had felt the depression most, and an almost stationary situation in Somerset. These figures do not, of course, include the handloom weavers, of whom there were still a large number. Though population was slowly declining, except in a few towns, this appears to have been due to concentration and an increased use of machinery rather than to further decay of the industry. Stroud, Trowbridge, and Frome all showed very

[1] See Table IV, p. 220, and p. 186. Kingswood had been transferred to Glos. in 1844.

[2] *Gloucester Journal*, 20 and 27 Feb. 1847.

[3] B. Little, 'History of the Sarum Fine Woollen Company' (typescript). I am indebted to Mr. Little and the Company (lately dissolved) for permission to quote it. It is not clear when Overbury & Matravers stopped working. There was a rumour that they were about to do so in 1847 but this was contradicted (*Bath Chronicle*, 18 Nov. 1847) and they defaulted again on the interest in 1851. Later Matravers was working a third, smaller mill (Town Mill) in Westbury, burnt down in 1861, after which he removed to Melksham, see below, p. 209.

[4] A. T. Playne, op. cit., p. 156.

[5] *Repts. Insp. Facts.*, 31 Oct. 1850 (H.C. 1304), p. 29.

[6] See Table I, p. 220.

small increases in 1851, but mills had been closed in several villages round Frome, and Bradford, Westbury, Calne, and Melksham had all lost population owing to emigration. In Gloucestershire the lower region continued to lose at a higher rate than Stroudwater, by nearly 11 per cent against 3½ per cent; but decline was noted in Horsley where eighty members of the Shortwood Baptist chapel had emigrated to Australia before 1850,[1] and in Bisley, Minchinhampton, and Avening owing to the failure of the cloth trade there.[2]

The Great Exhibition of 1851 resulted in nine prize medals for western manufacturers out of the eighteen who were exhibiting, as well as two others for cloth made in the west but exhibited by London wholesale houses, a grand total of eleven awards out of eighty-nine, given for woollen and worsted cloth.[3] Western productions were highly praised, but the Jury noted that the Stroudwater manufacturers had not understood that the object of the Exhibition was to show variety of production, and had exhibited only cloth of a pre-eminent character instead of showing their whole range.[4] All the other western towns which retained the manufacture, with Trowbridge at their head, received praise for excellent examples of cloth; and, among others, the only firm remaining at Chippenham, Pocock & Rawlings, obtained a medal for 'a variety of very beautiful cloths of great merit and permanence of dye and finish'. The awards were spread very evenly over the whole area and show that the traditional productions, fine broadcloths and many varieties of cassimeres and fancy cloths for trousers and waistcoats were still to the fore. Only two novelties had been introduced in the past ten or twelve years. One was the stout beaver cloth for winter wear known as 'patent double cloth' in which one side was coarse thick and warm while the other was very fine. This was a material especially liked by foreigners. It had been patented by J. C. Daniell in 1838 and developed by him

---

[1] Stroud P.L., *News Clippings relating to the Stroud Area* iii. 13 (Art. on the Free Churches at Nailsworth from *Stroud Journal*, Aug. 1960).

[2] See *Notes to Population Tables, W. Midland Div.* 1851, p. 25 (1852–3, H.C. 1631).

[3] The complete list of British awards in Class XII (Woollen and Worsted) is in *Ann. Reg.* 1851, ii, 425. For the total awarded in this class see *Suppl. Vol. to Catalogue of the Great Exhibition*, 1851, p. 196. *Catalogue* ii. 486 ff, gives names of British exhibitors.

[4] *Repts. by Juries appointed . . . for the Exhibition of 1851*, p. 351.

in conjunction with Charles Wilkins of Twerton.[1] The other, still in its infancy, was the elastic gloving cloth also used for trousers and later for great coats, made by Charles Hooper at Eastington, for which he obtained a medal. Later known as 'Hooper's lustres', it formed a very popular article in the trade for the next twenty years.[2]

Successful as exhibitors were, it was later said that the whole production of Gloucestershire at this time was only worth £900,000 a year.[3] On a very rough estimate, this must have been some £300,000 less than the value produced in the very prosperous year of 1836.[4] No figures are obtainable for the rest of the area and it is impossible to make any accurate estimate on the basis of the number of spindles employed. The total for Wiltshire and Somerset was about 91 per cent of those in Gloucestershire and it might be reasonable to conclude that about 75 per cent of them came from the area we are dealing with. More narrow cloth was made in the two southern counties which meant that the value was less; but the quality was as high as that of Gloucestershire. Nevertheless, it can easily be seen that western production now formed a very tiny part of that of the whole country. In 1850 the west had only 9 per cent of the spindles and employed only 17 per cent of the operatives in England and Wales, while Yorkshire had 68 per cent of the spindles and 63 per cent of the operatives.[5] (The greater number of operatives per spindle in the west may in part be accounted for by the more elaborate finishing processes used there.) Yet, owing to the nature of its products, the west continued to be treated as far more significant than its share in production would suggest. The credit of the industry at International Exhibitions largely depended upon it; and although

---

[1] Ibid., pp. 350–1. A strong cloth, scarlet on one side and blue on the other, was, however, being made in Gloucester especially for the East as early as 1805, Nemnich, *Neueste Reise*, p. 224.

[2] *Catalogue of Gt. Exh., 1851* ii. 496. According to the description of these 'lustres' in *Official Reports on . . . the London International Exhibition of 1871*, ed. Lord Houghton, ii. 13, they were knitted in the round, cut to make a single piece and finished like cloth. In view of the absence of any reference to machine knitting in Glos., this description may be due to a misunderstanding. There appears to be no patent for such cloth which Hooper could have used.

[3] *Repts. by Juries on the Int. Exh. of 1862*, Class XXI, p. 11.

[4] See App. V. Taking broadcloth as averaging 16s. a yd., narrow cloth at 7s. and stripes at 8s. the value of the cloth produced in 1836 would come to *c.* £1,280,000

[5] See Tables II and IV, p. 220.

the proportion of its production to that of the whole country shrank progressively during the following twenty years, it held its place as the 'prestige section'.

The next decade was a period of great activity. New machines were introduced and improvements to those already in use, such as the powerloom, speeded up production and reduced the labour force necessary to make any given quantity.[1] The early fifties were a time of recovery everywhere. 'During the last few years', wrote Howell in 1853, 'progress has been so energetic that places from which manufacture had almost disappeared have resumed industrial activity. The town of Bradford, Wilts., is a remarkable instance.'[2] Westbury was another. In 1849 Angel mill, which had become a corn mill when Overbury and Matravers left it in 1845, came into the hands of Abraham Laverton, a self-made man, the son of a weaver, who reconverted it to cloth and started a career of remarkable prosperity, which included the acquisition of the second mill formerly in the possession of the same firm, and ended with his election as M.P. for Westbury in 1875.[3] The later years of the decade were not so busy although the Crimean War provided a demand for uniforms; and the crisis of 1857 led to short-time working which lasted until the spring of 1858.[4] By 1859 Baker, who had succeeded to Howell's district, again noted that there had hardly ever been a year of more constant employment for the people or of more legitimate demand for the product.[5] The price of wool was high and an advance in wages must have stimulated the installation of labour saving machinery. Outlying villages, both in Gloucestershire and on the Wiltshire–Somerset border continued to decline[6] but, as before, this was only a symptom of greater concentration.

It was during the later fifties that the introduction of powerlooms was accelerated. In the area as a whole there were almost

[1] *Repts. by Juries . . . 1862*, Cl. XXI, pp. 4–5.
[2] *Repts. Insp. Facts.*, 31 Oct. 1853 (H.C. 1712), p. 25.
[3] B. Little, op. cit.
[4] *Trowbridge Advertiser*, 27 Mar. and 8 May 1858. Recovery was complete by the end of October, ibid. 30 Oct. 1858.
[5] *Repts. Insp. Facts.*, 31 Oct. 1859 (H.C. 2594), p. 47.
[6] See Population Tables in *V.C.H. Glouc.* ii. 175 ff.; *Wilts.* iv. 339 ff. *Som.* ii. 340 ff.

three times as many in 1861 as there had been in 1850. One Trowbridge firm could say in 1863 that the handloom weaver was almost forgotten,[1] but this was certainly an exaggeration. It may, however, have been generally true (as was said of the village of Broughton Gifford near Trowbridge in 1859) that it was only the fancy narrow cloth which was now woven on the handloom, because manufacturers were too uncertain of the fashions to risk installing suitable powerlooms,[2] which had been improved during the fifties to weave elaborate patterns.[3] Powerlooms with jacquard attachments were being used in Trowbridge by the seventies,[4] but there is no information about the date of their introduction. The last handloom weavers did not disappear until after 1880 but this was a case of survival only. With other machinery it is difficult to establish the date of adoption. It is clear that the slubbing billy was being superseded in the late fifties by other methods of making a continuous slubbing. Of these the piecing machine was certainly in use in Wiltshire and probably elsewhere in the west, though references to it (as everywhere) are few.[5] Much more important was the condenser, which drew off the wool from the carding engine in continuous rolls and wound them straight on to cops ready for spinning. Originally an American invention, it was quickly adopted by European manufacturers; but their English counterparts were very suspicious of it.[6] By 1853 it was being mentioned with approval as eradicating many of the defects incident to billy piecing,[7] but, although at least one

[1] Speech at opening of Salter's new factory, *Trowbridge Advertiser*, 12 Dec. 1863.

[2] Rev. J. Wilkinson, *History of the Parish of Broughton Gifford* (1859), p. 105 (W.A.S. Libr., Devizes, Wilts. Tracts VII). But when the machinery at Staverton was advertised in 1847 it included 'powerlooms . . . to weave any description of fancy patterns', *Gloucester Journal*, 22 Feb. 1847.

[3] *Repts. by Juries, Int. Exh. of 1862*, Cl. XXI, p. 5.

[4] e.g. *Trowbridge Advertiser*, 28 Aug. 1875, 'the property of James Cogswell retiring'.

[5] Ibid., 12 Dec. 1863; 31 July 1869. See J. A. Iredale, 'The last two piecing Machines', *Ind. Arch.* iv. 1 (1967), 51, which contains a photograph and description. It is mentioned in 1853 by J. Ibberson, *The Woollen Manufacturers' and Overlookers' Guide*, p. 13, and by C. Vickerman, *Woollen Spinning*, pp. 217–18, who says it was invented between 1830 and 1840.

[6] Several English inventors tried to produce a machine of this kind, including W. J. Dowding of Poulshot nr. Devizes, in 1827 (Patent no. 5566). That of Charles Wilson of Kelso, patented in 1834, is described by Ure, op. cit., pp. 181–3.

[7] Ibberson, op. cit., p. 13; C. Tomlinson, *Cyclopaedia of Useful Arts* ii. 1035–6.

Yorkshire firm bought a machine in that year,[1] it was by no means common until the later fifties. It arrived in the west about this time and superseded the billy or the piecing machine in the larger mills during the sixties. This is not the conclusion to be drawn from the official factory returns. In 1867, the first year in which the condenser is mentioned, not one was entered from the west against over 1,000 in Yorkshire. In 1871 a mere four were shown in Gloucestershire and one in Wiltshire against 1,651 in Yorkshire.[2] One can only suppose that western manufacturers saw no reason to let their neighbours know what they were doing (though they did not object to an occasional mention in public).[3] In fact, the machine making firm of James Apperley of Dudbridge, well known for its very successful patent feeding apparatus, which could be used either for carders or condensers and for which they obtained a medal at the Exhibition of 1862,[4] had patented four improvements to the condenser between 1856 and 1858 and exhibited one at the same Exhibition.[5] It would hardly have done so had the machine been unknown in Gloucestershire. Castle mill, Trowbridge, had one in 1858[6] and at least two other Trowbridge firms had adopted it by 1862.[7] One at Melksham was for sale in 1861.[8] There are also mentions of it in Gloucestershire in the sixties.[9] In fact, the official report, by George Leach, on carded wool and yarns exhibited at the Paris International Exhibition in 1867[10] included a long rebuke to northern manufacturers for their neglect of the condenser from which the west was explicitly exempted; for there, according to the writer, 'a system

---

[1] Brookes of Honley, Crump and Ghorbal, op. cit., p. 120.

[2] *Returns of No. of Cotton, Woollen, etc. Factories subject to the Factories Acts,* 1867–8 (H.C. 453); 1871 (H.C. 440).

[3] *Trowbridge Advertiser,* 12 Dec. 1863 (see p. 200, n. 1). The machine makers, Listers of Dursley, were making it in 1864 when their factory was burnt down, *Trowbridge Advertiser,* 13 Mar. 1864.

[4] See *Repts. by Juries...1862,* Cl. XXI, p. 4.

[5] Nos. 2666 of 1856; 1398 and 2785 of 1857; 1135 of 1858. See *Repts. by Juries... 1862,* Cl. VII, p. 2.

[6] *Trowbridge Advertiser,* 23 Oct., 1858.

[7] Clark and Salter, see p. 200, n. 1 above; Clark Papers, Machinery List, Wilts. C.R.O. 927.

[8] *Trowbridge Advertiser,* 25 May 1861.

[9] *Stroud Journal,* 30 Nov. 1867; 7 Mar. 1868.

[10] *Repts. on the Paris Universal Exh. 1867* iii. 67 ff., mainly reproduced in the *Stroud Journal,* 12 Oct. 1867.

of carding is carried on almost identical with that of our foreign competitors', and the latter had adopted the machine at a very early date. It is difficult to know how seriously to take this statement in view of the figures given above; especially as a professional writer on spinning made a violent attack on the condenser as late as 1894 on the ground that its use made it impossible to produce superfine English broadcloth 'in its old strength of fabric and fullness of face, lustre, and suppleness'.[1] As this was the material which Gloucestershire was most proud of, one might have expected some firms to have delayed installing it until the fashion for such cloth was on the wane.

Another machine which seems to have been quite as usual in the west as in the north was that for fulling, which had been invented by a Trowbridge engineer some twenty years earlier,[2] but did not come into general use in England until the mid-fifties.[3] The Clarks had ten, eight of them by the original inventor, in their Stone mill in 1860.[4] The fulling stocks were, however, still in use, and advertisements for fullers often required them to be familiar with both systems.[5]

In 1862 the Jurors for the International Exhibition in London reported that Trowbridge and Westbury had fully kept pace with the times and showed considerable progress in manufacturing power, increase of trade, and economy of production since 1851.[6] The other Wiltshire towns though praised for the excellence of their products, were, by implication, more backward in introducing new machinery, as may indeed be seen in some cases by sales catalogues of a later date. Wiltshire as a whole was, however, far in advance of Gloucestershire in the use of steam power; at 87½ per cent it equalled Yorkshire in 1861, when Gloucestershire had only just over 50 per cent,[7] and this inferiority persisted through the seventies. Though all the large firms there seem to have possessed steam engines, they had water wheels also and may have used steam only as an auxiliary when water failed. The advent of the railway must

---

[1] C. Vickerman, op. cit., pp. 218–24.
[2] For its early history see below, pp. 298–9.
[3] C. Tomlinson, op. cit. ii. 1037.
[4] Clark Papers, Machinery List, and see p. 201, n. 7.
[5] e.g. *Stroud Journal*, 11 Apr. 1868.
[6] *Rept. by Jurors for the Int. Exhibition 1862*, Cl. XXI, p. 11.
[7] See Table V, p. 221.

have cut coal prices but Yorkshire still had an advantage in that respect. It is not clear, however, that the use of water put manufacturers at a disadvantage provided they had the means of supplementing it when it failed.

According to the same report, Gloucestershire, or at least the Stroudwater region (and there was not much left of the industry elsewhere) had concentrated almost entirely on blue, black, and medley broadcloth, with scarlet for uniforms and hunting coats, some liveries and billiard cloth. The larger manufacturers had made great additions to their mills and had laid out capital freely to secure the newest and best machinery. This had resulted in a decrease from the level of 1850 of 22 per cent in the total number of persons employed, while the average per mill had risen from 75 to 95. In Wiltshire there had been an increase of 8 per cent in the number employed and the average per mill had risen from 80 to 98.[1] On the other hand, the value of production in Gloucestershire had only increased by £100,000 since 1851, 'far below the average increase in some of the other large manufacturing districts', and this was attributed to 'the universal taste of late years being for fancy and undressed goods a class which Stroud does not produce'.[2] The introduction of 'Meltons', without a glossy surface but with a softer and more pliable finish, especially associated with the use of Australian wool, had to some extent deflected public taste from the old-fashioned broadcloth to which Gloucestershire remained faithful.[3] Meltons had first been made in the west, yet only two firms, and those not from Gloucestershire, the Carrs of Twerton who obtained a medal, and Messrs. Sheppard of Frome who gained an Hon. Mention, appear to have exhibited any in 1862.[4] By 1871 they are included in a list of West of England cloth,[5] but in spite of their

---

[1] See Table IV, p. 220. The numbers per mill were far larger than in Yorks. (av. 55) or any in the kingdom except for Lancs., Derby, and Durham. The very large decrease in the number of mills in Glos. was mainly the result of concentration, but all the same 49 seems remarkably low as compared with 62 five years later.

[2] *Rept. by Jurors for the Int. Exh. 1862*, Cl. XXI, p. 11.   [3] Ibid., p. 6.

[4] For the Carrs see ibid., p. 15; for Sheppard *Trowbridge Advertiser*, 19 July 1862.

[5] Marling & Leonard of Stanley mills had some in the Paris Exhibition of 1867 and so had Laverton of Westbury, *Stroud Journal*, 29 June 1867. See also *Off. Repts. of the Int. Exh. of 1871 . . .*, ed. Lord Houghton, ii. 13, and *Stroud Journal*, 10 Aug. 1878.

popularity they formed only a small part of later production. Manufacturers appear to have been satisfied with the extent of their business as it was, for broadcloth kept a steady market even if it was not an expanding one. 'Business was booming in those days', said Sir Percival Marling writing of the sixties (he was born in 1861), 'and, as I am told, the buyers from London would come and mark the cloth in the loom before the piece was finished and gave large orders for West of England cloth.'[1] Playne's output too, was frequently sold as soon as it was finished to large wholesale houses in London, Manchester, and Scotland.[2] Indeed, Playne called the whole period of forty years from 1848 when, owing to a change of fashion, West of England broadcloth had come into prominence again, 'the palmy days of the Stroud valleys'; and although prosperity for the trade as a whole ended at least ten years before 1888, it is possible that some firms which had established their reputations managed to keep up profits until that date. This reluctance to introduce new and possibly speculative products was responsible for the very modest expansion in the number of spindles between 1850 and 1861, which showed an increase of 14·5 per cent over the whole region against one of 40 per cent in Yorkshire.[3]

After the depression in 1861–2, partly due to the new American Tariff, which caused some distress in Trowbridge[4] though its trade was said to have suffered less than that of the north,[5] there was a recovery to another period of prosperity in the mid-sixties. The healthy state of the industry from 1863 to 1865 was noted in the Factory Inspector's reports and the West of England was said to be in no way behind other clothing districts in 'manipulation', presumably indicating that its machinery was as up-to-date as it was elsewhere.[6] Trowbridge and the neighbouring village of Hilperton, together with Frome, Twerton, and the tiny village of Farleigh Hungerford, where a mill was working, were the only places in the southern area where an increase of population owing wholly or in part

[1] Sir P. Marling, *Rifleman and Hussar* p. 3.
[2] Playne, op. cit., p. 156.
[3] See Table II, p. 220.
[4] *Trowbridge Advertiser*, 31 Aug. 1861, 11 and 18 Jan. 1862.
[5] Ibid., 28 Sept. 1861, 18 Jan. and 14 June 1862.
[6] *Repts. Insp. Fact.*, 31 Oct. 1865 (H.C. 3622), p. 67.

to the prosperity of the manufacture was noted in the Census of 1871. Bradford had declined owing to emigration of weavers; and in Gloucestershire there had been emigration from Uley and Wotton, though Cam, with a successful mill, was said to have grown through removals from Dursley where mills had been closed.[1] The Stroudwater region showed an increase of nearly 8 per cent, but this was not solely due to the growth of the manufacture since many new industries had been introduced.

While the largest and most competent firms undoubtedly did well during the mid-century, the general state of affairs was probably less satisfactory than it seemed. A large number of mills were burdened with mortgages, many incurred as far back as the depression of 1837–42. Changes in interest rates also caused difficulties.[2] There must have been other manufacturers like William Barnard, a partner in Hunt & Barnard of Lodgemore mills, who had, on his own confession, lived on the edge of bankruptcy for years before it actually happened in 1860.[3] He had formed a second partnership with T. Sampson of Ham mills, who was already in difficulties when the shawls which he was making went out of fashion. William Barnard was awarded only a second-class certificate by the Bankruptcy Court owing to some dubious transactions in which he seems to have used the name of his other partnership, without Hunt's knowledge, to back up the failing credit of Sampson and himself.[4] Many others must have failed to retrieve their fortunes and have maintained an unstable position, liable to fall victim to later crises. Some were possibly operating on too large a scale for their capital. After the failure of J. & E. Hayward of Trowbridge in 1879, the auctioneer, an old friend, hinted that it might have been due to the rebuilding of their mill on a large scale and their investment in new and expensive machinery.[5]

[1] *Notes to Popn. Tables S.W. Div.*, 1871, 220, b and f; 253, i and m; 256, h; *W. Midland Div.* 279, i, j, k (1872 H.C. 67b).

[2] High discount rates are mentioned in 1861 as a cause of difficulties, *Trowbridge Advertiser*, 31 Aug. 1861; and there were frequent changes in Bank Rate in 1864, *Ann. Reg.*, 1864, i. 168–9.

[3] See report of bankruptcy proceedings, *Stroud Journal*, 25 Aug. 1860.

[4] Bankruptcy proceedings (see above note) and information from Mr. Waldron from a pamphlet written by Sampson in answer to accusations by Barnard.

[5] *Trowbridge Advertiser*, 1 Nov. 1879.

The amount of capital employed was very varied. Beginners with skill and judgement, not to mention good luck, could work their way up with a much smaller sum than that needed by established manufacturers with more extensive premises. How small was the amount upon which it was thought that a man might begin operations may be seen from an advertisement in 1871 which offered a small mill with the most modern machinery for making eighteen to twenty pieces a week as ‘a first class opportunity for a man with about £2,000’. The mill could be rented and part of the cost of the machinery left on mortgage.[1] Again, when John Libby (who was already in partnership with Hugh Pearce in a cloth factor’s business in Stroud with a joint capital of £8,000) arranged to begin clothmaking on his own account but still in the same partnership, it was stipulated that the capital he should invest in it should not be less than £2,000; but in this case he appears to have owned the mill already.[2] A man who started with nothing but £2,000 would have been in a very unsafe position in bad times, but if he was lucky, with a few prosperous years to start with, he might become very successful. Abraham Laverton, who had been in the employ of the Sheppards at Frome, can hardly have had so much when he started at Westbury, and he became one of the most successful manufacturers in the area.

At the other end of the scale, the Marlings, the early stages of whose business have already been described, were recognized in the mid-century as the most prominent manufacturers in the area.[3] The capital of Marling, Strachan, & Co. of Stanley mills before Strachan left the partnership was over £160,000 and after Stanley & Ebley mills and the two branches of the family were united in 1869 it was £176,000.[4] That of the Wiltshire manufacturers was more modest. Thomas Clark had £59,000 in the business when he retired in 1857 and in 1869 his three sons and their two sisters had over £95,000.[5] The Clarks were

[1] Ibid., 28 Jan. 1871.

[2] Glouc. C.R.O., D.1159 Acc. 1753. Articles of partnership between J. Libby and H. Pearce, 1864.

[3] Tucker, Reminiscences, 23 Oct. 1843; 1 May 1844.

[4] E. Moir, Typescript History of Marling & Evans in possession of the firm to whom and to the author I am indebted for permission to quote it.

[5] £22,444 of this belonged to the sisters and was gradually repaid to their heirs in the next ten years.

among the larger Trowbridge manufacturers, and in 1872, when several of the latter gave evidence on the Trowbridge Water Bill, the capital represented by their mills was given at £40,000 to £50,000 apiece,[1] but this was presumably only the fixed capital; the Clarks for instance gave theirs at £50,000, about £40,000 lower than the whole sum involved.

Below these came a group of men of whom we know little, whose whole capital may have been between £10,000 and £40,000. Ezekiel Edmonds of Church Street Mills, Bradford, bankrupt in 1865, the last member of a family which had had a successful career since 1791 at least, had £25,000 in his business, of which £7,000 was borrowed on bond.[2] Joseph Harrop of Boyers' mill, Westbury, which he rented at £400 per annum, said in 1872 that he had invested £16,000 and that the plant was worth £7,000 more.[3] When Staverton mill was eventually bought by a northern manufacturer who, after trying to find a tenant without success,[4] put in a manager and ran it himself, he thought that £16,000 would be an ample investment (presumably without including the value of the mill), but five years later he had invested £50,000–60,000, though this had partly been provided on the advice of a manager who proved to be fraudulent.[5]

Only one firm, the Clarks, has preserved any account of profits, and it seems impossible that they can be typical. The mid-fifties and mid-sixties were reckoned good years everywhere, but the Clarks never again reached the level of 1845. The highest amount realized by Thomas Clark senior between that date and his retirement in 1857 was just over 8 per cent in 1849; otherwise it varied from 3 to 5 per cent. When his three sons took over the business, they bought Studley Mills and rebuilt them, investing a good deal of money in the process. They paid 4 per cent interest on the capital invested by them and their two sisters and divided any profit above this sum between the three brothers who took an active part in running the business. Only once, in 1872, did they make as much as 8½ per cent, including the interest. Generally it was much less. From 1874 to 1880 they did not even make the interest, which varied

---

[1] *Trowbridge Advertiser*, 13 Apr. 1872.
[2] Ibid., 13 Apr. 1867.
[3] Ibid., 13 Apr. 1872.
[4] Ibid., 30 Dec. 1871.
[5] Ibid., 14 Apr. 1877.

between 2s. 8d. per £100 in 1875 to 3¼ per cent in 1880; but they never made a loss. The Clarks claimed to want not a large but a regular business.[1] They had large funds invested outside it and seem to have been content to go on working their mills as long as they did not lose by them. If their profits were, in fact, typical of those made by other manufacturers, one cannot wonder at the willingness of the latter to retire when any diminution of them occurred; but they probably were not or one would not find new men entering the business. These were not many, but among them were men like Libby, already mentioned, Strachan,[2] and Walker, who had all been previously engaged as cloth merchants or factors. George Tucker, also, must have anticipated a good return when he bought Wallbridge mill, Frome, for his son in the early seventies; and Arthur Tucker had his first successful year in 1875[3] when the Clarks paid only 2s. 8d. in the £100.

One form of organization which the west steadfastly refused to adopt was the joint stock undertaking. Two efforts were made to form companies of this kind. The first, an attempt to introduce the process of manufacturing cloth by felting, seems to have been inspired by Ezekiel Edmonds in hopes of retrieving his bankruptcy; but it never produced any cloth although the expensive machinery was installed, not at Staverton mill as advertised, but in Edmonds' own mill in Bradford.[4] After this failure there was another attempt, which initially had also something to do with Edmonds, to form a joint stock company for clothmaking, and operations were carried on at Staverton for more than a year; but obviously the public did not subscribe and the Company went into liquidation within three years of its foundation.[5]

While large mills such as Vatch mills, New mill, and Ham mill, all near Stroud, and Cam mill at Dursley were bought either by new firms or by manufacturers already established who formed new partnerships, several lay on hand for some time before being reoccupied. Staverton mill seems to have remained empty from 1847 until about 1850 when it was

[1] Ibid., 2 Dec. 1865.   [2] Moir, op. cit.
[3] Tucker MSS., last entry.
[4] *Trowbridge Advertiser*, 27 Feb. 1864; 20 Feb. 1866.
[5] Ibid., 9 and 18 Feb. 1867; 9 Mar. 1867; 25 June 1867; 5 Mar. 1870.

acquired for the rubber manufacture[1] but it had again been empty for a long time in 1864.[2] None of the cloth enterprises later connected with it succeeded. Castle St. mill in Trowbridge, put up for auction after John Stancombe's death in 1858, had been built at a cost of over £10,000, mortgaged for £5,000, and finally, after a second auction, was bought in at £3,950 by W. J. Stancombe, John's brother.[3] Melksham mill was put up for sale in 1861, but no bid reached the reserve of £3,600 and it was finally rented to Matravers whose mill at Westbury had just been burnt down.[4] Outlying mills without steam power, if sold at all, were not bought by cloth manufacturers. Monks' mill at Alderley attracted no tenant when it was offered on lease with the machinery as a going concern in 1868, and, after a year's delay, the owner removed the machinery to another mill at Stonehouse.[5] Bratton mills were sold to an agricultural machinery maker in 1859[6] and there are many other examples. A frequent successor to cloth was the manufacture of flock which had begun in the thirties and increased greatly in the middle of the century.[7] There were many other purposes for which former cloth mills were acquired, silk everywhere, rubber in Wiltshire, elastic in Gloucestershire, and, especially in the latter county, timber, bone turning, manure-making, and so on, which diversified the industrial scene and had the useful result of making the area less dependent on a single industry.

The latter, however, continued to increase up to 1867, though not in such a spectacular way as in some other parts of the country.[8] In spite of some difficulties created by the financial crisis of 1866, it was stated to be thoroughly sound and the *Trowbridge Advertiser* was told that autumn that 'our

---

[1] W. Woodruff, *The Rise of the British Rubber Industry*, pp. 20 n. 4, 219–20.

[2] *Trowbridge Advertiser*, 27 Feb. 1864.

[3] Ibid., 23 Oct. and 27 Nov. 1858; 25 June 1859.

[4] Abstract of Title in possession of Avon Rubber Co., kindly made available to me by Professor J. E. Woodruff. See also *Trowbridge Advertiser*, 27 Apr., 11 and 18 May 1861, which says that Matravers bought the mill, but in fact he did not do so until 1875 when he bought it for £4,800, of which £3,600 remained on mortgage which was never repaid.

[5] *Stroud Journal*, 28 Mar. 1868; J. Tann, op. cit., p. 98.

[6] *Trowbridge Advertiser*, 30 July and 20 Aug. 1859.

[7] Walker MSS. Walker began his career as a traveller in cloth and flock and had a great success with the latter, since it was needed for the beds of the navvies making the railway from Yeovil to Exeter.

[8] See note to Table II, p. 220.

staple trade was never so prosperous as at present'.[1] A year later the Stroud trade was depressed,[2] but at the beginning of 1870 S. S. Marling could say at an Oddfellows dinner that 'the manufacturing trade of the district was steadily increasing and their present position contrasted most favourably with that of their less fortunate friends in the north'.[3] On such occasions cheerfulness was perhaps to be expected, for in fact trade was depressed, though perhaps less so in Gloucestershire than elsewhere. The figures given in the Factory Returns for the end of 1870 show a drop of 16,853 spindles in the county, or nearly 26 per cent since 1867.[4] In Wiltshire the drop was not so great but far more spindles were idle, 10 per cent as against just under 4 per cent in Gloucestershire. The decrease in Gloucestershire is not altogether easy to account for, though outlying mills continued to close. Park mills, Kingswood, were for sale in 1867[5] and so was Mill-end mill at Eastington just before Charles Hooper's death, after a long illness, in 1869;[6] but the business was carried on by his son at the other mills he had occupied. The machinery at Abbey Mills, Kingswood, was also advertised for auction in 1870.[7] A few others may have closed as well, but the whole number of closures would hardly account for such a large drop in spindles. Similarly in Wiltshire no mill was advertised for sale in these five years, and only one small one in Bradford was burnt down.[8] So far as one can tell, the closures which did take place were only a continuation of the trend towards centralization; but it may be that, for the first time since 1850, there were no extensions to existing mills. The only suggestion of bad times was the auction by the Apperleys in 1868 of Dudbridge Lower mill, after it had failed to let; for this was a newly built mill filled with modern machinery.[9]

[1] *Trowbridge Advertiser*, 8 Oct. and 10 Nov. 1866.

[2] *Stroud Journal*, 2 Nov. 1867.

[3] Ibid., 22 Jan. 1870.   [4] See Table II, p. 220.

[5] *Stroud Journal*, 12 Oct. 1867. They were bought or leased by T. and R. Porter of Walk Mill nearby, but in 1869 they left a list of debts and liabilities with the Bankruptcy Court, *Gloucester Journal*, 13 Mar. 1869. They seem to have been still there, however, in 1870, *Stroud Journal*, 2 July 1870.

[6] *Gloucester Journal*, 17 July 1869. For Hooper's death see ibid., 25 Sept. 1869.

[7] *Stroud Journal*, 29 Jan. and 12 Feb. 1870.

[8] *Trowbridge Chronicle*, 17 July 1869.

[9] *Stroud Journal*, 7 Mar, 20 June, and 4 July 1868.

Trade revived after the end of the Franco-German war and prosperity lasted until 1875.[1] In 1871 Trowbridge was singled out as containing 'the largest manufacturers of the superior class of fancy goods in England, if not in Europe'.[2] In Stroud that year was one of 'commercial prosperity and industrial activity'.[3] One or two observers were prescient enough to scent danger. 'Fine cloth is gradually declining,' said James Ferrabee, the iron-founder and manufacturer in 1871, 'and another thirty years will probably see it confined to two or three large manufacturers or altogether vanished from the neighbourhood.'[4] If others agreed with him they took no steps to avert the danger. In 1870 Mr. Cole, one of the Commissioners for the International Exhibition of 1871, was told in Bradford that nothing new had been done since 1862; and S. S. Marling agreed that Gloucestershire was in very much the same position.[5] Their staple products continued to win more medals at Exhibitions than those of any other woollen manufacturing area. In 1867 fourteen exhibitors from the west had gained between them nine medals in Paris.[6] *Galignani's Messenger* remarked that Marling's black and blue broadcloth was the best the writer had ever seen, 'holding a middle place between the extreme glossiness of the French and Belgian cloths and the dullness of the Saxon'. Nevertheless, it expressed surprise at seeing far less that was new or remarkable than it had expected to find in the English section.[7] At the London International Exhibition of 1871, when no medals were awarded and exhibits were selected by local committees, the Official Report again characterized the best West of England cloths as superior to most others,[8] and *The Times* said that there was nothing in the building to equal the combination of fineness and softness with firmness of texture and the rich but not excessive lustre of the first qualities of the Stroud black and blue superfines.[9]

---

[1] Cf. *V.C.H. Glouc.* ii. 193.

[2] Article in *Bristol Times and Mirror*, quoted *Trowbridge Advertiser*, 3 Nov. 1871.

[3] *Stroud Journal*, 30 Dec. 1871.

[4] Ibid., 19 Aug. 1871.

[5] Ibid., 2 July 1870.   [6] Ibid., 28 Sept. 1867.

[7] Quoted ibid., 29 June 1867. Cf. Official Report by Thos. Nussey and George Leach, *Reports of Paris Exhibition, 1867* iii. 61, 73.

[8] *Official Reports on the various Sections of the Exhibition of 1871* ii. Woollen and Worsted Fabrics, by Professor T. C. Archer, p. 13.

[9] Quoted *Stroud Journal*, 5 Aug. 1871.

In the return of mills for 1874, published in 1875,[1] it was no longer thought necessary to list counties separately, and Gloucestershire was included in the West Midlands while Wiltshire and Somerset were combined with Cornwall, Devon, and Dorset in the South-western division. At first sight it looks as if this was a symptom of further decline; but an analysis of the figures, as compared with those of 1871, shows that the other counties included in the West Midlands division had retained so little of the industry at that time that the figures for 1874 must refer almost entirely to Gloucestershire. They might indicate a rise in spindles of as much as 40 per cent, and even if there had been an increase in the other counties, Gloucestershire's share in the total rise must have been very considerable. It is more difficult to estimate the increase in Wiltshire and Somerset, since Devonshire had also a sizeable woollen industry; but it is clear that here too the prosperous years from 1872 to 1874 had induced manufacturers to extend their operations.[2]

Decline began towards the end of 1875 but, if measured by the number of spindles in existence, it had not gone very far by 1879 even in Gloucestershire; while those in the south-west had actually increased, as had the number of powerlooms in both cases. Unfortunately there are no statistics of the number at work, and it is probable that the increase took place before the end of 1875 when trade was still good. Advertisements of mills for sale increased all over the region up to 1880. They included, almost for the first time since the early forties, those of some of the larger and well established manufacturers. Southfields and Churches mills at Woodchester were put up for auction in October 1875 owing to the death of one of the partners, Messrs. Bubb;[3] the Vatch mills of Messrs. Hastings suffered the same fate in July 1877,[4] and Nailsworth mill, owned by Flint & Son in January 1878.[5] S. Long & Co. let their Charfield mill to elastic manufacturers in the same year.[6] The

---

[1] *Factory Return* 1875 (H.C. 393) dated 'up to 31/10/1874'. Gloucestershire was grouped with Herefordshire, Salop, Staffs., Worcs., and Warwickshire.

[2] See Table VIII, p. 222.

[3] *Stroud Journal*, 7 Oct. 1876.

[4] *Trowbridge Advertiser*, 21 July 1877 and 6 Nov. 1877.

[5] *Stroud Journal*, 12 Jan. 1878.

[6] Ibid., 20 July 1878. They continued in business at Kingswood New Mills until 1885 at least, but had gone by 1902.

Sheppards' two establishments in Pilly Vale and Spring Gardens, Frome, were also for sale in July 1879,[1] thus ending a connection with the trade which had lasted since the early eighteenth century at least. None of these mills were bought by cloth manufacturers and Spring Gardens mill, which was a mile or so outside Frome, was demolished. The sales were due to death or retirement not to bankruptcies; but there were at least two of the latter in Trowbridge, those of Gabriel & Maddox in 1876[2] and of J. & E. Hayward, already mentioned, in 1879.[3] At least three country mills in Wiltshire or Somerset were also up for sale in the latter year owing to the insolvency of their owners.[4] The textile manufacture was 'notoriously unprofitable' in 1877[5] and nothing occurred in 1878, 'a year of exceptional disaster',[6] to improve the situation. Nevertheless Gloucestershire manufacturers were congratulating themselves in November that trade was not so bad as in the north, and that the local situation was one of 'comparative prosperity'; but these remarks were made in speeches at local meetings where cheerfulness was in order.[7] The depression did, of course, affect the whole country as is shown by the far smaller increase of spindles in Yorkshire in 1878 as compared with four years earlier, but the two western divisions had together suffered a small decline, though it was under one per cent.[8] The impression that Wiltshire suffered more than Gloucestershire is reinforced by the statement that there was little more than half work in Trowbridge in March 1879, though one firm had returned to full time.[9]

In spite of brave claims there had been a suspicion for some time, voiced earlier in Wiltshire than in Gloucestershire, that

[1] *Trowbridge Advertiser*, 5 July 1879.

[2] Ibid., 22 Apl. 1876.

[3] *Stroud Journal*, 4 Oct. 1879. See p. 205.

[4] Freshford mill, *Trowbridge Advertiser*, 3 Mar., 19 July, and 2 Aug. 1879; Rockabella mill nr. Rode, ibid., 10 May 1879 and Hawkridge mill nr. Westbury, ibid., 16 Aug. 1879. Freshford mill was sold to flock manufacturers but the others remained unsold.

[5] Ibid., 5 Jan. 1878.

[6] Ibid., 4 Jan. 1879.

[7] *Stroud Journal*, 16 Nov. 1878 (at a Liberal meeting); 8 Mar. 1879 (at an Oddfellows meeting).

[8] See Table VIII, p. 222.

[9] *Trowbridge Advertiser*, 11 Jan. and 22 Mar. 1879. The firm was Brown and Palmer.

something more than trade depression was at the back of the lack of demand for western products. The rise of fancy coatings made in Yorkshire of a mixture of woollen and worsted, which cost 25 per cent less than West of England broadcloth, was beginning to affect the market for the latter after 1875,[1] though there appears to have been no public mention of it before 1879.[2] Possibly this was the reason which impelled Messrs. Laverton of Westbury to experiment with worsted as early as 1875. Worsted yarn appears in their stockbook in January 1876 and they continued to use it, perhaps not very successfully at first, since its value dropped from £673 in 1876 to £152 in January 1879, though it rose again to £527 in 1881.[3] There is no other evidence of such trials before 1880, though it seems possible that some other firms may have made experiments.

Trowbridge seems to have suffered more from Scottish competition in tweeds than from that of worsteds. It was being talked of as early as 1876 when a local newspaper published an article[4] pointing out that in the past year or so the demand for the high-priced cloth which Trowbridge produced was declining in face of the less durable but cheaper and more varied cloth made in Scotland. 'Where one piece of West of England cloth is sold now, a hundred pieces of the lower-priced fancy Scotch are readily purchased.' Some Scottish firms were even sending down goods to be manufactured in the west;[5] and if they found that this paid them, surely western manufacturers could make the goods themselves. Too many hoped that the preference for Scottish goods was merely temporary and failed to take into account the fact that the rise of the ready-made clothing industry, which had begun some twenty years previously after the invention of the sewing machine, had completely altered methods of production. Fewer men now went to their tailors; far more bought ready-made suits of a cheaper

[1] J. Libby, *Twenty Years' History of Stroud, 1870–90*, pp. 81–2.

[2] *Stroud Journal*, 8 Feb. 1879 in a pamphlet by Rowland Smith of Stonehouse.

[3] Books of A. Laverton & Co. recently deposited in Wilts. C.R.O.

[4] *Trowbridge Advertiser*, 12 Feb. 1876.

[5] As early as 1848 Peghouse mill nr. Stroud was making yarn for the Scotch market, *Gloucester Journal*, 15 Jan. 1848. In 1869 the wool at Holcombe mill, Nailsworth, insured for £400, was owned by a Huddersfield firm, Books of T. W. Newman, an Insurance agent and wool broker, in possession of Messrs. Newman, Hender & Co. I am indebted to Mr. Ponting for letting me see them and to the firm for permission to quote them.

and lighter cloth, less durable perhaps, but made in a much greater variety of patterns. One Trowbridge manufacturer who had moved with the times and adapted his patterns to the prevailing demand had obtained more orders than he could execute.[1]

These opinions excited much comment, a good deal of it favourable; but many doubts were expressed about changing the style of manufacture. If producers altered their machinery to suit new demands, was there not a danger of losing their old reputation which might never return. Even these doubters conceded, however, that there was room for improvement in design and the management of colours.[2] The whole area was far behind Yorkshire in technical education.[3] Classes in chemistry and in textile design were held in Stroud from the autumn of 1877 by Bristol University College in co-operation with a local committee and with the financial assistance of the Clothworkers Company.[4] Attendance was small, but the level reached was satisfactory, and though only the elementary stages of design were taught, at least a beginning had been made; but there were no further developments up to 1890.[5] Trowbridge was more backward still, though the occasional lectures on chemistry given with the help of the Gilchrist Trustees seem to have become a course by 1879.[6] Weaving classes only began in 1891.[7] Nothing had been done about textile design by 1880, though some manufacturers were anxious to start a class on it.[8]

Perhaps one cannot be surprised at the reluctance to change. The staple western products were as good as ever. Fewer manufacturers than in former years exhibited at the International

---

[1] No name is given but from the description of the goods at the Paris Exhibition of 1878 the firm would appear to have been Salters, which exhibited 150 varieties of trouserings and coatings in wool and silk mixtures for which a gold medal was awarded, see below, p. 216, n. 1.

[2] *Trowbridge Advertiser*, 26 Feb. 1876. Lr. from Bradford.

[3] Although the report on the Paris Exhibition of 1867 said that Stroud and Trowbridge, like Leeds and Huddersfield, possessed Schools of Art (*Catalogue of the British Section at the Int. Exh. at Paris, 1867*, p. 79), no use of them was made in respect of textile design.

[4] *Stroud Journal*, 5 Mar. and 27 July 1878. See also *Trowbridge Advertiser*, 13 Aug. 1877.

[5] Libby, op. cit., p. 83.

[6] *Trowbridge Advertiser*, 22 Feb. 1879.

[7] Article on Wiltshire Woollen Industry, *Wiltshire Times*, 28 Dec. 1929.

[8] *Trowbridge Advertiser*, 1 and 22 Feb. 1879.

Exhibition in Paris in 1878, four from Gloucestershire, three from Trowbridge, and Messrs. Carr & Co. from Twerton.[1] They gained four gold, one silver, and three bronze medals out of a total of nine, twenty, and sixteen respectively awarded to English manufacturers. A report in the *Leeds Mercury*[2] found Hooper's exhibit, which included his elastic cloth and a diagonal coating woven under a new patent 'by far the most remarkable in the place'. Other western exhibits earned much praise, but there was an ominous note in the conclusion: 'The productions of the West of England rank second to none in the world, though few but Englishmen can afford to wear them. French and German goods may be preferred for price but not for quality. When the fine cloth trade of America was transferred from the West of England to Germany it was a matter rather more of price and finish than of quality and make.' It is not certain when or to what extent this transfer took place, for there are few references to exports in the mid-century. Up to 1860 at least the American tariff was not high enough to keep out English goods and the finest broadcloth was not made there at all. The duties rose during the Civil War and were levied partly by the yard and partly *ad valorem*; and they were finally codified in 1867 at levels which resulted in a total of 60 to 70 per cent on the export price.[3] It may have been during this period that American buyers began to substitute the cheaper European cloth for the best English, but the change was certainly not a complete one. It was only after 1880 that the tariff was felt as a real grievance.

Any account of the western industry after 1880 would almost necessarily resolve itself into a history of individual firms. Some disappeared for reasons unconnected with the trade, while others continued to be successful for many years. There were prosperous times during the eighties and nineties when considerable fortunes were made. Production may well have been as great as it had been in the seventies, for the firms which sur-

---

[1] *Rept. of British Commission for the Paris Universal Exhibition*, 1878, pp. 446–7.

[2] Quoted *Stroud Journal*, 10 Aug. 1878. It seems to be part of the official report by J. Wrigley and C. E. Bousefield, the latter having been one of the jurors for the woollen exhibits.

[3] F. W. Taussig, *The Tariff History of the United States*, 8th ed., pp. 195–206.

vived enlarged their premises and increased their machinery. There were over 13 per cent more powerlooms (though fewer spindles) in the West Midland division in 1890 than in 1878, though the South-western division showed a decrease of nearly 7 per cent in spindles and 15 per cent in looms. Messrs. Evans of Brimscombe mills maintained in 1904 that their production was four times as great as formerly, and Apperley, Curtis & Co. at Dudbridge claimed that their progress had been particularly rapid since 1872, when a new member of the family, Sir Alfred Apperley (as he afterwards became), had taken charge.[1] Ever since the fifties at least production had been progressively speeded up. It was estimated that Bradford was making, or could make, about 15,000 yards a week in the later seventies and eighties;[2] and if Bradford, with only three or four factories, could produce 780,000 yards a year, the production of the whole region must have been far above the three million or so yards of the thirties. This, indeed, may have been part of the difficulty. The market had expanded but probably not to that extent, and could not absorb further increases in the specialities produced by the west. This was probably the main reason why, with one or two exceptions,[3] no new firms appeared to take over premises which had been vacated, and the industry never looked like an expanding one. For the most part it continued to make fine and expensive cloth, the market for which was limited by the number of those who could afford to wear it; and since the American market was important in this respect, it was at the mercy of American tariff policy. Duties rose again in 1883 and still further in 1890; and these high rates encouraged the manufacture of fine cloth in the United States.[4] A fall in rates during the mid-nineties preceded a restoration of the higher ones in 1897;[5] and by 1906 Marling & Co. were exporting only 35 per cent of what they had sent abroad in the easier period ten years earlier.[6] Further variations up to 1930, when the *ad valorem* rate was 60 per cent,[7] stimulated or depressed the

[1] *Industrial Gloucestershire*, p. 28 (G.C.L., J.V.13.1).

[2] *Wiltshire Times*, 28 Dec. 1929.

[3] One firm, Humphreys & Co., moved from Narberth to Woodlands mill shortly before 1904 (*Industrial Gloucestershire*, p. 28) but it seems to have disappeared by 1907. Trowbridge had one new firm in the late nineteenth century, taking the place of one which disappeared.

[4] Taussig, op. cit., pp. 234–66.

[5] Ibid., pp. 292–333.

[6] E. Moir, MS. History of Marling & Evans.

[7] Taussig, op. cit., p. 514.

export level; but from 1885 at least the United States could no longer be regarded as a reliable market.

Some firms which tried making worsteds had considerable success. Laverton's experiments must have paid off after 1881 since in 1883 worsteds had taken first place in their output. In 1880 Marling & Co. made an agreement with a man from Huddersfield to join the mill for five years; and in 1881 worsted formed about 20 per cent of their output.[1] Some other firms also tried making them, Salters of Trowbridge, where they appear to have been found unsatisfactory and were discontinued,[2] P. C. Evans of Brimscombe (which was united with Marlings after 1920) and the old-established firm of R. & S. Davis of Stonehouse, which was making them in 1904 but closed two years later.[3] Worsteds never became a very large part of western production, although Lavertons had a great success after 1922 with a very fine make which sold well in America, and some other firms have continued to produce them. The distance of the west from the centre of the industry in Yorkshire, combined with the fact that in normal times there was enough demand for woollens to employ the much smaller body of manufacturers without requiring so great a change in technique, are probably the reasons which have kept the output small.

Western manufacturers were often attacked for not adapting themselves to the manufacture of the cheap cloth so successfully carried on in Yorkshire. In 1889 George Holloway, a highly controversial character who had built up a large ready-made clothing business in Stroud, castigated them for refusing to provide for the market which lay in front of them, and declared that out of some 11,000 pieces of cloth which he had purchased in the past year less than 600 had come from Stroud. It was true, he added, that many manufacturers who had already tried to change over to making goods which were popular and fashionable had found that they could not make them as cheaply as their rivals, but they should go on trying.[4] At a later date some did, and in 1907 the manufacture of tweeds and rough coatings was being taken up with success by the more pro-

[1] Moir, op. cit.
[2] Information from Salters.
[3] *Industrial Gloucestershire*, pp. 25, 28.
[4] *Stroud News and Advertiser*, 22 Feb. 1889 (Stroud P.L., *Cuttings*, iii. 25).

gressive firms in Gloucestershire, some of whom were using English wool.[1] This was a more hopeful development than trying to compete with Yorkshire in low qualities of broadcloth, as the last manufacturer in Bradford did without success.[2] Although the advent of railways had reduced the cost of coal in the west, Yorkshire still had advantages, not least of experience, in producing this kind of cloth, which were bound to defeat such experiments.

In fact, although the decline of the west as a cloth-producing region was due in part to economic disadvantages, it was also partly caused by the same factors which had given the region a new lease of life more than 200 years earlier. Just as, in the seventeenth century, western manufacturers had seized trade from the decaying centres of Kent, Suffolk, and Berkshire by introducing a new type of lighter cloth, so they, in their turn, lost trade in the nineteenth century to Scotland and to the worsted manufacture of Yorkshire by delaying change until it was too late. Even if the disadvantages might have frustrated earlier attempts to produce a different kind of cloth, far more could have been done with new patterns and with materials not greatly removed from their existing range. The success of those who did venture into this field shows that it would have been worth trying by a greater number.

[1] *V.C.H. Glouc.* ii. 195, 197.
[2] *Wiltshire Times*, 28 Dec. 1929. According to the writer all the firms there were prosperous until 1894, but all except one had closed by 1898. The last closed in 1906.

Size of the industry in the west as compared with Yorkshire and the total in England and Wales[1]

I. Number of mills

	Glos.	Wilts.	Som.	total W.	percent. of total E. & W.	Yorks.	percent. of total E. & W.	total England and Wales
1850	80	36	31	147	11·2	880	67·3	1,306
1856	64	27	24	115	9	806	62·9	1,282
1861	49	32	26	107	7·3	924	63·4	1,456
1867	62	25	29	116	8·2	818	57·6	1,420
1870	28	17	28	73	4·7	956	61·6	1,550

II. Spindles

	Glos.	Wilts.	Som.	total W.	percent. of total E. & W.	Yorks.	percent. of total E. & W.	total England and Wales
1850[a]	61,896	33,804	22,604	118,304	8·7	925,449	68·2	1,356,691
1856[a]	63,256	34,473	22,879	120,608	8	992,897	66	1,499,949
1861	59,986	44,825	31,401	136,212	7·3	1,296,190	70	1,846,850
1867	65,094	43,607	40,469	149,170	3·9	1,342,690	35	3,822,916
1870	48,241	38,817	39,066	126,124	6·5	1,468,130	70	2,081,931

III. Powerlooms

	Glos.	Wilts.	Som.	total W.	percent. of total E. & W.	Yorks.	percent. of total E. & W.	total England and Wales
1850	224	170	27	421	4·6	3,849	41·9	9,170
1856	421	252	251	924	6·7	6,275	45·6	13,726
1861	618	549	401	1,568	7·7	11,405	56	20,344
1867	1,231	770	609	2,610	6·1	20,028	47	42,571
1870	878	585	657	2,120	5·7	24,033	64·3	37,356

IV. Numbers employed

	Glos.	Wilts.	Som.	total W.	percent. of total E. & W.	Yorks.	percent. of total E. & W.	total England and Wales
1847	5,308	3,265	2,180	10,753	17·2	38,737	61·7	62,687
1850	6,043	2,877	2,175	11,095	17·2	40,611	63	64,426
1856	5,409	2,709	1,843	9,961	14·4	42,982	62·2	69,130
1861	4,687	3,130	2,267	10,084	13·2	50,473	66·1	76,309
1867	6,368	3,192	2,518	12,078	11·8	59,602	58·4	101,938
1870	3,848	1,639	2,591	8,078	8	70,625	70·1	100,640

[a] Includes doubling spindles, see *Rept. Insp. Facts.* 31 Oct. 1862. (1863, H.C. 3076, 510. This also affects the number of spindles as compared with persons employed in 1850 and 1856, see Table VII.

[b] Total swollen by large increases in Lancashire, Cheshire, and Derbyshire which may have been the result of including worsted spinning in woollen mills, since a total of 36 combing machines in these counties is also recorded. By 1870 these had altogether vanished in Cheshire and Derbyshire and had greatly diminished in Lancashire.

[1] From the official Factory Returns:

1847 (H.C.294) *B.P.P.* 1847, XLVI (Numbers employed only).
1850 (H.C.745) *B.P.P.* 1850, XLII
1856 (H.C. 7) *B.P.P.* 1857, i XIV
1861 (H.C. 23) *B.P.P.* 1862, LV
1867 (H.C.453) *B.P.P.* 1867–8, LXIV
1870 (H.C.440) *B.P.P.* 1871, LXII. Return dated Xmas 1870.

V. Power employed

A. In west

	Glos.			Wilts.			Som.		
	h.p.		percent.	h.p.		percent.	h.p.		percent.
	steam	total	steam	steam	total	steam	steam	total	steam
1850	806	2,291	35	632	791	79·9	218	546	40
1856	740	1,904	38·8	674	752	89·6	259	525	49·5
1861	1,079	2,124	50·8	929	1,062	87·5	335	632	53
1867	1,954	3,244	60·2	1,012	1,123	90·1	644	999	64·4
1870	922	1,489	62	633	695	91·1	503	836	60·2

B. West as compared with Yorkshire and total in England and Wales

	W.			Yorks.			Total England and Wales		
	h.p.		percent.	h.p.		percent.	h.p.		percent
	steam	total	steam	steam	total	steam	steam	total	steam
1850	1,656	3,628	45·6	9,347	12,153	76·9	12,567	19,454	64·6
1856	1,673	3,181	52·6	12,124	14,853	87	16,265	22,526	72·2
1861	2,343	3,818	61·3	19,634	22,450	87·4	25,233	31,908	79·1
1867	3,610	5,366	67·2	21,029	23,803	88·3	34,880	42,506	82
1870	2,058	3,020	68·1	36,671	39,802	92·1	45,148	51,833	87·1

VI. Spindles and Powerlooms running and standing, 1870 (1870 is the only year for which this is given)

	Spindles			Powerlooms		
	running	standing	percentage of standing to running	running	standing	percentage of standing to running
Glos.	46,406	1,835	3·9	852	26	3
Wilts.	35,277	3,540	10	534	51	9·5
Som.	38,206	860	2·2	624	33	5·3
Total W.	119,889	6,235	5·2	2,010	110	5·5
Yorks.	1,353,850	114,280	8·4	21,613	2,420	11·2
Total E. and W.	1,939,368	142,563	7·3	33,792	3,564	10·5

VII. Number of spindles and of persons employed per unit of power

	Number of spindles per unit			Persons employed per unit		
	W.	Yorks.	total England and Wales	W.	Yorks.	total England and Wales
1850	36·2	76·1	69·2	3·4	3·3	3·3
1855	37·8	66·8	66·5	3·1	2·9	3
1861	35·5	57·7	57·8	2·6	2·3	2·4
1867	27·8	56·4	90[a]	2·3	2·5	2·4
1870	T41·8	36·9	41·6	2·7	1·8	1·9
	(R39·7	34	37·4)			

[a] See p. 220 n. b.

16—C.I.

VIII *West Midlands and South-western Divisions as compared with Yorkshire and the total of England and Wales after 1870*[1]

	Spindles				Powerlooms			
	W. Mid.	S.W.	Yorks.	Total E. and W.	W. Mid.	S.W.	Yorks.	Total E. and W
1870	49,001[a]	94,371[b]	1,468,130	2,081,931	894[c]	1,575[d]	24,033	37,356
1874	70,773	140,793	1,886,066	2,604,610	1,226	2,586	30,684	45,025
1878	66,684	143,281	1,969,616	2,738,381	1,186	3,042	35,927	50,249
1890	53,010	133,493	1,774,948	2,477,964	1,342	2,582	36,577	51,070

	Numbers employed			
	W. Mid.	S.W.	Yorks.	Total E. and W.
1870	3,957[e]	5,524[f]	70,625	100,640
1874	4,978	7,688	75,354	105,371
1878	4,081	7,575	80,597	109,702
1890	4,183	6,689	86,796	114,209

[a] Includes besides Glos. 760 spindles in Shropshire.
[b] Includes besides Wilts. and Som. 14,756 spindles in Devon and 1,732 in Cornwall.
[c] Includes besides Glos. 16 powerlooms in Warwicks.
[d] Includes besides Wilts. and Som. 297 powerlooms in Devon and 36 in Cornwall.
[e] Includes 13 persons employed in Shropshire and 96 in Warwicks.
[f] Includes 1,202 persons employed in Devon and 92 in Cornwall.

[1] The figure for 1870 has been calculated by adding those for the counties included in 1874.

1874 (H.C.393) *B.P.P.* 1875, LXXI (dated 'up to 31/10/1874')
1878 (H.C.324) *B.P.P.* 1878–9, LXV (dated 'up to 31/10/1878')
1890 (H.C.328) *B.P.P.* 1890, LXVII (Aug. 1889–July 1890).

VIII

MARKETING AND LABOUR IN THE NINETEENTH CENTURY

I. MARKETING

THE new century saw no great change in marketing methods, but the practice of engaging directly in the export trade seems, so far as one can tell, to have diminished during the first half of the century. It had always been confined to a few large firms and experience had shewn how dangerous it could be. Some firms were trading directly to China in the 1840s and relations with overseas buyers were resumed later in the century, but, owing to lack of evidence, one cannot be certain when or to what extent this took place.

The London factors still did a substantial part of the business, but as time went on, if the Clarks' practice is any guide, manufacturers became far less ready to trust any one of them with a substantial part of their stock. One of the most noticeable features of the Clark's stockbook[1] is the number of houses at which stock was 'resting' at each year's stocktaking, a number which grew progressively larger in the later years. Thus in 1805 stock for sale was lying at four London houses; in 1823 a much larger stock was in the hands of no less than twenty-five firms, as well as with at least one country agent. These firms varied in the way they described themselves from Blackwell Hall factors, merchants, and warehousemen, to woollen drapers and even one 'worsted web warehouse'[2] but, whatever their description, they received cloth to sell on commission and paid for it only after they had sold it. Messrs. Rawlings of Frome appear to have been distributing their stock in the same way between 1821 and 1824, and in some cases to the same firms; but they also sold cassimeres to a Trowbridge firm of manufacturers, John Cooper & Co., and in 1825 paid for scribbling and carding done for

---

[1] W.A.S. Rec. Brch. vi.
[2] *From Holden's Triennial Directory*, 1817–19.

them by the same firm partly in cassimeres and partly in cash.[1] If London factors failed (and many of them did so in the bad years of the twenties and thirties) the manufacturer could repossess himself of the cloth resting and might lose only part of the price of the goods which had already been sold. The fact that such failures do not appear to have been followed by an increased number of bankruptcies among manufacturers suggests that many of them followed the Clarks' pattern.

A Gloucestershire manufacturer, said Miles in 1839, except for some of the largest firms, could not make out his own invoice for the London market but had to leave it to the factor who made large deductions for blemishes.[2] This was merely a continuation of the system over which there had been squabbles ever since the custom of selling through factors in the London market had begun; but Yorkshire manufacturers, according to Miles, were free from it (though when they dealt through the same factors, as some were certainly doing in the 1790s, they must have been subject to the same rules). But the practice no doubt encouraged those who could afford it to open their own warehouses in London[3] as the Clarks did in 1826.[4] Large firms had depots in other places also. In 1836 Charles Stephens of Stanley mills had two, one in Scotland and another, just opened, in Manchester.[5] To distribute stock among a number of agents for sale appears to have been a safer method of trading than to sell direct to shopkeepers; yet the latter practice seems to have become even more prevalent as the century progressed. Its dangers are well illustrated by the Austin accounts already discussed.[6] Yet the numerous advertisements from experienced men having good connections with buyers, who were anxious to travel for manufacturers, show that much business must have been done in this way; and its extent can be seen in George Tucker's reminiscences. His employer, William Stancombe of

---

[1] Sales Book in the possession of Messrs. Rawlings & Co., Cardmakers of Frome, to whom I am indebted for permission to quote from it. The name of the firm in 1825 is not given but it may have been G. & D. Rawlings.

[2] *Repts. Asst. Commrs. Hdloom Weavers*, 1840, Pt. V, p. 358.

[3] Cf. ibid., p. 367, Ev. of W. Playne.

[4] They began to inquire for one in 1824 but did not finally settle until two years later, Wilts. C.R.O., 927, Clark Papers, Lr. of 30 June 1826 to Kendall.

[5] Min. of Ev. before the H. of L. Ctee on the Cheltenham and G. W. Union Rly. Bill, 1836, p. 10 (*H. of L. Sess. Papers*, 1836, vol. xxxi).

[6] Glouc. C.R.O., D.2078. See above, pp. 183–4.

Trowbridge, seems to have entrusted almost all his sales business to such men, but he also sent Tucker to sell direct for him in Bath and Bristol in 1841 and in Manchester and Liverpool in 1843.

There was also an increasing number of country merchants. Several appear in the bankruptcy lists in Gloucestershire and others are known to have existed in Wiltshire in the thirties and later.[1] Such men may have begun by acting as agents but they also built up businesses of their own. Their advantage presumably lay in having a larger stock of goods to show than any single manufacturer would be likely to possess. The process may again be illustrated from the case of Tucker himself. He started such a business while still working for Stancombe and devoted himself entirely to it from 1849 onwards. In the prosperous years of the fifties and sixties he did well enough to see his daughter married to one of the larger Trowbridge manufacturers and to buy a mill in Frome for his son in the early seventies. Walker, whose career has already been mentioned, also built up a successful business of this kind before becoming a manufacturer.[2]

In the last resort, manufacturers with stocks unsold might send them to one of the London auctioneers who held regular sales—'an eligible method of dealing with them' according to one advertisement[3] but likely to be ruinous to the seller, even if he did receive the proceeds as cash down. Or they might even try to sell retail as did J. F. Lewis of Ebley in 1841, offering fine Saxony broadcloth in lengths of two yards for coats and waistcoats and the same quantity of cassimere for trousers, in order, he said, 'to circumvent the enormous profits required by retailers';[4] but this expedient did not save him from bankruptcy later in the year.

Another development in the early years of the century was the establishment of factories by London firms, often by forming a partnership with local manufacturers; though Carrick &

---

[1] e.g. Peter Anstie and George Wansey, both named as such by Tucker. There are also several advertisements by such men in the *Trowbridge Advertiser* of the fifties and sixties, and similar mentions appear in the *Stroud Journal* and in the *Directories*.

[2] For both Tucker and Walker see above p. 131, notes 5 and 7.

[3] *Gloucester Journal*, 25 Aug. 1816; 21 Nov. 1825.

[4] Ibid., 8 May 1841.

Maclean, who had a large factory in Trowbridge from before 1815 until they sold it in 1818, seem to have operated it themselves, probably through a local manager.[1] They were probably the same men who entered into partnership with G. D. Harris and Charles Stephens in 1813 to buy and operate Stanley mills; if so, they were Blackwell Hall factors.[2] Another purely London firm was Divett, Price, Jackson, & Co. who established themselves in Bradford in the first decade of the century and whose renewed efforts to introduce finishing machinery in 1808 caused a riot;[3] in 1818 they were woollen drapers in Smithfield. William Ireland, a Blackwell Hall factor of Gloucestershire origin, had partners in Chalford making cloth for the East India Company[4] whom he probably financed; and several other partnerships of this kind may be detected in the bankruptcy lists, some being family ones.[5] Some others may, in reality, have been cases of 'commission houses', noted in 1839 as operating throughout the region.[6] These, of course, were not partnerships at all, since the London end furnished the wool and the country manufacturer made it up at a fixed price, becoming merely the employee of the merchant and unable to make a profit out of his judgement in wool buying. An undoubted example may be seen in an advertisement which appeared in the *Gloucester Journal* in 1819 asking anyone who was prepared to manufacture a quantity of merino wool into superfine cloth to send the advertiser his terms.[7] Another advertisement, which suggests a severely cut price for the manufacturer, offered unlimited bank notes for any quantity of cloth

[1] *Salisbury Journal*, 28 Sept. 1818. It had a capacity of 80 to 100 ends per week, an end being half a piece.

[2] E. Moir, MS. History of Marling and Evans. The names of both Carrick and Maclean appear in the subscription list to the Wool Ctee in 1802, *Gloucester Journal*, 11 Oct. 1802.

[3] See below, p. 231. They operated Kingston mill and still owned it in 1848, W. Woodruff, op. cit., p. 20, n. 5.

[4] *Rept. on the State of the British Wool Trade*, 1828, p. 315. Ireland owned land in Chalford including Sevill's Upper Mill, *Gloucester Journal*, 30 Oct. and 6 Nov. 1841. His partners were H. & J. Davis who operated the mill and were bankrupt in 1838 after his death.

[5] e.g. S. & W. Hambidge, Fetter Lane and Stroud, 1806; J. D. Hayward & J. Pinniger, Calne and Coleman Street, 1811; John Davis & T. H. Lloyd, Holt and Blackwell Hall Factors, 1812; H. S. & J. Joyce, Freshford, and T. Joyce, Bucklersbury, 1824.

[6] *Repts. Asst. Commrs. Hdloom Weavers*, 1840, Pt. V, p. 358; ibid., Pt. II, p. 408.

[7] *Gloucester Journal*, 2 Aug. 1819.

'if at a price equivalent to the peculiar advantage of a return in Bank post bills weekly or oftener throughout each year'.[1] The existence of such opportunities, however specious they might be, may perhaps explain how so many small manufacturers were able to start again after having become bankrupt, and also why men with very little capital could enter the trade; but those who did so and prospered (and some did) must have been able to cut themselves loose very quickly. In fact, it looks as if Miles overestimated the difficulties experienced by manufacturers in selling their goods, for no doubt they were as anxious as they had always been to blame the factors for their misfortunes and lost no opportunity of impressing their grievances on an official observer.

All these methods of marketing appear to have continued throughout the century. Possibly the practice of dealing with shopkeepers may have fallen into abeyance in Gloucestershire during the middle of the century, since Hunt & Winterbotham of Cam mills claimed to have been the first firm to adopt 'the system of dealing with the retailer direct' in 1864;[2] but Tucker had been contacting such people on behalf of his employer in the forties and so had Walker on his father's behalf. Even in Gloucestershire the intermission must have been a very short one. Apart from this, advertisements of country dealers frequently appear in the local press and dealings in London and the country seem to have continued without complaint; but the very old practice of allowing one yard in twenty continued, with some firms at least, up to the beginning of the second world war.[3] It was, of course, allowed for in the price and it does not appear to have been a real grievance; but, as a cumbrous method of doing business, the trade is all the better without it.

II. LABOUR

There is a mass of evidence about wages in the early nineteenth century, but most of it concerns weavers and much is conflicting. What is certain is that in Gloucestershire there was no agreed rate for weaving any given species of cloth (except perhaps for 'stripes'), as might be inferred from the pamphlet written by

[1] Ibid., 1 Feb. 1819.
[2] *Industrial Gloucestershire*, p. 24.　　[3] Private Information.

Timothy Exell[1] for the benefit of the Commissioner for Hand-loom Weavers in that county in 1839. In 1825 and both before and afterwards there was a wide difference, amounting to 12s. or 13s. per piece, between the sums paid by different manu-facturers for the same kind of cloth.[2] It must be emphasized that high rates of pay did not necessarily mean high earnings for they could be offset either by poor materials taking longer to weave or by greater deductions; and wages always depended on the speed with which a cloth was woven. But weavers naturally preferred high rates and were always campaigning to get those of the lower paying masters up to the highest level. In Wiltshire and Somerset the range of rates was much more restricted and most manufacturers, with the exception of some small employers, seem to have paid roughly the same rates for the same kind of cloth, though these were reduced at different times in the various centres of the industry. Rates of pay for factory workers appear to have varied much less between employers, and there was far less agitation over them.

It was the constant over-supply of weavers which prevented them from receiving the full benefit of increased production in the nineties. Scribblers displaced by machinery found work largely in cassimere weaving,[3] but this was balanced by the departure of men into the armed forces. Above 800 from Frome had entered the army by October 1795[4] and there was much enlistment from other centres especially after 1797.[5] The supply of weavers, which included many women,[6] was, however, sufficient to fill the gaps, except perhaps during short periods of particularly good trade. Rates of payment for superfine cloth remained unchanged in Wiltshire and Somerset. In Gloucester-shire, although one manufacturer said that an additional penny per ell had been offered for some articles in order to get wea-

---

[1] T. Exell, *Brief History of the Weavers of the County of Gloucester.*

[2] *Repts. Asst. Commrs. Hdloom Weavers*, Pt. V, p. 451; Cf. P.R.O., H.O.40/18, fol. 377 where weavers for one employer were said to make about a guinea a week while others got 14s.

[3] Probably in loomshops where experience was not required, *Ev. on Woollen Trade Bill*, 1803, p. 318.

[4] Eden, *State of the Poor* ii. 643.

[5] *Ev. on Woollen Trade Bill*, 1803, pp. 171, 262; *C.J.* lviii. 889 (Ev. of C. Brooke). It is more likely that greater enlistment after 1797 arose from unemployment owing to the scarcity of money than from a scarcity of Spanish wool, as Brooke stated.

[6] *Ev. on Woollen Trade Bill*, 1803, p. 336 (Trowbridge); *C.J.* lviii. 884 (Glos.).

vers,[1] the only rates we know of are not higher than those assessed in 1756;[2] but since the latter were never paid it may be that an advance had really taken place. In both counties weavers had the benefit of using machine-spun yarn which did not break so easily,[3] and it appears to have been more common to finish a cloth in a fortnight than had been the case earlier in the century.[4]

A weaver in the double loom cannot normally have kept for himself more than 10s. to 12s. per week if he had to pay a journeyman, who would get from 6s. to 8s. If, as most weavers did, he employed his children or apprentices instead, he might, in favourable circumstances, make 18s. 6d. to 21s. at the cost of feeding them; and a man with two or more looms (and many had at least two) might do pretty well. With the fly-shuttle he could do even better, though some did not. One witness in 1803 thought it might save a quarter of the time taken to weave a cloth, but an employer believed that the saving was one-third.[5] Many weavers, on the other hand, took longer than in the double loom.[6] Those who made the best use of it might earn about 18s. a week if fully employed; but one Gloucestershire weaver said in 1806 that the men in his neighbourhood made only 11s. to 13s.[7] Weavers, of course, were determined to mention only the lowest sums they made and there was always some confusion between gross and net receipts. Not all were poverty stricken. Timothy Exell who gained the title of 'King of the Weavers' in the strike of 1825[8] was the son of a weaver with a large family 'who had accumulated sufficient property by that trade to live in comfort';[9] and a Painswick weaver left £50 to Gloucester Infirmary in 1819.[10] 'There were many master weavers who were rather respectable men and who kept four to six looms in their houses if they had room' said the

---

[1] *Ev. on Woollen Trade Bill*, 1803, p. 265.

[2] See App. IV, Tables M and N for this and other statements made below about weavers' and clothworkers' wages down to 1806.

[3] *Ev. on Woollen Trade Bill*, 1803, pp. 28, 300.

[4] Ibid., p. 13.   [5] Ibid., p. 300.   [6] Ibid., p. 10.

[7] *Ev. on State of the Woollen Manufacture*, 1806, p. 338.

[8] See Brief for prosecution of rioters at Epiphany Sessions in Gloucester, 1826, G.C.L., R.V.354.3 (63).

[9] T. Exell, *A Sketch of the Circumstances which . . . led to the Repeal of the Corn . . . Laws* in 1847, p. 7 (Repr. 1903 as a free trade pamphlet) G.C.L., J.13.7).

[10] *Gloucester Journal*, 10 May 1819.

writer already quoted in the *Stroud Journal* in 1868, whose memory went back to the eighteenth century. 'They kept journeymen and women and gave the journeyfolk about two thirds the price of the work. Some ill feeling always existed on account of this, for the master weaver always became too pressing.'[1] Such masters might end up as clothiers,[2] probably rather precariously; and the less respectable among them sometimes relied on embezzled yarn or 'slinge' as part of their raw material.[3] No doubt all these were the exception rather than the rule, but extreme poverty does not seem to have been normal before 1826. In that year Cobbett, coming down into the manufacturing district by Nailsworth and Woodchester, remarked that though there was suffering at present 'the people seem to have been consistently well off. A pig in every cottage sty; that is the infallible mark of a happy people'.[4]

Clothworkers had gained more as a result of the pressure they had begun to put upon their masters;[5] but very varying statements were made about their earnings early in the century, ranging from not over 12s. a week in Trowbridge to 18s. and 20s. in Uley. Uley was a place where Sheppard, at least, paid high wages; and it was said that shearmen there had earned up to two guineas a week before 1820.[6] It seems probable that there was a considerable rise during the Napoleonic wars, since in 1814 Joyce's shearmen at Freshford were making 20s. to 22s. where formerly they had earned 12s.;[7] and wages in Trowbridge must also have increased substantially by that date if the stories told by Walker (himself the son of a shearman) of men who spent up to 15s. or even 20s. a week on drink are true.[8]

---

[1] *Stroud Journal*, 4 July 1868, see above, p. 129, n. 1.

[2] e.g. Thos. King of Rodborough, *Ev. on Woollen Trade Bill*, 1803, p. 4.

[3] *Stroud Journal*, loc. cit. Such masters got their cloth finished at one of the many small fulling mills and by local clothworkers.

[4] *Rural Rides* (Everyman ed.) ii. 104.   [5] *V.C.H. Wilts.* iv. 166.

[6] Lrs. from T. B. Lloyd Baker to *Gloucestershire Chronicle*, 24 Jan 1871 and 28 Feb. 1872. (*Materials for a History of Gloucestershire* collected by A. J. Dunkin, G.C.L. 29498.)

[7] *2nd Rept. from Committee on the Growth, Commerce and Consumption of Grain*, 1814 (H.L. 26), 28.

[8] W. Walker, 'Early Recollections of the Woollen Trade'. The date is approximately fixed by the story that one of the Trowbridge manufacturers who was successfully established there by the early twenties began his career as a shearman of temperate habits who used to lend 2s. to other shearmen at the beginning of the week and receive back 2s. 6d. at the end of it.

The termination in 1809, in favour of the employers, of the long dispute over the restrictive statutes left a legacy of resentment among the workers which can be traced beneath the surface for many years. The characteristic behaviour of the two areas remained the same for some time. Gloucestershire, on the whole, was peaceful; Wiltshire and Somerset were not. No doubt the greater prosperity of Gloucestershire had something to do with this distinction; machinery had proved its value there while further south workers were still disposed to resist it by force. During the war there was only one short outburst of rioting in Wiltshire, in the depressed winter of 1807–8, caused by the efforts of another firm in Bradford to adopt the gigmill;[1] but bad feeling between masters and men was acute. When Nemnich, the Secretary of the Hamburg Chamber of Commerce, was shown round the Sheppards' mill at Frome about 1806 he was warned not to mention machinery in the men's presence; and at Staverton Jones told him that if the buildings were not already there he would never embark upon such an enterprise again.[2] The comparative absence of finishing machinery in Wiltshire and Somerset and its adoption without much difficulty in Gloucestershire accounts for the fact that the west remained peaceful in 1812 when the Luddites were burning mills in some parts of Yorkshire. The only sign of unrest was a letter signed 'E. Lud' addressed to John Lewis of Brimscombe threatening to burn down his mills if the workers in them, particularly those at the shearing frames, were not better paid.[3] This proved to have been written by a boy of fifteen who was thought to have been used as a tool by older men. No violence followed. It seems probable that other employers besides William Playne suffered from strikes if they paid less than the usual rates, but his experience, again in the depressed year of 1808, is the only one of which there is any record during the war.[4] The high prices of 1812 produced a humble petition purporting to come from the weavers of the whole region, begging their employers to give a rise in rates of pay which, they said, had not been altered for twenty-five years, although the

---

[1] P.R.O., H.O.42/95, Lr. from Jones & Bush, 28 July 1808. *Salisbury Journal*, 21 Mar. 1808 and *Gloucester Journal*, 19 Oct. 1807. See above, p. 226.

[2] Nemnich, *Neueste Reise*, pp. 218, 222.

[3] *Gloucester Journal*, 29 July 1812. The boy was transported for 15 years.

[4] *Repts. Asst. Commrs. Hdloom Weavers*, 1840, Pt. V, p. 469.

cost of living had soared tremendously. 'Your petitioners,' they added, 'deprecate every idea of dictating, of combinations, riot or tumultuously turning out from their labour,' and they hoped that by coming forward they would not become 'objects of resentment'.[1] Whether this petition evoked any response is unknown, but again there were no strikes or violence. The fall in the price of bread in 1813 must have brought them some relief; and in Wiltshire and Somerset at least the boom of 1814 produced a rise in some quarters of a penny per yard for weaving cassimeres.[2]

After the end of the war the same peaceful conditions continued in Gloucestershire, which exhibited a great contrast with the turbulent scenes in the north and midlands. There was a small disturbance at King's Stanley in 1819;[3] and a strike against Edward Sheppard at Uley is rather vaguely recorded at some date before 1820.[4] Another in 1821 led to the imprisonment of eleven weavers on a charge of combination.[5] All are said to have been undertaken in order to raise wages, but it is more probable that they broke out in resistance to a fall;[6] and peace seems to have been very quickly restored. On the other hand, riots were frequent in Wiltshire. Detachments from various regiments were stationed in Trowbridge from 1819 to 1837, although, to the disgust of the inhabitants, they had to be quartered in public houses, since the barracks had been pulled down in 1816.[7] The disturbances already mentioned,

---

[1] *Gloucester Journal*, 29 June 1812.

[2] *2nd Rept. from Committee on the Growth, Commerce, and Consumption of Grain*, 1814, pp. 28–29.

[3] P.R.O., H.O.41/4, fols. 292–4, 299. The curate of King's Stanley had totally forgotten this disturbance when he remarked in 1833 on the peaceful history of the village, *First Rept. Fact. Com.*, 1833, B.1, 45.

[4] Lrs. from T. B. Lloyd Baker to *Gloucestershire Chronicle*, 24 Oct. 1871 and 28 Feb. 1872. (See p. 230, n. 6.) It is clear he is referring to a strike before 1820, but it seems incredible that Sheppard could have agreed to a ten per cent advance. Baker was an old man when these letters were written and he may have been confusing this strike with that of 1825 when an advance was given.

[5] *Gloucester Journal*, 16 July 1821.

[6] Exell implies that an attempt to lower wages in 1821 was successfully resisted (*Brief History*, p. 7), but as the charge against the prisoners was combining to raise wages it looks as if the fall had taken place before the strike began. This is possibly the same disturbance which Miles placed 'about 1823', *Repts. Asst. Commrs. Hdloom Weavers*, 1840, Pt. V, p. 451.

[7] P.R.O., H.O.41/4, fols. 376, 386. H.O.42/190 Lr. from A. Ludlow 23 July 1819. For the removal of the troops in 1837 see H.O.41/12, fol. 446.

in 1818 and 1819,[1] were connected with contested elections for the county, which contributed to give them a political flavour;[2] but there was nothing in the way of political agitation to compare with the movements in the north. Outside Trowbridge and Westbury there appears to have been none at all.

There is much confusion over dates for the fall in wages. In Gloucestershire it may have begun as early as 1816, when a letter from 'an old manufacturer' noted a proposal for a weavers' benefit club as 'occasioned most likely by a person of inferior note as a manufacturer endeavouring to reduce their wages';[3] and as he particularly mentioned 'stripes' it seems very likely that the decrease in demand from the East India Company after 1813[4] had led to a lowering in rates for weaving them. Miles drew up an elaborate table of wages from 1808 to 1838 which shows a decrease in 1819 for almost every description of work, whether in the factory or out of it, and again for many occupations in 1829 and 1836,[5] but this can only be regarded as a very rough guide. Information about Wiltshire and Somerset is also conflicting. It looks as if the rate for weaving superfine broadcloth had decreased everywhere by 1830, from the very long-established level of 1s. 3d. per yard to 1s.,[6] but when this took place in Trowbridge is not at all clear. It had happened in Bradford, in some quarters at least, by 1822 and in Frome in that year;[7] but the unemployed Bradford weavers, whom Cobbett treated to breakfast at Heytesbury when he met them out nutting in 1826, said that the reduction had taken place at Christmas 1825.[8] Lower rates can easily be found,[9] but according to Austin in 1839 the majority of reputable manufacturers continued to pay what they had paid in the past, being more concerned to keep up the quality than

[1] See above, p. 160.
[2] P.R.O., H.O.42/190 Lr. from Ludlow, 20 July 1819.
[3] *Gloucester Journal*, 19 Aug. 1816.
[4] See above, pp. 157–8.
[5] *Repts. Asst. Commrs. Hdloom. Weavers*, 1840, Pt. V, p. 374.
[6] Ibid., Pt. II, p. 409. In the tables given (ibid., pp. 439–41) of the time taken for the various operations at different dates a reduction of 4s. per piece is shown after 1796 when the fly-shuttle was regarded as having been introduced, but this is far too early for Wilts. and Som.
[7] P.R.O., H.O.40/17, fols. 9, 49; *Repts. Asst. Commrs. Hdloom Weavers*, 1840, Pt. II, p. 434.
[8] *Rural Rides* (Everyman ed.) ii. 65.
[9] *Repts. Asst. Commrs. Hdloom Weavers*, 1840, Pt. II, p. 436.

to avoid being undersold by others who gave less than they did.[1]

It is sometimes thought that handloom weavers were too numerous and too scattered to combine;[2] but the history of strikes in Gloucestershire does not bear this out. It is remarkable that, although factory workers also experienced a reduction in wages, the only strikes we know of were either conducted by weavers only or were led by them. Those who worked in their own homes were, of course, the worst-paid workers in the industry and it was they who were foremost in striking. Shop weavers, who were only paid at journeymen's rates but often earned more than master weavers at home because they were more constantly employed, took little part, although they were said to be the most discontented.[3] There were many more loomshops by the end of the thirties than in 1803, though the increase of them in Gloucestershire appears to have been checked in the years immediately after the war. It was said in 1839 that there had been none round Stroud until after the strike of 1825;[4] but that, and the disturbance of 1829, convinced employers that it was wise to keep some weaving under their own control. By 1839 twenty-nine of the principal employers had over 1,000 shop-looms between them, or about one-third of the looms in the county.[5] In Wiltshire and Somerset the existence of shops, for cassimere weaving at least, seems to have been continuous since they were first set up in the 1780s; and resentment was chiefly directed against those outdoor masters who kept ten or eleven looms, or who took out more chains than they could weave themselves and farmed them out to other weavers, of course at a lower rate.[6] Unions, necessarily clandestine and conducted under other names, were certainly in being before the repeal of the Combination Acts in 1824. The riots in Warminster and Frome in 1822 over the lowering of rates for weaving and the introduction of the fly-shuttle[7] may have been spontaneous; but an effort in the following year to get back to

---

[1] Ibid., p. 450. 'The past' apparently extended back to 1828, see p. 245, n. 1, below.

[2] This was Austin's opinion (ibid., p. 438) and in spite of the Frome strike he had some justification for it in his district.

[3] Ibid., Pt. V, p. 388.   [4] Ibid., p. 436.   [5] Ibid., p. 378.

[6] Ibid., Pt. II, pp. 417, 451 (Frome), p. 456 (Trowbridge).

[7] See above, p. 161.

the former price was clearly initiated by a Union, which impressed observers with its systematic organization. The men's proceedings began by being entirely peaceful, but weavers who took out work at the current price were immediately induced to return it. Daily meetings in the fields, secrecy about their leaders, and intimidation of any weavers who opposed them greatly alarmed the authorities, and several men were gaoled for combination; but it was the magistrates themselves who provoked disturbances by yielding to the representations of manufacturers and countenancing the use of force for the recovery of cloth in the weavers' houses. For this illegal action they were severely reproved by Peel at the Home Office, who also impressed on a delegation of manufacturers the importance of abiding by the law, even if the result was that the strikers appeared to triumph.[1] The Government is not generally regarded in a favourable light by those who chronicle the hardships of the working population in the early nineteenth century, but both here and on later occasions one is forcibly impressed with the good sense of ministers as opposed to the often oppressive actions and intentions of the men on the spot. But the Government had also to keep order, and Peel sanctioned the use of the military, so that the Somerset Yeomanry and finally a troop of dragoons put an end to the disturbances. The weavers later issued a dignified statement of their sufferings from truck which appears to have been fully justified, calling for help in establishing a fund to enable them to withstand it.[2] The magistrates succeeded in convicting one manufacturer on such a charge and the weavers, with their consent, established a society for its suppression; but in the middle of the worst years which Frome had ever known, it is not likely that such a society could have effected its object.

It was not until 1825 that a serious strike took place in Gloucestershire. Its object, according to Exell, was to obtain a rise in rates to compensate for harder work made necessary by finer spinning and the weaving of more weft into the piece;[3] but in the minds of many strikers it was also intended to bring the

---

[1] P.R.O., H.O.40/18, nos. 52–6, 64, 84; H.O.41/7 fols. 90–94.

[2] Som. C.R.O., DD/LW 239, Paper headed 'To the Gentlemen, Tradesmen and others of the Town of Frome'.

[3] The same change took place in Wilts. but no strike occurred there.

rates of the lower-paying employers up to those of the higher-paying ones.[1] This strike was also notably well organized, every weaver in the region being made to surrender his shuttles, so that even those who wished to work could not do so.[2] Sheppard, who usually took the lead among the Gloucestershire manufacturers, signed a document which, as he said later, gave the weavers two-thirds of what they asked, with the proviso that the advance should remain in force 'while the trade and the corn laws remain in their present state only'.[3] The greater part of the employers in his neighbourhood followed his example and the weavers, feeling that they had won the victory, restored the shuttles to their owners. This strike has been described by the Hammonds, but they were in error in thinking that the victory was complete.[4] Sheppard's action created great indignation among Stroudwater manufacturers and William Playne wrote furiously to explain that such rates could not be paid by those who were under contract to the East India Company.[5] In fact he had some justification, for the weavers were again asking for rates by the hundred, without taking into account the very different types of cloth which might be woven with the same number of threads in the warp. As the increase was by no means universally given, the strike dragged on until the autumn, with riots in Stroud and Chalford in June[6] and an outburst of violence at Wotton-under-Edge in November, when a mill was attacked and several people wounded by a shot from the owners defending it.[7]

Like that at Frome two years before, the union made an immense impression upon observers. As many as ten thousand people (surely an exaggeration) were believed to have attended some of its meetings on Stinchcombe Hill; but what frightened magistrates above all was its boast that it corresponded not only with the Yorkshire unions but with every other combination in

---

[1] *Repts. Asst. Commrs. Hdloom Weavers*, Pt. V, p. 451.

[2] P.R.O., H.O.40/18, no. 376, Lr. from T. B. Lloyd Baker, 4 May 1825.

[3] Ibid., no. 410.

[4] *The Skilled Labourer*, p. 162.

[5] P.R.O., H.O.40/18, no. 422.

[6] Ibid., nos. 472, 476, 482, 490, 494, 506 (Stroud). For Chalford, where a magistrate was accused of abetting the rioters but acquitted at the Assizes, see *Gloucester Journal*, 10 Apr. 1826.

[7] P.R.O., H.O.40/18, nos. 876, 880; G.C.L., R.V.354.3, Brief for prosecution of rioters.

every trade existing in the country.[1] In effect it was by no means
so powerful as was feared. In a community where weavers were
always too numerous there were plenty who were willing to
work at rates under those which the Union demanded,[2] and
not everyone who did so was victimized. As Exell eventually
discovered, 'a combination takes up a deal of precious time and
money',[3] and the strike, with the sporadic violence which
accompanied it, petered out as the depression of 1826 began to
develop.[4] Sheppard's action, which he represented himself as
having taken with some reluctance believing it to be the only
way to prevent a stoppage at a particularly inconvenient time,[5]
was interpreted as active encouragement of the weavers in
order to avoid being undersold by manufacturers who paid less
than he did. It became a matter of common belief, not only in
Gloucestershire but in Wiltshire, that, as Playne said, 'there
has not been a strike but what some masters were at the bottom
of it',[6] and there seems to have been just enough truth behind
this statement to make the generalization plausible.[7]

The weavers' organization remained ready to resume its
activities when conditions became more favourable. At the
beginning of 1829 a more ambitious attempt was made to unite
workers over the whole area. There had already been two
attempts in the north to form a General Union of Trades, one
in 1818 which had not lasted long, and one in 1826 of which
little is known.[8] The latter must have persisted in some places,
for in January 1829 clubs modelled, it was said, on those at
Saddleworth in Yorkshire appeared simultaneously in Wiltshire
and Gloucestershire, complete with ritual oath-taking in a
setting likely to convince the neophyte of its importance, and
ceremonies which were impressive, at least to those who took
part in them. Their objects were to do away with truck and to
resist reductions in wages; and the Trowbridge magistrates
believed that these secret combinations were intended 'to

---

[1] P.R.O., H.O.40/19, fols. 17 ff.

[2] *Repts. Asst. Commrs. Hdloom Weavers*, 1840, Pt. V, p. 505.

[3] *Brief History*, pp. 8–9.

[4] P.R.O., H.O.40/19, fols. 263–4.

[5] P.R.O., H.O.40/18, fols. 411–12.

[6] *Repts. Asst. Commrs. Hdloom Weavers*, 1840, Pt. V, p. 449. In Wilts. it was 'the
more considerable manufacturers of Gloucestershire', ibid., Pt. II, p. 450.

[7] See remarks of J. F. Lewis quoted by Miles, ibid., Pt. V, p. 450.

[8] G. D. H. Cole, *Attempts at General Union, 1818–1834*, pp. 8–9, 13.

include the whole labouring population in the manufacturing counties of Wiltshire, Somerset, Gloucestershire, Lancashire, and Yorkshire'.[1] Agricultural labourers, farmers, shopkeepers, doctors, and attorneys 'of the lowest sort'[2] joined in, under compulsion according to the Gloucestershire manufacturers since Union members would not deal with them otherwise;[3] but an account from Trowbridge suggests that the organization was as welcome to the lower ranks of the middle classes as it was to the workers. 'About this time the ill-fated Union was in all its glory,' wrote George Tucker, then a junior clerk in the counting house of John Stancombe, under the date of March, 1829. 'It was liberally patronised by the tradespeople and the middling classes;—prayer meetings were held in its behalf and the principal members walked in solemn procession headed by one of the members apparelled as a bishop.'[4] The method by which the Union hoped to attain its objects was to strike against one master at a time; and in Gloucestershire the first to be attacked was a man named Haigh who was forced to sign an agreement covering wages and hours to be worked at his factory, promising to abolish his shop looms and to pay only in cash.[5] In Wiltshire the first strike was against Matravers and Overbury of Westbury, and in March their workpeople were coming over to Trowbridge to receive their strike pay.[6] It was afterwards recalled that the sums paid out depleted the funds of the Union so alarmingly that payments were stopped and the treasurer left for America with the balance;[7] but if this is the strike which was mentioned in 1839 (and we know of no other) the workers remained out for nine weeks and mules were installed in the factory, after which forty-one spinners were dismissed.[8]

[1] P.R.O., H.O.40/23, fol. 9, 83 ff. [2] Ibid., fol. 83. [3] Ibid.

[4] G. Tucker, 'Reminiscences of Departed Years', March, 1829.

[5] P.R.O., H.O.40/23, fols. 54–58. There was a man of this name at Rooksmoor mill, Woodchester, who appears to have been a commission clothier and whose machinery was sold up under a distress for rent at the end of 1829, *Gloucester Journal*, 12 Dec. 1829. Exell (*Brief History*, p. 9), represents the movement as having started in June 1828 as resistance to an attempt by Dursley clothiers, to reduce rates by 10 per cent in order to compete with the commission clothiers who were underselling them.

[6] Tucker, loc. cit.

[7] *Trowbridge Advertiser*, 24 May 1862. Reminiscences of J. Foley, retiring Chief Constable of Trowbridge.

[8] *Repts. Asst. Commrs. Hdloom Weavers*, 1840, Pt. II, p. 459. The name of the manufacturer is not given.

The Gloucestershire manufacturers seem to have been still more alarmed than their counterparts in Wiltshire. Among some of the magistrates, however, the old suspicions of them were still in evidence, and those of the hundreds of Longtree, Bisley, and Whitstone met without their manufacturing brethren to consider a statement which the Union had sent to one of them. They interviewed three of the heads of the Stroud Club and were fully convinced of its harmlessness. 'The spokesman who is a grocer at Stroud and worth some tens of thousands of pounds stated in the most candid and open manner that the principal object of the Union was to abolish Truck and Trust and they were willing to lay aside everything respecting wages for the present'; and if there proved to be anything illegal in their oath they were willing to reconstitute their organization entirely. 'I feel sure', wrote one of the magistrates, 'when the Club is established as a legal one, not only many clothiers but many gentlemen and magistrates will join it to endeavour to put down the nefarious system of truck which appears to have been the root of all the evil.' Some of the clothiers, he added, were of the same opinion, 'and Phillimore Hicks (of Eastington) is decidedly in favour of the Association and did not hesitate to say that many reports which were sent to Mr. Peel were without foundation'.[1] The Justices of the Stroud division, who were nearly all clothiers, had written in a much more alarmist tone, and the report of Francis Fagan who was sent down from Bow Street to investigate, did something to confirm their fears.[2] There can be no doubt that the majority of the members wanted to raise wages, to prevent the use of power-looms (then only in the offing) and to abolish shop looms; but the middle class element was afraid of such actions and wished to be assured that they were not being led into anything illegal. The rules of the Stroud Club were revised to confine its objects to suppressing truck and enforcing the payment of wages when due; it is significant that a clause 'to obtain that fair remuneration for labour which honourable manufacturers give' was struck out. The principal Gloucestershire manufacturers sent up a memorial asking for stronger measures against truck, but Peel was not hopeful about the effectiveness of further

[1] P.R.O., H.O. 40/23, fol. 107. Lr. from J. Kingscote Jr. 25 Mar. 1829.
[2] Ibid., fol. 115. See summary in *The Skilled Labourer*, pp. 163–4.

legislation. Truck continued to form a considerable element in the wages of those who worked for the smaller and less successful manufacturers. One who was still making stripes for China in 1839 said that he saw no future for the trade without it,[1] and another confessed that he only made cloth to get a profit on truck and labour.[2] In Bisley, a place with many small manufacturers, where, in 1839, only one was paying in money, it was said by the overseer to have become prevalent only in the early thirties,[3] perhaps after the cessation of the East India Company's orders; but some truck is likely always to have been present. The great stress laid upon it in 1829 suggests that it had increased in the bad times after 1825. Ten years later there was no complaint of it by Trowbridge weavers (which is surprising since their wages were occasionally paid in cloth),[4] but it was prevalent in Frome where there were still a few small masters making goods of lower quality. Austin considered that truck formed part of the wages of one in ten among the Wiltshire and Somerset weavers.[5]

The action of some of the Gloucestershire magistrates in meeting without the attendance of their manufacturing colleagues shows that the difference already noted between Gloucestershire and Wiltshire in the attitude of the Bench to the industry was still in being, although it was declining with the appointment of more manufacturers as Justices in Gloucestershire. In west Wiltshire they still consisted largely of manufacturers and the latter were the magistrates most readily available in Trowbridge and Bradford. If we may believe the denunciations of the Reverend H. C. Daubeny, who lived at South Wraxall in Bradford parish but some three miles from the town, this situation was seriously prejudicing the administration of justice in 1820.[6] Daubeny was outraged by the necessity of paying rates which were spent in the town of Bradford and not in the purely agricultural area where he lived; but his picture of the tyranny exercised by a magistrate who was also one of the principal Bradford manufacturers, though possibly

---

[1] *Repts. Asst. Commrs. Hdloom Weavers*, 1840, Pt. V, p. 364. This manufacturer, N. Jones of Chalford, kept a shop where the articles were said to be as good and the prices no higher than at other shops.

[2] Ibid., p. 399.   [3] Ibid., p. 461.   [4] Ibid., Pt. II, p. 457.

[5] Ibid., p. 468.

[6] P.R.O., H.O.40/13, fols. 603 ff.; H.O.52/1, Lr. of 16 May 1820.

exaggerated, must have contained a good deal of truth. To take a case to Quarter Sessions was no remedy, 'one magistrate will not fly in the face of another'; but his plea for a Bench uncontaminated by 'trade' had no more effect than earlier complaints of the same sort.[1] In 1829, it is true, the Trowbridge division numbered only three magistrates who were active manufacturers, though several of the remaining eight came from families who had made their money in the trade;[2] but others still in the business continued to be appointed throughout the thirties; and up to the sixties, at least, justice in Trowbridge was generally administered by two manufacturers sitting alone.

To return to the question of labour relations, the Union was, no doubt, engulfed in the depression of the latter months of 1829; but even if this had not been the case, the removal of the oath with its solemn ceremonial and the renunciation of any aspiration to deal with wages must have robbed it of much of its attractiveness for the workers and demonstrated to them how difficult any association with the middle classes must be. There were no more purely industrial movements covering the whole district, but the minor depression of 1834 led to strikes against individual masters in Gloucestershire. Of one, against an attempted reduction in rates by Sheppard,[3] no further information is available. That against the related firms of William Playne and Playne & Smith of Longford and Dunkirk mills respectively, began over the price for weaving stripes, but one of the motives of its organizers was again to raise the rates for other goods to the level of those paid by Stephens at Stanley mills, which were probably the highest in the district.[4] The final settlement, which seems to have embraced other firms besides the Playnes, showed a considerable decrease, and in 1838, when rates were lower still, the decline from those agreed after the strike of 1825 was 35 per cent for broadcloth, 38 per cent for cassimeres, and 50 per cent for stripes: since, however, the agreed rates had never been generally paid, the actual decrease was in most cases a good deal lower.[5] Playne

---

[1] See above, p. 117.
[2] See signatures in P.R.O., H.O.40/23, fol. 9.
[3] *Repts. Asst. Commrs. Hdloom Weavers*, 1840, Pt. V, p. 453.
[4] *Gloucester Journal*, 15 and 22 Feb. 1834.
[5] *Repts. Asst. Commrs. Hdloom Weavers*, 1840, Pt. V, p. 398. In Marling's case it was 24, 27, and 20 per cent respectively for the three varieties.

and other successful manufacturers, such as the Marlings and perhaps the Stantons,[1] seem to have succeeded in keeping their rates low and this may be one reason for their success; but Charles Hooper at Eastington, also a very successful manufacturer and very popular with the workpeople, had not lowered his up to 1841. Nor apparently had Stephens who retired in that year.[2]

In addition to low rates of pay, loom rents appear to have been exacted in some cases, especially for shop looms.[3] This custom must have grown up since 1803 when it was almost unknown in Gloucestershire.[4] In Wiltshire, weavers' debts for looms amounting to £20 appear in the Clarks' accounts in 1814; but this is the only specific mention of them and they seem more likely to be owed for looms supplied to men returning from the army than to represent a regular rent.[5] By 1839, however, hire of a loom and tackle at 2s. 6d. per week seems to have been common in Frome though it is not mentioned elsewhere.[6]

It is difficult to understand why Austin, the Commissioner for Handloom Weavers in the south-west, declared that the weavers of these counties were not at the low ebb of those in Gloucestershire[7] (unless he was thinking of stripe weavers who could hardly make 6s. a week when in full work). In general, outdoor weavers there if fully employed were said to earn about 9s. 8d. a week[8] while the average in Wiltshire and Somerset was given as 11s. 8d., though with good material the piece

---

[1] Stanton was accused at an anti-Corn Law meeting in 1841 of lowering wages five years previously when wheat fell in price and refusing to raise them again later when it rose; but he afterwards issued a denial. *Gloucester Journal*, 22 and 29 May 1841.

[2] At the same meeting Hooper was saluted 'in a gratifying manner by the title King of the Clothiers' and stated that he had never lowered rates since he began weaving. Stephens did not make such a claim but he was not accused of doing so and was not interrupted by the audience as Stanton was.

[3] *Repts. Asst. Commrs. Hdloom Weavers*, 1840, Pt. V, pp. 359, 389. In some cases 3s. a week was charged.

[4] *Ev. on Woollen Trade Bill*, 1803, p. 321.

[5] W.A.S., Rec. Brch. vi. p. 111. 'Rent of jenny' appears on p. 92. The small sums due from a number of persons, apparently workpeople, which are entered almost (but not quite) every year seem more likely to represent either advances of pay or the value of work temporarily in their hands.

[6] *Repts. Asst. Commrs. Hdloom Weavers*, 1840, Pt. II, p. 435.

[7] Ibid., p. 438.

[8] Ibid., Pt. V, p. 385.

could be woven more quickly and a good deal more could be got.[1] But since there was greater redundancy of weavers in the two latter counties, estimated at one-third of the whole number as against 16 per cent for Gloucestershire,[2] the average earnings for the whole body were much smaller—a net 3s. 6½d. in Trowbridge[3] and 6s. 1½d. in Frome[4] (where rather unexpectedly trade was said to be comparatively prosperous),[5] against 8s. 1½d. in Gloucestershire.[6] Shopweavers averaged more. Such looms were generally given preference in employment and men worked more steadily at them; but the work was less skilled, since the weaver neither sized his warp[7] nor put it into the loom. It was perhaps the pride of the outdoor weaver in his skill, almost as much as the fear of losing his independence, which kept him at work in his own cottage in spite of the cruel disadvantages of remaining there.

The weavers' plight was only a further development in a situation which had always existed. Wages of other adult workers in the industry were mostly appreciably higher. In 1825 before the great fall in rates of pay, one country gentleman, afterwards a magistrate, remarked that factory workers, men and even women, could in some cases earn 20s. to 30s. a week or more.[8] By the thirties ordinary workers did not earn nearly so much though a few skilled ones may have done so. It was said in 1833 that wages for these men were higher than ever; but for work requiring no skill able-bodied men were usually paid 12s. and the more infirm 10s. 6d.[9] There was, too, a certain amount of redundancy caused by new machinery. The mule displaced labour by 60 per cent.[10] The rotary cutter worked more quickly than the shearing frame and men were dismissed when it was introduced.[11] Fullers in the west were accused of employing boys who could find no work when they grew up, a problem which did not exist in Yorkshire where the nature of the cloth required the labour of two men instead of a man and a boy.[12]

[1] Ibid., Pt. II, p. 399.   [2] Ibid., 437, Pt. V, p. 419.
[3] Ibid., Pt. II, p. 425.   [4] Ibid., p. 417.
[5] Ibid., pp. 420, 425.   [6] Ibid., Pt. V, p. 404.
[7] See below, p. 291.   [8] P.R.O., H.O.40/18, fol. 377.
[9] *First Rept. Fact. Com.*, 1833 E, p. 11.
[10] *Repts. Asst. Commrs. Hdloom Weavers*, 1840, Pt. V, p. 370.
[11] See report on Dunkirk mill, Freshford, *First Rept. Fact. Com.*, 1833, B2, p. 82.
[12] Rept. of R. J. Saunders, 14 July 1843, *Fact. Insp. Repts.*, 1843 (H.C. 523), p. 38.

All this, added to the bad times, meant a fall in wages for factory workers too, though not so heavy a one as for weavers. In 1839 Miles believed that, in general, money wages in Gloucestershire had fallen by 30 per cent below those paid in 1820;[1] and one manufacturer put the decline in weavers' real wages at 55 per cent.[2] Wages in Yorkshire also declined, but they remained appreciably higher than in the West. In 1834 tables were drawn up from returns made by certain mills to the Factory Commission, showing average wages received by workers in different age groups; but as they come from comparatively few mills and cover only a minority of workpeople, the figures are somewhat suspect.[3] The returns from Gloucestershire did not include any from high-paying employers such as Sheppard, the Hicks, Stephens, or R. & S. Davis of Stonehouse, while from Somerset only four were received one of which came from Charles Wilkins of Twerton, a very good employer whose payments must have raised the average considerably. The following table shows the average of men's earnings at various ages (there is no particular significance about the age groups), but the difference between the western counties should not be stressed since they are probably due to the smallness of the sample.[4]

Average wages paid to male factory workers in Yorkshire and the west, 1833

Aged	*21–26*	*26–31*	*31–36*	*36–41*	*41–46*
Yorks.	19s. 6¼d.	22s. 5¼d.	22s. 6d.	22s. 6¼d.	22s.
Glos.	11s. 5½d.	12s. 11¾d.	15s. 3½d.	14s. 4¼d.	13s. 8d.
Wilts.	11s. 6¾d.	13s. 10½d.	15s. 5d.	13s. 7¾d.	14s. 8d.
Som.	14s. 10¾d.	16s. 3½d.	17s. 10½d.	19s. 9d.	16s. 10½d.

[1] *Rept. Asst. Commrs. Hdloom Weavers*, 1840, Pt. V, p. 380. Rather different estimates are given in other sections and 30 per cent seems to be an average of men (over 25 per cent), women (over 33 per cent) and children (under 25 per cent), ibid., p. 375. See also p. 418.

[2] Ibid., p. 404. This figure was arrived at by calculating wages at 25 per cent lower and wheat at 30 per cent higher.

[3] *Suppl. Rept. Fact. Com.*, 1834, i., 39–41. The number of firms given in the Appendix, p. 68, were: Yorks. and adjacent counties, 27; Glos., 17; Wilts., 16; Som. 4. In the table the heading for the north is Leeds, but apparently this covers all the northern firms which sent in returns.

[4] The causes assigned in this Report (p. 41) for the low rate of wages in Glos. and Wilts. as compared with Somerset must be disregarded, for the returns are too scrappy to enable a true average to be calculated.

In some cases these sums were eroded still further in the next six or seven years;[1] but the lower level in the west was a recognized fact which helped to compensate the manufacturer for the higher price of coal and transport.[2]

Only in one respect, that of the hours worked, can the bad times be said to have advantaged the workers, or rather, perhaps, their children. The usual period in the west, said a Gloucestershire manufacturer, J. W. Partridge of Bowbridge, giving evidence to the Central Board of the Factory Commission, was $10\frac{1}{2}$ hours.[3] This may have been his own experience, but instances of 12 can very easily be found (6 a.m. to 8 p.m. with two hours for meals).[4] A variation in hours worked had been common for a long time, for in 1816 and for some years before that nineteen mills in Wiltshire and Somerset had worked 10 hours excluding meals, one $10\frac{1}{2}$, eleven for 11 hours and one (the Clarks) for 12.[5] This did not, of course, exclude much longer hours when orders were heavy or time had to be made up.[6] Even in 1833 a sudden rush at shipping times might mean that a mill worked 14, 16, or 20 hours, but at least one Gloucestershire firm employed a relay of children when this occurred.[7] Only at Trowbridge was a regular 13 hours being worked by some manufacturers, two of whom readily abandoned the practice of not stopping for meals when its objectionable nature was pointed out to them.[8] In all three counties only one mill, which was working a continuous 15 hours and had previously worked 16, was condemned by the Commissioner,[9] and this contained only fulling and finishing machinery on which children under twelve were not employed. Longer hours were often worked in finishing departments, especially on the gigmill,

---

[1] See tables of wages at different dates given by Miles, *Repts. Asst. Commrs. Hdloom Weavers*, 1840, Pt. V, p. 374. Austin said there had been no decrease for weaving after 1828, ibid., Pt. II, p. 441.

[2] Ibid., Pt. V, p. 514, Lr. from S. Sevill.

[3] *First Rept. Fact. Com.*, E, p. 9, Ev. taken before Central Board. Cf. Ev. of the engineer W. Lewis, ibid., B1, p. 50.

[4] Ibid. B1, pp. 37, 47, 56, 66.

[5] *Rept. on State of Children in Manufactures*, 1816, pp. 308–9.

[6] e.g. $14\frac{1}{2}$ hr., 'but not now for the last year', *First Rept. Fact., Com.*, 1833, B1, p. 59.

[7] Ibid., E, p. 9; *Suppl. Rept.*, 1833, II *Answers to Queries*, B1, p. 15.

[8] *First Rept. Fact. Com.*, 1833, B1, p. 90.

[9] Dunkirk Mill Freshford, ibid. B2, p. 82.

than in carding and spinning,[1] and it was working this machinery for overlong periods which had caused some of the worst deformities suffered by young people in Yorkshire.[2] No injuries solely attributable to factory work were recorded in the west though some children had suffered from malnutrition in earlier life.[3]

This evidence, however, applies only to cases where mills were worked by steam. The irregularity of water power caused 'making up time' to be a regular feature in water-driven mills at some seasons of the year; and if children sometimes only worked 3 hours a day and often only 6,[4] at other times they had to do 12, 14, or even 19. At Eastington work in dry weather could not begin until 1 p.m. and at Painswick the water would flow from 10 a.m. or noon until 10 p.m. or midnight, 'and if not used would be an entire loss'.[5] When the greater part of the work was done by manual labour, said a Trowbridge manufacturer in 1833, they worked from 1 a.m. to 7 p.m.[6] Even when the water was not flowing they often had to be on the premises waiting for it. These conditions sometimes had their lighter side; the writer of 1868, already quoted, described how the children used to look at the millpond and would make joyful signs to each other when the water was getting low and they could look for a break.[7] Another description written about 1880 by a resident of Frome, who had made inquiries about the Spring Gardens mill, is not so cheerful. 'The workpeople were sometimes called at midnight on Sunday to use the water that had collected and they would work till 10 a.m. Monday when the water was getting low. They would start again about 5 p.m. and go on as long as there was any water. If they lived at a distance they often slept in their clothes, and an old woman assured the writer that all the girls doing such work never took their clothes off in the week.'[8] This situation was not entirely remedied by the Factory Act. Water mills were still allowed to

---

[1] *Suppl. Rept. Fact. Com.*, 1834 ii, Answers to Queries (H.C. 167), B1, p. 97. *First Rept. Fact. Com.*, 1833, B1, p. 46.

[2] *Rept. on Children in Facts.*, 1832 (H.C. 706), pp. 33, 45.

[3] *First Rept. Fact. Com.*, 1833, B1, p. 110.

[4] Ibid. B1, p. 54.   [5] Ibid. B1, p. 46; *Suppl. Rept.* 1833 ii, B1, p. 18.

[6] Ibid. B1, p. 96.   [7] *Stroud Journal*, 18 July 1868.

[8] Som. C.R.O., DD/LW 244, Scrapbook of E. R. Singer. Cf. *Rept. Fact. Com.*, 1833, B1, p. 104, where a man at Westbury had often, in the past, been called at 2 a.m.

make up lost time up to 60 hours a week and in 1836 young people of twelve to eighteen years of age were found in some cases to have worked 72.[1] All the same, conditions in the west were a very mild edition of those to be found in Yorkshire.

Nearly all the western manufacturers said that they would prefer not to employ children under nine years of age, and ascribed the presence of younger ones in the mill to their parents' desire for their wages and their inability to leave them at home alone. They were just as adamant as their northern competitors on the argument that children must work before they were twelve or they would never learn habits of industry or skill in the trade. They had kept an eye on possible Government interference since the introduction of Pitt's Act to protect children in cotton factories, introduced in 1816 but not finally passed until 1819.[2] In 1833 they were outraged at having to repudiate, as Edward Sheppard put it, 'the charges of cruelty towards those persons whom it has been the practice of their lives to rear up, to protect and to support';[3] but in this case the Factory Commissioners agreed with them. Neither Horner nor Woolrich thought there was anything in the area which called for legislative interference[4] and Woolrich wrote a remarkably favourable report. He had not been prepared, he said, to find 'groups of rather unusually healthy looking children turned out of these much abused mills';[5] and neither he nor Horner had ever seen a factory child in rags.[6] The great employers were generally benevolent and anxious for the welfare of their employees. Corporal punishment was often forbidden and very seldom excessive. At Stanley mills, when serious punishment was needed, a jury of children decided upon it 'with the most salutary results'.[7] If the smaller manufacturers did little or nothing for their workers, there were no cases of aggravated cruelty or neglect.

---

[1] *Repts. Insp. Facts.*, Feb. 1836 (H.C. 78), p. 14.
[2] G.C.L., J.V.13.2 (11). In 1816 three manufacturers from Glos. were deputed to attend the House of Commons. Wilts. and Som. sent a solicitor with a statement, *Rept. on State of Children in Manufactories*, 1816, pp. 307 ff. See also Lr. from Henry Sheppard to Paul Methuen, M.P. 4 Apr. 1818, Corsham Papers, No. 5868.
[3] G.C.L. (H), F.1.8. *Facts and Reasonings submitted by the Woollen Manufacturers of Gloucestershire. . . .* (by Edward Sheppard).
[4] *First Rept. Fact. Com.*, 1833, B1, p. 30.
[5] Ibid. B1, p. 111.   [6] Ibid. B1, p. 60.
[7] *Suppl. Rept. Fact. Com.*, 1834, ii, *Answers to Queries*, B1, p. 19.

After the passage of the Act very few violations took place, although in 1836 when trade was brisk there was much grumbling that children of eleven and twelve were restricted to 48 hours a week. There were some prosecutions for minor offences and, after 1844, when a new Act directed the fencing of certain parts of the machinery, several cases of neglecting to do so occurred.[1] There were also occasional difficulties in getting convictions from magistrates who were often in the business themselves.[2] But, as compared with the north, the violations were few. It is true that a large number of children under eleven, and in some cases all under thirteen, were at once turned off in order to avoid compliance with the education clauses of the Act,[3] and this, at the prevailing level of wages, may perhaps have meant more hardship for the family than their remaining in the mill. 'If children were worked to death before, they are starved to death now,' said a Frome employer in 1839.[4] When in 1836 the limitation of hours for children under thirteen came into force, it caused the discharge of many of them but not all, since there were not enough of thirteen and over to carry on the industry;[5] but where there were 1,386 children under thirteen employed in the west in 1835, there were only 88 in 1846.[6]

Later legislation seems to have been accepted without question and the Ten Hours Act in 1847 went almost unnoticed. The Act of 1874 produced a letter from a Gloucestershire manufacturer complaining of the provision that no child, young person, or woman should work more than four and a half hours without a break of half an hour.[7] This compelled them to begin earlier and get home later and the employees resented it as much as their masters, since the married women

---

[1] *Repts. Insp. Facts.*, 31 Oct. 1850 (H.C. 1304), p. 26; 30 Apr. 1852 (H.C. 1500), p. 19; 30 Apr. 1853 (H.C. 1642), p. 36; 31 Oct. 1854 (H.C. 1881), p. 34; 30 Apr. 1856 (H.C. 2090), p. 26; 30 Apr. 1858 (H.C. 2391), pp. 30–1.

[2] *Return of persons summoned*, 1837 (H.C. 120), pp. 50–3; and esp. *Repts. Insp. Facts.*, 31 Oct. 1847 (H.C. 900), pp. 14–15 for a case at Trowbridge.

[3] Ibid., 1834 (H.C. 596), p. 23. *Second Rept. on Mills & Factories* 1840 (H.C. 227), p. 14. In the case of scattered country mills there was a genuine difficulty in obtaining education for the children.

[4] *Repts. Asst. Commrs. Hdloom Weavers*, 1840, Pt. II, p. 462.

[5] *Rept. Insp. Facts.*, 31 Dec. 1836 (H.C. 73), p. 27.

[6] *Factory Return*, 1836 (H.C. 138), p. 13; 1847 (H.C. 294), p. 611.

[7] *Repts. Insp. Facts.*, 31 Oct. 1875 (1876, H.C. 1434), p. 82.

found it difficult to get earlier to the mill and were unable to have their tea at home as they had been accustomed to do. But this seems to have been the only manifestation of resentment against the regulation of hours for women and it was a question of convenience not of principle. The movement against interference with the hours which women might choose to work, begun by the Women's Rights supporters in the later seventies,[1] evoked no response among women workers in the west.

Unrest died down in the two prosperous years after 1834, but the depression which began in 1837 encouraged the progress of the movement for the People's Charter, founded in 1836. Chartists were active in Wiltshire from the autumn of 1838 and in Gloucestershire in 1839. One of the national leaders, the printer Henry Vincent, appears to have come originally from Wotton-under-Edge,[2] and Wotton was the centre of Chartism in Gloucestershire.[3] In Wiltshire the local leader was a man named Carrier of Trowbridge, described as a hatter but previously a gigman, perhaps thrown out of that employment by new machinery. Both were supported by other leaders from Bath and Bristol; and Vincent, who edited the *Western Vindicator*, filled it with accounts of successful meetings in the cloth-manufacturing areas and with inflammatory language against the working man's oppressors. Chartism was, of course, primarily a political movement, but both Vincent and a local Gloucestershire magistrate could agree, from different stand-points, in emphasizing the low remuneration of the workers as a root cause of the agitation.[4] The most prominent leaders did not come from the cloth industry, though in Wiltshire some minor ones were described as spinners or weavers.[5] Timothy Exell, it may be noted, who had played such a large part in the strike of 1825, was strongly opposed to Chartism and appears to have argued forcibly against it among the weavers. He asked for, but did not obtain, a reward for his exertions towards suppressing it.[6]

[1] See Hutchins and Harrison, *History of Factory Legislation*, pp. 183 ff.
[2] P.R.O., H.O.40/42, fol. 665.
[3] Ibid., fols. 585, 773, 797.
[4] Ibid., fol. 525 (*Western Vindicator*); 753 (J. Purnell, Stinchcombe).
[5] P.R.O., H.O.40/48, fol. 248.
[6] P.R.O., H.O.41/15, fols. 309, 322, 403–4, 416.

In Stroud the agitation died down fairly quickly[1] and throughout Gloucestershire, in spite of the magistrates' apprehensions, the movement was completely peaceful.[2] Elsewhere, what violence there was appears to have been the result of provocation.[3] Trowbridge was inclined to riot but very little damage was done. The movement was checked by the imprisonment of its leaders, but some activities continued until 1842, taking the form in Gloucestershire of infiltration into meetings called by the manufacturers to petition for the abolition of the Corn Laws,[4] this being the period when Chartist policy was to make common cause with the Tories on the ground that the abolition of the Corn Laws would only result in lowering wages. A Chartist Society continued to exist in Gloucester, but when the movement revived in 1848 it found no support in western manufacturing districts. The leader of the Gloucester Chartists seems to have been a reformer of the mildest kind, who disapproved entirely of the language used by some visiting speakers and felt that, over the years, some working people in the cloth industry had done better for themselves than some of their masters.[5]

This may have been true of a few skilled operatives, but throughout the nineteenth century wages continued to be low, much lower than in Yorkshire, though it is difficult to obtain precise evidence. One account for Stroud in 1871[6] gives wages for men as 14s. to 16s. a week though some, presumably foremen or with exceptional skills, might earn 22s. to 35s. Women weavers were said to make 10s. to 13s. and girls up to the age of twenty 8s. to 10s. Boys earned 5s. and 7s. The average wage of labourers in other Stroud industries in 1870 was said on another occasion to be 12s. to 14s.[7] and in 1868 clothworkers' earnings fluctuated between these sums.[8] Rates seem to have

---

[1] P.R.O., H.O.40/42, fols. 537, 585, 741.

[2] Ibid., fols. 511, 585, 641, 649–51.

[3] See R. B. Pugh, 'Chartism in Wiltshire', *W.A.M.* liv, 169–84.

[4] *Gloucester Journal*, 22 May 1841.

[5] Ibid., 22 Apr. 1848.

[6] *Stroud Journal*, 9 Sept. 1871. This came from one of the sisters at a local convent who was working among the poor. It caused considerable annoyance but remained uncontradicted.

[7] Ibid., 28 June 1879. Other evidence shows much the same level. In 1872 wages in the building trades were 3s. a day (ibid., 27 July 1872).

[8] Ibid., 11 Apr. 1868.

been much the same in Wiltshire and Somerset.[1] In a country mill in Corsley some men earned 20s. or even 30s. but others 13s. to 14s.[2] There were certainly variations between employers, some paying less than others,[3] but there were no further strikes to equalize rates. Gloucestershire remained peaceful throughout. Wiltshire workers occasionally struck against individual masters; but most of their strikes were not for wages but against unsatisfactory conditions in the mill. Perhaps the most notable occurred in 1863 when a Westbury manufacturer who had come from Yorkshire tried to impose excessive fines for lateness on his women power-loom weavers, which excited much unfavourable comment.[4] In 1864 a 'United Weavers' Association' (apparently male) was formed in Trowbridge as a result of a strike. It was still in being a year later when its object was stated as being to arrange things with the masters and prevent strikes, in which it had been successful in the past year.[5] A Working Men's Association was mentioned again in 1869, which had supplied funds to unemployed men,[6] but it is not known whether this was the same Society or how long it remained in being.

At least one Gloucestershire manufacturer realized that low wages were less of a benefit to the industry than was believed. Speaking at a dinner given to his workpeople in honour of his daughter's marriage in 1872, John Libby thought it would be far more advisable to raise wages than to reduce hours of work, and offered to give an advance of 10 per cent if others would follow suit[7] (which they do not appear to have done). He returned to this theme nearly twenty years later in the account which he wrote of Stroud between 1870 and 1890, pointing out that what the industry needed was not a low-paid labour force

[1] See *V.C.H. Wilts.* iv. 175. The average of 23s. a week for men given by the U.S. Consul in 1886 must have included a good many of the more highly paid artisans in engineering.

[2] M. F. Davis, op. cit., p. 45.

[3] See letters in *Trowbridge Advertiser*, 22 and 29 Oct. 1859, suggesting that Bradford rates were lower than those at Trowbridge.

[4] Ibid., 21 Nov. and 5 Dec. 1863. For strikes at other mills see ibid., 16 Dec 1867 (Salters, Trowbridge); 25 Feb. and 4 Mar. 1871 (Lavertons, Westbury); 20 Apr. 1872 (Brown & Palmer, Trowbridge). These were all settled amicably within a few days.

[5] Ibid., 23 Apr. 1865.

[6] *Trowbridge Chronicle*, 6 Feb. 1869.

[7] *Stroud Journal*, 29 June 1872.

but a well-educated one.[1] It could hardly be said that children who had worked half-time in the mills from the earliest age allowed were educated even in elementary subjects. In 1876 the inspector visiting Stroud to grant labour certificates to children over thirteen, under the Act of 1874, found that out of seventy-eight examined only four could pass the fourth standard, which was usually reached at ten or twelve by children who had full-time schooling.[2] Things may have been as bad in Yorkshire, but with higher wages and far greater opportunities of attending technical classes, the workers were more fitted to appreciate and take part in innovations in the industry.

[1] J. Libby, *Twenty Years' History of Stroud, 1870–1890*, p. 83. S. S. Marling had thought in 1870 that an Education Bill was needed, since English operatives were often inferior in education to those on the Continent, *Stroud Journal*, 13 Aug. 1870.

[2] Ibid., 29 July 1876.

PART III

Raw Materials and Processes

IX

WOOL

DURING the period dealt with in this book, at least up to 1825, wool was divided into short wool suitable for carding and long wool used for combing. The epithets 'fine' and 'coarse' were applied to these two categories, and, generally speaking, the shorter the staple (or length of the hair) the finer the wool will be. It will also contain more serrations to the inch which gives it its felting properties. During the last 150 years, with extensive breeding for quality and the use of modern machinery, the epithets fine and coarse can no longer be applied to carding and combing wool respectively, for very fine wool can now be combed; but during the seventeenth, eighteenth, and early nineteenth centuries 'fine' wool denoted carding wool, though within this category the qualities of coarse (or 'low') and fine were also distinguishable.

Dr. P. J. Bowden has produced evidence which goes to show that the greater part of the wool grown in England during the Middle Ages was short, although the longer stapled kinds might be used either for woollens or worsteds.[1] Under the conditions in which sheep were kept, the potentially long-woolled breeds did not produce a fleece with a really long staple.[2] But there is some evidence that, up to the end of the sixteenth century, there was little differentiation between wool from different parts of the country or different breeds of sheep. No distinction between carding and combing wool was made in Leiden which had always imported its wool from England;[3] and as late as 1639 three Leeds clothiers equated wool from

---

[1] P. J. Bowden, 'Wool Supply and the Woollen Industry', *Econ. Hist. Rev.* (2nd ser.), ix(1), 44–58. In 1828 it was said that, before the invention of machine combing, wool of 5 in. staple could be combed. *Rept. on State of British Wool Trade*, 1828, p. 313. J. Luccock in 1805 gives the length for combing as 'upwards of four inches', *Nature and Properties of Wool*, p. 155.
[2] R. Trow-Smith, *A History of the British Livestock Industry to 1700*, p. 161.
[3] N. W. Posthumus, *Geschiedenis van de Leidsche Laken-industrie* ii. 13.

counties which were later looked upon as producing long wool with that of others which, in the eighteenth century, were the home of short-woolled sheep.[1] None the less, it is certain that by this time the enclosure policy of the early sixteenth century, by providing better pasture and making it unnecessary for sheep to wander far in search of food, had changed the nature of much of the wool, which had become longer and coarser; but all sheep bear wool of varying staples and qualities and even when, in general, the fleece is getting longer, there may be still much wool in it which is suitable for carding.[2]

According to the clothiers already quoted, the wools of Leominster, Cotswold, Hampshire, and part of Wiltshire stood in a class apart as capable of making the finest cloth. This belief comes as no surprise so far as Leominster wool is concerned. Wool from the Ryeland breed of sheep remained the finest in England up to the end of the eighteenth century, after which cross breeding and higher feeding caused it to degenerate.[3] The others were not all of the same quality. Where Herefordshire fleeces sold for 35s. to 36s. a stone of twelve pounds just before the Civil War,[4] best Hampshire wool was selling at 1s. 2d. a pound at Kingsclere in 1635;[5] but 'Hampshire' probably includes the Isle of Wight, the wool of which was reckoned in the seventeenth century 'the best after that of Lemster and Cotswold'.[6] The order in which the wools are placed may reflect the quantity of the finest wool which could be got from the fleeces; but we know very little of the individual properties of wools at any time before the last quarter of the eighteenth century. When full descriptions began to be written enclosure and, still more, cross breeding had so changed the character of the sheep that any attempt to describe the quality of earlier fleeces must contain a large amount of guesswork. There is much evidence of weight and, in general, the length of the staple will vary with the weight; but history is almost entirely silent about the other qualities, softness, tenacity, elasticity (or the lack of it), and felting properties, which any

[1] P.R.O., E.134/14, Car. I, Michaelmas 20. Answers to Int. 36.
[2] Cf. the remarks of the Staplers in 1652, P.R.O., S.P.18/25/42.
[3] Trow-Smith, *A History of the British Livestock Industry, 1700–1900*, p. 132.
[4] Bodl. Libr., MSS. Aubrey 2, fol. 153. [5] *C.S.P.D. 1634–5*, 106.
[6] *Camden's Britannia*, tr. with additions and improvements by Edmund Gibson (1695), p. 127. This observation seems to have been added by Gibson.

clothier must have looked for in selecting wool suitable for his purpose. We do know that Cotswold wool was renowned for its whiteness,[1] a valuable quality where dyeing in the piece was practised, and it probably felted better than wool grown in chalky counties. These properties may have contributed to the esteem in which it was held in the Middle Ages. For Cotswold wool offers a well-known problem. Coming from what has been said to be potentially a long-woolled sheep[2] its appears to have changed its character completely between the sixteenth and the eighteenth centuries. All the evidence shows that it was in high regard for clothmaking up to the early seventeenth century, but, although it has been classed as a long wool,[3] its capacity for making fine cloth shows that it cannot have been similar to other long wools. In 1614 it held a place just below Ryeland wool[4] and as late as 1726 Defoe still placed it there;[5] but long before this it was only used in Gloucestershire for making the medium-quality cloth which was sent to the Levant and to India, while the finer kinds were made of Leominster or Spanish wool.[6] In 1779 Rudder, the historian of Gloucestershire, declared that 'it was never fine in the memory of any man I have conversed with',[7] and it had become even coarser by cross breeding with Leicesters; but the shorter parts of the fleece were still used for making cloth for the Army and India. Some light is thrown on this change by an agricultural writer in 1794,[8] who says that Cotswold sheep in their unimproved state were small and light, 'having in the memory of an experienced agriculturist now living a fleece of fine wool about three pounds weight, but lighter and finer before that period'. He added that the introduction of rams from Warwickshire and other counties and the progress of enclosure since the 1740s had increased the weight of the carcass and the coarseness of the wool within a comparatively short time. Although this does not explain the apparent degeneration of the fleece during the seventeenth

---

[1] Ibid., p. 238. ('Candidissimum' in original Latin text of 1586, p. 193.)

[2] Trow-Smith, *British Livestock Industry to 1700*, pp. 165–6.

[3] E. Power, *The Wool Trade in English Medieval History*, pp. 21–2. Cf. Trow-Smith, loc. cit.

[4] G. Markham, *Cheap and Good Husbandry*, p. 65.

[5] Defoe, *Plan of the English Commerce* (1928 ed.), p. 198.

[6] P.R.O., C.104/44, Waste Book of Jacob Turner (1677–85).

[7] *History of Gloucestershire*, p. 23.

[8] G. Turner, *A General View of the Agriculture of the County of Gloucester*, p. 9.

century, he was told that in an earlier period the sheep were 'cotted' or housed during the winter, which would have made the wool much softer than when it came to be exposed to all weathers.[1] In fact, if Cotswold wool was finer at an earlier period but rather longer than some other English fine wool, its value in the Middle Ages can perhaps be explained, since the longer parts of the fleece were always chosen for making warps and it was sometimes stipulated that these should be made of combed wool; a greater length of staple combined with the qualities of fineness and softness would therefore have been particularly valuable. It is however possible that it was the improvement in cloth, rather than the degeneration of the wool, which explains the fact that it was no longer used for the best cloth by the end of the seventeenth century.

The other two fine wools mentioned in 1639 also declined in quality. In 1805 Hampshire wool, including that of the Isle of Wight, was ranked above that of Dorset but below Wiltshire.[2] By 1767, according to Elderton, the best Wiltshire wool was not good enough to make cloth at 9s. 6d. a yard,[3] and Anstie in 1787 placed it in the third class of English wools.[4] It had been rivalled in the 1690s by Southdown wool[5] which had scarcely been mentioned at the beginning of the century; and in 1791 Southdown, of all the English wools, was said to be most like Spanish in closeness of texture, although it was not so fine.[6] It is strange that Temple, the Trowbridge clothier, does not mention it in the list of wools from the southern counties which he gave during his controversy with Smith in 1750, especially as he had used it himself.[7] He placed the wools he did mention in order as Gloucestershire, Berkshire, Wiltshire, Hampshire, Wight, and Somerset, of which the prime was worth from 1s. to 1s. 6d. a pound 'by a gradation of about 1d. per lb.'.[8] It

[1] The excellence of Saxony wool in the nineteenth century was largely due to 'cotting' as well as to careful breeding and feeding.

[2] Luccock, op. cit., pp. 267, 269, but he admitted that he had never seen it.

[3] Som. C.R.O., Elderton Lr. Book. To J. Watts, 11 June 1767.

[4] J. Anstie, *A General View of the Bill*, pp. 47–8.

[5] *Econ. Hist. Rev.* (2nd ser.) ix(2). 242; *The Clothier's Complaint*, p. 28.

[6] J. Anstie, *A Letter to the Secretary of the Bath Agricultural Society*, pp. 29–30.

[7] W. Temple, *A Refutation of one of the principal Arguments in the Rev. Mr. Smith's Memoirs of Wool*, p. 13. For his use of it see his books among the Clark Papers, Wilts, C.R.O. 927.

[8] Ibid., p. 7.

looks as if this was intended to be an ascending order of fineness, though Smith in his reply took the opposite view.[1] There appears, however, to have been no set gradation of quality between the wools of various counties and it is obvious that some places in each might produce better wool than others according to variations of soil and herbage.[2] A Shepton Mallet clothier purchased wool from dealers in Marnhull and Wimborne (presumably Dorset or Hampshire wool) between 1755 and 1764 at prices rather above those of Wiltshire wool,[3] though Luccock fifty years later ranks Dorset below Salisbury Plain in this respect.[4]

It seems probable that nearly all English wool grew somewhat longer and coarser between 1600 and 1800, owing partly to further enclosures and partly to cross breeding of which no account has been kept. From this general opinion one must except Herefordshire wool and perhaps the improved Southdown. Herefordshire wool of the Ryeland breed remained not far behind Spanish in fineness. The main difference seems to have been the greater softness and pliability of Spanish wool which gave the cloth a 'feel' and lustre which were unobtainable if only English wool was used,[5] and this seems to have been the main reason why Spanish was preferred.

The prohibition placed on the export of wool in 1662, not for the first time,[6] aroused no protests for some years. Since the opinion was held on all sides that foreign competition with English woollen goods was nourished by the use of English wool, it seemed a sensible measure to prevent the foreigner from getting it. This opinion, one had almost said superstition, can be traced back at least to 1571[7] and may have originated

---

[1] J. Smith, *The Case of the English Farmer and his Landlord*, p. 67.

[2] Cf. Anstie's remark that a small area in Wiltshire produced much finer wool than the rest of the county, *A Letter to the Secretary of the Bath Agricultural Society*, p. 28.

[3] P.R.O., C.110/119, Pt. II. Wool Account (Long narrow book fol. 66 ff.). From 1755 to 1760 'running fine', a medium grade of wool, from Dorset was priced above that from Wilts. by 5s. to 25s. per pack, though Westley once noted it as 'very dear'.

[4] Op. cit., p. 285. He notes also the presence of a different variety from the Dorset breed round Poole and Wareham.

[5] Ibid., p. 169.

[6] For the previous history of this measure see P. J. Bowden, *The Wool Trade in Tudor and Stuart England*, Ch. VII.

[7] B.M., MS. Lansd. 100/25.

in the first half of the sixteenth century.[1] When Spanish wool was first introduced into Flanders at the end of the fifteenth century it could not compete with English and was relegated to the villages, where it was used for the new draperies;[2] but it was later forced on Flemish and other continental cloth manufacturers by the scarcity of English wool. It was greatly improved in the first half of the sixteenth century; but it is probable that manufacturers had, to begin with, the same difficulty in spinning warps from it as faced English clothiers when they began to use it nearly a hundred years later.[3] Continental makers had surmounted this difficulty by that time, and it was totally untrue that English carding wool was necessary to them.[4] In fact, it was clearly recognized in England as early as 1669 that it was only long combing wool which was smuggled abroad,[5] and this was again emphasized by John Munn in 1739;[6] but since the decline in exports affected only goods made with short wool, it was convenient to ignore the distinction. The cry that foreigners could compete because they got English wool was such a convenient excuse for falling exports that few people troubled to distinguish what kind of wool they meant.

The policy of forbidding export aroused some doubts when the price of wool continued its decline from the high level at which it had stood in 1650,[7] and the severe fall in the 1670s caused a sharp reaction among landowners. Although most pamphleteers took the view that evasion of the prohibition by smuggling lay at the root of the fall,[8] other and more logical reasons were found by some in the facts that the number of sheep in the country had greatly increased, that being in enclosed pastures they were bearing more wool, that the thinner

[1] 'A Treatise concerning the Staple,' Tawney and Power, *Tudor Economic Documents* iii. 102.

[2] H. Pirenne, *Histoire de Belgique* iii. 242.

[3] Cf. Rees' *Cyclopaedia*, Vol. 38, under 'Woollen Manufacture'.

[4] William Carter's argument in 1671 that the French carded English short wool with Spanish as English clothiers did (Smith, *Memoirs of Wool* i. 239) is unsupported by any other evidence.

[5] *H.M.C., 8th Rept.* (H. of L. MSS), p. 127.

[6] Smith, op. cit. ii. 319 ff.

[7] The decline was not continuous; in 1669 wool was said to be dear, *H.M.C. 8th Rept.*, loc. cit.

[8] The argument ran that smuggling increased foreign competition which led to the decline of the manufacture in England and thus to a lack of demand for wool.

cloth now fashionable consumed less of the raw material, and finally that the increase of imports from Ireland was adding to a supply which had outrun the demand.[1] The latter was the result of the prohibition placed on the import of Irish cattle in 1667[2] in the interests of certain English graziers, which had led to a revolution in Irish agricultural practice. Where previously farmers had kept cattle for export they were now forced to rely on wool, and in a few years the quantity imported to England rose sharply.[3] Wool fetched very low prices in 1672[4] and the depression which lasted until 1674 did nothing to raise them; but the full effect of the influx of Irish wool in the shape of a fall in rents, may not have been felt so soon owing to the rot of sheep in England in the winter of 1673–4.[5] From 1675 onwards the low price and the state of the industry were continuously discussed in Parliament. It is clear that there was a movement of opinion in favour of reversing the prohibition,[6] and it was said in 1678 that a clause had been prepared for addition to a Bill before the House providing that export should be permitted when the price fell below a certain point.[7] It is a measure of the anxiety felt by the country over the decay of the old markets that a Parliament of landowners could reject such a course; but there was already a suspicion in the minds of some that it was the clothiers and not the nation who benefitted.[8]

After a spectacular rise in 1681 wool fell still lower in the depressed period of the mid-eighties, when, as far as Gloucestershire and Wiltshire wool was concerned, the diminished exports of the Levant Company added to the general failure in demand.[9]

[1] Smith, op. cit. i. 285–7, 297 ff. Cf. *C.S.P.D. 1677–8*, p. 37.

[2] 18 Car. II, c. 2, reinforced by 20 Car. II, c. 7.

[3] See Smith, op. cit. i. 244–5 note. It was used throughout the South-west cloth area, as well as elsewhere. P.C.2/72, fol. 469.

[4] *C.S.P.D. 1672*, p. 205.

[5] *H.M.C. Portland* iii. 345; *Som. Rec. Soc.* 34, p. 150. Cf. Smith, op. cit. i. 261, where the author of 'Reasons for a Limited Exportation of Wool' puts it in 1672 ('about five years ago from 1677').

[6] Grey, *Parliamentary Debates* iii. 430 ff.; v. 157. Cf. preface to (W.C.), *England's Interest in securing the Woollen Manufacture* (1689).

[7] 'A Narrative of the whole Proceedings of the last two Sessions of Parliament ending 15 July 1678, concerning the Transportation of Wool' (on back of *Some Considerations . . . upon a Bill about Transportation of Wool*). Cf. Smith i. 252 ff.

[8] *A Treatise of Wool and the Manufacture of it*, p. 4.

[9] Cf. Aubrey, *Natural History of Wilts.*, ed. Britton, Pt. II, Ch. X.

After 1688 there was another rise in which, no doubt, a part was played by the improvement in trade immediately after the Revolution; but one of the main causes must have been the interference with exports of wool from Ireland caused by William III's campaign there.[1] There was little Irish wool on the market in the mid-nineties.[2] Prices regained the level of the sixties and rose higher still during the period of inflation in 1695; nor did they drop to any great extent after the recoinage,[3] although by 1697 Irish wool had returned to the market in even greater quantities, especially after the ban imposed on Irish woollen goods in 1698.[4] This continued high price was behind the agitation against wool broggers which began in 1692. Such attacks were natural in times of high prices and there had been a prolonged one at the end of the Civil War when the rot of 1648, coming after the great destruction of sheep by the armies, had made wool much dearer.[5] Whether any western clothiers took part in this earlier movement is doubtful,[6] but in 1692 the attack was led by those of Gloucestershire in connection with the campaign against the Blackwell Hall factors.[7] It met with no more success than had attended earlier attempts to suppress wool broggers; and after the Blackwell Hall Act had passed in a form which excluded any mention of wool, organized petitions to the House of Commons from Worcester, Cirencester, Devizes, and Kidderminster in 1698 resulted in the appointment of a Parliamentary Committee which, in spite of evidence from Blanch and others about the profits made by the broggers, reported that the grower should be left free to sell to any buyer he chose.[8]

The gradual change from the system prevalent at the beginning of the century when wealthy clothiers were accus-

---

[1] (W.C.) *England's Interest in securing the Woollen Manufacture*, note to preface.

[2] From 1693 to 1695 only 140,000 stone were imported, *H.M.C., H. of L. MSS.* (N.S.) v. 70. Cf. Smith, op. cit. i, 388 n.

[3] *Econ. Hist. Rev.* (2nd. ser.) ix (2). 242–3.

[4] 217,678 stone in 1697 according to a writer of 1738, Smith ii. 244. From 1699 to 1701 imports averaged 312,269 stone per annum, *H.M.C., H. of L. MSS* (N.S.) v. 70.

[5] See Bowden, *The Wool Trade in Tudor and Stuart England*, pp. 175–80.

[6] The lead was taken by Coggeshall clothiers. Three signatures to the petition of 1652 (P.R.O., S.P.18/25/33) are identical with those of Gloucestershire clothiers flourishing twenty years before or after this date, but the surnames (Davis, Fletcher, West) are too common for positive identification.

[7] *C.J.* x. 590. See above, pp. 73–4.   [8] Ibid. xii. 91, 122, 277.

tomed to buy their wool from the growers at shearing time was distasteful to men like Blanch who believed that it was due to the machinations of the factors; but in fact the variety of the goods made, and the increasing number of gradations of quality to be found in the same fleece, must have made it much more convenient to buy wool ready sorted. In the mid-seventeenth century the Staplers claimed to divide short wool into four or five sorts;[1] but the broggers who frequented country markets seem to have divided it into not more than four in a rather rough and ready way.[2] Presumably they knew their customers and could judge what sort of wool they needed. These men, who bought up local wool and also dealt in suitable wool from other parts of England, were of much the same status as clothiers. In the seventeenth century and the earlier part of the eighteenth the industry, apart from the superfine section of it, relied quite as much upon them as it did on the London wool merchants. The number of occasions on which a country stapler is found among the creditors of a bankrupt clothier shows how necessary these men were to the trade. By the mid-eighteenth century the local markets, to which country people had been in the habit of bringing their wool, were decaying. In 1756 a notice appeared in the *Gloucester Journal* to the effect that 'wool jobbing and forestalling' had grown to such a pitch as greatly to injure the trade, and that several principal clothiers and woolstaplers had entered into a covenant to pay a penalty if they bought wool so jobbed.[3] Such an agreement could do nothing to arrest the tendency and may well have first been broken by those who subscribed to it. None the less, to judge from notices in provincial papers, some local fairs retained their importance, at least as price indicators, well into the nineteenth century; and so did Bristol fair which one Dorset woolstapler was attending in 1812, but rather because it was a centre at which the news could be heard and customers discovered than because substantial business was to be done there.[4] Most purchases were effected by orders through the post. Clothiers sometimes bought unsorted wool from farmers, as did William Westley between 1751 and 1763, but

---

[1] P.R.O., S.P.18/25/42.　　[2] *Econ. Hist. Rev.* (2nd. ser.) ix (2). 242.
[3] *Gloucester Journal*, 6 July 1756.
[4] Dorset C.R.O. Colfox Papers, Lrs. of 27 Aug. 1806 and 5 Feb. 1812.

it was a very small amount compared with the sorted wool which he got from staplers in Wiltshire, Dorset, Hampshire, and Worcestershire.[1] In the early nineteenth century a Wiltshire firm was sending wool direct to cloth manufacturers in Frome and Gloucestershire as well as in the north;[2] and a Dorset one was dealing both with the London wool merchants and with a wide variety of country manufacturers including some from Gloucestershire.[3]

Classification was only partly standardized. In the mideighteenth century Worcester and Pershore staplers were selling head, second (sometimes divided into 'fine' and 'low'), and so on by number; others, especially in Wiltshire, dealt in superfine (or best fine), running fine, and seconds; while a Dorset man from Marnhull offered 'choice locks' or 'superfine locks', which, by the end of the century had become recognized names for the best sorts.[4] Even by the nineteenth century there was no complete standardization of carding wool though more grades were recognized. Before 1780 a Devizes stapler had made eight grades.[5] Luccock, writing in 1805, gives a list of ten as used in the east and north, but said that few staplers recognized less than nine, while some distinguished as many as seventeen.[6] Some of the western grades, as shown in the surviving woolstaplers' books for the early nineteenth century, bore different names from those given by Luccock, but they also comprised ten varieties.

In the eighteenth century and earlier many clothiers who made medium cloth bought their yarn ready spun.[7] William Palling of Painswick, whose cloth was of the kind which was sent to the Levant and to India, was supplied by yarnmakers from Devizes and Cirencester, who sometimes haggled keenly over the price as may be seen from the following letter:[8]

[1] P.R.O., C.110/119, Pt. II, Wool Account. See above, p. 259, n. 3.

[2] Books of J. & T. Beavan of Holt, Wilts. They were primarily leather manufacturers (as they still are) but dealt in wool as a sideline. I am indebted to Mr. F. W. Cooper of Melksham for letting me see these books.

[3] See p. 263, n. 4.

[4] See above, n. 1. These were all different qualities of carding wool. For combing wool see Luccock, op. cit., p. 141.

[5] *Letters and Papers of the Bath and West of England Society* viii (1798). 76.

[6] Op. cit., pp. 142–3.

[7] See E. Coward, 'William Gaby, His Book', *W.A.M.* xlvi. 50 ff.

[8] Palling Papers.

CHAPMAN PAULING,   May 30, 1720

Since I had not the opportunity of seeing thee again yesterday I was willing to give thee these Lines only for the sake of thy Redy mony will beat (?abate) thee one half crown in each Pak more than I sayd I would so that it's now if I mistake not five shillings p. pack between us and inasmuch as I think thee Can not be unsensible how little incouridgement I have to make yearne for so Little proffit (I hope you) will be willing to Complay with me at this Low price.

                                                        JOHN LEWIS

After the ban placed on Irish woollen goods in 1698, Irish yarn began to arrive in quantity, and in 1699 the yarnmakers of Tetbury and Cirencester were complaining that the poor were ready to perish for lack of work owing to its competition.[1] Irish yarn was chiefly worsted, but a quantity of woollen yarn was included,[2] and this soon proved indispensable to Gloucestershire clothiers making medium cloth, possibly because the price was lower than that of English yarn by up to £4 per pack.[3] In 1708, when it was proposed to place an additional duty on imported wool and yarn, Cirencester and Tetbury still insisted that they were being ruined by it,[4] but Gloucestershire clothiers, like many others, declared that not enough hands could be found to spin Irish as well as English wool and that interference with imports of yarn would mean a shortage for the manufacture.[5] Its continued importance in the making of cloth for the Levant and East India Companies may be gauged from the many petitions sent up from the region in 1731 for the removal of the duty on its import.[6] This agitation followed one begun in Devonshire in 1729 for the abolition of the export duty paid in Ireland,[7] which was considered, no doubt correctly, as a positive incentive to the Irish to send their yarn elsewhere. This duty was removed by the Irish Parliament in 1730, but yarn

---

[1] *C.J.* xii. 387, 423.

[2] 'Bay yarn' was made from noils (the short hairs combed out of long wool) and this counted as woollen yarn, *C.J.* xviii. 705. But there was also some yarn spun from carding wool.

[3] *C.J.* xii. 387. The price of spinning in Ireland was said to be above one third cheaper than in England, *H.M.C., H. of L. MSS.* (N.S.) iii. 108.

[4] *C.J.* xv. 477, 490.

[5] Ibid. 566, 568. The proposal was negatived in the H. of L., *L.J.* xviii. 560; and a second attempt in the following year failed in the Commons, *C.J.* xvi. 189.

[6] *C.J.* xxi. 603, 612, 639, 660.

[7] *J.C.T.P.*, 1722–34, pp. 77–9, 85.

still paid about a penny per pound on entry to England[1] and all attempts to remove this duty were unsuccessful. Irish yarn continued to be extensively used in Gloucestershire as late as 1756[2] but by the eighties the decay of the export trade in coarse cloth had diminished the need for it in the west and much less was imported owing to the growth of the Irish manufacture.[3]

Spanish wool was of many qualities, but only the finest kind, Segovia, sorted into three grades, Refine, Fine, and Terceira, was used in England. One writer gives its staple as from half an inch to one and three quarter inches and that of Hereford wool as beginning at one and a half inches.[4] Before the Civil War it seems to have been little dearer than the latter. The best quality, sent by Edward Ashe to his father and brother John in 1642, cost 3s. 3d. per pound,[5] and it seldom rose above that figure.[6] The price already mentioned for Herefordshire wool about 1637 would have resulted in one of over 3s. a pound for the prime after sorting. But it was already feeling Spanish competition.[7] By 1685 (when prices were low in any case) it fetched only 20s. to 22s. per stone of twelve pounds, or 1s. 8d. to 1s. 10d. per pound unsorted;[8] and it remained at under 2s. up to 1790 except during wars which made Spanish wool scarce, as in the early forties[9] or the mid-eighties[10] of the eighteenth century. The gap between its price and that of Spanish wool was not, however, excessively wide, for the price of the latter fell also and was generally under 3s., often 2s. 6d. or 2s. 9d., in

---

[1] Smith, op. cit. ii. 248.

[2] In 1756 the weavers asked for higher rates if Irish yarn was used, see App. IV, Table M.

[3] Cf. Lord Sheffield, *Observations on the Objections made to the Export of Wool from Gt. Britain to Ireland*, p. 30. He dates the decrease from 1768.

[4] *Excidium Angliae* by the Cheshire Weaver (J. Digges Latouche), p. 5.

[5] P.R.O., C.107/20, Groot Boek, fol. 135.

[6] In 1676 the superfine quality was said to have sold at 4s. and 4s. 4d. a pound in 1660 (Smith, op. cit. i. 312) but it cannot have remained long at that price. That in the Ashe books for 1659–60 is 2s. 9d. and in Aug. 1660 Refine was selling at 2s. 6d. (P.R.O., C.107/18, Large Day Bk., fols. 200, 336). Depression in trade had reduced it to 2s. 2d by 1667, Rees, *Cyclopaedia*, Vol. 38, under Woollen Manufacture.

[7] *C.S.P.D. 1636/7*, pp. 415–16.

[8] Bodl. MSS. Aubrey 2, fol. 153.

[9] In 1742 Hereford wool rose to 55s. a tod or just under 2s. a pound, while the prime was worth 2s. 6d. or even 3s.; but it fell to 37s. per tod. the next year when the import of Spanish wool was permitted, W. Temple, *A Refutation . . .*, p. 11.

[10] At Ross wool fair in 1785 the price of fine Hereford wool was 25s. 6d. per stone (12 lb.) or just over 2s. 1½d. per lb., *Gloucester Journal*, 25 July 1785.

the eighteenth century. In 1760 William Westley paid £22 per pack or 1s. 10d. per pound for prime Herefordshire wool and 2s. 5d. for highest quality Spanish (R), but the next quality (F) was only 1s. 9d.[1]

Imports of the latter came, mainly direct from Spain, to London, Bristol, or Exeter, by far the greatest part of them to London.[2] It was part of the attack on the Blackwell Hall factors to allege that, by engrossing the wool, they made it impossible for clothiers to buy direct from the importers or to get the wool elsewhere than in London;[3] but the factors' monopoly was not quite so complete. Even at the end of the seventeenth century clothiers could buy from other people,[4] and in the eighteenth it was common to buy in Bristol or Exeter (though the latter market seems to have ended later in the century), or from a London merchant, provided that the clothier was not in debt to his factor and thus obliged to do what the factor wanted. By the later eighteenth century factors seem to have given up any attempt to force clothiers to buy through them,[5] and the latter often resorted direct to the importers, the first approach being made through a broker who was asked what wool was in the market.[6] The importing firms were large and the wool was often sold by auction. Brokers were not always what they seemed. In 1802 a well-known one, Charles Brooke, a candidate for election to Parliament at Chippenham, brought a libel action against a clothier who had accused him of acting as a principal in transactions with clothiers in contravention of his broker's oath. Nominally the wool he sold them was the property of a Spanish consortium which kept an agent in London to dispose of it, but evidence given at the trial was to the effect that much of it had been sold outright to Brooke and resold by him.

[1] P.R.O., C.110/119, Pt. 2, Wool Account, fols. 66–7. The highest price he ever paid for best or 'Head' Hereford wool was £23 per pack or 1s. 11d. per lb. in 1763, ibid., 25 July 1763.
[2] In 1699, 1683 bags of 200 lb. each came to London and only 509 cwt. (c. 285 bags) to the Outports, Customs 3/3.
[3] *The Clothier's Complaint*, p. 5; *Reasons for restraining the Factors at Blackwell Hall from dealing in Spanish and English Wool* (J. Blanch); *Reasons for preserving the public Market at Blackwell Hall and restraining the Factors from dealing in Wool*.
[4] *Econ. Hist. Rev.* (2nd ser.) ix (2). 248.
[5] W.A.S. *Rec. Brch.* xix, nos. 13, 14, 91, 153; Som. C.R.O. Elderton Lr. Book, esp. to S. Perry, 26 Nov. 1767 and 14 Jan. 1769.
[6] Bath Cent. Ref. Library, Books of Stevens and Bailward of Bradford.

He lost his action and was fined £500 by the City;[1] but he gained the election (though unseated on petition) and his firm was still active in the 1820s, though apparently as wool merchants.

Up to the middle of the eighteenth century the importance of the ban on the export of English wool was still generally accepted. Increased competition from the Continent, of which clothiers were very conscious, brought renewed schemes all through the thirties for the prevention of smuggling; and when the Commissioners for Trade and Plantations issued a request for them after the severe crisis of 1740–1, the stream increased to a flood.[2] The report which the Board prepared for the House of Commons recommended a register for wool,[3] but this proposal was disliked by everyone[4] and, although approved by the House, the resulting Bill failed to get through by the end of the session. Improving trade in 1743 appears to have lessened the sense of urgency; and the whole agitation is perhaps most remarkable for the appearance of the Reverend John Smith of Lincoln, who in 1744 sent in an alternative scheme[5] and published his well-known work, *Chronicon Rusticum Commerciale or Memoirs of Wool*, three years later. In this remarkable book he examined the history and literature of wool from as far back as he could trace it, and applied his acute critical powers to demonstrating the fallacies with which pamphleteers had bolstered up the thesis that foreigners could not make cloth without English wool. It took a long time for his views to take effect, although Temple found in 1750 that the book was 'looked upon as an unanswerable piece of argument'.[6] Smith knew far less about carding wool than about the long wool grown in Lincolnshire,[7] and the lack of distinction between

---

[1] See *The Libel Action of Brooke v. Guy*, 1802, and H. Guy, *An Answer to an Address from Charles Brooke*, 1802 (both in W.A.S. Libr., Devizes, Wilts. Tracts XXVIII). Some letters to Brooke in 1792 from the Dursley clothier J. Wallington, which elucidate the transactions of which Guy accused Brooke during the Chippenham election of 1802, are in the Glouc. C.R.O., D.149, F.189.

[2] *J.C.T.P.*, 1734–41, pp. 393–5, 410–11; ibid., *1742–49*, pp. 4, 7.

[3] Smith, op. cit. ii. 398–405.

[4] Ibid. ii. 287; *J.C.T.P.*, 1734–41, pp. 405, 412.

[5] *C.J.* xxiv. 542. The scheme was probably that which appears in *Memoirs of Wool*, ii. 557 ff. proposing to give a premium on exports of woollen goods and allowing the export of wool under a duty.

[6] *A Refutation of one of the Principal Arguments . . .*, preface.

[7] As he himself confessed, *The Case of the English Farmer and his Landlord in Answer to Mr. Temple*, p. 11.

carding and combing wool (in which the pamphleteers whom he examines were equally deficient) produced some minor errors in his observations. Temple attacked Smith with his customary violence, but he was right in pointing out these errors, especially that of comparing the sum given for the unsorted Herefordshire fleece with that fetched by the prime variety of Spanish after sorting. Nor was Temple guilty, as Smith alleged, of comparing the price paid for Spanish wool 'in its dirt' before washing (which was done after shearing and in which the wool lost about 53 per cent in weight) with that of English wool washed on the sheep's back and, when shorn, said to be 'in its grease'.[1] The main point, however, was not mentioned by either side; it was the fact that continental manufacturers did not need English carding wool. They used any they happened to find in a long-woolled fleece[2] but this was very different from a deliberate attempt to get the finest English wool, which, in fact, was not at all affected by whatever smuggling took place. Combing wool was in a different position since it was really needed in France, where there was none so good, even at a price much above that of French wool;[3] and combing wool was what Smith was really interested in.

By the eighties the country gentry had thoroughly absorbed Smith's work. In 1781-2 when the Lincolnshire sheepowners were suffering from a prolonged fall in the price of their wool, a scheme for export was brought forward, but the general sentiment of the country was still against it and the promoters were forced to recognize that it had no chance of success.[4] The controversy made little impact in the west, for it was only the price of long wool which had fallen. That of short wool was

---

[1] 'Here then was Mr. Temple's fraud,' Smith, *Memoirs of Wool* (2nd ed. 1757), ii. 251 n.

[2] *Observations on British Wool by a Manufacturer of Northants.* (2nd ed. 1739), p. 4. The account of English wool by Savary des Bruslons lays great stress on the combing wool smuggled from Canterbury and on that used for hosiery, but though the finer kinds are mentioned the French are not depicted as using them. *Dict. univ. de commerce* ii. 955. Roland de la Platière definitely states that only combing wool was exported from England, but some English carding wool was occasionally used for the warp of fine cloth, *Encycl. méth.* i. 74*, 118.

[3] According to Roland its price in England was 100 per cent below that of French wool in France, but 80 per cent above it in France; and it was well worth this high price, ibid. i. 77*.

[4] *A Short View of the Proceedings of the several Committees* (1782) (by Edmond Turner Jr.).

19—C.I.

rising,[1] no doubt because of the adoption of the spinning jenny in Yorkshire. Two years later, in 1784, when the price had risen still higher, the improbable reason alleged by western clothiers was extensive smuggling to France.[2] Some Wiltshire clothiers did, in fact, believe that carding wool was not affected by smuggling,[3] but the Committee of Western Manufacturers was not so enlightened,[4] even though its chairman, John Anstie, who gave evidence to the Parliamentary Committee on the subject, admitted that carding wool was not necessary to the French. They used it at Elbeuf for the warp of heavy cloth[5] and Anstie maintained that no other wool was so suitable for making second and livery cloth;[6] but French sources give no grounds for believing that the import was large or that it had recently risen. On the other hand, smuggling probably supplied a great deal more combing wool than the landowners allowed, although hardly as much as the 13,000 packs at first suggested by the clothiers. Even the 11,000 packs (over two and a half million pounds) finally suggested was a gross exaggeration; but the French official figure of 286,328 pounds (1,193 packs) imported in 1783, which Sir Joseph Banks obtained from the French Bureau of Commerce,[7] was probably much too low. The French could draw upon smuggled Irish wool as well as on English and they must have got a good deal of both, for, as Roland said, 'the love of gain, subduing fear, generally procures us English wool when and as much as we want it'.[8]

The more stringent provisions against smuggling which were finally embodied in a Bill passed in 1788[9] aroused passionate feelings among landowners; and the pamphlet war which attended the proceedings was remarkable for the bitter attacks on western clothiers made by Lord Sheffield, Thomas Pownall, Arthur Young, and others, who insinuated that their object in promoting the Bill was aimed not so much at the prevention of

---

[1] *Salisbury Journal*, 4 Feb. 1782.   [2] *Gloucester Journal*, 30 Aug. 1784.

[3] *Wool encouraged without Exportation* (H. Wansey), p. 24.

[4] *Gloucester Journal*, 13 Sept. and 13 Dec. 1784; 14 Mar. 1785; 20 Mar., 10 and 24 Apr., and 12 June 1786.

[5] *C.J.* xliii. 277.   [6] *A General View of the Bill*, pp. 43–4.

[7] Bischoff, *Comprehensive History* i. 243. This was the year when the figures were highest.

[8] *Encycl. méth.* i. 77*.   [9] 28 Geo. iii. c. 38.

smuggling wool to France as of its transport to rivals in York-shire.[1] A difference of opinion between western and Yorkshire clothiers[2] lent some colour to these attacks, but agreement between them was finally reached in 1787.[3] Anstie challenged Young to withdraw his allegations (which were quite un-founded)[4] but he did not do so. It is not likely that the new Act would have ended what smuggling there was, but in a few years the French Revolution had put a stop to fears of competition. Even in 1791–2, when the price of wool rose sharply in response to a heavy demand, it was not imputed to smuggled exports. The slump of 1793 brought a fall, and fine English wool does not appear to have risen above the level of 1792 until early in 1799, when the best varieties stood at 2s. 3d. and 2s. 6d. per pound.[5] All the same, there was not much justification for the agitation of 1800 against the proposal to allow free export of wool to Ireland as part of the arrangements in connection with the Union. The manufacturers made great play with the scarcity of wool in England and claimed that its production had declined since 1743;[6] but, in fact, the scarcity seems to have been the result of the shortage of Spanish wool in the previous year, owing to the outbreak of war with Spain. It lasted no longer than July 1799 when imports from any place, in ships of any nationality were permitted;[7] and imports, at nearly five million pounds reached a level slightly higher than in any

[1] T. Pownall, *Live and Let Live*; *The question of Wool truly stated* (A. Young); *A Speech on the Wool Bill that might have been spoken . . . on May 1st . . . 1788* (Young); *A Comparative View of the present Laws against the Illicit Export of Wool* and many others against the Bill, which was defended by Anstie in *A General View of the Bill* and also from Norwich in *While we Live Let Us Live*. See also *Gents. Mag.* 56 (July–Dec.), 1136; *Observations on a Bill . . .* (G. King); A. Young in *Annals of Agriculture* vii. 134.

[2] They had at first been in sympathy with the west (*Gloucester Journal*, 13 Dec. 1784), but there was a misunderstanding over a draft Bill prepared by a Customs officer which was, in fact, disliked by Anstie as much as by everyone else, J. Hustler, *Observations upon the Bill . . . for preventing the Exportation of Wool* (Bradford, Yorks. n.d. but in fact 1787), pp. 17 ff., *Gloucester Journal*, 20 and 27 Feb., 20 Mar., 24 Apr., 12 June, and 11 Sept. 1786, Anstie, *A General View of the Bill*, p. 13.

[3] *Salisbury Journal*, 22 Oct. 1787; Bischoff, op. cit. i. 241.

[4] *Gloucester Journal*, 22 Jan. 1787; *A General View of the Bill*, p. 121.

[5] Arch. B. and W. iii, Lr. of 14 May 1799 to John Fanshawe. These were 'choice locks' presumably Ryeland. There is a considerable difference between Marshall's prices of Southdown wool (see Ashton, op. cit., Table 15) and those given in the *Gloucester Journal*, and by Lord Sheffield, *Observations on the Objections made to the Export of Wool from Gt. Britain to Ireland*, p. 47, the two latter being much higher.

[6] *Account of the Proceedings of the Merchants*, pp. 45, 49, 105, 125–6.

[7] *C.J.* liv. 701, 709, 737.

preceding year.[1] To some extent these imports were taking the place formerly held by fine English wool, for there is little doubt that the quality of the latter was continuing to decline. Farmers were becoming more interested in producing mutton for the consumption of the growing artisan classes;[2] and every step in the way of crossing breeds or providing better food to increase the size of the carcass tended to reduce the fineness of the wool.

It was the high price of Spanish wool which aroused the interest of many western clothiers in the efforts being made to improve the quality of English wool by importing Spanish sheep. This enterprise had originated with Sir Joseph Banks, whose interest in wool had been stimulated by the Lincolnshire controversy of 1782, and whose acquaintance with French savants who were trying to do the same thing led to his receiving, in 1785, two Spanish sheep bred there.[3] It was at his instigation that George III obtained direct from Spain a ram and two ewes in 1789, and many more later. Through John Maitland, the Blackwell Hall factor and M.P. for Chippenham, Banks was enabled to get some of the first wool obtained from these sheep manufactured by western clothiers;[4] but the main centre of experiments in the west was the Bath and West Society, which received two of the King's rams in 1792[5] and several more at later dates. Ewes were sent to them from a number of breeders including some clothiers, both active and retired. It was in this way that Dr. Caleb Parry of Bath built up his well-known flock and conducted one of the best-known and most minutely documented experiments in crosses between Spanish and Ryeland sheep.[6] Others tried crosses between Spanish and Southdown, and there were flocks of the pure Spanish breed as well. The Society's Wool Committee, which included many clothiers, regularly inspected specimens of such wool and con-

[1] See Table in Bischoff, op. cit. i. 330.

[2] Ibid. i. 334.

[3] See H. B. Carter, *His Majesty's Spanish Flock*, pp. 47-8.

[4] Carter, op. cit., pp. 167 (Hawker of Dudbridge), 174 (Walker of Painswick). Earlier, wool from Banks's flock had been manufactured by Matthew Humphreys of Chippenham and Henry Wansey of Salisbury, ibid., pp. 153, 164-5.

[5] Arch. B. and W. v. fol. 23. Banks had written to the Society in 1791, ibid. ii. 320.

[6] See his 'Essay on the Merino Sheep' in *Communications to the Board of Agriculture* v., Pt. II (1806).

firmed the improvement in its value, but it was not until 1798 that a report was obtained on cloth made from it by a member of the Society, Thomas Joyce of Freshford,[1] one of the chief supporters of the experiment in Wiltshire and Somerset. By 1799 the Wool Committee which included Joyce, J. W. Yerbury of Bradford, and J. G. Everett of Heytesbury, considered Parry's wool the finest they had ever seen from the west and 'equal to the general growth of Spain';[2] but a draper to whom in 1800 Parry showed cloth made by Joyce from this wool thought it worth 5s. a yard less than that made of the best imported Spanish.[3] Parry believed this to be mainly due to lack of proper sorting, but in general the opinion of merchants and woolstaplers, perhaps owing to their vested interests, was more adverse to the cross-bred wool than were those of the manufacturers who composed the Society's Wool Committee.[4] When Lord Somerville became President of the Board of Trade in 1798 he added the weight of his influence to the efforts to find a substitute for wool from Spain, and he acquired a flock of Spanish sheep for himself which he kept pure bred.[5] Two notable recruits to the number of breeders were secured in 1800 and 1801 in the influential manufacturers from Uley, Edward Sheppard and Daniel Lloyd.[6] From 1800 onwards the Bath Committee regularly held trials of Anglo-merino wool from various flocks, getting it manufactured by Joyce, Lloyd, Henry Hicks of Eastington, John Waldron of Trowbridge, Francis Naish of Twerton, and Samuel Yeats of Monks' Mill, Alderley, the latter of whom reported in 1806 that the wool was of the finest quality in spite of having been unskilfully sorted.[7] In the same year the Society, at Billingsley's instigation, established an

[1] *Letters and Papers of the Bath and West Society* ix. 344.

[2] Arch. B. and W. v. 339.   [3] Carter, op. cit., p. 242.

[4] Ibid., pp. 160–4, but in one case of a cloth made in 1794 by H. Wansey of pure Spanish wool from Banks's flock, his draper's opinion was very favourable. Rees (*Cyclopaedia*, under 'Wool') states that the wool was commonly sold unwashed and the great amount of dirt prejudiced buyers against it, but its continued high price suggests that this was not the case in the west.

[5] Carter, pp. 249–50. He certainly had a flock (as Carter suspects) before 1802. It was mentioned at a meeting of the B. and W. Soc. on 4 Nov. 1800. See Arch. B. and W. v. 312.

[6] Carter, pp. 261–9. Lloyd's mills were at Uley but he farmed at Bowldown near Tetbury, see above, pp. 181–2. Sheppard favoured a Spanish and Ryeland cross but Lloyd used Southdown as his English breed.

[7] Arch. B. and W. vii. 238–41.

annual fair for the wool in Bath;[1] and during the shortage of
Spanish wool in 1807–9 it attracted a fair number of buyers.[2]
Some was also sold in London and at the annual wool fairs in
the west, where the price was always above that of pure Ryeland wool, by 6s. per stone (of 12½ lb.) at Ross in 1808 and by
8s. to 13s. in 1809.[3] But in 1810 Spanish wool was again available and interest in Anglo-merino fell off. Sales at the Bath wool
fair were a great disappointment that year,[4] and although the
wool still sold at an advanced price of 13s. per stone over that
of Ryeland wool at Ross[5] and at 3s. per pound over Southdown
at Hounslow,[6] the fall in the price of Spanish wool consequent
on the rise in imports diverted the interest of buyers. The experiment had always been unpopular among a farming community
which was finding mutton more profitable than wool; and the
slovenly appearance of the sheep, together with the small size
of its carcass and the difficulty of fattening it, was a great
hindrance to its acceptance.[7] Sheppard himself finally abandoned his flock feeling that the wool got worse every year as
the sheep increased in size.[8] The Bath and West Society did not
publicly recognize the failure of the experiment until 1828[9]
when premiums for the wool and for cloth made of it were
discontinued. In their place one was offered for an essay on
the possibility of producing fine wool in England; but those
received did not justify confidence in success.[10] There was,
however, at least one instance of a pure-bred Spanish flock
which came to produce fine wool of a length suitable for
combing,[11] a satisfactory result for the owner but not what the
experiment had been designed for.

[1] Ibid. 267, 280. For Billingsley see above, p. 127. n. 1.

[2] *Gloucester Journal*, 8 Aug. 1808; 17 Aug. 1809.

[3] Ibid., 27 June and 25 July 1808; 10 and 24 July 1809. The increase in the
Herefordshire stone since the seventeenth century is in line with other increases,
such as that of the 'weight' of wool from 30 lb. to 31 lb.

[4] Arch. B. and W. vii. 516.

[5] 60s. against 47s., *Gloucester Journal*, 23 July 1810.

[6] 6s. against 3s., ibid., 6 Aug. 1810.

[7] See Carter, esp. Ch. XIII; Arch. B. and W. iii, Lr. of 31 May 1802 to Lord
Somerville.

[8] *Ev. on the State of the British Wool Trade*, 1828, p. 296.

[9] Arch. B. and W. xvi., Min. of A.G.M. Dec. 1828, Item 14.

[10] Ibid., Min. of A.G.M. 1829, Item 10. Two essays by R. Pitter and G. Webb-
Hall were published in the *Letters and Papers of the Bath and West Society* xv. (1829),
75, 92.

[11] Bischoff, op. cit. ii. 258 (J. K. Trimmer).

By that time a revolution, and indeed more than one, had taken place in the supply of carding wool. The greater part of the imports now came not from Spain but from Saxony, where Spanish sheep, presented to the Elector in 1765 and 1778, had been carefully bred and tended until their wool was finer and more silky than most of what came from Spain.[1] Imports of this wool had begun about 1800[2] and had reached well over half a million pounds by 1806 as compared with over five millions from Spain;[3] and its qualities were recognized both in Yorkshire and the west, although manufacturers did not like using it because it was dirtier than Spanish wool and therefore wasted more in manufacturing.[4] War conditions after 1806 interfered with the supply until 1814, but imports rapidly increased afterwards, all the more because in Spain the number of sheep had decreased and the quality of the wool had declined in the course of the war.[5] In 1820 imports of German wool were for the first time greater than those of Spanish, and by 1827, at over 21 million pounds, they formed 72 per cent of the total wool imports, against 15 per cent from Spain and Portugal together.[6] Not all this total was of the finest quality. Foreign wools of a lower description were superseding English wool in the manufacture of cloth from 5s. a yard upwards, owing to the deterioration of English carding wool which became more marked soon after 1820.[7] Southdown wool was a drug in the market between 1826 and 1829 and farmers and wool-staplers[8] attributed the low price to the large quantities of foreign wool imported, being very reluctant to recognize that their own actions in producing a sheep which would fetch more money as mutton had interfered with the quality of the wool.

In 1816 the agricultural interest had attempted to obtain a duty on wool which would protect the sheepowner to the same extent as the Corn Laws protected the arable farmer. The

[1] Ibid. i. 386 ff.

[2] *Ev. on the State of the British Wool Trade*, 1828, p. 41.

[3] This figure and those below are drawn from the above Report, App. I.

[4] Nemnich, *Neueste Reise*, p. 7. Cf. *Ev. on the State of the British Wool Trade*, 1828, p. 41.

[5] *Rept. on Manufactures, Commerce, and Shipping*, 1833 (H.C. 690), p. 81.

[6] Portuguese wool was similar to Spanish though less fine.

[7] *Ev. on the State of the British Wool Trade*, 1828, pp. 299, 317.

[8] Dorset C.R.O., Lrs. of Thomas Colfox, 29 Sept. 1823 and 20 Jan. 1824.

petition failed, and the price of Southdown wool, which had fallen to 1s. 6d. a pound in the depression of 1816 (a fall of 50 per cent since the great shortage of Spanish wool in 1809) rose in 1817 and reached 2s. 6d. a pound in 1818,[1] a year of much speculative activity. The influences which produced this rise worked also towards the import of cheaper wool which would compete with Southdown; and when the latter dropped in price in the great slump of 1819 it was natural to blame the imports, which had risen to over 24 million pounds the year before. Lord Sheffield, that protagonist of the fine-woolled sheep breeders, once again raised the question of a tax, but ministers seemed to be against it. Manufacturers were startled to discover a little later that the Government had changed its mind and, in return for an agreement by the landed interest to a tax on malt, was laying a duty of 6d. a pound on foreign wool.[2] Attempts to get it withdrawn met with no success until 1823, when, in connection with protests against the ware-housing bill (which allowed cloth and other merchandise to enter in bond for re-exportation later), manufacturers were informed that the Government would abolish it in return for their acquiescence in the export of English wool.[3] Gloucester-shire clothiers, who had stated as early as 1815 that they re-gretted the prohibition of export as 'the last act of an exploded system which they would readily consent to the repeal of',[4] agreed at once to this proposal and, although they were accused by the northern worsted manufacturers of wishing to get rid of the tax at any price,[5] the motive behind their agreement was simply the fact that English wool was no longer a matter of importance to them.[6] The tax was reduced to its former level

[1] Prices are taken from Bischoff, op. cit. ii., Table VI.

[2] Ibid. i., Chs. X and XI. The additional tax was about 5d. since 1d. per lb. had been imposed for revenue purposes in 1802, Smart, *Economic Annals* i. 685. (Bischoff speaks of 'the late tax' as one of 7s. 11d. per cwt. or about ¾d. per lb., op. cit. i. 461.)

[3] Bischoff, op. cit. ii. 37.

[4] Resolutions passed at a meeting of Woollen Manufacturers, 8 Mar. 1815 (against the Corn Laws), G.C.L., J.V.13.2(10).

[5] Bischoff, op. cit. ii. 46. Leeds manufacturers who used short wool decided that its export would be a lesser evil than the wool tax, ibid. ii. 40.

[6] The use of English wool in Gloucestershire appears to have declined from c. 1823. The Dorset woolstapler, Thomas Colfox, sent samples to a Painswick clothier in that year in response to a request, but the county is never mentioned again in his correspondence.

of 1d. from December 1824 and export of wool was permitted at the same duty.[1]

While the export of long wool slowly increased, short wool remained almost unaffected. The imports of foreign wool, on the other hand, grew from an average of 20 million pounds per annum during the last three years of the tax to one of over 29 million between 1825 and 1827.[2] The fact that this coincided with another serious fall in the price of Southdown wool from about 1s. 3d. or 1s. 4d. per pound to a maximum of 9d., confirmed the sheepowners in their belief that importation was the cause of their distress. In 1828 they made a renewed effort to get the tax re-imposed, which led to an inquiry in the House of Lords[3] but did not prevail on the Government to alter its policy. The complainants were nearly all breeders of Southdown sheep, and they were all convinced that their wool had improved rather than deteriorated; but as they did not sort it themselves it is probable that they were not aware of the problem. As one woolstapler said, he now got none of the finest quality wool out of Southdown fleeces from a certain Wiltshire farm, whereas in 1815 the proportion had been 6 per cent; while of the second quality he now got 29 per cent against a former 50.[4] In the past the price obtained for the finer kinds had sufficed to afford a good sum for the fleece as a whole, but now there was hardly any of the higher priced wool to raise the general level.

After 1825 very little English wool was used in the west except for such army cloth as was still made for the Government or the East India Company. Saxon wool had established its superiority over Spanish by 1820 and by the early thirties wool from Germany (not all, of course, of the finest quality) formed 65 per cent of the total imports while Spanish had sunk to 7 per cent. Australian wool formed nearly 8 per cent[5] but the west was slow to experiment with it. It had first been seen in London in 1803 when Captain MacArthur produced some specimens from his merino flock which made a good impression on the manufacturers' committee which was pursuing the

---

[1] Bischoff, op. cit. ii. 66.   [2] Ibid. ii. 97.

[3] *Report from the Select Committee of the House of Lords on the State of the British Wool Trade*, 1828.

[4] Ibid., p. 190.

[5] *Accounts of Foreign and Colonial Wool imported 1816–1843* (1844, H.C. 306). Averaged 1830 to 1834 inclusive.

repeal of the restrictive statutes.[1] It appeared commercially in
1807 and by 1818 about 65,000 pounds were imported. At
first it was of very varying quality and almost always too dirty
to command the entire approval of manufacturers, though they
appreciated the peculiar softness of the wool imparted to it by
the climate. MacArthur's wool and that of one or two other
large growers soon commanded a price above that of Spanish
wool, but below that of the best Saxony; but the buyers came
almost entirely from the north. Donald Maclean of Stanley
mills seems to have been the first western manufacturer to take
an interest in it; but in general western buyers were put off by
its appearance which did not reveal its real quality. In 1824
Hicks of Eastington was the only man in the west besides
Maclean who knew anything of it. By 1827 Edward Sheppard
was buying and the following year Stanton was a convert, but
a year later it could be said that few western manufacturers
knew its nature except from hearsay.[2] As late as 1872 German
and related wools seem to have been much more extensively
used in Gloucestershire than Australian, although between
1865 and 1874 German wool formed only $2\frac{1}{2}$ per cent of the
imports to 58 per cent of Australian.[3] The books of one broker
operating in Gloucestershire[4] show sixty-three sales of German,
Austrian, or Hungarian wools between 1860 and 1872 against
eleven of wool from Sydney and Tasmania. The reason was,
no doubt, the suitability of German wool for making the highly
dressed broadcloth which was still the staple production of the
county. Australian wool was less suited to such material. It
made 'soft, elastic and pliable fabrics'[5] which came increasingly
into fashion after the middle of the century, but those Gloucestershire manufacturers who clung to the cloth for which they
had received so many awards chose the wool which was best
for making it. Wiltshire and Somerset, with a larger production of fancy goods, seem to have adopted Australian wool to
a much greater extent.

[1] E. M. Onslow, *Some early Records of the MacArthurs of Camden*, p. 65.

[2] Ibid., pp. 415, 420, 425–6, 438.

[3] Averaged from figures in Statistical Abstract, 1875. Wool from Austria and
Hungary is not separately entered, but the whole import from Europe formed only
12 per cent of the total.

[4] Books of T. W. Newman, in possession of Messrs. Newman, Hender, & Co.

[5] *Reports by Juries on the International Exhibition of 1862*, Class XXI, p. 3.

The mention above of a broker in foreign wool operating in the country points to one of several changes in the methods of buying wool which took place in the early part of the nineteenth century. After 1815 wool was sent from Spain and Germany to factors who allowed bills to be drawn on them at once but gave long credit to their customers.[1] Some German wool producers sent their own agents to London, who distributed samples to the four large firms which dealt in foreign wool; but in 1821 one of the latter was said to be about to by-pass the agents and establish his own house on the Continent to buy direct from the growers.[2] Wool auctions were held in London at regular intervals and were attended by manufacturers from the west and north. Others, beginning, it is claimed, with William Playne in 1824, made their own expeditions to buy wool by visiting the great Silesian estates which produced it,[3] but there is no evidence that this was a common method of obtaining it. In 1836 Charles Stephens spoke of buying by sample from London and of the dissatisfaction felt when the wool was not up to sample;[4] but as he was emphasizing the advantage which a railway would give of getting to London and back in a day and so facilitating inspection, he may have exaggerated the extent to which wool was purchased in this way. Some manufacturers seem to have attended the quarterly London auctions of foreign wool all through the century, but by the thirties at least brokers were established in the country from whom those who could not spare the time or money to go to London could order their requirements. One such was J. Bleeck of Warminster who gave evidence at the railway inquiry of 1835, and he was not the only one, as may be seen from a glance at current directories. By the mid-century there were a far larger number of houses in London, including many German ones, who imported foreign wool; but there seems to be no evidence to show whether some manufacturers dealt direct with them or whether it was the universal custom to employ brokers in London or the country.

---

[1] *Rept. on the Law relating to Merchants, Agents, or Factors*, 1823 (H.C. 452), p. 14.
[2] Onslow, op. cit., pp. 395–6.
[3] Playne, op. cit., p. 154. W. R. Stanton also went to Germany in 1828, Onslow, op. cit., p. 425.
[4] *Rept. on Cheltenham and Great Western Union Rly. Bill*, 1836 (H.L. 78), pp. 11, 23.

X

THE PROCESSES OF MANUFACTURE

CLOTH-MANUFACTURING processes have often been described and the only apology which can be offered for doing so again must be that more detailed information than is usually given will enable the reader to understand better the repeated charges about bad making. It also seems worth while to record, as far as information is available, some facts about the machinery invented or used in the west, which may be more conveniently discussed here than in the narrative.

A. CLEANSING AND SCOURING THE WOOL

The preparatory processes of picking the wool to remove hairs or other extraneous objects, scouring it in running water, often in a stream, drying it, and willeying or beating with rods to open up the staple were mechanized at different dates after the arrival of spinning machinery. The willey or devil, of which there were several models, had arrived in Yorkshire by 1800 and in the west in 1804,[1] but many western manufacturers seem never to have used it. This may not have been due to backwardness, since fine wool was said not to require its use, scribbling itself being a sufficient preparation.[2] Machinery for picking and wool-washing was not produced until well on in the nineteenth century,[3] and though it was invented in Yorkshire the west does not appear to have been backward in acquiring it. Picking machines were in use in Trowbridge by 1858[4]

---

[1] *Rept. Asst. Commrs. Hdloom Weavers*, 1840, Pt. V, p. 369. Nemnich saw the machine at Frome in 1806, *Neueste Reise*, p. 220, and it is mentioned several times afterwards in Gloucestershire, e.g. *Gloucester Journal*, 24 Oct. 1808 and 23 Sept. 1811.

[2] *Encyclopaedia Britannica*, 1841, quoted Bischoff, *Comprehensive History* ii. 391.

[3] Machines for both are mentioned as recent in *Repts. by Jurors . . . on the Int. Exhibition of 1862*, Cl. XXI, 4.

[4] *Trowbridge Advertiser*, 27 Nov. 1858.

and wool-washers are mentioned in 1857,[1] but washing could still be done in the river Avon at Bradford in 1869.[2] Drying the wool, which before the machine age was done either in the open air or in buildings heated by stoves,[3] was performed in many different ways by 1862,[4] and it is impossible to say what methods were generally adopted in the west.

The ingredient employed for scouring and for many other purposes where an alkali was required was the stale urine known as 'sig', a natural source of ammonia. This was also eventually dispensed with, but not until the later years of the nineteenth century, in favour of a chemical alkali such as some form of soda. It was not only conservative workmen who preferred the old method. The author of a professional treatise on spinning in 1894 greatly regretted the disuse of sig on the ground that the ammonia in it was volatile and passed off, leaving the wool 'kind and soft to the touch', whereas a fixed alkali such as soda might do damage if used to excess.[5]

Fine wool wasted considerably in scouring. In the early nineteenth century English wool was said to waste 25 per cent, Saxony wool 20 per cent, and Spanish 12 per cent;[6] but in 1828 Saxony wool was said to waste about one-eighth more than English.[7] These differences depended upon the state in which the wool arrived. English wool, washed on the sheep's back, was not so clean as Spanish which was washed after shearing, while Saxony wool arrived in the fleece, apparently unwashed, and was generally the dirtiest of all. Other estimates are $12\frac{1}{2}$ to 25 per cent for English wool given by a Devizes woolstapler about 1780[8] and 15 to 20 per cent for Spanish given by Joyce the Freshford manufacturer in 1798,[9] which seems high and

[1] Ibid., 10 Oct. 1857.

[2] Ibid., 20 Nov. 1869.

[3] The round houses of which a few remain in Gloucestershire and Wiltshire may have been used for this purpose, see K. Ponting, 'Some Questions about Round Towers', *Ind. Arch.*, 4 (1). 60–2; also a ref. in 1855 to 'a round wool stove now used as a workman's cottage' at Holcombe mill, Nailsworth, G.C.L., R.V.205.5. But they may also have been used for bleaching, J. Tann, 'The Bleaching of Woollen and Worsted Goods, 1740–1860', *Textile History* i. (1969), 2. 158 ff.

[4] See *Repts. by Jurors . . . for the Int. Exh. of 1862*, Cl. XXI, 4.

[5] C. Vickerman, *Woollen Spinning*, pp. 73–4.

[6] *Recs' Cyclopaedia*, vol. 38, under 'Wool'.

[7] *Rept. on State of British Wool Trade*, 1828, p. 314, Ev. of W. Ireland.

[8] *Letters and Papers of the Bath and West Society* viii. 80.

[9] Ibid. ix. 344–5.

much above the $12\frac{1}{2}$ per cent for a lower quality of Spanish wool mentioned in 1828.[1]

B. CARDS, OIL, AND SPINNING

After scouring the wool could be dyed at once, or dyeing could be left to be done in the piece, which was necessary if the colour was a light or bright one. Grease in some form, preferably oil, had then to be added. In the early seventeenth century whale oil seems to have been frequently used for making the ordinary 'sorting-pack cloth' for export, and it was sometimes mixed with hempseed oil, which was forbidden in 1632.[2] Other forms of grease such as butter were often employed, especially, it may be conjectured, by those who sold their yarn in the market. Markham recommended goose or swine's grease to housewives spinning their own wool if they had no access to rape oil,[3] but this did not meet with approval when the cloth was destined for sale. Benedict Webb, inspired by his observation of the rape oil used in France, took out a patent for making it in 1624;[4] but he seems to have been unaware that it was already being produced in East Anglia[5] and used in Suffolk and the north of England.[6] Webb's neighbours approved of his oil, although some of them had tried imported rape oil and found it unsatisfactory;[7] but rape oil was not subsequently used for making fine cloth in the west though it could be employed for cheaper kinds either alone or mixed with Seville oil.[8] From a very early date in the history of Spanish cloth the

---

[1] *Rept. on State of the British Wool Trade*, 1828, p. 267, Ev. of J. C. Francis. Both he and Ireland (see p. 281, n. 7) spoke only of 'foreign' wool but Bischoff explained the discrepancy in their evidence by saying that Ireland was speaking of German and Francis of Spanish wool, *The Wool Question Considered* (1828), p. 92.

[2] P.R.O., P.C.2/42, fol. 336.

[3] G. Markham, *The English Huswife* (1615), p. 67; *C.J.* i. 552.

[4] Patent no. 30, see E. Moir, 'Benedict Webb, Clothier', *Econ. Hist. Rev.* (2nd ser.), 10 (2) (1957), 256–64.

[5] G.C.L., S.Z.23.2 (10). I owe this reference to Mr. J. P. Cooper.

[6] Markham, loc. cit., speaks of it as the usual oil.

[7] P.R.O., E.134/2, Car. I, Easter 19, Answers to Interrogatory 2. This ref. also comes from Mr. J. P. Cooper.

[8] In 1711 H. Wansey had some at 3s. 2d. per gall. when Seville oil was 4s. 4d. to 4s. 8d. and his son mentioned it once, Wilts. C.R.O. 314/1/3. See also J. Tann, op. cit., p. 152 and *Wilts. Arch. Soc. Rec. Brch.* xix. no. 475. Oil made from grain was said to be sticky and might injure the cloth, *Ency. méth.* i. 122.

superfine clothier depended entirely on olive oil from Italy, Spain, or Morocco, and in the early nineteenth century western manufacturers would go to considerable lengths to ensure that the Gallipoli oil which they preferred was pure and unmixed with rape.[1] Stale or bad oil could do much damage. Elderton's remarks to his relatives on the 'stinking oil' used in making some of their cloths were picturesque though perhaps exaggerated. 'A draper sold some (of your cloths) but . . . one day when I called he had no less than fifteen suits of cloth lay on the counter. There, Sir, says he, all these are returned on my hands, the Gentlemen will not suffer their servants to be in the room with 'em, they stink so.'[2] Even what might appear to be the best oil could turn out to possess properties which injured the cloth. 'Mr. Packer was so unfortunate as to purchase a pipe of oil at £42 per ton which appeared so exceeding fine and good that he reserved it for his fine yarn; what was the cause he cannot tell but it occasioned more rows than he usually made in 500 cloths,' wrote Mrs. Packer to a Blackwell Hall factor in 1768.[3]

The quantity of oil used is variously stated, but after the introduction of machinery it diminished, as indeed one would expect, since the constant handling of the wool was much lessened when spinning machines were adopted. At Leeds in 1588 the proportion was four gallons of Seville oil to 12 stone of wool, or a gallon to 32 pounds.[4] The example of manufacturing costs in 1723 preserved in the Clark Papers is unsatisfactory in this respect, because of the uncertainty about the actual amount of wool oiled;[5] but a petition of 1730 gives a gallon to 40 lb.[6] Other pre-machine estimates are a gallon to 24 lb.[7] and (for farmhouse spinners) 8 lb. of grease to about 27 lb.[8] None of these statements refers specifically to the western district which, as late as 1894, was said to use more oil than other areas.[9] A

---

[1] *1st Rept. from Ctee on Seeds and Wool*, 1816 (H.C. 272), p. 203.

[2] Som. C.R.O., Elderton Lr. Book, To N. Cockell, 26 Jan. 1769.

[3] Glouc. C.R.O., D.149, F.114, Lr. to T. Misenor, 21 July 1769. 'Rows' were lines of raised wool which had escaped the shears.

[4] Tawney and Power, op. cit. i. 217.

[5] See App. III, Table H.

[6] *C.J.* xxi. 692.

[7] T. Hale, *Complete Body of Husbandry* (2nd ed., 1759), iii. 306 (a pint to every 3 lb.).

[8] G. Markham, *The English Huswife*, p. 88 (3 lb. of grease to 10 lb. of wool).

[9] Vickerman, op. cit., pp. 139–40.

statement circulated by Wiltshire clothiers in 1798, after spinning was done by machinery, gives about two gallons for 100 lb. of wool;[1] while the Commissioner for Handloom Weavers in Gloucestershire in 1859 gives figures which result in from just under two to two-and-a-half gallons to the hundred.[2] Both these are above the modern proportion of one-and-a-half gallons per hundred.

The price of oil fluctuated a good deal. When it was low it formed a very small element in the cost of making a cloth, but a rise was felt as a burden. In 1725–6 there was a concerted effort by the clothiers of Wiltshire and Somerset to get rid of the import duty on oil;[3] and during the war with Spain in 1743 there was a general protest from the west against the rise in price, said to have been from £26 to over £60 per ton, owing to the prohibition of imports from Spain and the failure of the olive harvest in the province of Naples, whence Gallipoli oil came.[4] This complaint was thoroughly investigated since Parliament was considering the state of the industry, but no action was taken; and the London merchants alleged that the quantity used was so little that no great burden resulted from a high price.[5] It reached £70 to £75 per ton in 1800[6] but even this formed a very small element in the increased price of cloth beside the rising cost of wool.

After being oiled, the wool was scribbled in the clothier's workshop. In the late seventeenth and eighteenth centuries the scribbling horse was an upright frame covered with leather leaves set with iron teeth over which the wool was repeatedly drawn with smaller hand cards. This process might be repeated several times for fine cloth using wire teeth of different sizes.[7] The date when scribbling became general is uncertain. Thoresby in 1715 called it a 'new invention whereby the differ-

---

[1] Glouc. C.R.O., D.1759 (1 gall. to 51 lb. wool). See App. III, Table J.

[2] *Repts. Asst. Commrs. Hdloom Weavers*, 1840, Pt. V, p. 370.

[3] *C. J.* xxii. 601, 637, 660, 671.

[4] Ibid. xxiv. 401, 409, 420, 422–3.

[5] Ibid. 413.

[6] Glouc. C.R.O., D.149, F.189, Lrs. of Bell, Davies, Vaughan, Van der Horst & Co. of Bristol to Sheppard & Hicks, 10 and 15 Nov. 1800. The cost formed about 1·8 per cent of the whole cost of cloth in 1798. See App. III, Table J.

[7] *Encycl. méth.* i. 108 ff. This is the best description, with several references to the English practice, but according to it wool was not oiled before scribbling either in England or in Languedoc.

ent colours are delicately mixed'[1] and so, no doubt, it was in Yorkshire at this time; but it must have been adopted earlier in the west and other places which made medleys. A preliminary carding on a stockcard—a process which cannot have been much unlike scribbling—is described by Markham in 1615 as necessary for all medleys[2] and in 1641 the stockcarding of Spanish cloth made in Shepton Mallet seems to have been equivalent to scribbling.[3]

The wool was then given out to the spinners. For superfines in the eighteenth century the proportion was two-thirds for weft and one-third for warp,[4] but the cassimeres introduced in 1766 required equal quantities and approximately the same degree of twist in each.[5] Except in this case, wool intended for warp was more tightly twisted than that for weft and in the opposite direction. For coarser cloth the warp seems sometimes to have been formed of two threads twisted together,[6] but in general when this was done it was for specialized kinds of material such as rateens. The tendency for warp spinning to be entrusted to specialists has already been noted. For weft superfine clothiers often formed groups of spinners in country places. Surviving accounts suggest that five or six women might undertake the weft for one superfine cloth.

The first duty of the spinner was to card the wool again on hand cards. For superfine cloth these were supplied by the clothier; for coarser cloth spinners might be obliged to find their own.[7] The wire for the cards, and frequently the cards themselves, were often imported up to the end of the seventeenth century, in spite of several prohibitions beginning in the reign of Richard III. In 1711 foreign wire was still said to be the

---

[1] Quoted Crump, op. cit., p. 18.   [2] G. Markham, op. cit., pp. 86–7.

[3] R. Watts, op. cit., p. 43.

[4] Markham writing for housewives in 1615 said that a half-and-half division was most satisfactory, op. cit., p. 90. Petty in 1661 seems to suggest the same, T. Birch, *History of the Royal Society*, p. 57. But the weight specified for the weft in the Wilts. wage assessment of 1603 must mean that in 'sorting-pack cloth' the weft formed approximately two-thirds of the total, and existing clothiers' books prove that this was always the case in making superfine broad-cloth in the eighteenth century.

[5] Patent no. 858, 26 Aug. 1766.

[6] An account of processes in the Stourhead Papers (Wilts. C.R.O. 383/908) treats this as the only way of making warps. There are other references in the third G. Wansey's ledger (Wilts. C.R.O. 314/2/1), and to 'mill twist' in *Ev. on the Woollen Trade Bill*, 1803 (H.C. 95), p. 62.

[7] *The Clothiers' Reasons against passing the Bill . . .* (1711).

best, but it was alleged that, owing to the improvements made by the Dutch who had arrived in the seventies, none had been brought into Frome 'since that which was hid in the meeting house six and twenty years ago', nor had foreign woolcards been imported.[1]

Woolcards were made in many parts of England but by the end of the seventeenth century Frome stood out as the chief cardmaking town in the region,[2] probably because iron was found in the neighbourhood and wire drawers practised their trade on the spot. The cardmakers there were capitalists employing large numbers; one, John Glover, in the early eighteenth century is said to have had 400 work-people. Dursley was also a cardmaking town and the cardmakers intermarried with the families of the clothiers.[3] Much information about the trade is contained in pamphlets issued in connection with an attempt by Frome cardmakers in 1709 to ban the age-old practice of refurbishing old cards and selling them for use in making coarser cloth.[4] Whatever the merits of this controversy, it is clear that proper carding was the foundation of good clothmaking, and that many of the faults complained of might be traced to thick spinning due to wool insufficiently or improperly carded, sometimes with wire which had split or become hammerheaded. Bad cards and inefficient scribbling may be one reason not only for the faults of the white cloth made for export in the sixteenth and seventeenth centuries but also for the unfavourable comparison of English spinning with French in the cheaper cloths exported to the Mediterranean.[5] French cards, at least in Rouen, were considered inferior to English in the eighteenth century;[6] but English cloth of the coarser kinds was frequently made with bought yarn, either English or Irish, and the carding may have been very inefficiently done.

Cards needed to be renewed frequently. A French estimate

---

[1] *A Dialogue between Dick Brazenface the Cardmaker and Tim Meanwell the Clothier*, p. 2.

[2] *The Voyage of Don Manoel Gonzales*, p. 100. When many other towns sent up petitions about the sale of old cards in 1605 (P.R.O., S.P. 14/17/107), Frome was not mentioned by name so that presumably the industry was not yet important there.

[3] *Glouc. N. and Q.* ii. 619.   [4] See *V.C.H. Som.* ii. 425–6.

[5] Above, p. 4.

[6] A. P. Wadsworth and J. de L. Mann, *The Cotton Trade and Industrial Lancashire*, pp. 461, 517. Roland suggests the same thing where superfine cloth was concerned, *Ency. méth.* i. 109.

gives two hundred pounds of wool, probably Spanish, as the most which could be scribbled with one pair of scribblers,[1] and it was said in 1709 that not more than forty pounds of English wool was generally carded in new hand cards.[2] The quantity of Spanish wool was probably less. Scribbling cards cost from 4s. 3d. to 4s. 9d. in the early eighteenth century and small cards for spinners from 24s. to 27s. per dozen,[3] but this must be offset for the Spanish wool clothiers by small receipts from the sale of old cards.[4]

Spinning was done on the 'great wheel' which stood about five feet high and entailed walking to and fro as the spinner drew out and twisted the thread and then wound it on the spindle.[5] The small wheel which enabled the spinner to sit at her work was, no doubt, sometimes employed, but more work could be done at the large wheel because the spinner had a longer range.[6] The Saxony wheel with the flyer, which enabled the yarn to be spun and wound at the same time, was not well suited for carded wool and appears never to have been used for it. Its tendency would have been to lay the hairs too straight and to place too much strain on the yarn.[7]

After spinning, the yarn was wound on reels which figured among every spinner's equipment.[8] Reels with a clock to show the number of revolutions were certainly used in Trowbridge and, no doubt, elsewhere, by the 1750s.[9] It is not known in what way the Dutch reel, introduced to Trowbridge by the Dutch immigrants in the 1670s and used there as long as hand spinning continued,[10] differed from the English one.

---

[1] Ibid. i. 123. An English source suggests 240 lb. English wool in refurbished scribbling cards and forty in small cards, *A Dialogue. . . .*, p. 5.

[2] *Remarks made by the Wier Drawers, Cardmakers and English Wool Clothiers on a pretended dialogue set forth by the Spanish Clothiers* (1711), p. 2.

[3] Wilts. C.R.O., 314/1/3, Wansey Papers.

[4] See W.A.S. Rec. Brch. xix. no. 171.

[5] Cf. J. Blanch, *Hoops into Spinning Wheels*, p. 13, where the courtesan confesses 'In my youth I ran at the wheel.'

[6] Wadsworth and Mann, op. cit., pp. 411–12. Cf. H. Lemon, 'The Development of Spinning Wheels', *Textile History* i. 1. 88, on the productivity of the great wheel.

[7] Ibid., 91.

[8] Often only as 'spokes', see Trowbridge Par. Reg., Inventories, Wilts. C.R.O. 206/95.

[9] References to 'snap reels' and once to a clock appear in the above inventories about 1749–50.

[10] J. Bodman, *History of Trowbridge*, p. 23.

By the end of the eighteenth century all the above processes were carried out by machinery. Carding and scribbling engines and the spinning jenny need no description, but the apparent inefficiency of the jenny in spinning fine yarn in 1777 demands some attention, though the explanation can only be guessed at.[1] In the first place the carding engine, at Chard at least, was of very primitive construction. In Cook's words (although the copyist has been unable to read one of them) it was 'a frame that takes 3 or 4 pairs of cards; the upper cards are hung in a kind of (blank) and all worked at once. The under cards are fixed in a movable part of the frame and all turned at once by a motion of the foot as a woman turns a card upon her knee.'[2] Whether this denotes a cylinder card at all seems doubtful; if it does it would resemble a primitive form of Arkwright's machine with a flat over the barrel rather than the roller and clearer card which emerged as the most suitable machine for carding wool. The carders introduced in other parts of the west may, of course, have been of a more developed type, but it is also possible that the absence of any device for the speedier production of a slubbing was a more important element in the failure. This intermediate process between carding and spinning was, so far as we know, unnecessary in the woollen industry before machinery was introduced, although it was already an element in the production of fine cotton yarn.[3] The slubbing billy is said to have appeared in cotton in 1786[4] and it must have been introduced into the woollen industry almost immediately. No doubt it contributed to the success of the second attempt to introduce machinery; but it must not be forgotten that the jenny itself had also been much improved from the earlier version.[5]

While the scribbling and carding engines were almost always worked by power the billy and jenny remained hand-operated machines for a long time. By 1840 power could be applied to

---

[1] See above, pp. 126–7.

[2] Arch. B. and W. I, fol. 30, Lr. of 29 Nov. 1777. Cook's improvement in the jenny was to place the spindles horizontally. Mr. C. Aspin, author, with S. D. Chapman, of *James Hargreaves and the Spinning Jenny*, considers that this model would spin better than that described in Hargreaves' patent.

[3] Wadsworth and Mann, op. cit., p. 176.

[4] G. J. French, *Life and Times of Samuel Crompton* (Reprint 1970), p. 90.

[5] See Aspin, op. cit.

both,[1] and power-driven billies and jennies appear in an advertisement of machinery for sale in Trowbridge as late as 1856.[2] By this time, as already described, the condenser was beginning to supersede the billy and the mule had been generally adopted in place of the jenny by the more progressive manufacturers.[3]

These mules were not self-actors, which did not begin to be common in the Yorkshire industry before the fifties and even then were not suitable for all kinds of spinning.[4] References to them in the west are found in 1867 and 1872,[5] but when they were first installed is unknown. The mule employed before that time was that to which power had been applied in the 1790s, in which the pushing in of the carriage and the guiding of the faller wire were left to the skill and judgement of the spinner.[6] It was not, however, the only machine of the kind known in the district. Apart from the jenny, some use was made of the 'jack', which is found in Gloucestershire, though not in Wiltshire or Somerset, during the first half of the century. What is apparently the only one now in existence[7] is very similar in appearance to the mule; but it dispenses with the rollers and uses the clasp, as on the jenny, to hold the sliver fast while the outward movement of the carriage attenuates it. The jack used in Gloucestershire, however, seems to have been more like a billy. It was a peculiarity of the industry there to use slubbing instead of yarn for the coarser cloths[8] a practice which had begun in 1802 when Uley weavers struck against it.[9] In 1839 the jack was described as

---

[1] *Special Repts. of Insps. of Facts. on Prevention of Accidents*, 1841 (H.C. 311), p. 23; also (for billies) *6th Rept. on Regulation of Mills & Facts.*, 1840 x. (H.C. 504), pp. 60–1, 126. See also Crump and Ghorbal, *History of the Huddersfield Woollen Industry*, p. 118.

[2] *Trowbridge Advertiser*, 5 July 1856.   [3] See above, pp. 187–8, 200–1.

[4] *Repts. by Jurors . . . on the Int. Exhibition of 1862*, Cl. XXI, 4.

[5] *Stroud Journal*, 30 Nov. 1867. (Cam Mills), 12 Oct. 1872. Lavertons at Westbury had several shops for self-actors in the latter year. (Records recently deposited in the Wilts. C.R.O.)

[6] *History of Technology*, ed. C. Singer, iv. 288–90.

[7] In the Welsh Folk Museum, St. Fagans, Glam. See description in J. G. Jenkins, *The Welsh Woollen Industry*, p. 61. 'Jack' is said to have been the name by which the semi-power-driven woollen mule was known in the U.S.A. and in N. Lancs. (A. H. Cole, *The American Wool Manufacture*, p. 113; Aspin, op. cit., p. 60), but it seems questionable whether the machine so called was not always either that described by Mr. Jenkins or the one used in Glos.

[8] *Repts. Asst. Commrs. Hdloom Weavers*, 1840, Pt. V, p. 370.

[9] *Ev. on Woollen Trade Bill*, 1803, p. 34.

a machine worked by the slubber 'which twists and lengthens the rollers into a long weak thread', and it is implied that the rollers obtained from the carding machine were pieced up upon it in the same way as they were on the billy.[1] The jack, therefore, only made the slubbing easier to weave by imparting a rather greater degree of twist and by winding the sliver directly on to a bobbin ready for the weaver instead of on to a cop to be further spun on a jenny or a mule.[2] This was probably the machine 'which both slubs and spins' seen by Nemnich about 1806, and it was still in use in the forties.[3]

C. WARPING AND WEAVING

The yarn spun for warp (called 'chain' in the west) was first wound from the skein on to spools and then warped in the clothiers' workshops, frequently, it would seem, by the weavers themselves.[4] Up to late in the nineteenth century warping was done by winding the yarn round two bars or pegs placed a certain distance apart, so that a given number of turns made up a known length of warp.[5] Spooling, too, seems often to have been done by the weaver before he warped the yarn,[6] and in the 1790s some weavers were refusing to take out warps without the customary allowance for it.[7] In 1798 the Bath and West Society offered a premium for a machine to save the expense of spooling, by connecting the spool with a warping bar or machine 'properly constructed to receive worsted or yarn and put it into chains of any description which may be required'; and in 1800 a committee of clothiers inspected a machine for spooling which was reported to have much merit and received a reward of ten guineas.[8] Whether this was the 'spooling tommy' which appears

---

[1] See p. 289, n. 8.   [2] *Special Repts. Fact. Insp.*, 1841 (H.C. 311), p. 23.

[3] Nemnich, *Neueste Reise*, p. 225. Newspaper mentions begin in 1808 and continue at least until 1841 (*Gloucester Journal*, 24 Oct. 1808; 20 Mar. 1841). See also G.C.L., V.F.5.1(11), Advt. of his inventions by James Dutton, *c.* 1844.

[4] *Ev. on Woollen Trade Bill*, 1803, p. 84. Cf. Pressnell, op. cit., p. 90.

[5] A. T. Playne who entered the family business at Longfords mill, Minchinhampton, in 1865 remembered this being done, *Minchinhampton and Avening*, p. 143.

[6] Thomas Long's books frequently show the weaver as having done the spooling, but it was occasionally performed by someone else. No price is given. Wilts. C.R.O. 947.

[7] Pressnell, op. cit., p. 95. In 1623 unpaid spooling was a grievance, *H.M.C. Var.* i. 94.

[8] Arch. B. and W. v. 233, 340.

in Gloucestershire from 1807 onwards[1] is not certain; but in 1839 spooling was done by girls at 3s. a week and warping was also done by women on the employer's premises.[2]

In order to strengthen the warp it had to be sized. With cheaper cloth this could be done by passing a brush dipped in paste over it in the loom or by steeping it in chalk and water beforehand;[3] but a fine warp had to be sized in glue. By whom this was done is not always clear. In the books of Usher & Jeffries and of Thomas Long several warps are marked 'sized in skein' but there is no difference in the rate for weaving them and that for others not so marked. In 1756, however, weavers were asking for an additional payment for 'sized in skein'[4] which suggests that they must have done it themselves, presumably in the clothiers' workshops before they spooled the yarn. In the early nineteenth century it seems to have been the general practice for the weavers to do the sizing by immersing successive portions of the warp in glue after they had taken it home;[5] and in the few cases where they took it out already sized they received only journeymen's wages.[6] Nevertheless, in the great Gloucestershire strike of 1825 they were trying to insist that the employers should do it (presumably without reducing the rate for weaving), 'a thing quite unprecedented' according to Henry Wyatt of the Vatch mills near Stroud.[7] In the next ten or twelve years the position changed,[8] possibly owing to the introduction of more sophisticated methods;[9] and some weavers were deploring the fact that sizing by the masters had reduced their earnings.[10]

[1] G.C.L., R.X.319.4. Advt. of sale of goods, 22 Feb. 1807, and frequently later.

[2] *Repts. Asst. Commrs. Hdloom Weavers*, 1840, Pt. V, p. 371; ibid., Pt. II, p. 439.

[3] T. Birch, *History of the Royal Society* i. 57–8. See below, p. 292. According to the author of *Excidium Angliae* (p. 5), sizing was only necessary for Spanish warps but he may only have meant sizing in glue.

[4] See below, App. IV, Table M.

[5] *Ev. on Woollen Trade Bill*, 1803, p. 64. But according to Britton in 1801 (*Beauties of Wilts*. ii. 307) the weaver sized the chain and got it spooled by a woman before warping. Where this was done is not stated.

[6] *Ev. on State of the Woollen Manufacture*, 1806, p. 335.

[7] *Gloucester Journal*, 20 June 1825, Lr. from H. Wyatt and Sons.

[8] *Rept. Asst. Commrs. Hdloom Weavers*, 1840, Pt. V, p. 391. See also Pt. II, p. 275 on Wilts. where the change was not complete.

[9] See Tomlinson, op. cit. ii. 957 for a description of the process as practised by the Sheppards of Frome in 1854.

[10] Petition of the Broad Weavers, n.d. but possibly *c*. 1837–9, preserved by Messrs. Strachan of Lodgemore Mills, Stroud, to whom I am indebted for knowledge of it.

Care was also necessary for 'turning on', or the insertion of the warp into the loom, for each of the threads, of which there might be any number up to over 4,000,[1] had to be given an equal tension. About 1743 a Devizes clothier, Richard Brooks, invented a device for turning on, and realizing that the weavers who would use it would be too poor to pay his fees, got 148 signatures of masters and journeymen from several Wiltshire towns to a suggestion that those who had the good of the industry at heart might consider how he could be remunerated for making it public.[2] As might have been expected this evoked no response, and Brooks died soon afterwards. His device might probably have been pirated with impunity, but there is no evidence that it was.

The weft yarn ('abb' in the west) was given out in skeins and was wound on a quill to be placed in the shuttle by a child employed by the weaver, working a simple instrument called a swift. The quill was supported at both ends in such a way that it could turn freely as the flow of weft from it pulled it round; but some care was needed to wind the yarn so that it would come off always at the same angle. For this it was necessary to build up a cone at each end of the quill and then to fill the 'valley' between them, 'so nice a business' said Sir William Petty (who was the son of a Romsey clothier and wrote an account of clothmaking for the Royal Society in 1661) 'that the poor boys who work at it do often feel the penalties of miscarriage'.[3] In the 'bobbin(g) shuttle' used in Gloucestershire by some weavers in 1756, the bobbin did not revolve but was fixed at one end, and the fact that it tapered towards the free end allowed the yarn to slip off freely. It could be wound in sections, probably a much easier task than winding the quill.[4]

The greatest fault in weaving was probably that of leaving broken threads unmended. Another was due to the fact that, in weaving broadcloth, the sley, being pushed up by a man at each end, might meet the weft with greater force at the sides than in

---

[1] With the 'hundred' containing 190 threads a cloth of 2,200 would have over 4,000 warp threads and one of 1,600 (the most common superfine in the eighteenth century) over 3,000.

[2] *Gloucester Journal*, 19 Mar. 1744.

[3] Birch, op. cit. i. 59.

[4] The bobbin was also used with the fly-shuttle and was similar to that in use today.

the middle of the cloth. When the fly-shuttle was used the reverse was the case, and weavers sometimes grumbled that, with it, the cloth was more loosely woven at the sides which were the most easily seen. Either fault made for uneven weaving which would cause trouble later. Another difficulty with handloom weaving was that of striking up the weft with exactly the same force after an intermission.[1]

The invention of the power loom owed nothing to western enterprise, but it is interesting to note that J. C. Daniell was experimenting with it from 1824 onwards.[2] As he was associated with Charles Wilkins at Twerton, it seems possible that the semi-powerloom in use there in the thirties was one of his products.[3]

D. SCOURING, BURLING, AND FULLING

The cloth which came from the loom in the 'say' as it was called, was first scoured to remove the oil and grease used in spinning[4] and then fulled to felt and shrink it. Both were done in the fulling mill with heavy wooden hammers or stocks, the scouring first, according to Petty, with a slow motion of the hammers 'leisurely without such violence as heats it much'; and the fulling followed with quick heavy strokes which heated the cloth and shrank the fibre.[5] Heat was regarded as supremely important, and Yarranton, writing about 1680, attributed the soft feel of Dutch cloth to the fact that the trough in which it was fulled was kept closely covered, the stocks falling through apertures made to fit them; whereas in England the trough was open to the air which was brought down on the cloth by their fall.[6]

Petty treats these two operations as continuous, and this is the

---

[1] W. Cooke Taylor, *Handbook of Silk, Cotton, and Woollen Manufactures*, p. 164.

[2] Patents nos. 4987, 7 July 1824; 5266, 13 Oct. 1825; 5679, 5 Aug. 1828.

[3] See above, p. 189.

[4] The term 'braying' was often used in the west to denote scouring, e.g. R. Watts, *The Young Man's Looking Glass*, p. 43. Cf. *Trowbridge Advertiser*, 5 Feb. 1871, 'the offensive liquid from the braying machines'. In other cases braying seems only to mean removing hairs or something of the same nature as burling.

[5] Birch, op. cit., p. 61.

[6] A. Yarranton, *England's Improvement*, pp. 107–9. The open trough continued to be normal in England, cf. Playne's remarks about workmen falling onto the stock-pit, op. cit., 146.

impression left by all early references. He represents the burling, or taking out of knots and other objects which might have become embedded in the cloth (now called 'knotting') as being done before scouring;[1] and this appears to have been a wide-spread practice.[2] In Gloucestershire it was done at that point in 1802.[3] In 1641, however, the fine Spanish cloth made in Shepton Mallet was burled, as it is today, between scouring and fulling,[4] and this was certainly the case with the fine cloth made in the eighteenth century even in Gloucestershire, since the anonymous writer of 1868 speaks of burling as having been an unhealthy occupation done by women in attics over the fulling mill when the cloth was wet, 'there being hardly any convenience for drying cloth as there is now'.[5] When men set up as burlers they probably employed women, and in this case the cloth must have been removed from the mill to be sent to them.[6] Burling might also be done after shearing and it is probable that fine cloth was burled more than once in the course of manufacture.[7]

Fulling could be done either with stocks which fell vertically into a trough or with hammers which pounded the cloth at any angle at which the operator liked to set them.[8] Roland de la Platière, the French Inspector of Manufactures, who in the mid-1780s wrote the section of the *Encyclopédie méthodique* dealing with the textile industries, believed that in England hammers were more common than stocks.[9] English sources give no information on this point, though both were in use about 1800, the former being more generally used for scouring.[10]

---

[1] Birch, op. cit. i. 60.

[2] Posthumus, op. cit. ii. 234 speaks of burling before scouring in Leiden, and in France, about 1785, cloth was burled in the say as well as after scouring and after dressing, *Encycl. méth.* i. 290.

[3] *Ev. on Woollen Trade Bill*, 1803, p. 303.

[4] R. Watts, *The Young Man's Looking Glass*.

[5] *Stroud Journal*, 11 July 1868.

[6] As was done by G. Wansey who employed a male burler in Warminster *c.* 1700, Wilts. C.R.O. 314/1/3. In Yorkshire in 1806 fine cloth was brought home to be burled after scouring. *Ev. on the State of the Woollen Manufacture*, 1806, p. 7.

[7] Ibid., p. 296.

[8] A. Kilburn Scott, 'Early Fulling and its Machinery', *Trans. Newcomen Soc.* xii. 38; L. F. J. Walrond, 'Early Fulling Stocks in Gloucestershire', *Ind. Arch.* i. 9.

[9] *Ency. méth.*, i. 290 ff.

[10] According to *Rees's Cyclopaedia* (*c.* 1819) the oblique or 'driving stocks' were always used for scouring and the upright ones for fulling, s.v. 'Woollen Industry'.

Fuller's earth, which was often advertised in the *Gloucester Journal* at about 40s. per hundredweight, was generally used as a detergent in scouring, but Petty suggests that, in default of it, other and less savoury ingredients such as sig or swine's dung might be employed. In the west in the early nineteenth century fine wool-dyed cloth was scoured twice, once with sig, after which it was burled, and again with fuller's earth in warm water, the latter process being known as 'pizing'.[1]

Most mills in the west had more than one pair of stocks, but none so far discovered before 1790 had more than five.[2] After the use of spinning machinery had increased production, a larger number is sometimes found; the largest known up to the present was at Tellisford Mill on the Somerset Frome, which was insured for twelve in 1821.[3] Occasionally mills are described as having a half or even a three-quarter stock.[4] Possibly these were under the usual size, intended for fulling narrow cloth.

The problem in fulling was to ensure that the cloth shrank evenly. After the first hour and again at intervals of about two hours it was taken out and 'readed' to see if this was the case. Surviving clothiers' books show that the fine medley broadcloth made in the early eighteenth century shrank rather less than half its width and about one-third of its length.[5] Shrinkage, however, was proportioned to the texture of the cloth and the length of the fulling process, and different authorities often give different figures.[6] Generally speaking, the thinner the cloth the less the shrinkage would be. The time taken for fulling also varied, partly with the length of the cloth, partly according to the texture desired. The medleys made in Wiltshire in the eighteenth century, if well woven, might be finished after five or six 'readings', or in as little as nine hours, but when the length and breadth did not shrink proportionately, as was apt to happen with a badly woven cloth, the process would take

---

[1] *Repertory of Arts* (2nd ser.), 37. 70. (in Lewis's patent for scouring).

[2] J. Tann, op. cit., p. 159 (Fromehall mill, 1687).

[3] Som. C.R.O., DD/LW, 41, Papers of an Insurance Agent.

[4] St. Mary's mills, Chalford had 'two whole stocks, one three quarter stock and one half stock' in 1775, *Gloucester Journal*, 15 May 1775.

[5] Long's cloths sometimes shrank under one-third in length, but one of 42·2 yds. before fulling shrank to 25½ and another of 40 yds. to 23·2. Wilts. C.R.O. 947.

[6] e.g. *Repts. Asst. Commrs. Hdloom. Weavers*, 1840, Pt. V, p. 372 (26 per cent in length and 41 per cent in breadth). Bischoff, op. cit., p. 398 (50 per cent and 45 per cent).

much longer. Gloucestershire cloth seems to have been more heavily fulled, but it may be that the longer time said to be taken was due to its greater length. In 1839 twenty-four hours was given as normal for a white cloth and thirty-six for a coloured one.[1] Special kinds might take much longer. There are references in the nineteenth century to boxcloth being milled for a fortnight, while even an ordinary cloth, if 'obstinate', might take a week.[2]

Cloths could easily be damaged in fulling and Petty suggests that tearing and working the surface into flocks might be prevented by throwing in 'oatmeal, (fuller's) earth and sig at convenient times'. The Devizes clothier, Richard Brooks, treats the use of one of these agents as normal, but only for fulling coarse cloth.[3] Oatmeal was used by some of the early Spanish clothiers apparently with impunity,[4] although it was otherwise forbidden as tending to deceit.[5] For fine Spanish cloth an oil soap was a necessity and in the 1630s the Spanish clothiers were insisting upon it.[6] But even in the nineteenth century the use of the less savoury ingredients continued in Gloucestershire, where most of the cloth was milled before dyeing; and in the opinion of old and conservative workmen they did the work much better than any new-fangled chemicals.[7]

When the cloth came out of the fulling mill it was hung on the tenters to dry. Cloths should not have been stretched in length more than one yard in twenty, but they were often drawn out much further. Those intended for the Levant in the later seventeenth century were sometimes stretched eight yards in forty.[8] Another reason for stretching was the fact that

---

[1] *Repts. Asst. Commrs. Hdloom Weavers*, 1840, loc. cit. Austin on Wiltshire gives 13 hrs., ibid., Pt. II, pp. 280–1. Luccock in 1805 gives 30 hrs. 'in the last age, but now 7–8,' op. cit., p. 167.

[2] *Trans. Newcomen Soc.* xii. 51; Playne, op. cit., p. 146.

[3] R. Brooks, *Observations on Milling Broad and Narrow Cloth*, p. 10.

[4] *C.S.P.D. 1629–31*, 406, 418. Possibly makers of the cheaper Spanish cloth could not afford imported soap and substituted oatmeal. For its use see *Encycl. méth.* i. 300.

[5] J. May, *A Declaration of the Estate of Clothing*, p. 26.

[6] P.R.O., S.P. 16/366/76 (Castille or Venice soap). In the eighteenth century it was usually Alicante soap but Marseilles and Joppa soap were also used.

[7] *Repts. Asst. Commrs. Hdloom Weavers*, 1840, Pt. V, p. 392; Playne, op. cit., p. 146.

[8] *C.J.* x. 169.

fulling sometimes left the sides of the cloth longer than the middle.[1] In such a case the centre was pulled out by means of a rope and pulley fixed to a board at the end of the tenter.[2] Such straining did much damage, sometimes breaking the ground of the cloth and accentuating any thin places. Moreover, if over-strained, the cloth would shrink to the original size when wet, and this was the source of the endless contention between drapers and clothiers which led to so many disputes and deductions.

Gloucestershire seems to have taken the lead in the mechanization of scouring, as Wiltshire did with fulling. In 1816 William Lewis of Brimscombe patented a machine consisting of two revolving cylinders through which the cloth was pressed. He claimed that it dispensed altogether with the use of sig and avoided the partial felting which often occurred in scouring and made burling more difficult afterwards.[3] Several other patents followed, among them one by Alfred Flint, a Uley engineer;[4] and machines after another patent of William Baylis Jr. of Painswick were being used by manufacturers in that neighbourhood in 1823.[5] Apart from these, the first mention of 'cloth washers' so far found is in 1829 at Dudbridge mills,[6] and ten years later they appear to have been in general use.[7] It looks as if Yorkshire was still depending on the fulling mill since there is no mention of any other method of scouring in the *Encyclopaedia* of 1841.

Before 1820 stocks in Gloucestershire were coming to be be made of iron and attempts were being made to supply additional heat by means of steam conducted through the heads of such stocks. A patent for this was taken out in 1815 by

[1] This was mainly caused by stretching during the reading, Brooks, op. cit., pp. 18–19.

[2] This implement must be the the 'skee' or 'skey' which some Exeter merchants wished to ban in 1696 but which was defended by clothiers as essential. *C.J.* xi. 459, 487, 494. For its use in Gloucestershire see *Gloucester Journal*, 29 Mar. 1790. Brooks gives this as the usual method of stretching cloth which had been woven unevenly, op. cit., p. 22.

[3] No. 4013, 5 Apr. 1816. See *Repertory of Arts* (2nd ser.), 37. 69 ff. Fulling was included but does not seem to have been a success.

[4] No. 4721, 1 Nov. 1822. A double cloth washer by Flint was in Lower Mills, Dursley, in 1844, G.C.L., R.X.115.13(52).

[5] *Gloucester Journal*, 10 Feb. 1823.

[6] Ibid., 29 Aug. 1829.

[7] *Repts. Asst. Commrs. Hdloom Weavers*, 1840, Pt. V, p. 392.

James Dutton of Hillsley in conjunction with George Austin[1] whose engineer he was, but Austin's death almost immediately afterwards robbed Dutton of patronage and he had no capital to push his invention.[2] In 1825 William Hirst, who claimed to have introduced so much machinery into Leeds, took out a patent for the same process[3] and was attacked not only by Dutton but by John Price the Stroud engineer, who claimed to have a patent himself and ascribed the original invention to Stephen Clissold, a manufacturer of Ebley.[4] The process seems to have been laid aside in Gloucestershire where it was thought to have been only partially successful, but in Yorkshire it was developed by the firm of Willans & Ogle, which bought Dutton's patent in 1826 so that by claiming the ownership of one previous to Hirst's they might protect themselves against a prosecution for infringement.[5] In 1841 it was well enough known to appear in the *Encyclopaedia Britannica's* account of clothmaking, and the best stocks for the purpose were said to come from this firm.

The production of a machine for fulling was longer delayed. The first patent to have possibilities was obtained in 1833 by John Dyer, a Trowbridge engineer.[6] He sold it in the following year, and it came into the hands of a man named Chevalier, who also acquired a somewhat similar one taken out in 1841 by Luke Hebert of Birmingham, apparently acting for an inventor abroad.[7] Chevalier was advertising this invention in the *Leeds Mercury* in 1843,[8] and in 1847 advertisements began to appear in Gloucestershire from Robert Wood & Sons of Hunslet, who depicted their machines as 'preferred by most of the first manufacturers in the West Riding'.[9] Dyer had reserved the right to make his machine himself, and he must have incorporated into it various additions and improvements probably made elsewhere, since many of the machines used in Trowbridge

---

[1] No. 3960, 23 Nov. 1815. See *Repertory of Arts* (2nd ser.), 28. 328–31.

[2] G.C.L., V.F.5.1(3).

[3] No. 5118 with J. Wood, 5 Mar. 1825.

[4] *Gloucester Journal*, 30 May, 6 and 27 June 1825.

[5] Their patent was no. 5245, 20 Aug. 1825. See G.C.L., V.F.5.1(11).

[6] No. 6460, 13 Aug. 1833.

[7] No. 9088, 20 Sept. 1841.

[8] E. Kilburn Scott, op. cit., p. 44 ff. Dyer negotiated the right of receiving £3 for each machine sold during the term of the patent.

[9] *Gloucester Journal*, 8 May 1847.

after 1850 came from him.[1] It was, however, a long time before
the fulling mill was abandoned in Gloucestershire where, in
1871, it was said that cloth was first fulled in the mill and then
passed through the machine,[2] possibly because the use of the
stocks was necessary to produce the proper texture of superfine
broad-cloth.

E. RAISING, SHEARING, BRUSHING, AND PRESSING

The original method of raising the nap on cloth, generally
called rowing, was to damp it and hang it over a bar while a
man drew a frame known as a 'handle' set with teazles over it.
When cloth was thus hung up it was said to be 'perched' and it
might be perched for other reasons, such as inspection or
burling. In Wiltshire and Somerset, however, the word perching became synonymous with rowing and was so used as late
as 1774.[3] Towards the end of the eighteenth century it became
more usual, at least in Gloucestershire, to raise the nap of fine
cloth by laying it over a board and drawing the handles over it
in a more or less horizontal position. This was known as
'dubbing' and was, according to Roland writing about 1785,
a peculiarly English practice.[4] In some cases perching continued
or at least alternated with dubbing,[5] for a system of rollers
round which the cloth was wound, so that fresh surfaces could
be drawn down and kept taut, was in use both in Yorkshire and
Wiltshire in the early nineteenth century;[6] but in Gloucestershire it looks as if dubbing was the only process employed.[7] The
choice of teazles needed care for it was easy to ruin a cloth by

---

[1] See p. 202.

[2] *Official Repts. on the various Sections of the Exhibition* (of 1871), ed. Lord Houghton:
II, *Woollen and Worsted Fabrics*, by Prof. T. C. Archer, p. 11. In some cases the
process was reversed, the driving stocks being used to press out mill-wrinkles made
by the machine, Walrond, loc. cit.

[3] W.A.S. Rec. Brch. xix. no. 650.

[4] *Encycl. méth.* i. 304, quoting Duhamel, 'L'Art de draperie'.

[5] See Crump, op. cit., p. 301, for Gott's practice in Leeds.

[6] This was known as a 'temenog' in Wilts., a term borrowed from the Navy
and probably introduced by returning sailors about 1802. See Daniell's patent no.
5598 (1828) with a drawing, Bodington, Notes for *Wilts. V.C.H.*, and Tucker's
Reminiscences. The apparatus seems to be similar to that called the 'nelly' in
Huddersfield, Crump and Ghorbals, op. cit., p. 96.

[7] No other method is mentioned by the anonymous writer in 1868, *Stroud
Journal*, 11 July 1868.

beginning with hard new heads which would tear the substance.[1] In a fine cloth the raising alternated with shearing several times, the nap being sometimes raised in both directions and sometimes only in one, the latter being known as 'mozing'.[2] The number of courses given with the handles varied with the quality of the cloth and was sometimes large; mention of twenty-six- and twenty-nine-course handles can be found.[3]

In the early seventeenth century clothiers, forbidden to use the gigmill, often tried to conceal it under the name of 'mozing mill';[4] and this would seem to imply that it performed the mozing. In 1802, however, a Dursley clothier said that it had not been so used until recently though rowing had always been done by it;[5] but it is not easy to see why this was so. The mill was generally powered by water through gearing connected with the wheel which drove the fulling mill. In the arguments of 1802-3 purporting to show that the gigmill then used could not be the same as that forbidden by the statute of Edward VI, it was pointed out that it had then been described as an instrument 'for perching and burling', neither of which was done by the machine currently in use. If the word 'perching' is taken in the Wiltshire sense of 'rowing' it would denote exactly what the gigmill performed in 1802. As for burling, when cloth was burled before scouring, as described above,[6] the use of the gigmill for this purpose would no doubt take out knots quickly at the cost of injuring the cloth,[7] and this would explain the prohibition; but it must be remembered that cloth made for export in the early seventeenth century was thicker in texture than that produced at the end of the eighteenth century, and the damage might not have been so great.

After 1800 a large number of patents was taken out for improved gigmills, many by inventors from the west. The first appears to have come from Thomas Jotham, a Bradford clothier,[8] but it is impossible to say whether this or how many of

---

[1] Playne, op. cit., p. 147. Cf. Posthumus, op. cit. ii. 248.

[2] Bischoff, op. cit. ii. 401. Mozing was done after the first shearing.

[3] Catalogue of stock and machinery for sale at New Mills, Dursley, 16 Mar. 1789, G.C.L., R.115. 118, p. 20.

[4] P.R.O., S.P.16/180/71.

[5] *Ev. on Woollen Trade Bill*, 1803, pp. 269, 306.

[6] Above, p. 294.

[7] *C.J.* lviii. 885. See also K. G. Ponting, op. cit., p. 43.

[8] No. 2539, 15 Sept. 1801.

the later patents were actually brought into operation. Some worked the surface at different angles, or from the centre outwards, but these do not appear to have been an improvement upon the ordinary method.[1] The price of teazles, which fluctuated enormously and could rise to £22 per pack,[2] inspired many attempts to use iron wire for rowing. The patents of John & William Lewis and William Davis of Brimscombe taken out in 1817 and 1819 appear to have been at least in partial use;[3] but no early attempt seems to have been completely successful in Gloucestershire.[4] Wire was used in Wiltshire on occasion,[5] and since teazles and wire produce surfaces of a different nature,[6] wire may have been unsuitable for Gloucestershire broadcloth.

Of all the operations of clothmaking, shearing the nap was probably that which required most skill and judgement in the workman. Anyone who looks at a pair of shears must wonder how they could be used with such precision to produce an even surface, and will not be surprised to hear that surfaces were often far from even. The blades, connected by an iron bow, were set at an angle to each other, the lower one being held down to the cloth by a leaden weight attached to it. The portion of cloth to be shorn was placed over a table with a top in the form of a cushion, and the depth of the cut was determined by the degree to which the cushion was stuffed combined with the varying weight of the leaden attachment.[7] The angle at which the table was set to ensure an easy movement of the shears was another important factor in cutting superfine cloth.[8] In the eighteenth century cloth was usually shorn wet, though some

---

[1] For an account of some of them see A. Ure, *Dictionary of Arts, Manufactures and Mines*, ed. R. Hunt (1860), iii. 1055–6.

[2] Bischoff, op. cit. ii. 399. They went as low as £2. 10s. 0d. per pack in 1829, *Gloucester Journal*, 21 Nov. 29.

[3] Nos. 4189, 19 Dec. 1817 and 4379, 19 June 1819. See Rees's *Cyclopaedia*, vol. 38 under Woollen Manufacture; *Repertory of Arts* (2nd ser.), 37. 149–50; 38, 79 ff. The Lewises brought an action against Harris and Co. of Stanley Mills in 1819 for using their machine. A crank machine for dressing cloth with iron cards was for sale in Chalford in 1829. *Gloucester Journal*, 19 Sept. 1829.

[4] See Lr. from S. Sevill, *Gloucester Journal*, 13 Feb. 1830, and Dutton's circular in support of his inventions *c.* 1844, though he claimed to have a satisfactory machine himself, G.C.L., V.F.5.1.(11).

[5] See Daniell's patent no. 5795 of 26 May 1829.   [6] Ponting, loc. cit.

[7] Birch, op. cit. i. 63–4; Posthumus, op. cit. ii. 251.

[8] *Encycl. méth.*, i 312.

cuts may have been made when dry.[1] In the seventeenth century and earlier the shearman opened and closed the blades by the strength of his hand alone, but in England, towards the end of it, a wooden crook was attached to the upper blade, by using which the operator could open and close it more easily.[2] This not only abridged the time taken but also facilitated the shearing of the nap very close, so that it could ultimately receive a more brilliant surface. The refusal in 1718 of the Leiden shearmen to adopt the 'so-called English method' of the crook and of wet shearing is said to have been one cause of the decline of the industry there.[3]

Shearing was among the first of the finishing processes to be mechanized, but not quite as early as is suggested in some continental histories of technology, which elevate the gigmill set up at Horningsham by William Everett in 1767 and destroyed by a mob into the first example of a shearing machine.[4] This is due to misleading information given to Roland de la Platière and copied by other writers from the *Encyclopédie méthodique*.[5] In fact, France preceded England in the production of mechanical means of shearing,[6] but it seems improbable that the first English inventor, John Harmer, had any knowledge of this. An Independent minister of Sheffield, he took out a patent in 1787 for mechanical shears described as for cutting fustian.[7] Very little is known of him, and although Sheffield was obviously a suitable place for making machinery, there is no information about the reasons which inspired his interest in the process. His invention does

[1] In the directions for shearing given by George Wansey c. 1700 'wetting' is only mentioned occasionally for some cuts in the better cloth, *Wilts. C.R.O.* 314/1/2.

[2] Posthumus, op. cit. ii. 252. When the 'crook' was introduced is unknown. Petty in 1661 mentions a 'querret' moving 'on the outward side or back of the shears' which might be the crook, but this date seems rather early, Birch, op. cit., p. 63.

[3] Posthumus, loc. cit., also iii. 1107. Cf. Onslow Burrish, *Batavia Illustrata*, 2nd ed. (1731), pp. 374–5. The crook was used in Amsterdam.

[4] See above, p. 142.

[5] *Encycl. méth.* i. 312. Roland gave the date as 1758 and altered the size of the mob from 300 as given in the *Bath Chronicle*, 6 Aug. 1767, to 500. Since this pseudo-invention is mentioned by C. Ballot, *L'Introduction du machinisme dans l'industrie française* (1923), p. 180, n. 4, it must be emphasized that there is no trace in English sources of any riot in Wilts. in 1758 or of Everett's having received a reward of £15,000 from the Government and re-establishing the machine. See J. Pilisi, 'Le Tondage dans l'histoire des techniques', *L'Industrie textile*, Jan. 1955, p. 51.

[6] Pilisi, loc. cit. [7] No. 1595, 20 Mar. 1787. See pp. 149–50.

not appear to have been suitable for cloth until his patent of 1794 had introduced improvements.[1] The machine merely replaced human agency by mechanical means in working the shears and cut the cloth from list to list. Later patents by others (among which was one taken out by J. C. Daniell in 1810)[2] enabled the cloth to be drawn from end to end, passing under a fixed blade against which a movable one worked continuously; but though this was satisfactory for narrow cloth it was less so for broad.[3] In Gloucestershire some use was made of a machine patented in 1801 by a local man, I. Sanford, but its production ceased in 1809, probably with the maker's death.[4] In that county it was noted about 1806 that the first two cuts were made from end to end and later ones from list to list.[5]

The invention of the rotary cutter working on the principle of the lawn mower which was, in fact, derived from it, is generally attributed to John Lewis, a manufacturer of Brimscombe near Stroud; but many people had worked on rotary machines before Lewis took out his first patent in 1815. He appears rather to have been in the position of Arkwright, whose main service was the making of previous ideas useful. The first rotary machine was invented in the United States by S. G. Dorr of Albany and patented in England by the inventor himself in 1793 just before his death.[6] His son and others improved the machine in America and the specification was brought to England in 1811. Several patents embodying the principle were then taken out, and a model, cutting from list to list, worked for a time in a Bermondsey factory, probably about 1812–13. A Yorkshire manufacturer also had one copied from a model at Utica, N.Y., but forbore to work it for fear of the Luddites.[7] Both appear to have been far from perfect.

---

[1] No. 1982, 29 Mar. 1794.

[2] No. 3348, 19 June 1810. Advertised in the *Gloucester Journal*, 14 Sept. 1812.

[3] See description in Rees's *Cyclopaedia*, vol. 38, under 'Woollen Manufacture'.

[4] No. 2558, 14 Nov. 1801. An advt. in the *Gloucester Journal*, 2 Jan. 1809 offers 'the last of the make that will ever be offered', but a man who understood the working of it was advertised for in 1812, ibid., 24 Feb. 1812.

[5] Nemnich, *Neueste Reise*, p. 225.

[6] No. 1945, 9 Apr. 1793. His death is mentioned in No. 1985, 7 May 1794.

[7] See T. Webster, *Reports and Notes of Cases on Letters Patent for Invention* i. 492; Statements made below about the rotary cutter, not otherwise documented, are drawn from the above and from *Repertory of Arts* (3rd ser.), viii. 105 ff. and ix. 38 ff.

Lewis's first patent was for lengthways cutting with a rotary cutter[1] and it was followed less than a month later by a similar one taken out by the Stroud engineer Stephen Price.[2] Whether either of these machines was satisfactory is doubtful. Hirst in Leeds said they were not,[3] but Hirst is not always reliable. In 1818 Lewis, with his brother William and their engineer William Davis, took out a second patent to cut from list to list, the most satisfactory method for shearing fine cloth, but the machine could also be adapted to cut lengthways.[4] Meanwhile, another patent to cut lengthways had been obtained in 1816 by John Collier, an Englishman who had set up as a machine maker in Paris and had introduced improvements into the American machine which had been taken there in 1812;[5] and he obtained a second patent to cut from list to list on the same day as Lewis in 1818.[6] According to Hirst, he set up the machine in Bristol and invited western clothiers to inspect it. They did not buy, and Collier afterwards offered it on trial to Hirst, who subsequently ordered another.[7] Meanwhile, Lewis and his brother bought out Davis's interest in their patent in 1819, and the latter, after taking out two more patents, left Gloucestershire for Leeds.[8] He bought up Price's patent; and his machine, which he claimed as his own, differed from that of Lewis in several respects. In 1823 he was advertising it in the *Leeds Mercury* at £420, 'half the price of the French one'.[9] Collier, who had also secured a third patent in 1822,[10] challenged Davis with having merely copied his invention, but his residence in France probably made it difficult for him to carry on legal proceedings. Eight of his machines had been imported by 1825

[1] No. 3945, 27 July 1815.
[2] No. 3951, 12 Aug. 1815. Minutely described in Rees's *Cyclopaedia*, vol. 38, which ignores Lewis's patent.
[3] *Gloucester Journal*, 26 Dec. 1829.
[4] No. 4196, 15 Jan. 1818. See *Repertory of Arts* (2nd ser.), 37. 327 ff.
[5] A. H. Cole, op. cit., p. 132.
[6] No. 4020, 1 May 1816, and no. 4195, 15 Jan. 1818. For Collier see J. J. Hemardinguer, 'Une Dynastie de méchaniciens anglais en France: James, John et Juliana Collier, 1791–1847', *Rev. d'histoire des sciences*, 17 (2), July–Sept. 1964.
[7] See Hirst's letter to the *Gloucester Journal*, 26 Dec. 1829 (also printed in the *Leeds Mercury*, 24 Dec. 1829).
[8] Nos. 4487, 11 July 1820 and 4820, 24 July 1823. He obtained other patents from Leeds for processes not connected with shearing from 1825 to 1839.
[9] See *Gloucester Journal*, 3 Feb. 1823.
[10] No. 4702, 27 Sept. 1822.

and they had also been made in England,[1] but they were said to have been superseded by a very good American machine known as the Miles cutter, which was introduced in 1823.[2]

Among all these machines it was that of Lewis which made most way in Yorkshire, so much so that in 1831 the only rotary cutters mentioned in the Report of the Committee on Children in Factories were known as 'lewises'.[3] Upwards of a thousand had been sold by 1829.[4] On the other hand, the Clarks of Trowbridge sold one of unspecified origin in 1826 and bought one by Davis,[5] and by 1860 they had several of them.

The Miles cutter had no connection with Lewis, but a new Gloucestershire patent obtained in 1824 by Gardner and Herbert, a smith and a carpenter respectively of Stanley St. Leonards, took his machine as a basis for improvements.[6] In 1829 Lewis brought two actions for infringement, the first against William Davis a Nailsworth manufacturer, the second against N. S. Marling, both of whom were using this machine. Several witnesses gave evidence that the features of Lewis's machine were drawn from various earlier patents; but the fact that his engineer, also William Davis, had worked for a time with the man who had made the machine in Bermondsey was only discovered after the trial had ended with a verdict in Lewis's favour. An application for a new trial failed, a decision which evoked some unfavourable legal comment. Though it was clear that Lewis was not the sole inventor, it was generally agreed that he was the first person in England to produce a machine which cut the cloth effectively from list to list.

Perhaps because of his lawsuits, Lewis's machine was far from universal in Gloucestershire. It shared the field with the Miles cutter which is frequently mentioned, and with that of

---

[1] *Ctee. on Artisans and Machinery,* 1824, 1st Rept. (H.C. 51), p. 21; *Rept. of Ctee. on Export of Tools and Machinery,* 1825 (H.C. 504), pp. 44, 139.

[2] Patented in England by Thos. Miles, clothdresser of Dudbridge 'in consequence of communications made to him by certain persons residing abroad', No. 4799, 3 June 1823. Cole, op. cit., p. 132, says that he was the agent of the American inventor Beriah Swift. See also *Rept. of Ctee. on Export of Tools and Machinery,* 1825, p. 44.

[3] *Rept. from Ctee on Bill to regulate the Labour of Children in Mills and Factories,* 1831–2, pp. 14, 31, 65.

[4] Webster, op. cit. i. 491.

[5] W.A.S., Rec. Brch. vi. p. xxiii.

[6] No. 5059, 18 Dec. 1824. See *Repertory of Arts* (3rd ser.), 9. 76 ff.

Gardner and Herbert which also appears, though less often, in lists of machinery for sale. Another machine, that patented by George Oldland of Hillsley in 1830 and 1832,[1] which was highly praised in the *Encyclopaedia Britannica* of 1841, has not been found in such lists, but this does not mean that it was not in use. The two latter patents, however, were merely additions to that of the Lewises, and in 1854 it was stated that theirs was the one most generally employed.[2]

Mechanical brushers, apparently first used in Yorkshire, had made their appearance in the west before 1802, since Paul Bamford had one at Twerton before his bankruptcy in that year.[3] Later they were common throughout the region, the most usual in the thirties being the 'Jones patent brusher' from Yorkshire. Pressing had always been done by inserting parchment between the folds of the cloth and placing it in a press for several days; if hot pressing was required, heated iron plates were inserted at the top and bottom and in the middle. Hot pressing gave a gloss to the surface which could not be obtained in any other way. Its drawbacks were that it rendered any rainspots much more visible[4] and also tended to decay the wool and make it harsh;[5] but although forbidden by the Edwardian statutes, the advantage of the gloss had carried the day by the later eighteenth century and cloth was not saleable without it, according to a witness in 1803.[6]

A new process for giving the cloth a permanent damp-resisting surface was, as already mentioned, the work of that prolific inventor J. C. Daniell.[7] First patented in 1819, it involved rolling the cloth round a hollow cylinder and plunging it into hot water; but it only became widely known after the inventor's association with Charles Wilkins of Twerton, who learnt of its existence when trying the same method himself. But in 1826

---

[1] No. 5960, 22 July 1830, improved by no. 6236, 3 Mar. 1832. See Bischoff, op. cit., p. 400; Ure, *Philosophy of Manufactures*, pp. 197 ff.

[2] C. Tomlinson, op. cit. ii. 1039.

[3] *Gloucester Journal*, 1 Feb. 1802.

[4] *C.S.P.D.*, *1667–8*, 423.

[5] *Reasons for the Bill . . . for Improvement of the Woollen Manufacture* (1689), p. 3.

[6] *Ev. on the Woollen Trade Bill*, 1802–3, p. 381.

[7] Patent no. 4391, 17 July 1819 (also concerned with wire cards). Daniell took another, No. 5038, 20 Nov. 1824, presumably after his association with Wilkins. See above, p. 189 and *Reports by Jurors appointed . . . for the Exhibition of 1851*, Cl. XII, p. 350.

the patent was cancelled, partly on the ground that the specification was insufficient but also because the method had already been employed by a Yorkshire manufacturer in 1807, although he had not persisted in using it.[1] In spite of this, the general opinion was that Daniell was the real author of 'one of the most useful inventions ever introduced into the woollen trade',[2] and it is satisfactory to know that among all his patents there were at least two which brought him some recognition.[3] A method of blowing steam through the cloth instead of boiling it had been patented in 1824 by J. C. Fussell, an edge-tool maker of Mells, but this was cancelled in 1826, mainly because the specification was considered insufficient.[4] The process was in use in England by 1854 and was said to save time,[5] but it had not achieved the success it had had on the Continent where roll-boiling was unknown. The reason, according to a Huddersfield manufacturer in 1855, was probably because in England the steam was not applied at a sufficiently high pressure, as it could be in the 'decatiering' machine used at Verviers and over the rest of Europe, which had the advantage of being able to give the cloth any amount of lustre desired without injuring it.[6] English manufacturers subsequently copied continental methods and both processes are still in use, although the fashion for glossy cloth has disappeared and they are now employed for other purposes than those for which they were originally designed.

[1] W. Carpmael, *Law Reports of Patent Cases* i. 450, 453 ff.

[2] Ibid., 457 note; *Repts. by Jurors . . . for the Exh. of 1851*, loc. cit.

[3] For the other see pp. 197–8.

[4] No. 4999, 11 Aug. 1824. See Carpmael, op. cit., pp. 449–53. Wilkins had already tried steam but turned to hot water after associating himself with Daniell.

[5] Tomlinson, op. cit. ii. 1040.

[6] *Paris Universal Exhibition, 1855*, Pt. I, p. 148. (Report on Woollen Manufactures and Machinery by the Huddersfield Chamber of Commerce.) But in 1867 'the baked and lustrous glare' imparted by the 'decatting' machine was contrasted unfavourably with the finish of Stroud blue and black broadcloth, *Reports on the Paris Universal Exhibition, 1867* iii. 73.

APPENDIX I

EXPORTS

TABLE A

Quantity of cloth exported from London 1662–3, compared with an average for the years 1699–1701 from London and Outports separately

	1662–3[a] Mich.–Mich. London only (pieces)	annual average, 1699–1701[b] Xmas–Xmas			
		London (pieces)	per cent inc. or dec.	outports (pieces)	total (pieces)
long cloth	12,548	33,300	+165	2	33,302
short cloth	16,901	15,408	−8·8	2,003	17,411
Spanish cloth	16,283	10,404	−36	317	10,721
broad cloth	—	—		403	403
TOTAL	45,732	59,112	+29	2,725	61,837

[a] Add. MSS., 36,785.

[b] Averaged from Customs Ledgers (Customs 3/3–3/5). The totals for 1700 and 1701 from which this average is derived correspond closely with those given in E. B. Schumpeter, *English Overseas Trade Statistics, 1697–1808*, Table XIV, which does not give separate figures for London and Outports; but those for 1699 do not, except for Spanish cloth. The difference is as follows:

	Ledger, Customs 3/3	Schumpeter
long cloth	31,324	29,996
short cloth	18,823	12,977
Spanish cloth	11,912	11,915
broad cloth	231	367
	62,290	55,255

The difference is partly due to the apparent omission of white cloth which is entered separately in 1699 though not again until 1710 when a tax was imposed upon its export in exchange for the payment previously made to the patentees.

TABLE B

*Comparative exports of cloth, old drapery, and new drapery by value in
1700, 1720, 1775, and 1790*
(figures from Schumpeter, op. cit., Tables XII and XIII)[a]

Cloth	1700 (£)	percent. of total	1720 (£)	percent. of total	1775[c] (£)	percent. of total	1790[c] (£)	percent. of total
broad	15,380		9,220		—		—	
long	336,651		476,133		513,250		1,107,782	
short	169,212		178,632		620,775		1,246,638	
Spanish	195,300		234,100		68,620		48,520	
white	b		8,664		2,112		1,520	
	716,543	25·4	906,749	28·2	1,204,757	24·5	2,404,460	41·5
old drapery								
N. dozens	220,440		238,740		343,734		365,718	
Devon doz.	22,374		—		—		—	
frize	31,420		35,637		12,626		15,050	
flannel	20,146		46,149		46,964		70,814	
kerseys	116,078		127,446		42,642		15,146	
cottons	35,118		24,774		88,588		57,205	
	445,576	15·8	472,746	14·7	534,554	10·9	523,933	9
new drapery								
bays (all kinds)	366,741		453,103		732,871		739,598	
serges and perpets	930,198		632,546		661,586		868,058	
says	70,398		45,880		232		—	
stuffs	289,415		707,484		1,779,915		1,257,701	
	1,656,752	58·8	1,839,013	57·1	3,174,604	64·6	2,865,357	49·5
TOTAL	£2,818,871		£3,218,508		£4,913,915		£5,793,750	

total woollen goods exported (including hosiery):

£2,989,394	£3,999,633	£5,144,136	£6,207,854

[a] A small number of goods omitted.

[b] Not separately entered.

[c] Computed Value. This was considerably above the official value in 1775 and 1790,
but in 1700 and 1725 the real value was much nearer to the official value than at the end of
the century.

TABLE C

Annual average of cloth exported per decade by quantity
(figures from Schumpter, op. cit., Table XIV)

	1701–10[a] pieces	1711–20 pieces	1721–30 pieces	1731–40 pieces	1741–50 pieces	1751–60 pieces
broad	430	444	159	577	125	70
long	39,994	37,187	31,570	30,728	28,835	39,710
short	14,949	10,815	11,700	14,762	18,463	31,607
Spanish	12,757	16,655	10,229	12,735	5,654	7,998
white	[b]	1,765	986	674	845	550
	68,130	66,866	54,644	59,476	53,922	79,935

	1761–70 pieces	1771–80 pieces	1781–90 pieces	1791–1800 pieces	1801–7 pieces
long	34,983	37,388	59,217	102,375	31,400
short	41,363	41,991	53,662	90,279	21,402
Spanish	5,842	3,168	1,711	3,443	7,615
white	384	287	149	57	—
	82,572	82,834	114,739	196,154	60,417

[a] Average of nine years, 1705 missing.
[b] Separately entered for 1710 only (2,862 pieces).

APPENDIX II

QUALITY AND WEIGHT OF CLOTH

A. QUALITY

THE fineness of cloth was related to the number of warp threads in a given width. These were reckoned by the 'hundred'; but other circumstances must be taken into account, and the Gloucestershire clothiers were right in protesting in 1756 that this was not the only consideration in fixing the rate for weaving. Nevertheless, the hundred is probably a better guide in the case of the simple type of cloth produced in the early sixteenth century than it would be later. The term indicates far more than a hundred threads, but there is no evidence of the actual number until 1756, when the Gloucestershire weavers gave it as 190.[1] In the nineteenth century it was sometimes 200.[2]

In one of the four draft Bills produced for the proposed legislation on wages in 1593, and in the rates agreed by the Trowbridge clothiers and weavers in 1602 and 1605, payment was regulated by the hundred, which ran from cloth of 700 to cloth of 1,400.[3] Some finer cloth was made, for the final version of this draft gives the very high rate of 6s. 8d. per ell for the finest sort and 4s. for the second, where that for the ordinary 'sorting-pack' cloth as made in the west was only 2s. These rates may refer to the 'especial fine clothes made of the principal of the wool' mentioned in 1591,[4] but in 1639 it was said that very few fine cloths were made in comparison with the coarser ones.[5]

Western 'narrow list sorting-pack cloth' was stated in the Wiltshire wage list to run from 700 to 1,000, and 'broadlist', which was of better quality,[6] from 800 to 1,200. It seems reasonable to conclude that the finer cloth made there (nos. 4 to 6 in the Table D below)

[1] *C.J.* xxvii. 732. Also in Glouc. C.R.O., D.149, B.8, Petition of 22 Aug. 1755.
[2] *Repts. Asst. Commrs. Hdloom Weavers*, 1840, Pt. II, p. 434.
[3] Bland, Brown and Tawney, *English Economic History, Select Documents*, pp. 336–343; *H.M.C. Var.* i. 162 ff. In the draft the rates by the hundred have been struck out and replaced by rates for five qualities ranging from 6s. 8d. per ell (1½ yd.) for the best to 1s. 6d. per ell for 'narrow list sorting-pack cloth'.
[4] *A.P.C.* xxi. 99.
[5] P.R.O., E.134/14, Replies to Interrogatory 36.
[6] Ehrenberg, op. cit., p. 269.

ran from 1,200 to 1,400. The books of Thomas Long and Usher & Jeffries, the Wiltshire clothiers making superfine cloth in the early eighteenth century,[1] show that it was normally a '1600' cloth, although 1,900 for 'drabs'[2] is occasionally found. Both made cheaper sorts, from 1,200 upwards, but nothing below. In 1728 the Gloucestershire magistrates approved a wage rate for cloth of 2,200,[3] but such a very high hundred appears to have been unusual. In 1839 the kinds most usually made there ran from 1,700 to 2,000.[4] Although the hundred is not the only criterion, these figures do give some idea of the relative coarseness of most Tudor and Jacobean cloth in comparison with that of the eighteenth and nineteenth centuries.

B. WEIGHT OF CLOTH

The length and breadth of broadcloth was regulated in the Middle Ages and the weight was laid down in the statute of Edward VI in 1552. All these were re-enacted, with some alterations, up to 1624.[5] Their enforcement had always presented difficulties, and it is probable that the quantity of cloth which did not conform to official standards was at least as great as that which did. Aulnage and customs duty were paid on the cloth of assize which was officially 24 yards long; and for this purpose cloths of other sizes were converted into cloths of assize and paid duty accordingly.[6] There was much fraud, especially as the seals were often sold in bulk to clothiers and could thus easily be falsified.

The quantity of wool necessary to make a short cloth is variously stated; but three tod (84 lb. or one quarter of a sack) is the most general estimate.[7] There was a tendency to put more weft into the better quality cloths, from the standard 54 lb. up to over 60 lb. in 1605 and over 70 in 1655,[8] so that in many cases their weights must have been greater than provided for in the statute.

In the table on the next page the official weights given in the statute

---

[1] See above, p. 13, n. 3 and p. 71, n. 6.

[2] Drabs (derived from the French 'drap') were a very stout and closely woven cloth. Some patterns are in the cloth book of Usher & Jeffries, Wilts. C.R.O., 927.

[3] See below, App. IV, Table M.

[4] *Repts. Commrs. Hdloom Weavers*, 1840, Pt. V, pp. 392–5; Pt. II, p. 434.

[5] The final statute of 1624, 21 Jas. I, c. 18, made no change in weight or dimensions from that of 1607, 4 Jas. I, c. 2.

[6] A list of these proportions will be found in Supple, op. cit., p. 257.

[7] P.R.O., S.P.14/80/16. Also in Tawney and Power, *English Economic Documents* i. 180 (1547); *H.M.C., 3rd Rept.* (H. of L. MSS), 50 (1591); *C.J.* i. 769 (1624) and L. Roberts, *The Merchant's Mappe of Commerce* (1638), p. 250.

[8] *H.M.C. Var.* i. 168.

TABLE D

I. Statutory weight of broadcloth when dyed and finished

1607		wet length yd. (37 in.)[a]	dry length yd. (37 in.)	breadth qrs. (9 in.)	weight	
					per piece lb.	per sq. yd. of 36 in. oz.
1. broad-listed sorting-pack cloth, white and red	made in Wilts. Glos., Som., and Oxon.	26–8	29	6½	64 (60)[b]	19·8
2. narrow-listed do.		26–8	29	6½	61 (57)[b]	18·8
3. plunkets, azures, and blues from Wilts. and Somerset		26–8	29	6½	68 (64)[b]	21·1
4. fine cloth with plain lists from Wilts., Glos., and Somerset		29–32	33	6½	72 (67)[c]	19·4
5. stoplists (mainly Worcesters but some from Wilts.)		30–3	34	7	78 (73)[c]	19·1
6. long Worcesters (from Worcester, Coventry, and Herefordshire)		30–3	34	7	78 (73)[c]	19·1
7. long broadcloth of Kent, Reading, or Yorks., made of dyed wool in mingled colours		30–4	35	6½	86	23·6
8. short Suffolk sorting cloth coloured or white		23–6	27	6	64	24·6
9. fine short Suffolk coloured or white		23–6	27	6½	64	22·7
10. plunkets, azures, and blues from Norfolk, Suffolk, and Essex		29–32	33	6½	80[d]	23·2
11. Yorkshire medleys (if half pieces = dozens)		23–5	26	6½	66	24·3

[a] Including usual allowance of 1 in. per yd.
[b] Allowance of 4 lb. to cover loss in dressing. The figure in brackets has been used for the calculation.
[c] Allowance of 5 lb. for same purpose.
[d] No allowance made since most were exported fully finished.

TABLE D (*cont.*)

II. Later non-statutory weights

	dry length yd. (37 in.)	breadth qrs. (9 in.)	weight per piece lbs.	per yd. (37 in.) oz.	per sq. yd (36 in.) oz.
12. Spanish cloth					
1632[1]	18	6½e	30		16
1660[2]	not over 25	6½e	43		16·5
1667[3]		(6–7) say 6½		finest 20 coarsest 28	12 16·7
1691[4]	i. 20–24	6½e	under 30 (say 30)		c. 11·9–14·
	ii. 26–30	6½e	30–34		c. 10·8–11
fine Salisbury	over 24 (say 25)	6½e	c. 30		c. 11·5
13. Glos. long cloth, exported to Levant, 1689[5]	c. 44	6	72		c. 17
14. superfine broadcloth 1806[6]		7		19	10·5
do. finest for shawls, Vigonia wool		8		11	5·5
15. modern cloth (heaviest, for men's overcoats)		6		25–6f	16·6–17·

e No mention of breadth but it has been assumed to be the usual breadth for Spanish cloth.

f Weight per yd. of 36 in.

of 1607 have been reduced to weight per square yard for comparison with Spanish and modern cloth. The statutes prescribed that length and breadth should be measured in water, but the weight taken when the cloth was dry. The dry length therefore is always uncertain. Stretching up to one yard was permitted but, as already stated, cloth was often stretched far more, up to six or eight yards in some cases;

[1] Supple, op. cit., p. 267, n. 2. By 1640 the weight was established at 32 oz. to the yd for Customs purposes; it had varied considerably before.

[2] For Customs purposes, in the Book of Rates, 12 Car. ii. c. 4.

[3] In the abortive draft Bill of 1667 (see p. 99), Arch. H.L., 8 Nov. 1667, no. 106.

[4] *H.M.C., 14th Rept.*, App. VI (H. of L. MSS.), p. 37.

[5] *C.J.* x. 169. These measurements are those of the cloth seized in an aulnage dispute Other slightly different measurements were also given but incompletely.

[6] *Ev. on State of Woollen Manufacture*, 1806, p. 425.

and that this was officially recognized is shown by the grant of a 'toleration' for the over-stretching of cloths for export to certain countries.[1] In the table the dry length has been taken as being one yard above the highest wet length allowed, and this gives what was probably the lowest legal weight per yard, but the result can only be regarded as an approximation.

[1] B.M., Galba, E.i, 320b and Vesp. F.ix, 285, where Benedict Webb argued strongly against straining. The cloth affected came from Suffolk, but as more and more Gloucestershire cloth came to be exported, the toleration extended to it.

APPENDIX III

NUMBERS EMPLOYED AND COST OF PRODUCTION

A. NUMBERS PER LOOM

ESTIMATES of the number of persons employed by one loom[1] were often made for propaganda purposes. In some cases the variation between them is due to the omission or inclusion of certain processes; but the fact that such workers as fullers and shearmen would perform their tasks on any one cloth much more quickly than spinners or weavers is seldom stated. The fuller, even if he burled the cloth as well, could full in two or three days a cloth which had occupied two weavers and several spinners for at least a fortnight and probably longer. Only Sir Matthew Hale's estimate of 14 persons to a loom (Table G on p. 318) seems to take account of this; and he may have underestimated the number of spinners.

TABLE E

Various estimates of the number employed by each loom

Unfinished Cloth		
1615 (Glos.)[2]	spinning, weaving, and fulling	14
1622 (Wilts.)[3]	weaving, spinning, and spooling (but really *c.* 18, —44 looms and 800 people)	'20 at least'
1622 (Glos.)[4]		'16 and upwards'

Other later estimates are based on the number employed by one pack of wool (240 lb.) and were intended to show how much was lost to the nation by smuggling wool abroad. The basic one was

[1] The estimates quoted by Lipson, *Economic History of England* ii. 17, are not comparable with those given here. That for Suffolk in 1618 (25 person to a loom) includes loom and spinning wheel makers and carriers; and Sir E. Sandys's estimate of 40, in 1621, seems wildly improbable.

[2] P.R.O., S.P.14/80/16. The number was designedly kept low for unfavourable comparison with the new draperies.

[3] *H.M.C. Var.* i. 94.

[4] P.R.O., S.P.14/128/49 (2).

drawn up by John Haynes, one of the Commissioners for the prevention of smuggling, for presentation to Parliament in 1701–2,[1] but by 1706 he had revised the allocation of labour and reckoned that one pack would make four instead of three cloths.[2] In 1736 another pamphleteer re-issued the statement in a slightly different form, adding prices for each operation.[3]

TABLE F

Estimates of the number employed for each pack of wool

	Haynes			1736			
				numbers	price £. s. d.		
	1702	1706			£.	s.	d.
sorting	} 3 men	3	sorting	1		8	0
dyeing, etc.			dyeing	—	1	10	0
scribbling	5 men	5		6 (4 men 2 boys)	2	8	0
spinners	} 20 women	35		30	6	0	0
carders	} 20 girls						
weavers	6 men	8		8	4	16	0
quilling	2 boys	4		4		10	0
burling	⎫		burling	4 women		12	0
scouring	⎪		scouring	⎫			
fulling	⎬ 8		fulling	⎪			
dressing	⎪ 7 (6 men		rowing	⎬ 5	3	4	0
racking	⎪ and 1 boy)		shearing	⎪			
pressing	⎭		racking	⎪			
			pressing	⎭			
	63	63		58 (without dyeing)	19	8	0

For superfine cloth the wool was spun finer which probably meant more spinners. In the books of Thomas Long of Melksham about 1713[4] six to eight women were employed to spin the weft for a superfine medley, about 20 to 25 yards when finished. On the few occasions when the names of individual warp spinners are mentioned the number is about the same but they each took only about half the weight taken by the weft spinners. If one adds three (two men and a boy) for weaving, two for washing and picking the wool, two for fulling, one for burling and four for finishing, this would give a total of 24 to 28 people employed on one superfine medley cloth

[1] *C.S.P.D., 1702–3*, 519.   [2] *A View of the Clothing Trade*, p. 9.
[3] *The Golden Fleece*, p. 9.   [4] Wilts. C.R.O. 947.

(excluding the dyeing of the wool); but nine of these would only be employed for a relatively short time.[1]

Coarser cloth did not need such fine spinning and on the basis of 1 lb. a day as the most which could be done by one spinner,[2] some 80 lb. of wool, as used for a white sorting-pack cloth in the early seventeenth century, could hardly occupy fewer than five spinners for three weeks and probably several more, as few women were in a position to work the whole time. This gives a minimum of 12 persons for a 'white' cloth, and suggests that an estimate of 14 or even 16 to such a cloth may not be inaccurate, though the fullers would only work on it for a day or two, and washing and picking the wool would take much less time than weaving.

B. COST OF PRODUCTION

Manufacturing costs are frequently given as half[3] to three-quarters[4] of the whole, depending on the price of the wool. Sir Matthew Hale's estimate of costs for a coarse Gloucestershire medley, 31 yd. long after fulling and woven in three weeks, is as follows:[5]

TABLE G

(*c.* 1659 or *c.* 1676.)	number employed	£.	s.	d.
90 lb. wool at 1s. per lb.		4	10	0
parting and picking	1		3	0
colouring	—		16	0
breaking and spinning the abb 54 lb. at 2½d. per lb.	6 spinners 2 breakers	1	7	9
breaking and spinning the warp 34 lb. at 5d. per lb.			18	6
cards and oil		1	0	0
weaving, spooling, and warping	3	1	1	3
fulling and burling	1		12	0
shearing and dressing	1		18	0
drawing	—		1	6
carriage and factorage			7	0
	14	11	15	0

[1] Wilts. C.R.O., 314/1/2, Books of the second George Wansey, which contain directions for dressing various kinds of cloth taking from 28 to 50 hr. Superfine cloth, which he did not make, might have taken longer and so would a cloth of greater length.

[2] See below, App. IV, p. 322.

[3] *Atkyns*, op. cit., p. 78. Cf. the estimate for Leeds in Tawney and Power, op. cit. i. 217.

[4] Smith, op. cit. i. 187.

[5] *A Discourse touching provision for the Poor*, pp. 45–8. For its date see above, pp. 102–3. Six spinners seems a low estimate for both warp and weft.

This seems rather underestimated, though in fulling (usually undertaken by two men) and dressing (by four) there may be an attempt to compensate for the fact that their whole time would not be occupied. In good times this cloth would sell for £13 and the profit would be about 10½ per cent on cost; but when Hale wrote it would only fetch £12. The manufacturing costs come roughly to 62 per cent and the wool to 38 per cent of the total. Labour alone, excluding dyeing, forms 43 per cent which shows the high percentage cost of the subsidiary materials used in the manufacture. This estimate was frequently copied in pamphlets and manuscripts for nearly a hundred years after it first appeared. Among other things, it shows that the clothiers' representations, as reported by Davenant, that spinning formed half the cost of a cloth[1] cannot be accepted.

When Spanish wool was used its high price meant that manufacturing costs formed a smaller proportion of the total. The following account of the cost of manufacturing two pieces of medley found among the Clark Papers[2] is puzzling because of the amount of

TABLE H

Costs of manufacturing two pieces of medley cloth c. 1724

	£.	s.	d.	
English wool 120 lb. at 1s. 3d.	7	10	0	
Spanish wool 120 lb. at 2s.	12	0	0	
beating of the wool		1	6	
picking of 113 lbs. at ¾d. per lb.		7	0¾	
scribbling the warp 42½ at 1½d. per lb.		6	2	(*sic*)
scribbling two abbs (weft) 90½ at 3d. 1 mixture	1	3	0	(*sic*)
cards		6	0	
warp spinning at 14½d (? per score)[a] 886 skeins	2	6	4	(*sic*)
abb spinning 87 (lb.) at 8d.	2	18	0	
cards		12	0	
spooling and weaving of 80 yd.	4	2	6	
oil, 20 lb. is 2½ gall.		8	9	
braying, burling, and milling		17	0	
soap, 8 lb. at 6½d.		4	0	(*sic*)
dressing of 54 yds. at 1s. 2d. yd.	2	14	0	}
more		9	0	}
seals, etc.		5	0	
dyeing	1	4	0	
	£37	14	3¾	

[a] For an explanation of this expression see below, App. IV, Table K.

[1] *Works* (ed. Sir C. Whitworth), ii. 252.
[2] Wilts. C.R.O. 927.

wool which appears to have been used; but it seems to be worth inserting for the sake of the other costs mentioned, though several items seem to be wrongly calculated.

In 1786 the Blackwell Hall factor, Thomas Everett, reckoned 'labour' (probably meaning manufacturing costs) at £30 per bag of Spanish wool containing 196 lb. and valued at £25 to £30 according to its quality.[1] Taking the medium price of £27. 10s. the wool forms 47 per cent and the other costs 53 per cent of the whole. He also calculated the profit as being nearly 40 per cent of the cost of manufacture; but here allowance must be made for interest, for cloth often 'rested' for many months before it was sold. Nevertheless, the profit, even though factorage had to be paid from it, is substantial enough to explain how it was possible to become rich by manufacturing such cloth.

After the introduction of machinery the relation of the different factors in production altered. Wool grew more expensive in proportion, labour less. It is interesting to compare the following account, emanating from Trowbridge in 1798,[2] with that in the Clark Papers over sixty years earlier, although they are not strictly comparable. The later one was intended to show that the price of cloth must rise owing to the rise in the cost of wool.

The two great changes here are in the cost of wool and of spinning. Scribbling, now done by machinery, costs 2½d. per lb. overall less than in 1724. Cards are much cheaper, and spinning, which in the earlier statement includes carding by hand, is less by 2½d. per lb. for weft but by as much as 8d. for warp. There is no great difference in the cost of the other processes, nor would one expect it, since so far they had not been mechanized.

The cost of labour alone, excluding dyeing, appears to be £7. 6s. 7d. or nearly 33 per cent of the whole cost (excluding rent, interest, and other charges) but is considerably more than half the cost of the wool. By 1825 Edward Sheppard thought it was half,[3] but it had fallen by that time owing to the introduction of mechanical shearing.

Other estimates are not exactly comparable. In 1806 a Taunton maker of superfines gave manufacturing costs as 35 per cent of the total for an ordinary superfine, but 45 to 50 per cent for a cassimere and even more for fancy cloth.[4] The former seems low by comparison with the account above since it would presumably include cards, oil

---

[1] P.R.O., B.T.6/114, fol. 106.
[2] Glouc. C.R.O. D.1759 (Austin Papers). It was circulated from Trowbridge in connection with a movement to raise the price of cloth.
[3] Bischoff, op. cit. ii. 74.
[4] *Ev. on State of the Woollen Manufacture*, 1806, p. 33.

TABLE J

1798. An estimate of the cost of manufacturing a superfine broadcloth

	£.	s.	d.
60 lb. wool at 4s. 2d.	12	10	0
carriage at 7s. per bag		1	9
trying at 5s. per bag		1	3
dyeing 60 lb. at 6d.	1	10	0
picking 51 lb at 1d. per lb.[a]		4	3
oil, 8 lb. at 1s. per lb. (8s. gall.)		8	0
scribbling 59 lb. at 2d.		9	10
carding 1½d. Slubbing 1½d. 59 lb. at 3d. per lb.		14	9
cards for both per piece		1	0
spinning warp, 440 skeins or 22 score at 3½d. per score		6	5
spinning abb, 34 lb. at 2½d. per lb.		7	1
weaving 40 yd. at 15d. per yd.	2	11	0 *(sic)*
list and forrel		3	0
braying 18d. and burling 6s.		7	6
milling 3s. inspector 2d.		3	2
soap 4 lb. at 13¼ lb.		4	5
dressing 30 yd. at only 15d. per yd.	1	17	6
drawing 1s. carriage and postage 2s. 3d.		3	3
paper and twine			4
discount for cash on £10. at 1d. per £.			10
	——	——	——
	22	5	4
expenses in rent, interest, factor's charges, insurance, allowance for damages, etc. on a trade of six cloths a week		3	13	7½
	——	——	——
value of cloth	25	18	11½
sale price of 29½ yds. at 16s. 6d.	24	6	6
	——	——	——
loss	1	12	5½

[a] The quantity shown as picked (51 lb.) is probably a mistake for 59 lb.

and soap, but the two latter seem exaggerated. By 1839 Miles reckoned labour at only a little over 20 per cent of the whole, against that of materials, including wool, at over 65 per cent.[1]

[1] *Repts. Asst. Commrs. Hdloom Weavers*, 1840, Pt. V, p. 374.

APPENDIX IV

WAGES

SINCE all prices paid for spinning and weaving relate to piece work, it is necessary to discover the time taken to perform these processes if any estimate of weekly wages is to be made. In the case of scriblers, fullers, and shearmen, and of some minor workers, the payments for the processes given in App. III are of no assistance in determining the earnings of the workers, since the time taken can only be vaguely estimated. Some statements about weekly wages taken from reports of travellers are printed below, but in most cases they are probably employers' estimates.

A. SPINNING

Two statements suggest that spinners could do about one pound a day, but both refer to yarn for only moderately fine cloth.[1] Wool for superfines could not be spun so quickly. During the controversy over the riots of 1738–9 the writer of the Essay on Riots stated that the wife and two daughters of his servant could not spin more in a day than 1⅓ lb. between them, or a little over 7 oz. each.[2] In fact, this was probably not far from his opponent's estimate that a woman could earn 2s. 6d. a week by spinning,[3] for Temple was probably reckoning payment at 9d. per lb. although the rate in Melksham had decreased to 6d. in the autumn of 1738. But it would mean a long day to spin ½ lb.—twenty hours said the Essayist, though this was perhaps an over-estimate. Nevertheless, fine spinning paid better than coarse and there are many references to the difficulty of getting spinners for coarser cloth when the fine trade was busy.

It is surprising to find that Eden, in describing the same village fifty years later, said that 1 lb. could be spun in a day,[4] since he must have been referring to fine yarn. His statement that a woman with children could not spin more than 2½ lb. in a week accords better

---

[1] At Bury St. Edmunds, 1575, *V.C.H. Suffolk* i. 677; Yorkshire early eighteenth century, H. Heaton, *Yorkshire Woollen and Worsted Industries*, p. 338.

[2] *Country Commonsense*, by a Gentleman of Wilts. (T. Andrews), p. 159.

[3] 'The Case . . . between the Clothiers and the Weavers', *Gentleman's Magazine* ix. 205.

[4] Sir F. M. Eden, *The State of the Poor* iii. 796.

with the earlier estimate but is still overstated. In 1793 it was said that when spinning had been plentiful a mother with her children could earn 4s. to 5s. a week;[1] and with the price at 11d. per lb. for weft[2] this would not have been impossible for an adult and two children.

Rates for spinning of any kind of wool were, of all the textile occupations, the most likely to fluctuate. A list of those which survive is given in Table K and the earnings from them may be roughly estimated from what has been said above. Those marked as 'assessed' may, of course, never have been paid.

B. WEAVING

The earliest statement of the time taken to weave a cloth comes from Gloucestershire, where, in 1544, William Ithell of Charfield 'for ten years past hath always occupied within his house two brode looms where yerely he and his have weaved three score clothes at the least'.[3] Thirty cloths a year for one loom is a high estimate and probably refers to a fairly coarse type of sorting-pack cloth, which would be about 40 yd. long before fulling.[4] In view of what is said below of superfine cloth it looks as if twenty to twenty-five white short cloths a year of the type exported by the Merchant Adventurers, taking finer and coarser together, might be a fair average, or even an overestimate, for the production of one loom which was constantly employed by an industrious weaver.

Hale gives three weeks for a coarse Gloucestershire medley of 32 yd. which was possibly 42 to 45 yd. before fulling.[5] In 1729 the Worcester weavers said that the long cloths which they had been making for the Levant, 44 yd. after fulling and probably 60 or more before it, took them a month each.[6] After this date our information relates only to fine Spanish cloth. Temple in 1738 thought it not uncommon for a fine medley, about 36 yd. before fulling, to be woven in three weeks, and a fine white cloth in rather less.[7] As far as Wiltshire is concerned, surviving records do not support the presumption that this rate of production was ever kept up throughout the year. Both Temple and the Worcester evidence suggest that the greatest length woven in a day was 2 yd. In 1803, when much longer hours were worked, but still without the fly-shuttle, $2\frac{1}{2}$ yd. appear

[1] *A Letter to the Wiltshire Landowners on the Alarming State of the Poor*, p. 11.
[2] See Table K.
[3] E. S. Lindley, 'Kingswood Abbey, its Lands and Mills', *B.G.A.S.* 75. 91.
[4] See pp. 296–7 for shrinkage.
[5] Hale, op. cit., p. 48.
[6] *C.J.* xxi. 292.
[7] *The Case . . . between the Clothiers and the Weavers*, p. 15.

TABLE K

Rates for spinning (per lb. unless otherwise stated)

Rates for warp spinning for fine cloth were paid by the 'score' of skeins, which gave an incentive to fine spinning. The pound seems to have made 20 to 30 skeins. For several cloths in Thomas Long's books 25 skeins, or $1\frac{1}{4}$ score, made 1 lb. The skein contained 320 yds.[1]

		warp	weft	not specified
1593[2]	assessed	$2\frac{3}{4}$d. to 3d.	$1\frac{3}{4}$d. to $2\frac{1}{2}$d.	
1605[3]	Wilts. assessed	2d. to 4d.	$1\frac{1}{2}$d. to $2\frac{1}{2}$d.	
1615[4]	'ordinary wools in the old drapery'			3d.
1655[5]	Wilts. assessed (coarse cloth)	3d.	$1\frac{3}{4}$d. to 2d. (cloth of 700–800)	
?1659[6]	Glos. coarse medley	5d.	$2\frac{1}{4}$d.	
1677[7]	Som. assessed			4d. English 10d. Spanish
1713–18[8]	supf. Spanish	1/- to 1s. 2d. per score (1s. 3d.–1s. $5\frac{1}{2}$d. lb.)	9d. to 10d.	
1723[9]		1s. $2\frac{1}{2}$d. per score (fine English)	8d. (Spanish)	
1725–6[10]		1s. 3d. per score (Spanish)	9d. (Spanish)	
⎧ 1738	Melksham		6d. (Spanish)	
⎨ 1739,				
⎩ March[11]	Melksham		7d. (Spanish)	
1760[12]	?Spanish or fine English	normally 11d. per score raised to 1s. 3d. and 1s. 5d. per score		
1760[13]		1s. 2d. per score (probably fine English)	8d. (prob. Spanish)	

[1] A. Young, *Annals of Agriculture* ix. 297.
[2] Bland, Brown and Tawney, op. cit., pp. 337–8.
[3] *H.M.C. Var.* i. 168.
[4] P.R.O., S.P.14/80/16.
[5] *H.M.C. Var.* i. 178.
[6] Hale, op. cit., pp. 45–7.
[7] Somerset Sessions Minutes, *Som. Rec. Soc.* 34. 224.
[8] Books of Thos. Long, Wilts. C.R.O., 947.
[9] Books of Usher & Jeffries, see App. III, Table H.
[10] Ibid., Wilts. C.R.O. 927.
[11] *Country Commonsense*, p. 159, n.
[12] *W.A.S. Rec. Brch.* xix. No. 203.
[13] Book of Joseph Udall of Melksham.

		warp	weft	not specified
c. 1774[1]		1s. 4d.–1s. 5d. per score (25 or 30 sk. to lb.) 1s.–1s. 1d. per score		
1789[2]			4d. to 11d.	
1785–90[3] 1797	} probably Spanish			1s.–1s. 2d. 5d.
1798[4]	(jenny)	6¼d. per score	5½d. (carding, slubbing, and spinning)	

to have been common, though 4 yd. could be done on occasion.[5] Two yards a day (taking the day as twelve hours) on the kind of cloth they were making represents about 6 picks (or throws of the shuttle) a minute,[6] whereas in 1840 it was reported that a weaver using the fly-shuttle could make 40 for a short period and could keep up an average of 30.[7] All the same, the average time for weaving a piece of broadcloth, 54 yd. long before fulling, was 150 hours, or about 2¾ yd. in a day of 12 hours, not much more than had been done in 1803, and, it was said, an able-bodied man in Trowbridge could not weave over 2½ yd. of cassimere in a day.[8] The time would, of course, vary widely according to the strength of the warp. One weaver said in 1839, what no doubt was true over all the centuries of weaving, that (using the fly-shuttle) one man might weave 6 yd. of white cloth in a day while another with different warp could only do three;[9] but the statement refers to shop weavers where the work was much more continuous than in the home.

We have no evidence for rates of payment by the piece which still

[1] A. Young, *Annals of Agriculture* ix. 297.

[2] Ibid. xi. 26. Owing to the finer spinning required and the use of less oil which reduced the weight of the wool, the price, though nominally the same as for many years past, was actually lower by one-third.

[3] Eden, op. cit. iii. 796.

[4] Glouc. C.R.O., Austin Papers, D.1759. See App. III, Table J.

[5] *B.P.P.*, *1802–3* vii. 20, 88. Cf. the 2 ells (3 yd.) suggested by a Glos. witness, ibid., 7.

[6] I am indebted to Mr. K. G. Ponting for working this out from contemporary patterns.

[7] *Repts. Asst. Commrs. Hdloom Weavers*, 1840, Pt. V, p. 382.

[8] Ibid., Pt. II, p. 297.   [9] Ibid., Pt. V, p. 383.

covered so much of the cheaper cloth in the eighteenth century. All we have are the sums rated by the magistrates a hundred years earlier, and these are a very poor guide since they were seldom paid. A comparison between them, however, shows something of the movement of rates for weaving. Table M showing the three Gloucestershire rates, the first rated in 1728, the second asked for in 1755, and the third rated in 1756 (none of which was ever paid) does give a measure of the fall in wages in that county up to the middle of the eighteenth century.

TABLE L

Rates for weaving

	assessed in Wilts.	1605[1]	1655[2]
cloth of	700	7s.	8s.
	800	8s.	9s.
	800 if broadlisted	9s.	
	900 narrow listed	9s.	
	1,000 narrow listed	10s.–11s. 4d. acc. to quantity of weft (54 to over 60 lb.)	
	1,100 narrow listed	12s.–13s. 8d. same provision	

If broadlisted from 900 to 1,100 weaver to have 1s. 6d. more. 6d. to be paid for every bear between 1,100 and 1,200 (5 bears to a hundred).
1s. to be paid for hanking.
Thus the highest earnings for a broadlisted cloth of 1,200 with over 60 lb. of weft would be 18s. 8d. For a piece of shortcloth, probably 36 yd. long before fulling, this would be a little over 6d. per yard. Usher & Jeffries of Trowbridge paid 1s. per yard in the 1720s for cloth of 1200, but it was almost certainly woven with finer yarn.

Spanish cloth

1704–26	*Books of Thos. Long of Melksham*
	18d. to 2s. 2d. per ell (1½ yd.) i.e. 1s. to 1s. 5¾d. per yd. apparently without relation to the hundred)
1727 Jan.	1s. 4d. per yd.
1728–9	21d. per ell, i.e. 1s. 2d. per yd.
	Books of Usher & Jeffries of Trowbridge
1720–5	Price paid per piece, apparently *c.* 1s. 2d. per yd.
1726	1s. 3d. for 1,400 to 1,600
	1s. for 1,200
	H. Coulthurst, Melksham[3]
1738	1s. 2d. per yd. apparently for 1,600
	Books of J. Udall, Melksham
1760	1s. 2d. per yd. for 1,500
c. 1770–1820	1s. 3d. per yd. for superfine cloth (1,600 upwards) in Wilts. and Somerset.

---

[1] *H.M.C. Var.* i. 168.   [2] Ibid. i. 173.   [3] Pressnell, op. cit., p. 72.

TABLE M

Gloucestershire weaving rates in the eighteenth century

(Rates for 1755 and 1756 are given for ells which have been re-calculated in yards for comparison with those of 1728)

Hundreds	1728[1] (assessed) per yard	1755[2] (asked for) per yard	1756 (assessed)[3]			
			hundred	white	hundred	medley
400–500 to 2,200	3d. to 2s.	2¼d. to 1s. 10⅔d.	900 to 2,200	4d. to 1s. 2¾d.	800 to 2,200	4d. to 1s. 4d.
(1,600	1s. 1¼d.	1s.		10d. to 1s.		11½d.)

In 1756 1d. extra per ell was asked for sized in skein (or ¾d. if the piece was under 1s. per yd.).

There was also a section in 1756 for 'clayed work' from 400 to 1000 for which rates ran from 4d. to 6½d., per ell; but 2s. per piece extra was to be given if the yarn was Irish, or 1s. if only the warp was Irish.

Rates paid in 1803[4] (not universal)

fly-shuttle ⎰ 1s. 4d. per ell = *c.* 10¾d. per yd. (kind of cloth not stated but probably 1,800 or more).
⎱ livery cloth, 34s. for 45 ells = *c.* 6⅕d. per yd. probably 1,000–1,200). This had been paid at 25s. in 1798.

---

[1] *A State of the Case*, p. 6.
[2] Glouc. C.R.O., D.149, B.8, Petition dated 22 Aug. 1755.
[3] *C.J.* xxvii. 732.
[4] *Ev. on Woollen Trade Bill*, 1803, pp. 301, 279.

TABLE N

Wages by the day or week

Spinning

1763[1]   Not over 6d. per day in Bradford and Trowbridge

1786[2]   4d. per day in Gloucestershire (Painswick and Northleach)

Weaving

1763[3]   8s. to 10s. per week for superfine in Bradford and Trowbridge. 6s. 6d., 7s. or occasionally 8s. per week for inferior cloths

1767[4]   10s. to 12s. on carpets at Wilton
7s. 6d. to 9s. on flannels and linseys at Salisbury

1803[5]   earnings stated by witnesses before Committee on Woollen Trade Bill:

	by weavers		*by Employers*
	Masters	*Journeymen*	
(a) double loom			
10s. (Bradford)		8s. to 9s.	10s. to 12s
7s. 6d. to 8s.	} (Road)		10s. to 14s.
10s. for cassimeres	}		£2. 5s. 4d. gross[a] per piece, i.e. *c*. 18s. 6d. per week net for two
15s. gross for two (Chippenham)			
20s. gross (Glouc. exceptional)		6s. to 8s.	
		10s. (exceptional, Glouc.)	£64. 15s. 2d. per yr. (£1. 4s. 11d. per week) gross or *c*.£1. 1s. per week net for two.
(b) fly-shuttle[6]			
	9s. to 11s.		18s. to 21s.
	10s. to 13s. (1806)		
			£50. 5s. 4d. per year, i.e. 19s. 11d. per week gross or *c*. 18s. 5d. net.
			21s. per week gross or *c*. 18s. net.

---

[a] Expenses were given as about 7s. for the piece plus 1s. 6d. for quilling for two looms if the weaver had no child to quill for him, *Ev. on Woollen Trade Bill*, 1803, p. 267. They have been taken here as equal to 4s. 3d. a week. Elsewhere they were given as 9s. 4d. on 44s (ibid., p. 321). One weaver thought they amounted to one-third of the gross payment, *Ev. on State of Woollen Manufacture*, 1806, p. 336. In 1839 the average deduction in Gloucestershire on an 1800 cloth was 5s. 7½d. *Repts. Asst. Commrs. Hdloom Weavers*, Pt. V, p. 387.

[1] *Propositions for improving the Agriculture, Industry and Commerce of Great Britain*, p. 31.

[2] A. Young, *Annals of Agriculture* vi. 34.

[3] *Propositions for improving . . .* , loc. cit.

[4] A. Young, *A Six Weeks' Tour through the southern Counties of England*, pp. 158, 171.

[5] *Ev. on Woollen Trade Bill*, 1803, Weavers, pp. 10, 20, 60, 77; Employers, pp. 252, 265; *C.J.* lviii. 884.

[6] *Ev. on Woollen Trade Bill*, 1803, pp. 10, 252, 300; *C.J.* lviii. 884; *Ev. on State of the Woollen Manufacture*, 1806, p. 33b.

TABLE N (*cont.*)

Shearmen

1677[1]	6s. per week (Trowbridge)
1739[2]	8s. to 10s. or possibly 12s. per week (Wilts.) These figures were hotly disputed.
1763[3]	14s. to 15s. per week.
c. 1770[4]	7s. (Glos.)
1795[5]	14s. to 20s. (Wilts.)
	Bradford 17s.; av. in Trowbridge, 14s.
1803[6]	2s. 6d. per day (Kingswood)
	not over 12s. (Trowbridge)
	15s. to 16s. (Chippenham)
	12s. to 15s. (Bradford) (after 4yrs. as a 'colt')
	14s. to 16s. (Dursley)
	18s. to 21s. (Uley)
1806[7]	14s. (av. 11s.) (Shepton Mallet)
	18s. (Wilts.)
1814[8]	20s. to 22s. (Freshford)

---

[1] *H.M.C. Var.* i. 155, and see p. 103, n. 5.

[2] 'The Case . . . between the Clothiers and the Weavers', in the *Gentleman's Magazine* ix. 205.

[3] *Propositions for improving* . . . p. 31.

[4] *Ev. on Woollen Trade Bill*, 1803, p. 307.

[5] Eden, op. cit. iii. 782, 800.

[6] *Ev. on Woollen Trade Bill*, 1803, pp. 115, 143, 196, 208, 255, 307.

[7] *Ev. on State of the Woollen Manufacture*, 1806, p. 436.

[8] See p. 230.

APPENDIX V

THE VOLUME OF PRODUCTION

ANY estimates of production can only be conjectural, since indications are too few to permit even of approximate accuracy, except partially for a few years in the nineteenth century. Nevertheless, it may be useful to make a guess if only to test the probability of the claims made for production in the area, particularly at the end of the seventeenth century.

A. LATE SEVENTEENTH CENTURY (c. 1690–1710)

The average export figure of 54,000 long, short, and Spanish cloths estimated for the west, including Worcester, in 1699–1701 and given above on p. 26 has been arrived at by taking 90 per cent of the long cloth, all the Spanish cloth and 75 per cent of the short cloth shown in Table A (App. I). The west was the only source of Spanish cloth, but Suffolk was still producing some long and short cloth, and what came from Yorkshire at this period was probably entered as long. (As explained above, the large exports of Yorkshire cloth to Europe via Hull were entered as 'dozens'.)[1] Cloth which may have come from other centres was probably short. There is no information about Dorset which still had a sizeable industry; but it is not easy to see where much more than the balance of 8,000 cloths could have come from, outside Gloucestershire, Wiltshire, Somerset, and Worcester.

In trying to estimate the whole production of the area it would be natural to turn to the only figures which exist for the country as a whole. These were given by the farmers of the aulnage in 1688–9; but they are not very helpful. They exist in two versions,[2] one of which, that in the Harleian MSS., gives larger quantities than the other; but the only category of cloth which is separately entered in both lists is that of long cloth, where the Harleian MSS. gives 48,260 pieces and the list in the State Papers 33,051. The difference is entirely accounted for by a higher estimate in the former for cloth

---

[1] See above, p. 31, n. 5.
[2] MSS. Harl. 1898, No. 61b; P.R.O., S.P.32/3/179. For the history of the aulnage from 1660 see *Cal. Treas. Papers*, 1697–1701/2, p. 46.

consumed at home; and since western long cloth seems to have been chiefly made for export, it would probably be safer to take the lower figure. Assuming that the west produced 90 per cent of it, we get a figure of nearly 30,000 pieces most of which came from Gloucestershire and Worcester. This is not incompatible with the estimate for the annual value of Gloucestershire's total production as £500,000, given in 1695 by Bishop Edmund Gibson in translating Camden's *Britannia*,[1] or with the figure of 50,000 cloths stated in 1712 by Sir Robert Atkyns.[2] The latter was said to be calculated 'by the seals of the aulnage and by the many waggon loads which go weekly to London, besides the cloth vended in this county, at Bristol and other places'; but Atkyns obviously had the previous estimate in mind, since he averaged the price at £10 per cloth, tacitly admitting that this was rather high[3] by including 'rugs and other incidents to the clothing trade' in the total.

Spanish cloth may be reckoned at the 30,000 pieces estimated for 1704;[4] but short cloth is almost impossible to estimate. It included Gloucestershire reds and other piece-dyed coloured cloth produced mainly for home consumption. These were about 30 yd. in length. So were Salisbury whites and much other white cloth made in Wiltshire or Somerset for dyeing in London; but one can only guess at their number.

In trying to arrive at an estimate for 1700 one must remember that some of the medleys made in Gloucestershire may have counted as Spanish cloth. It might therefore be advisable to take 45,000 as the total for Gloucestershire and to add the whole 30,000 Spanish cloths. Nearly 5,000 whites were still made for export in 1699,[5] and another 10,000 might be included for whites, not called Spanish, dyed either in the country or in London; but this is a pure guess which may be too high or too low. Assuming it to be correct we arrive at 90,000 cloths as a possible figure for the region as a whole.

Another method of calculation which can be used for comparison is to take the table of profits from the aulnage from 1686–8,[6]

---

[1] *Camden's Britannia*, tr. Bishop Edmund Gibson, 1695 (4th ed. 1772), p. 283. This passage was an addition by Gibson.

[2] *The Ancient and Present State of Gloucestershire*, p. 78.

[3] Most of the cloth made for the Levant was priced at £5. 10s. to £6. 10s. per piece white in Jacob Turner's books in the 1670s (see P.R.O., C.104/44), and the cloth for the E.I. Co., was similar. Finer white cloth was valued at £12 or £13 but it is doubtful whether there was enough of this and of what was dyed and finished in the county to bring the average up to £10.

[4] See p. 16.

[5] The amount (exported to Germany) was 4,642 pieces, Customs 3/3.

[6] *H.M.C., H. of L. MSS.* xiv. App. VI, p. 42.

according to which Wiltshire produced half as much as Gloucester-shire. Some of this would come from druggets and serges, so that, if we take Gloucestershire's production at 50,000 cloths, that of Wilt-shire might be 20,000. Somerset, on the basis of production in the mid-eighteenth century, might contribute another 15,000 pieces or more.[1] Worcester was sending some 4,000 cloths to London at the beginning of the eighteenth century, so that production for the whole area, including Worcester, again comes to just about 90,000 cloths. In comparison with the figures of cloth arriving at Blackwell Hall between 1713 and 1720 (see above pp. 31–2) these quantities seem to be underestimated for Wiltshire and Somerset (medleys) and some-what overestimated for Gloucestershire, though some of the medleys must have come from thence. But an average over-all surplus of about 27,000 cloths a year above what was sent to Blackwell Hall would account for the Gloucestershire cloths ordered directly for export and for the western cloths which were sold at fairs in the country, since the system of selling direct to country shopkeepers had scarcely developed by 1710. The medley section of the industry was also increasing rapidly in the second decade of the century, and produc-tion was less in 1700 than after 1713.

B. PRODUCTION IN THE EIGHTEENTH CENTURY

Had the returns of the inspectors of medley cloth, instituted under the Act of 1727,[2] been preserved, they would have provided an invaluable basis for the calculation of production, though the Act did not cover white cloth or that which was dyed in the piece. As it is, they only exist in Somerset for certain years. In Gloucester-shire it was decided that the Justices for the Berkeley division should apportion the districts of the six inspectors named in 1727.[3] By 1754 there were only three and their areas were:

1. Cam and North Nibley,
2. Dursley and Uley,
3. Wotton-under-Edge and places adjacent.

In 1763 the inspector for district 1 took over Wotton-under-Edge, but he is not mentioned after 1765. In 1770 the inspector of No. 2 district took over Cam and was reappointed until 1773, after which all mention ceased. It looks as if the production of medleys had decreased so much that it was not worth while for anyone to apply for the post.

---

[1] See below, Table P.   [2] See above, p. 53.
[3] Glouc. Q. Sess. Order Bk. (Glouc. C.R.O.), Midsummer Sess. 1727, fol. 410. Later entries at Easter Sess. in the years named.

In Wiltshire inspectors continued to be appointed,[1] but by 1790 they must have become very slack, for the Bench ordered directions to be printed and delivered to everyone newly appointed, and instituted fines for neglect in observing them.[2] In spite of this no figures have been preserved, though they appear to have been duly reported and were once referred to by the *Salisbury Journal*.[3]

In Somerset the districts were assigned as follows and £25, 'if the duty amount to it', was allowed for each inspector, except in division 5, where the sum was £30 each.[4] This would represent 25,200 cloths,

TABLE O

Production in Somerset in 1727–1728

	inspectors	amount[a] claimed (from July 1727 to Easter 1728)	number of cloths
1. Iford, Tellisford, Freshford, and Priston	1	£15	1,800
2. E. & W. Harptree, Chew Magna, Litton, and Littleton	1	£8	960
3. Mells to Frome, and Smith's mill[b]	1	£16	1,920
4. Mills from Smith's mill to Road Bridge, ten mills in all[c]	2	£14[d] £13	1,680 1,560
5. Shepton Mallet, Croscombe, Dinder, and all mills between Wells and Doulting; and at Stoke Lane, Batcombe, Westcombe, and Lovely	2	£30 (i.e. £15 each)	3,600
6. Kelston, Saltford, Keynsham, Twerton, Bath, and Bathford	1	£10	1,200
TOTAL (for period from 11 July 1727 to 30 Apr. 1728)			12,720

[a] Q. Sess. Order Bk. Easter Sess. 1728.

[b] These must have included Nunney, Whatley, and Hapsford. Smith's mill was later known as Leonard's mill and is now the Frome sewage works. (I owe this identification to Mr. K. H. Rogers.)

[c] Going down stream these were Frigglestreet, Wallbridge, Sanders', White's mill, Oldford, Lullington, Clifford, Shawford, Scutt's Bridge and Road. The town mill at Frome is represented by 'Sanders''; the mills were partially occupied by Thomas Sanders in 1727, Som. C.R.O., DD/LW 36, Frome Rate Book.

[d] £14 was for Frome. £13 for Beckington district.

[1] The divisions for Wilts. are given in *V.C.H. Wilts.* iv. 158.

[2] Wilts. C.R.O., Q. Sess. Order Bk., fol. 458, Mids. Sess. 1790.

[3] *Salisbury Journal*, 29 May 1808.

[4] Som. C.R.O., Som. Q. Sess. Min. Bk. Midsummer Sess. 1727.

but this was probably an outside estimate which can hardly have been reached even in the prosperous days before 1718. The total for 1727–8 can be estimated from the salaries actually claimed.

After 1728 no return has been preserved until 1753 and from that year up to 1769 the residence of the inspectors, but not their districts, is given, and the district must be discovered from a scrutiny of the new appointments. One cannot always be certain that the figures are assigned to the right district. Those with two inspectors were divided to make eight instead of six. The year ran from Easter to Easter, so that the period might vary, in extreme cases, between 11 and 13 months. There are several gaps in the middle of the century. The credibility of these figures depends on one's estimate of the trustworthiness of the inspectors. Only one detailed return has survived, that for the Lacock area of Wiltshire for the third quarter

TABLE P

Cloths sealed in Somerset, 1752–1809

(Many totals are obviously incomplete. Those in brackets, except for 1767–8, were not entered but have been calculated from the totals for the year.)

District[a]	1752–3[b]	1753–4	1754–5[b]	1755–6	1756–7[b]
1. Iford, etc.	1,447		1,116		1,336
2. Harptree	483		503		468
3. Mells	3,612		3,120		3,200
4. Beckington	2,894		2,564		2,659
5. Frome	2,684	(missing)	2,034	(missing)	1,957
6. Shepton Mallet	2,580		2,340		2,550
7. Batcombe	875		797		667
8. Bath	879		781		835
	15,454		13,255		13,672

District	1757–8[b]	1758–9[c]	1759–60[c]	1760–1[b]	1761–2[c]
1. Iford, etc.	1,094	1,093	1,162	1,605	1,584
2. Harptree	401	544	527	510	502
3. Mells	3,118	3,640	3,545	3,598	3,571
4. Beckington	2,686	2,896	2,600	2,358	3,205
5. Frome	1,936	2,206	1,828	1,799	1,903
6. Shepton Mallet	2,790	3,466	3,450	3,530	3,430
7. Batcombe	717	767	843	—	466
8. Bath	851	862	881	—	—
	13,593	15,474	14,836	13,400	14,661

Footnotes at end of table p. 337.

TABLE P (*cont.*)

District	1762–3[b]	1763–4[c]	1764–5	1765–6[c]	1766–7
1. Iford, etc.	1,220	1,347		958 ($\frac{1}{2}$ yr.)	
2. Harptree	503	520		521	
3. Mells	766	3,163		3,378	
4. Beckington	2,202	3,473		3,531	
5. Frome	1,951	2,379	(missing)	2,244	(missing)
6. Shepton Mallet	3,300	3,500		3,538	
7. Batcombe	590	645		1,067	
8. Bath	—	—		148 ($\frac{1}{4}$ yr.)	
	10,532	15,027		15,385	

District	1767–8[c]	1768–9[c]	1769–70[c]	1770–1[c]	1771–2[c]
	$\frac{1}{4}$ yr. only				
1. Iford	(589)	2,394	2,621	2,250	1,880
2. Harptree	(42)	70	204	262	—
3. Mells	(849)	3,025	3,414	2,944	3,465
4. Beckington	(766)	3,678	3,560	3,717	4,020
5. Frome	(603)	1,776	1,824	2,122	2,761
6. Shepton Mallet	(700)	3,638	—	4,356	4,394
7. Batcombe	(165)	935	—	860	431
8. Bath	—	—	—	308[d]	625
	(3,714)	15,516	11,623	16,819	17,576

District	1772–3[c]	1773–4[b]	1774–6	1776–7[b]	1777–8
1. Iford	1,520	2,051		3,500	
2. Harptree	—	—		—	
3. Mells	3,004	2,976		3,470	
4. Beckington	4,470	3,567		4,303	
5. Frome	2,839	2,447	(missing)	2,206	(missing)
6. Shepton Mallet	4,504	4,372		2,968	
7. Batcombe	796	714		507	
8. Bath	—	—		—	
	17,133	16,127		16,954	

Footnotes at end of table p. 337.

TABLE P (*cont.*)

District	1778–9[b]	1779–80[b]	1780–1[b]	1781–2[b]	1782–4
1. Iford	3,300	3,466	3,470	3,601	
2. Harptree	—	—	—	—	
3. Mells	4,524	4,099	4,026	4,509	
4. Beckington	3,702	2,862	3,051	2,444	(missing)
5. Frome	2,726	2,407	2,434	2,712	
6. Shepton Mallet	3,774	3,312	4,135	3,740	
	18,026	16,146	17,116	17,006	

District	1784–5[c]	1785–6[c]	1786–7[c]	1787–8[c]	1788–9[b]
1. Iford	3,354	1,660	—	2,722	2,490
2. Harptree	—	—	—	—	—
3. Mells	4,468	4,991	4,832	4,561	4,607
4. Beckington	3,802	3,976	3,572	3,353	3,556
5. Frome	2,847	2,457	2,196	(5,151)[e]	3,513
6. Shepton Mallet	3,502	3,332	3,490	3,463	3,559
	17,973	16,416	14,090	19,250	17,725

District	1789–92	1792–3[f]	1793–4[b]	1794–5[b]	1795–6[b]
1. Iford		2,710	4,309	4,297	4,790
2. Harptree		—	—	31	467[g]
3. Mells		3,755	3,609	3,182	3,364
4. Beckington	(missing)	3,784	2,489	1,866	2,535
5. Frome		3,560	4,240	4,327	4,420
6. Shepton Mallet		3,299	3,756	3,728	3,593
		17,108	18,403	17,431	19,169

District	1796–7[b]	1797–8[b]	1798–9[b]	1799–1800[b]	1800–1[b]
1. Iford	4,475	4,172	3,980	3,871	3,790
2. Harptree	541	554	431	248	806
3. Mells	3,795	4,236	4,326	4,508	4,114
4. Beckington	3,422	2,119	3,054	3,178	4,434
5. Frome	4,458	4,362	3,854	4,574	4,219
6. Shepton Mallet	3,641	3,928	3,296	3,880	3,696
	20,332	19,371	18,941	20,259	21,059

Footnotes at end of table p. 337.

TABLE P (*cont.*)

District	1801–2[b]	1802–3[b]	1803–4[b]	1804–5[b]	1805–6[b]
1. Iford	2,012	3,316	3,428	3,529	3,584
2. Harptree	520	346	—	775	506
3. Mells	3,347	4,118	4,567	4,724	5,022
4. Beckington	2,876	2,799	3,244	3,244	3,518
5. Frome	3,016	3,686	4,216	4,625	4,721
6. Shepton Mallet	2,513	2,444	2,552	2,815	3,520
	14,284	16,709	18,007	19,712	20,871

1. District	1806–7[b]	1807–8[b]	1808–9[b]
1. Iford	3,678	4,573	4,011
2. Harptree	517	523	527
3. Mells	5,172	4,854	4,622
4. Beckington	3,729	3,324	3,512
5. Frome	4,635	4,786	4,895
6. Shepton Mallet	2,403	2,700	2,991
	20,134	20,760	20,558

a These districts are often called after other mills in them, e.g. Shepton Mallet appears as 'Croscombe' and Iford as 'Road' or 'Tellisford'.

b From Sess. Rolls.

c From Sess. Min. Book.

d This and the following year's return came from a new inspector after a gap and there is nothing to show his district apart from the fact that the others were already represented.

e Not returned but calculated from total given.

f From return in Sess. Roll, Easter 1794.

g This figure is attributed to 'Harptree and Stoke', presumably Stoke Lane. In 1802–3 the division is called 'Batcombe', in 1806–7 and 1808–9 'Shepton', and in 1807–8 'Bath'. The inspector was the same throughout. Possibly he took over any scattered mills remaining in the whole area, but it seems more probable that the clerk did not know what division he represented.

of 1727, the first after the Act had been put into operation.[1] It shows that between August 7th and October 25th the inspector visited the three principal mills every two or three days, generally sealing one or two cloths at each visit. One other mill was only visited eight times and a fifth only twice, when two cloths were sealed. It seems probable that these two mills were usually dealing with white cloth, of which much had been made in the neighbourhood, at least up to

[1] Wilts. C.R.O., Q. Sess. Mich., 1727. See *V.C.H. Wilts.* iv, p. 158.

1711,[1] or with the druggets and serges made in Devizes and Calne, none of which were included in the Act. The 119 cloths sealed are therefore a credible number for the period; but inspectors just appointed were more likely to do their duty than after the Act had been in operation for some years. As late as 1770 an inspector measured and sealed cloth at Lullington and Clifford mills in the Frome and Beckington districts; but the millman who reported this to a House of Commons Committee in 1802 had never seen it done at any of the nineteen mills at which he had worked after leaving Clifford mill in 1774.[2] In 1803 it was said that 'the inspectors never perform any duty, they call for their twopence which is sometimes paid and sometimes not... they go on information from the millman'.[3] Some of the later figures look very much as if they were compiled in this way and a few of them may have been the result of juggling with those for the preceding year. But, on the assumption that they represent a minimum, one may build up a conjectural total of medley broadcloth produced in 1787–8 as follows:

	pieces
Somerset, 19,250 pieces, say at least	20,000
Wiltshire, at least as much	20,000
Gloucestershire, maximum ever mentioned, 50,000 pieces but supposing a loss in consequence of decay in the Levant and East India trades not fully made up by the inland trade	45,000
	85,000

The chances are that the Somerset inspectors missed much more cloth than the 750 pieces suggested, and the figure suggested for Wiltshire may also be too low. If 24,000 pieces of superfine cloth were made in these two counties,[4] 16,000 may seem rather a low estimate for the liveries and other inferior cloth made in Frome, Westbury, and other places, although there had been a great decrease in that manufactured for export. But it seems improbable that production had risen from the level of 1700, especially as nothing now came from Worcester. In fact, the total for Gloucestershire may be too high, since the county was still suffering from the effects of the loss of the export trade in medium cloth and the lower level of the East India Company's purchases. In all, one cannot

[1] *C.J.* xvi. 553.   [2] *C.J.* lviii. 885. Ev. of John King.
[3] *Ev. on Woollen Trade Bill*, 1803, p. 346. Cf. pp. 191, 382.
[4] See above, p. 62.

suppose that more than 90,000 pieces of broadcloth were made, if that, but the production of narrow cloth including cassimeres, may have been greater than it had been ninety years earlier.

Yorkshire's production in 1790 was 172,588 pieces of broadcloth and 140,407 of narrow cloth. Unfortunately no comparison of yardage can be made, but it was probably greater per piece in Yorkshire owing to the large amount of long cloth still made there.

C. PRODUCTION IN THE NINETEENTH CENTURY

The only figures in existence are those given for Gloucestershire between 1822 and 1838 by W. Miles, the Commissioner for Handloom Weavers; and an isolated one for 1841 given by S. S. Marling at the Free Trade meeting in January, 1842.[1] They were derived from the returns made by manufacturers to the Commissioners of Excise in order to obtain the drawback on the soap used in fulling. The returns were destroyed from time to time, and the fact that the first figures are for the half year May–October 1822[2] may be

TABLE Q

Production in Gloucestershire 1823–38

	broadcloth (yd.)	narrow cloth and cassimeres (yd.)	not distinguished (yd.)	felt (yd.)	stripes (yd.)	total (yd.)
1823	1,051,909	233,411	141,137	28,524	14,880	1,769,762
1824	1,209,827	210,682	289,352	31,259	—	1,741,100[a]
1825	1,189,086	200,691	332,580	37,886	—	1,750,243
1826	972,394	133,607	352,770	40,890	—	1,499,661
1827	704,908	140,629	519,914	58,724	—	1,434,175
1828	914,834	243,817	452,360	48,318	—	1,659,329
1829	914,741	216,211	355,018	21,298	9,984	1,517,252
1830	936,279	235,397	330,799	78,030	22,408	1,602,913[b]
1831	1,283,577	271,059	383,122	12,592	26,272	1,976,622
1832	1,323,664	381,653	433,181	23,680	7,162	2,169,340
1833	1,030,632	349,123	35,550	4,760	6,624	1,426,689
1834	1,499,676	453,868	—	7,770	5,532	1,966,846
1835	1,265,103	497,176	79,909	3,200	19,138	1,864,526
1836	1,285,771	457,475	141,589	8,913	22,770	1,916,518
1837	1,045,857	372,076	299,876	4,007	27,392	1,749,208
1838	863,443	398,968	284,620	6,040	39,523	1,592,594[c]

[a] 1,741,120 in list of totals.   [b] 1,602,953 in list of totals.
[c] 1,593,594 in list of totals.

[1] See p. 178.   [2] Not given in Table Q.

explained by the fact that these must have been the earliest ones extant.

Miles printed two tables, one giving total yardage, the other dividing the total into broadcloth, cassimeres, narrow cloth, felts, and stripes.[1] (Table Q) The latter presents some problems. In 1824, 1830, and 1838 the totals do not agree with the yardage given in the other table, but the differences are small and are probably errors in addition. The headings 'cassimeres' and 'narrow cloth' must refer to substantially the same product, for during this period no narrow cloth except cassimeres or cassinets is mentioned. Manufacturers, no doubt, called this cloth by either name and the Excise classified it accordingly. Finally, the yardage for 'stripes' is exceedingly small when compared with the number of pieces furnished to the East India Company as given by Miles in another table.[2] Most manufacturers must have classed their stripes as broadcloth (as it was) in claiming the drawback. Nothing is known of the material classified as felt.

TABLE R

Quantity of "stripes" supplied to the East India Company from Gloucestershire, Yorkshire, and other counties, 1820–38

	Gloucestershire (pieces)	Yorkshire (pieces)	other counties (pieces)	total (pieces)
1820	9,643	—	$425\frac{1}{4}$[a]	10,068
1821	10,460	1,250	—	11,710
1822	12,523	2,250	40	14,813
1823	9,952	59	33	10,044
1824	10,623	—	15	10,638
1825	11,049	1,300	—	12,349
1826	14,877	607	—	15,484
1827	5,960	400	—	6,360
1828	4,774	1,946	—	6,720
1829	11,048	$1,911\frac{1}{2}$	5	$12,964\frac{1}{4}$
1830	11,688	$622\frac{1}{2}$	—	12,310
1831	16,326	660	—	16,986
1832	$15,680\frac{1}{2}$	1,293	—	$16,973\frac{1}{2}$
1833	$69\frac{1}{2}$	—	—	$69\frac{1}{2}$
1834	60	—	—	60
1835	72	—	—	72
1836	199	—	—	199
1837	—	—	42	42
1838	$143\frac{1}{2}$	—	—	$143\frac{1}{2}$

[a] From London factors.

[1] *Repts. Asst. Commrs. Hdloom Weavers*, 1840, Pt. V, pp. 365–6.
[2] Ibid., p. 364. See Table R.

BIBLIOGRAPHY

I. MANUSCRIPT SOURCES (Other than those in the Public Record Office, British Museum, Bodleian Library, Somerset House, and the County Record Offices of Dorset, Gloucestershire, Somerset, and Wiltshire.)

1. Archives of the House of Lords. Chronological Series (petitions, draft Bills, Minutes of evidence on Railway Bills).
2. Commonwealth Office Library. East India Company Court Books.
   East India Company. Home Miscellaneous, vol. 16.
3. Institute of Historical Research. Notes by P. R. Bodington for the *Victoria County History of Wiltshire* (1909).
4. Record Office of the Corporation of London.
   Journals of the Court of Common Council.
   Repertories of the Court of Aldermen.
5. University of London Library. Letter from Lord Lansdown.
6. Bath Central Reference Library.
   Books of Stevens & Bailward, Bradford.
   Dyebook of Wallbridge Mill, Frome.
7. Bath and West of England and Southern Counties Society, Bath. Archives.
8. Devizes: Library of the Wiltshire Archaeological and Natural History Society. Diary of George Sloper.
   Everett, Wiltshire Wills.
9. Gloucester City Library.
   Smyth Papers.
   Documents relating to the Clothiers' Proceedings for the Repeal of the Woollen Statutes, 1802–3.
   Miscellaneous MSS. and printed matter.
10. Nottingham University Library. Letters of Henry Wansey Jr.
11. Salisbury City Muniment Room. Salisbury City Books.
12. Manuscripts in private hands.

Business Correspondence of James Harding of Mere (Catalogue with National Register of Archives)	Lord St. Aldwyn, Williamstip Park, Glos.
Corsham Papers	Lord Methuen, Corsham Court, Wilts.
Palling Papers (Catalogue in Gloucestershire C.R.O.)	Mrs. Smith, Painswick.

Wool Purchase Book of Messrs. Rawlings	Messrs. Rawlings, Cardmakers, Frome.
Books of T. W. Newman	Messrs. Newman, Hender & Co., Nailsworth, Glos.
Wool-sales Book of J. & T. Beavan, Holt	Messrs. J. & T. Beavan, Holt (Mr. F. W. Cooper, Melksham).
Books of J. Udall, Melksham	Late Mr. Stratton, Melksham.
Letter from Prince Rupert } Weavers' Petition *c.* 1840 }	Messrs. Strachan & Co., Lodgemore Mills, Stroud.
E. Moir, History of Marling & Evans (typescript)	Messrs. Marling & Evans, Stanley Mills, Glos. (to be published).
Recollections of J. Walker in *The Woollen Industry of the West of England* by K. G. Ponting (1971)	(Now published).
G. Tucker, Reminiscences of Past Years	(To be published).
B. Little, History of the Sarum Fine Woollen Company (typescript)	(Copy with Mr. K. G. Ponting, Pasold Research Fund Ltd. for eventual publication.)

II. BOOKS, PAMPHLETS, AND PERIODICALS (Calendars of documents in the P.R.O. and volumes published by the Historical Manuscripts Commission are omitted. A location is given for items not in the British Museum, the Bodleian Library, or the University of London Library).

Abstract of Inquisitiones post mortem from Gloucestershire, 1625–42, ed. W. P. Phillimore and G. S. Fry (1893).

An Account of the number of Woollen Cloths of all sorts exported by the Levant Company from England to Turkey in 46 years from Xmas 1671 to Xmas 1717 (?1718).

An Account of the proceedings of the Merchants . . . concerned in the Wool and Woollen Trade of Great Britain . . . that the laws respecting the exportation of Wool might not be altered in arranging the Union with Ireland (1800).

Analytical Index to the Remembrancia of the City of London, 1579–1664, ed. W. H. and H. C. Overall (1878).

Annual Register.

ANSTIE, J., *A general View of the Bill presented to Parliament during the last Session for preventing the illicit Exportation of British Wool and live Sheep* (1787).

——, *A Letter to the Secretary of the Bath Agricultural Society on the subject of a premium for the improvement of British Wool* (1791).

——, *Observations on the importance and necessity of introducing improved Machinery into the Woollen Manufactory; more especially as it affects the counties of Wilts., Gloucester and Somerset* (1803).

An Answer to those who have read Sir John Dalrymple's Pamphlet in support of a tax and permission to export raw Wool (1782).

ASHTON, T. S., *Economic Fluctuations in England 1700–1800* (1959).

ASPIN, C. and CHAPMAN, S. D., *James Hargreaves and the Spinning Jenny* (1964).

ASPINALL, A., *The early English Trade Unions* (1949).

ATKYNS, SIR R., *The Ancient and Present State of Gloucestershire* (1712).

AUBREY, J., *The Natural History of Wiltshire*, ed. J. Britton (1847).

——, *Wiltshire Topographical Collections*, corrected and enlarged by J. E. Jackson (1862).

BALLOT, C., *L'Introduction du machinisme dans l'industrie française* (1923).

Bath and West Society; Letters and Papers on Agriculture, Planting, etc. 14 vols. (1783–1815).

BELOFF, M., *Public Order and Popular Disturbances, 1660–1714* (1938).

BENSON, R. and HATCHER, H., *Old and New Sarum.* (1843).

Bibliotheca Gloucestrensis, ed. J. Washbourn Jr. (1825).

BICKHAM, G., *The British Monarchy, or a new chorographical description of all the dominions subject to the King of Great Britain*, 2 vols. (2nd ed., 1748).

BIGLAND, R., *Gloucestershire Collections*, 3 vols. (1771–1889).

BILLINGSLEY, J., *A General View of the Agriculture of the County of Somerset with Observations on the Means of its Improvement, drawn up in 1795 for the consideration of the Board of Agriculture* (3rd ed. 1798).

BIRCH, T., *The History of the Royal Society of London for the improving of Natural Knowledge*, vol. I (1756).

BIRD, J. T., *History of Malmesbury* (1876) (Devizes: W. A. S. Libr.).

BISCHOFF, J., *A Comprehensive History of the Woollen and Worsted Manufacture*, 2 vols. (1842).

——, *The Wool Question considered* (1828).

The Blackwell Hall Factors' Case (?1698).

BLANCH, J., *An Abstract of the Grievances of Trade which oppress our Poor* (1694).

——, *The Interest of England considered in an Essay upon Wool* (1694).

——, *The Beau Merchant* (1714).

BLANCH, J., *Swords into Anchors* (1725).

——, *Hoops into Spinning Wheels* (1725).

BLAND, A. E., BROWN, P. A., and TAWNEY, R. H., *English Economic History: Select Documents* (1914).

BODMAN, J., *A concise history of Trowbridge* (1814).

BOWDEN, P. J., *The Wool Trade in Tudor and Stuart England* (1962).

BOWDEN, WITT, *Industrial Society in England towards the end of the Eighteenth Century* (1925).

BOWMAN, W. D., *Bristol and America* (1929).

Bristol Poll Books 1722, 1734 (Bristol P.L.).

The British Merchant, or Commerce preserved, ed. C. King (1721).

BRITTON, J., *The Beauties of Wiltshire*, vols. I and II (1801).

(BROOKE, C.), *Proceedings of the Court of King's Bench . . . in an action brought by Charles Brooke, Woolbroker, versus Henry Guy, clothier . . . . for a Libel* (2nd ed. 1802) (Devizes: W.A.S. Libr., Wilts. Tracts, vol. 28).

BROOKS, R., *Observations on milling broad and narrow Cloth* (1743) (Devizes: W.A.S. Libr.).

BUNN, T., *A letter relative to the Affairs of the Poor of . . . Frome Selwood* (1834; 2nd ed. 1851).

BURRISH, O., *Batavia Illustrated* (2nd ed. 1731).

Diary of Thomas Burton, M.P., ed. J. T. Rutt. 4 vols. (1828).

Camden's Britannia, newly translated into English with large additions and improvements by E. Gibson, D.D. (1695; 4th ed. 1772).

CAMPBELL, R., *The London Tradesman* (1747).

CARPMAEL, W., *Law Reports of Patent Cases*, vol. I (1843).

CARTER, H. B., *His Majesty's Spanish Flock* (1964).

C[ARTER], W., *England's Interest in securing the Woollen Manufacture of this Realm against the artifices of France* (1689).

The Case as it now stands between the Clothiers and the Weavers and other manufacturers with regard to the late Riot in the County of Wilts., by Philalethes (W. Temple) (1739).

The Case of the Levant Company (1718).

The Case of several members of the Levant Company complaining of the Restraint of their Trade (1718).

CLAPHAM, J. H., *An Economic History of Modern Britain*: vol. I, *The early Railway Age 1820–1850* (1926).

CLARK, G. N., *The Later Stuarts* (1934).

The Clothier's Complaint (1692).

The Clothiers' Reasons against passing the Bill for prohibiting the importation of foreign wool cards and to prevent the abuses in making the same with old wire (1711).

The Clothiers' Reasons . . . for adding a clause to oblige buyers of Cloth upon credit to give notes (1714).

Cobbett's Complete Collection of State Trials (1809–26): (vol. 11 compiled by T. B. Howell).

COBBETT, W., *Rural Rides* (Everyman ed., 2 vols.).

COKE, R., *A Detection of the Court and State of England*, 3 vols. (4th ed. 1719).

——. *Reflections on the East Indy and Royal African Companies* (1695).

COLE, A. H., *The American Wool Manufacture* (1926).

COLE, G. D. H., *Attempts at General Union: A Study in Trade Union History, 1818–1834* (1953).

COLLINSON, J., *History of the county of Somerset*, 3 vols. (1791).

A Comparative View of the present Laws against the illicit Exportation of Wool (1788).

A Copy of some Reasons formerly offered by the Gloucestershire Clothiers to show the true cause of the decay of the Worcester trade, proper to be presented at the present time (?1743).

Country Commonsense, by a Gentleman of Wilts. (T. Andrews) (1739).

County Curiosities, or a new description of Gloucestershire (1757) (G.C.L.).

CRUMP, W. B., *The Leeds Woollen Industry, 1780–1820* (1931).

——, and GHORBAL, G., *History of the Huddersfield Woollen Industry* (Tolson Memorial Museum Handbooks no. 9, 1935).

CUNNINGHAM, W., *Growth of English Industry and Commerce:* vols. II and III *Modern Times* (1921, 1917).

CUNNINGTON, B. H., *Records of the Court of the County of Wilts, being extracts from the Quarter Sessions Rolls of the seventeenth Century* (1932).

——, *Some Annals of the Borough of Devizes 1553–1791* (1925).

DANIELL, J. J., *History of Chippenham* (1896) (Devizes: W.A.S. Libr.).

DAVENANT, C., *Works*, ed. C. Whitworth, 5 vols. (1771).

DAVIES, M. F., *Life in an English Village: an economic and social survey of the parish of Corsley, Wiltshire* (1909).

DAVIS, T., *A General View of the Agriculture of the County of Wilts.* (Agricultural Surveys, 1794, 1813 ed.).

DEFOE, D., *A Tour through the whole Island of Great Britain* (ed. G. D. H. Cole, 2 vols., 1927).

——, *The Compleat English Tradesman* (3rd ed., 2 vols. 1732).

——, *A Plan of the English Commerce* (1728).

——(?), *A Brief Deduction of the Original, Progress and Immense Greatness of the British Woollen Manufacture* (1727).

A Dialogue between Dick Brazenface the Cardmaker and Tim Meanwell the Clothier, fairly stated (n.d. ?1710).

DIRECTORIES. *A Collection of the Names of the Merchants living in and about the City of London* (1677).

Holden's Triennial Directory, 1817–19.

Pigot's Directory of Somerset, 1830, 1842.

Kelly's Directory of Somerset, 1875.

The Drapers' Bill, . . . with the Clothiers' Objections, 1714.

EDEN, SIR F. M., *The State of the Poor*, 3 vols. (1797).

EHRENBURG, R., *Hamburg und England im Zeitalter der Königin Elizabeth* (1896).

Encyclopédie méthodique: Manufactures, Arts et Métiers, vol. I (by Roland de la Platière) (1785).

An Enquiry into the Causes of the Encrease and Miseries of the Poor of England (T. Andrews, 1738).

Excidium Angliae, or a View of the fatal consequences attending the smuggling of Wool, by the Cheshire Weaver (J. Digges Latouche) (1727).

EXELL, T., *Brief History of the Weavers of the county of Gloucester* (1838) (G.C.L.).

——, *A Sketch of the circumstances which providentially led to the repeal of the Corn . . . Laws* (1847, repr. 1903) (G.C.L.).

Facts and Reasonings submitted by the Woollen Manufacturers of Gloucestershire in answer to the allegations made by the supporters of a bill to regulate the labour of children . . . in factories (E. Sheppard. 1833) (G.C.L.).

FIRTH, C. H., *Cromwell's Army* (1902).

——, (ed.), *Memoirs of Edmund Ludlow* (1894).

FISHER, P. H., *Notes and Recollections of Stroud, Glos.* (1871).

FOX, F. F. and TAYLOR, J. (ed.), *Some Account of the Guild of Weavers in Bristol* (1889).

FOX, H., *Quaker Homespun* (1958).

FRENCH, G. J., *The Life and Times of Samuel Crompton* (1859, repr. 1970)

FRIIS, A., *Alderman Cockayne's Project and the Cloth Trade* (1927).

FULLER, T., *The Church History of Britain* (1655: 1845 ed.).

——, *The History of the Worthies of England* (1662: 1811 ed.).

FURNISS, E. S., *The Position of the Labourer in a system of Nationalism* (1920).

GAYER, A. D., ROSTOW, W. W., and SCHWARZ, A. J., *The Growth and Fluctuation of the British Economy*, 2 vols. (1953).

The Gentleman's Magazine (1731–).

GILBOY, E. W., *Wages in Eighteenth Century England* (1934).

Gloucestershire Notes and Queries (1881–1902).

The Golden Fleece, or the Trade, Interest and Wellbeing of Great Britain considered (1736).

The Golden Fleece defended, or Reasons against the Company of Merchant

Adventurers, humbly offered to the consideration of the Hon. House of Commons (1647).

GRETTON, R. H., *Burford Records* (1920).

GREY, A., *Parliamentary Debates*, vol. 3 (1769).

Memoirs of the Family of Guise of Elmore (Camden Society, 3rd ser., vol. 28, 1917).

GUY, H., *An Answer to an Address from Charles Brooke to the electors of Chippenham* (1802) (Devizes: W.A.S. Libr., Wilts. Tracts, vol. 28).

HALE, SIR M. *A Discourse touching Provision for the Poor* (1683).

HALE, T., *A Complete Body of Husbandry*, 4 vols. (1756, 2nd ed. 1758–1759).

HAMMOND, J. L. and B., *The Skilled Labourer, 1760–1832* (1920).

HAYNES, J., *A View of the present State of the Clothing Trade in England* (1706).

——, *Great Britain's Glory* (1715).

HEATH, R., *Aleppo and Devonshire Square; English Trade to the Levant in the eighteenth century* (1967).

HEATON, H., *The Yorkshire Woollen and Worsted Industries* (Oxford Historical and Literary Studies, vol. 10, 1920).

HEWINS, W. A. S., *English Trade and Finance, chiefly in the seventeenth century* (1892).

A Hint to the Blackwell Hall Factors, being the true State of the case between Mr. Samuel Weatherhed, Blackwell Hall Factor, and Mr. John Heller, Merchant (1705).

HINTON, R. W. K., *The Eastland Trade and the Common Weal in the seventeenth century* (1959).

HOLDEN, J. M., *The History of Negotiable Instruments in English Law* (1955).

HOSKINS, W. G., *Industry, Trade and People in Exeter, 1688–1800* (1935).

HOUGHTON, J., *A Collection for the Improvement of Husbandry and Trade*, ed. R. Bradley (1727).

HUNTER, D. M., *The West of England Woollen Industry under Protection and Free Trade* (1910) (G.C.L.).

HUSTLER, J., *Observations upon the Bill . . . for preventing the export of Wool* (1787).

HUTCHINS, B. L. and HARRISON, A., *A History of Factory Legislation* (2nd ed. 1911).

HUTCHINS, J., *The History and Antiquities of the county of Dorset*, vol. II (1863).

IBBERSON, J., *The Woollen Manufacturers' and Overlookers' Guide* (1853).

Industrial Gloucestershire (1904) (G.C.L.).

INTERNATIONAL EXHIBITIONS:
Report by the Jurors appointed . . . for the Exhibition of 1851 (1852).

Official Catalogue of the Great Exhibition of 1851 and Supplementary Volume.

Paris Universal Exhibition 1855, Pt. I, Reports to Parliament, 3 vols. (1856).

Reports by Juries . . . on the International Exhibition of 1862, ed. J. F. Iselin and P. Le Neve Foster (1863).

Reports on the Paris Universal Exhibition 1867, vol. III (Official report on wool by T. Nussey and G. Leech)

Catalogue of the British Section, 1867.

Official Reports . . . of the London International Exhibition of 1871, ed. Lord Houghton, vol. II (Woollen and Worsted Fabrics by Prof. T. C. Archer).

British Commission Report on the Paris Universal Exhibition, 1878, 2 vols. (1880).

JENKINS, J. G., *The Welsh Woollen Industry* (1969).

JONES, W. H., and JACKSON, J. E., *Bradford-on-Avon*, annotated by J. Beddoe (1907).

KHAN, S. A., *The East India Trade in the seventeenth century* (1923).

KLEIN, J., *The Mesta, A Study in Spanish Economic History, 1273–1836* (Harvard Economic Studies, vol. 21, 1920).

LIBBY, J., *Twenty Years' History of Stroud, 1870–1890* (1890).

A Letter to the Landholders of the county of Wilts on the alarming state of the Poor (1793) (Devizes: W.A.S. Libr., Wilts. Tracts, vol. 16).

LINDLEY, E. S., *Wotton-under-Edge* (1962).

LIPSON, E., *The Economic History of England*, vols II and III, *The Age of Mercantilism* (3rd ed. 1943).

LUCCOCK, J., *The Nature and Properties of Wool* (1805).

MCCULLOCH, J. R., *A select collection of early English Tracts on Commerce* (1856)

——, *A select collection of scarce and valuable Tracts on Commerce* (1859).

MACDERMOT, E. T., *History of the Great Western Railway*, vol. I (1927).

MACLACHLAN, J. O., *Trade and Peace with Old Spain* (1940).

MACPHERSON, D., *Annals of Commerce*, 4 vols. (1805).

MARKHAM, G., *Cheap and good Husbandry* (1614).

——, *The English Huswife* (1615).

MARLING, SIR P. S., *Rifleman and Hussar* (1931).

MARSHALL, W., *The Rural Economy of the West of England*, 2 vols. (1796).

MASSON, P., *Histoire du commerce français dans le Lévant au XVII siècle* (1911).

Materials for a history of Gloucestershire, collected by A. J. Dunkin (G.C.L.)

MAY, J., *A Declaration of the Estate of Clothing* (1613).

Mercator, or Commerce retrieved, by W. Brown with the assistance of D. Defoe and others (1713).

Memoirs, Journals, and Correspondence of Thomas Moore, ed. and abr. by Lord John Russell (1860 ed.).

MOORE, J. R., *Defoe in the Pillory and other Studies* (University of Indiana Publications, Humanities series, no. 1, 1939).

MORSE, H. B., *The Chronicles of the East India Company trading to China, 1635–1834,* vol. I (1926)

NEMNICH, P. A., *Beschreibung einer im Sommer 1799 von Hamburg nach und durch England geschehenen Reise* (1800).

——, *Neueste Reise durch England, Schottland und Ireland* (1807).

News Clippings relating to the Stroud area, 1959–65 (Stroud P.L.).

NOAKE, J., *Worcester in olden Times* (1849).

Observations on a bill for explaining and amending . . . the several Laws . . . for preventing the exportation of live sheep, wool and other commodities, by G. King (1787).

Observations on British Wool and the Manufacture of it in this Kingdom, by a manufacturer of Northants (J. Munn) (2nd ed. 1739).

ONSLOW, E. M., *Some early Records of the MacArthurs of Camden* (1915).

PARIS, R., *Le Lévant* (Histoire du commerce de Marseille, vol. V, 1660–1789, ed. G. Rambert, 1957).

Parliamentary Register, vols. 82 (1803), 89 (1805).

PILE, C. C. R., *Cranbrook and the Clothmakers* (Cranbrook Notes and Records, no. 2. 1951).

PIRENNE, H., *Histoire de Belgique,* vol. 3 (1907).

Plain Reasons addressed to the people of Great Britain against the intended petition . . . from the owners and occupiers of land in the county of Lincoln for leave to export wool (1782).

PLAYNE, A. T., *A History of the parishes of Minchinhampton and Avening* (1915).

PLUMMER, A., *The Witney Blanket Industry* (1934).

PONTING, K. G., *A History of the West of England Cloth Industry* (1957).

PORTER, SIR J., *Observations on the Religion, Law, Government, and Manners of the Turks* (2nd ed. 1771).

POSTHUMUS, N. W., *De geschiedenis van de Leidsche lakenindustrie,* vols. 2 and 3 (1939).

POSTLETHWAYT, M., *The Universal Dictionary of Trade and Commerce* (4th ed. 1774).

POWER, E. E., *The Wool Trade in English medieval history* (1941).

POWNALL, T., *Live and Let Live* (1787).

Propositions for improving the Manufactures, Agriculture, and Commerce of Great Britain (1763).

The Proverb Crossed (1677).

350 *Bibliography*

J.R., *A Woollen Draper's Letter on the French Treaty* (1786).

RAMSAY, G. D., *The Wiltshire Woollen Industry in the sixteenth and seventeenth centuries* (1943).

Reasons for a general liberty to all Clothiers to sell their Cloth when, where, and as they please (1698).

Reasons for the Bill for improvement of the Woollen Manufacture and preventing the export of Wool (1689).

Reasons for preserving the publick market at Blackwell Hall and restraining the Levant Company . . . from deferring their shipping as long as they please (?1697).

Reasons for preserving the publick market at Blackwell Hall and restraining the Factors from dealing in Wool (?1697).

Reasons for restraining the Factors at Blackwell Hall from dealing in Spanish and English Wool (J. Blanch) 1698.

Reasons humbly offered against the Bill for explaining and amending the Act of 10 Anne relating to medley broadcloth (1714).

Reasons of the decay of the Clothing Trade, humbly offered to Parliament (1691).

REES, A., *Cyclopaedia*, vol. 38 (1819).

Remarks made by the Wier Drawers, Cardmakers, and English Wool Clothiers on a pretended Dialogue set forth by the Spanish Clothiers (?1711).

Remembrancia of the City of London, ed. E. K. Chambers and W. W. Greg (1907).

Repertory of Arts, 2nd series, vols. 37 and 38; 3rd ser., vols. 8 and 9.

The Reply of the Country to the kind reasons of the great City for a general Liberty to the Clothiers for selling their cloth when, where and as they please (?1698).

ROBERTS, L., *The Merchant's Mappe of Commerce* (1638).

ROBINSON, H., *The British Post Office* (1948).

ROGERS, J. E. T., *Agriculture and Prices in England*, vol. 6, 1583–1702 (1857).

RUDD, M. A., *Historical Records of Bisley with Lypiatt, Gloucestershire* (1937).

RUDDER, S., *A New History of Gloucestershire* (1779).

RUDGE, T., *The History of the county of Gloucester* (1803).

D. S., *To all the Clothiers of England; the state of the difference between the Clothiers and the City of London* (?1662)

SAINSBURY, E. B. (ed.), *A Calendar of the Court Minutes of the East India Company* (1907).

SAVARY, J., *Le Parfait Négociant* (1679: ed. 1749).

SAVARY DES BRUSLONS, J., *Dictionnaire universelle de commerce*, 3 vols., 1723–30 (ed. 1742).

SCHUMPETER, E. B., *English Overseas Trade Statistics* (1960).

Scott, W. R., *The Constitution and Finance of English Joint Stock Companies to 1720*, vol. 2 (1912).

Seasonable Observations on the present fatal declension of the general Commerce of England (1737).

Sheffield, Lord, *Observations on the Objections made to the export of Wool from Great Britain to Ireland* (1800).

Singer, C., *et al.*, ed., *History of Technology*, vol. IV (1958).

Smart, W., *Economic Annals of the nineteenth century*, 2 vols. (1910, 17).

Smith (Smyth), J., *Men and Armour for Gloucestershire in 1608* (pr. 1902).

Smith, J., *Chronicon Rusticum Commerciale or Memoirs of Wool* (1747, and 2nd ed. 1757).

——, *The Case of the English Farmer and his Landlord in answer to Mr. Temple* (1750).

Smith, W., *An Essay for the recovery of Trade* (1661).

Some Considerations . . . upon a Bill now depending about Transportation of Wool (1678).

Somerset Record Society, vols. 23, 24, 34: *Quarter Sessions Records for the county of Somerset*, 1607–25, 1625–39, 1666–1677.

Somerset and Dorset Notes and Queries, vols. II (1891) and III (1893).

A State of the Case and a Narration of facts relating to the late commotions and rising of the weavers in the county of Gloucester (J. Dallaway, 1757).

Stephens, W. B., *Seventeenth century Exeter* (1958).

Stevens, H. N., *The Dawn of British Trade to the East Indies, 1599–1603* (1886).

Stratford, F., *A Plan for extending the navigation from Bath to Chippenham* (1765) (Devizes: W.A.S. Libr., Wilts. Tracts 73).

Stratford, J., *Gloucestershire Biographical Notes* (1887).

Supple, B. E., *Commercial Crisis and Change in England, 1600–1642* (1959).

Sutherland, L. S., *A London Merchant, 1695–1774* (1933).

Tann, J., *Gloucestershire Woollen Mills* (1967).

Taussig, F. W., *The Tariff History of the United States* (8th ed. 1931).

Tawney, R. H. and Power, E. E., (ed.), *Tudor Economic Documents*, 3 vols. (1924).

Taylor, I., *Historical Memoirs of the Baptist Church Meeting in Castle St., Calne* (1778) (Devizes: W.A.S. Libr., Wilts. Tracts 3).

Cooke Taylor, W., *The Handbook of Silk, Cotton, and Woollen Manufactures* (1843).

Temple, W., *A Refutation of one of the principal Arguments of the Rev. Mr. Smith's Memoirs of Wool* (1750).

Thurloe State Papers, vol. V (ed. T. Birch 1742).

Tomlinson, C., *Cyclopaedia of Useful Arts*, 2 vols. (1852–4).

A Treatise of Wool and Cattel (George Clark, 1677).

A Treatise of Wool and the Manufacture of it (G. Clark, 1685).

TROW-SMITH, R., *A History of the British Livestock Industry to 1700* (1957).

——, *A History of the British Livestock Industry, 1700–1900* (1959).

The true State of the Dyers and Clothworkers.

TUCKER, J., *Instructions for Travellers* (1758).

TURNER, G., *A General View of the Agriculture of the county of Gloucester* (Agricultural Surveys, 1794).

TURNER, E., *A short View of the proceedings of the several Committees . . . held in consequence of the intended petition . . . from the county of Lincoln* (1782).

Two Letters sent from Amsterdam and read in Parliament, 11 June, 1642 (2nd letter to John Beauchamp).

UNWIN, G., *Industrial Organisation in the sixteenth and seventeenth centuries* (1904).

——, *Studies in Economic History* (1927).

URE, A., *The Philosophy of Manufactures* (3rd ed. 1847).

——, *Dictionary of Arts, Manufactures, and Mines*, vol. 3 (5th ed. R. Hunt, 1860).

VICKERMAN, C., *Woollen Spinning* (1894).

Victoria County Histories:

    Berkshire, vol. I (1906).

    Dorset, vol. II (1908).

    Gloucestershire, vol. II (1907).

    Hants., vol. 5 (1912).

    Somerset, vol. 2 (1911).

    Suffolk, vol. I.

    Warwickshire, vol. 2 (1908).

    Wilts., vol. 4 (1960), vol. 7 (1963), vol. 8 (1965).

A View of the Treaty of Commerce with France (1787).

VIOLET, T., *The Advancement of Merchandize* (1651).

The Voyage of Don Manoel Gonzales (late Merchant) of . . . Lisbon to Great Britain (1745).

WADSWORTH, A. P. and MANN, J. DE L., *The Cotton Trade and Industrial Lancashire, 1600–1780* (1931).

WANSEY, H., *The Journal of an Excursion to the United States of America in the summer of 1794* (1796).

WARNER, R., *Excursions from Bath* (1801).

——, *History of Bath* (1801).

WATTS, R., *The Young Man's Looking Glass* (1641).

WAYLEN, J., *A History of the Devizes* (1859).

——, *Chronicles of the Devizes* (1839).

WEBSTER, T., *Reports and Notes of Cases of Letters Patent for Invention* (1844).

While we live, Let us live (1788).

WILKINSON, REVD. J., *History of the Parish of Broughton Gifford, Wilts.* (1859) Devizes: W.A.S. Libr., Wilts. Tracts VII.

WILLCOX, W. B., *Gloucestershire, a study in Local Government, 1590 to 1640* (1940) (Yale Historical Publications, Misc. no. 39).

WILLIAMS, W. R., *The Parliamentary History of the county of Gloucester, 1213–1898* (1898).

Wiltshire Notes and Queries, 6 vols. (1905–16).

W.A.S. Record Branch (later Wiltshire Record Society):
    vol. 6, *The Trowbridge Woollen Industry, 1804–1824*, ed. R. P. Beckinsale (1951).
    vol. 13, *Progress Notes of Warden Woodward for the Wiltshire Estates of New College, Oxford*, ed. R. L. Rickard (1957).
    vol. 15, *Tradesmen in early Stuart Wiltshire*, ed. N. J. Williams (1960).
    vol. 17, *Wiltshire Apprentices and their Masters, 1710–1768*, ed. C. Dale (1961).
    vol. 19, *Documents illustrating the Wiltshire Textile Trades in the eighteenth century*, ed. J. de L. Mann (1964).

WOOD, A. C., *A History of the Levant Company* (1935).

WOODRUFF, W., *The Rise of the British Rubber Industry* (1958).

Wool encouraged without Exportation, by F. A. S. (H. Wansey, 1791).

YARRANTON, A., *England's Improvement by Sea and Land* (1677).

YOUNG, A., *Annals of Agriculture* (1784–1815).

——, *A Six Weeks tour through the southern Counties of England* (1768).

——, *A Speech on the Wool Bill that might have been spoken . . . on May 1st . . . 1788.*

——, *The Question of Wool truly stated* (1788).

III.   ARTICLES IN PERIODICALS AND COLLECTIONS.

AMBROSE, G., 'English Traders at Aleppo, 1658–1756', *Econ. Hist. Rev.*, vol. 3, no. 2 (1931).

BATES-HARBIN, D. W., 'Members of Parliament for the county of Somerset', *Proceedings of the Somerset Arch. and Nat. Hist. Soc.* 14 (1939).

BOWDEN, P. J., 'Wool Supply and the Woollen Industry', *Econ. Hist. Rev.*, 2nd ser., vol. 9, no. 1 (1956).

BROWN, W. E., 'Long's Stores, Devizes', *W.A.M.* 55 (1953).

BULLEY, J. A., 'To Mendip for Coal', *Proc. Som. Arch. and Nat. Hist. Soc.* 97 (1952).

COWARD, E., 'William Gaby, His Booke', *W.A.M.* 46 (1934).

DAVIS, R., 'England and the Mediterranean, 1570–1670', *Essays in the Economic History of Tudor and Stuart England presented to R. H. Tawney*, ed. F. J. Fisher (1962).

'*The Diary of Thomas Smith of Shaw House*', *W.A.M.* 11 (1869).

FAIRLIE, A., 'Dyestuffs in the eighteenth century', *Econ. Hist. Rev.*, 2nd ser., vol. 17, no. 3 (1965).

FRANCIS, SIR A. D., 'John Methuen and the Anglo-Portuguese Treaty of Commerce', *Historical Journal*, 3 (1960).

FISHER, H. E. S., 'Anglo-Portuguese Trade, 1700–1770', *Econ. Hist. Rev.*, 2nd ser., vol. 16, no. 2 (1963).

GILL, G., 'Blackwell Hall Factors, 1797–1799', *Econ. Hist. Rev.*, 2nd ser., vol. 6, no. 3 (1954).

'A Gloucestershire Mill in South Africa', *Ind. Arch.*, vol. 4, no. 3 (1967).

HARKNESS, D. E. A., 'The Opposition to the 8th and 9th Articles of the Commercial Treaty of Utrecht', *Scottish Hist. Review*, 21 (1924).

HÉMARDINGUER, J. J., 'Une Dynastie de mécaniciens anglais en France; James, John et Juliana Collier, 1791–1847', *Revue d'histoire des sciences*, vol. 17, no. 2 (1964).

HINTON, F. H., 'Notes on the Administration of the Relief of the Poor at Lacock, 1583 to 1834', *W.A.M.* 49 (1942).

IREDALE, J. A., 'The last two Piecing Machines', *Ind. Arch.*, vol. 4, no. 1 (1967).

KILBURN SCOTT, A., 'Early Cloth Fulling and its Machinery', *Trans. Newcomen Society*, vol. 12 (1931–2).

KITE, E., 'The Guild of Merchants in Devizes', *W.A.M.* 4 (1858).

LEMON, H., 'The Development of hand Spinning wheels', *Textile History*, vol. 1, no. 1 (1968).

LINDLEY, E. S., 'Kingswood Abbey; its lands and mills', *Trans. Bristol and Gloucestershire Arch. Soc.* 75 (1958).

MANN, J. DE L., 'A Wiltshire Family of Clothiers; George and Hester Wansey', *Econ. Hist. Rev.*, 2nd ser., vol. 9, no. 2.

——, 'Clothiers and Weavers in Wiltshire in the eighteenth century', *Studies in the Industrial Revolution presented to T. S. Ashton*, ed. L. S. Pressnell (1960).

MINCHINTON, W. E., 'The petitions of the Weavers and Clothiers of Gloucestershire in 1756', *Trans. Bristol and Gloucestershire Arch. Soc.* 73 (1955).

MOIR, E., 'Benedict Webb, Clothier', *Econ. Hist. Rev.*, 2nd ser., vol. 10, no. 2 (1957).

——, 'The Gentlemen Clothiers', *Gloucestershire Studies*, ed. H. P. R. Finberg (1957).

PARRY, C., 'Essay on the Merino Sheep', *Communications to the Board of Agriculture on subjects relevant to Husbandry*, vol. 5 (1806).

PILISI, J., 'Le Tondage dans l'histoire des techniques', *L'Industrie textile*, 1955.

PERRY, R., 'The Gloucestershire Woollen Industry, 1100–1690', *Trans. Bristol and Gloucestershire Arch. Soc.* 66 (1947).

PONTING, K. G., 'Some Questions about Round Towers', *Ind. Arch.*, vol. 4, no. 1 (1967).

PRIESTLEY, M., 'Anglo-French Trade and the "Unfavourable Balance" Controversy, 1660–1685', *Econ. Hist. Rev.*, 2nd ser., vol. 4, no. 1 (1951).

PUGH, R. B., 'Chartism in Wiltshire', *W.A.M.* 54 (1951).

RAMSAY, G. D., 'Industrial Laisser Faire and the Policy of Cromwell', *Econ. Hist. Rev.*, vol. 16, no. 2 (1946).

——, 'The Report of the Royal Commission on Clothing', *English Hist. Rev.* 57.

TANN, J., 'The Bleaching of woollen and worsted goods, 1740–1860', *Textile History*, vol. 1, no. 2 (1969).

TAWNEY, A. J. and R. H., 'An occupational Census of the seventeenth century', *Econ. Hist. Rev.*, vol. 5, no. 1 (1934).

WALROND, L. F. J., 'Early Fulling Stocks in Gloucestershire', *Ind. Arch.*, vol. 1, no. 1 (1964).

WATSON, C. E., 'The Minchinhampton Custumal', *Trans. Bristol and Gloucestershire Arch. Soc.*, 54 (1932).

WILSON, R. G., 'Transport Dues as Indices of Economic Growth, 1775–1820', *Econ. Hist. Rev.*, 2nd ser., vol. 19, no. 1 (1966).

WOLFF, P., 'English Cloth in Toulouse, 1380 to 1450', *Econ. Hist. Rev.*, 2nd ser., vol. 2, no. 3 (1950).

IV. PARLIAMENTARY PAPERS

Ninth Report from the Select Committee on East Indian Affairs, 1783, Misc. Repts., vol. vi.

Resolution of the two Houses of the Parliament of Ireland respecting a Union . . . Minutes of Evidence relating to Wool, BPP *1799–1800*, vol. cix.

Minutes of Evidence on the Woollen Trade Bill, 1803 (H.C. 95), BPP *1802–3*, vol. vii.

Minutes of Evidence taken before the Committee appointed to consider the State of the Woollen Manufacture, 1806 (H.C. 268), BPP *1806*, vol. iii.

Fourth Report from the Select Committee on East Indian Affairs, 1812 (H.C. 148), BPP *1812*, vol. vi.

Second Report from the Committee of the House of Lords on the Growth, Commerce, and Consumption of Grain, 1814 (H.L. 26), BPP *1814–15*, vol. v.

First Report of the Committee on Seeds and Wool, 1816 (H.C. 272), *BPP 1816*, vol. vi.

Minutes of Evidence taken before the Select Committee on the State of Children employed in the manufactories of the United Kingdom, 1816 (H.C. 397), *BPP 1816*, vol. iii.

Minutes of Examination taken before the Committee of the Privy Council for the Affairs of Trade, regarding the Wool Tax (H.C. 56), *BPP 1820*, vol. xii.

Third Report on the Foreign Trade of the Country (East Indies and China), 1821 (H.C. 746), *BPP 1821*, vol. vi.

Report on the State of the Law relating to Goods . . . entrusted to Merchants, Agents, or Factors, 1823 (H.C. 452), *BPP 1823*, vol. iv.

First Report from the select Committee on Artisans and Machinery, 1824 (H.C. 51), *BPP 1824*, vol. v.

Report of the Committee on the export of Tools and Machinery, 1825 (H.C. 504), *BPP 1825*, vol. v.

Report from the Select Committee of the House of Lords on the state of the British Wool Trade, 1828 (H.L. 515), *BPP 1828*, vol. viii.

First Report and Minutes of Evidence on the Affairs of the East India Company (China Trade), 1830 (H.C. 644), *BPP 1830*, vol. v.

Report from the select Committee on Manufacturers' Employment, 1830 (H.C. 590), *BPP 1830*, vol. x.

Minutes of Evidence on the East India Company's Affairs; II. *Finance and Accounts—Trade*, 1831–2 (H.C. 735), *BPP 1831–2*, vol. x, i.

Report from the select Committee on the Bill to regulate the Labour of Children in Mills and Factories, 1832 (H.C. 706), *BPP 1831–2*, vol. xv.

Report from the select Committee on Manufactures, Commerce, and Shipping, 1833 (H.C. 690), *BPP 1833*, vol. vi.

First Report of the Commissioners for inquiring into the employment of Children in Factories, 1833 (H.C. 450), *BPP 1833*, vol. xx.

Supplementary Report of the Central Board of Factory Commissioners, 1834 (H.C. 167), Pt. I, *BPP 1834*, vol. xix; Pt. II, *BPP 1834*, vol. xx.

Third Report from the select Committee on Agricultural Distress, 1836 (H.C. 465), *BPP 1836*, vol. viii.

Report of the House of Lords' Committee on the Cheltenham and Great Western Union Railway Bill, 1836, House of Lords Sessional Papers 1836, vol. xxxi (vol. xi in B.M. arrangement).

Reports of the Assistant Commissioners for Handloom Weavers, 1839–40, Pt. II, on S.W. England, by A. Austin (H.C. 43 I), *BPP 1840*, vol. xxiii.

Pt. III, on W. Riding of Yorks., by H. C. Chapman (H.C. 43 II), *BPP 1840*, vol. xxiv.

Pt. V, on Gloucestershire, by W. Miles (H.C. 220), *BPP 1840*, vol. xxiv.

Report on Handloom Weavers, by Hickson, 1840 (H.C. 639), *BPP 1840*, vol. xxiv.

Second Report from the Select Committee on the Act for the Regulation of Mills and Factories, 1840 (H.C. 227), *BPP 1840*, vol. x.

Sixth Report from the same (H.C. 504), *BPP 1840*, vol. x.

Report of the Commissioners for Handloom Weavers, 1841 (H.C. 296), *BPP 1841*, vol. x.

Special Reports of Inspectors of Factories on the practicability of legislative interference to diminish accidents to children . . . arising from Machinery, 1841 (H.C. 311), *BPP 1841*, vol. x.

Reports of Inspectors of Factories:
  1834 (H.C. 596), *BPP 1834*, vol. xliii.
  Half year ending Feb. 1836 (H.C. 78), *BPP 1836*, vol. xlv.
  Half year ending 31 Dec. 1836 (H.C. 73), *BPP 1837*, vol. xxxi.
  Quarter year ending 31 Dec. 1839 (H.C. 218), *BPP 1840*, vol. xxiii.
  Half year ending 30 June 1843 (H.C. 523), *BPP 1843*, vol. xxvii.
  Half year ending 31 Dec. 1843 (H.C. 524), *BPP 1844*, vol. xxviii.
  Half year ending 31 Oct. 1845 (H.C. 681), *BPP 1846*, vol. xx.
  Half year ending 31 Oct. 1846 (H.C. 779), *BPP 1847*, vol. xv.
  Half year ending 31 Oct. 1847 (H.C. 900), *BPP 1847–8*, vol. xxvi.
  Half year ending 31 Oct. 1850 (H.C. 1304), *BPP 1851*, vol. xxiii.
  Half year ending 30 Apl. 1852 (H.C. 1500), *BPP 1852*, vol. xxi.
  Half year ending 30 Apl. 1853 (H.C. 1642), *BPP 1852–3*, vol. xl.
  Half year ending 31 Oct. 1853 (H.C. 1712), *BPP 1854*, vol. xix.
  Half year ending 31 Oct. 1854 H.C. 1881), *BPP 1854–5*, vol. xv.
  Half year ending 30 Apl. 1856 (H.C. 2090), *BPP 1856*, vol. xviii.
  Half year ending 31 Oct. 1856 (H.C. 2153), *BPP 1857*, Sess. I, vol. iii.
  Half year ending 30 Apl. 1858 (H.C. 2391), *BPP 1857–8*, vol. xxiv.
  Half year ending 31 Oct. 1859 (H.C. 2594), *BPP 1860*, vol. xxxiv.
  Half year ending 31 Oct. 1862 (H.C. 3076), *BPP 1863*, vol. xviii.
  Half year ending 31 Oct. 1865 (H.C. 3622), *BPP 1866*, vol. xxiv.
  Half year ending 31 Oct. 1875 (H.C. 1434), *BPP 1876*, vol. xvi.

Return of Persons summoned for Offences against the Factory Acts, 1837–8 (H.C. 120), *BPP 1837–8*, vol. xlv.

Factory Returns:
  Persons employed in the mills and factories of the United Kingdom, 1835 (H.C. 138), *BPP 1836*, vol. xlv.
  Return of the number of Powerlooms in Factories, 1836 (H.C. 24), Ibid.

Return of the number of mills and factories within the district of each Inspector of Factories, 1836 (H.C. 122), *BPP 1837*, vol. l.

Return of Mills and Factories, 1838 (H.C. 41), *BPP 1839*, vol. xlii.

Return of the number of Persons employed in cotton, wool, etc. factories, 1847 (H.C. 294), *BPP 1847*, vol. xlvi.

Return of mills and factories
1850 (H.C. 745), *BPP 1850*, vol. xlii.
1856 (H.C. 7), *BPP 1857*, i, vol. xiv.
1861 (H.C. 23), *BPP 1862*, vol. lv.
1867 (H.C. 453), *BPP 1867–8*, vol. lxiv.
1870 (H.C. 440), *BPP 1871*, vol. lxii.
1875 (H.C. 393), *BPP 1875*, vol. lxxi.
1878 (H.C. 324), *BPP 1878–9*, vol. lxv.
1890 (H.C. 328), *BPP 1890*, vol. lxvii.

Accounts:
Account of the Quantity of woollen goods and yarn exported . . . in the years ending 5 Jan. 1813 and 5 Jan. 1815 (H.C. 467), *BPP 1814–15*, vol. x.

An account of the total quantity of woollen manufactures exported 1800 to 1821 (with details from 1816 to 1821) (H.C. 443), *BPP 1821*, vol. xvii.

Account of the quantities of British wool, woollen yarn, and woollen manufactured goods exported from the United Kingdom in each year from 1820 to 1832 inclusive (H.C. 526), *BPP 1833*, vol. xxxiii.

Accounts of foreign and colonial wool imported from 1816 to 1843 inclusive (H.C. 306), *BPP 1844*, vol. xlv.

Statistical Abstract 1875, *BPP 1875*, vol. lxxiv.

Census:
1821. Abstract of answers and returns (H.C. 502), *BPP 1822*, vol. xv.
1841. Abstract of answers and returns (H.C. 587), *BPP 1844*, vol. xxvii.
1851. Abstract of answers and returns (H.C. 1631), *BPP 1852–3*, vol. lxxxv.
1871 Population Tables (H.C. 676), *BPP 1872*, vol. lxvi.

INDEX